DESCRIBING FOREIGN POLICY BEHAVIOR

DESCRIBING FOREIGN POLICY BEHAVIOR

edited by

PATRICK CALLAHAN
LINDA P. BRADY
MARGARET G. HERMANN

SAGE PUBLICATIONS
Beverly Hills / London / New Delhi

To Richard C. Snyder
Our teacher, colleague, and friend

For information address:

SAGE Publications, Inc.
275 South Beverly Drive
Beverly Hills, California 90212

SAGE Publications India Pvt. Ltd.
C-236 Defence Colony
New Delhi 110 024, India

SAGE Publications Ltd
28 Banner Street
London EC1Y 8QE, England

Printed in the United States of America

Library of Congress Cataloging in Publication Data

Main entry under title:

Describing foreign policy behavior.

    1. International relations—Research. 2. International relations—Decision making. I. Callahan, Patrick. II. Brady, Linda P. III. Hermann, Margaret G.
JX1291.D47   327'.072   81-9231
ISBN 0-8039-1708-2   AACR2

FIRST PRINTING

Contents

Foreword

An extraordinary and intolerable gap exists today in the conceptual and empirical resources of those of us who seek to develop reliable generalizations and theories about foreign policy. We have no adequate concept of foreign policy that can be translated into units of analysis with dimensions or properties that are observable and important. The situation borders on the preposterous. Articles and books in endless number propose to explain, understand, and even predict foreign policy with the most superficial attention to the specification of foreign policy and its characteristics. Concern is lavished upon the explanatory variables and the theories intended to account for foreign policy—ranging from dependency theory to bureaucratic politics, from power and capabilities to ideology and leader personalities. But the neglect of what it is that these variables and theories are supposed to explain is so rampant that one wonders if we may all be subjects of the king with presumed fine garments. Where is the child who dares to shout that the emperor has no clothes—that our models and theories of foreign policy lack specification of the behavior to be explained?

Perhaps the above statement is an exaggeration, but I believe for most of the postwar period the description is not far wide of the mark. The inadequate specification of foreign policy and its qualities remains one of the most serious roadblocks to theory development in foreign policy today. Fortunately, the situation is beginning to change, and I believe this book, and the research it relates, contributes to a new and important trend. Before sketching the new development which this volume seeks to accelerate, let me mention some of the ways in which foreign policy is treated in most of the literature today and why it is inadequate.

Most studies of foreign policy conducted over the past several decades can be classified as fitting into one or more of the following categories: historical narratives of foreign policy interactions, evaluative and prescriptive analyses, case studies of a single policy episode, accounts of foreign policy organizations and processes, characterizations of the instruments used in statecraft, frameworks of the explanatory variables, and quantitative descriptions of behavior patterns or tests of hypotheses using quantitative data. For various reasons, the need to address the general concept of foreign policy or its various properties has not been necessary to realize the scholarly purposes commonly associated with most of the types of research. For example, with evaluations of prior foreign policies or descriptive narratives of the interactions between two countries or among multiple countries, usually the analyst wants to know why certain positions or actions were or were not adopted and the consequences. That activity which is foreign policy is a given as a matter of historical record. There is no obvious need to define it or establish a set of theoretically possible properties. Similarly, the study of a single case does not compel the investigator to consider of what general phenomena this case is a particular instance. By the same token, examinations of the institutions, processes, and instruments of foreign policy require the researcher to explore organizational theory, the capabilities of armies, or the skills necessary for effective negotiation.

If foreign policy research of the kinds noted above can realize worthwhile objectives without a direct consideration of foreign policy properties, it is more difficult to offer a similar defense for frameworks or theories that purport to explain foreign policy. These efforts typically devote nearly exclusive concern to independent variables—the factors that are assumed to shape foreign policy—without stipulating the nature of the policy to be explained. Of course, it is possible—and necessary—to improve our comprehension of the array of elements that can influence the actions and inactions of international actors. However, because the factors involved likely vary or combine in different ways depending on the nature and kind of policy stipulated, we must question whether such studies can be declared successful by their own standards and declared purposes.

Researchers who have used quantitative analysis to describe foreign policy or to determine its relationship in a hypothesis with other variables have been unable to neglect foreign policy in the way builders of frameworks have. Data analysts have specified a variety of measurable foreign policy behaviors and indicators. Among the most frequently used have been votes in national legislatures (on foreign relations) or in international organizations; foreign trade, assistance, and loan data; wars and conflict indicators; content analysis of documents for expressions of hostility or friendship; and event data. Although the necessity for quantifiable data has led to a variety of foreign policy behavior measures, researchers have seldom explored the relationships between different types of behavior or the relationships between the observable data and the more macro concept of foreign policy.

Despite the infrequency with which users of various kinds of foreign behavior data have asked more encompassing questions, I believe their efforts have contributed to a new consciousness about the need to examine what we mean by "foreign policy." There have been other factors at work as well. Increasing use of comparative case studies in foreign policy research has required researchers to specify the larger class of foreign policy behaviors shared by each case.

Furthermore, there have been changes in the concerns of those interested in studying foreign policy that have forced more attention to its meaning. The recognition of various kinds of international actors in addition to national governments has raised questions about the basic concept. Perhaps most individuals are prepared to agree that multinational corporations have foreign policies as do subnational governments. More reflection may be necessary, however, to answer such questions as: Does the private individual who systematically refuses to buy products from a certain country have a foreign policy? What about the parents of a youngster held in a foreign prison who intercede directly with foreign prison officials on their child's behalf? What about a church congregation that supports a medical missionary in another country? This expanded concern with the nature of international actors is necessitating attention to the concept of foreign policy and its properties.

Another development that has encouraged examination of the properties of foreign policy is the emergence of North-South issues in international relations and the emergence of international scholars from the Third World. The overwhelming preponderance of foreign policy research since World War II has been conducted by scholars in North America, Europe, Japan, and the Soviet Union. These researchers have understandably seen the Cold War, international politico-military crises, and war as the fundamental problems of international relations and foreign policy. Now some of these analysts, joined by a very small but growing cadre of Third World scholars, recognize that other foreign policy issues drive the behavior of policy-makers and publics in various parts of the world. Social and economic development, dependency, and social injustice have become increasingly important aspects of international relations that may not be captured by various measures of conflict, hostility, and crisis that have dominated our ideas of foreign policy.

At the same time, some scholars in industrialized countries have become concerned with economic interdependence and the so-called low politics issues. They have encouraged the idea—often without careful examination—that a meaningful distinction between domestic and foreign policy may no longer exist. (Since I would contend that foreign policy has remained an undefined term for most analysts, it may be difficult to argue that its distinction from something else is no longer valid, but presumably was in the past.)

In sum, there is great ferment in the study of foreign policy about the core concept and its properties. The developments described above are forcing inquiry about basic questions. What is foreign policy? What are the elements of foreign policy—both its dimensions that are present in varying degrees in all policies and the properties that may be present in some policies but not in others? How are the observable actions and indicators of policy to be connected to our concept of foreign policy? About which features of foreign policy would increased knowledge give us improved understanding of what actors have done and may do?

The contributors to this volume do not address all these questions with equal force. Foreign policy as a concept is treated implicitly in some chapters and explicitly in the last chapter. The bulk of the text, however, is devoted to articulating possible attributes of observable foreign policy behaviors. It is here that the authors seek to provide momentum to the trend for increased sophistication in our thinking and use of foreign policy related concepts. The array of attributes and measures developed here deserve to be examined for their own merits and as a challenge to the reader's imagination to devise other behavior attributes with both theoretical and empirical import.

In reading this book the reader should also consider the assumptions that all the contributors appear to share. Perhaps the most important of these is that one or more units of analysis can be devised to capture features of foreign policy activity.

Several of the contributors to the volume offer assurances that event data do not constitute the only candidate for such a unit. I share that conviction. Certainly a number of the attributes discussed could be operationalized in other ways, although it happens that one of the commonalities of the chapters is their use of event data to measure variation in each of the elements of behavior proposed.

Thus, it must be assumed that the contributors believe that event data constitute one possible unit of foreign policy behavior. That is an assumption I personally would support. Having said this, I must hasten to add that the potential of event data as a unit of analysis for foreign policy behavior has not yet been realized. In the late 1960s and early 1970s Professor Edward Azar hosted several conferences at Michigan State University to explore the common problems faced by many of the producers and users of event data. These occasions were important in numerous respects, but it must be noted that no agreement emerged on how an event should be conceptualized to constitute a unit of analysis. Given the quite different purposes of the participants, that inconclusiveness should not be surprising. More than a decade later, many ways of operationalizing an event can be found, but little has been done to conceptualize it as a unit of foreign policy. It simply is not possible to merge the various event data sets because they "mean" quite different things. Thus, the reader should be cautioned from accepting too quickly the idea that a variety of data sets exist today which share a common unit of foreign policy behavior in the form of an event. By the same token, I believe that many of the failings most frequently mentioned about event data can be attributed to these early generations of experiments with this unit of analysis rather than some intrinsic weakness. Of course, there are some vital philosophical questions that must be recognized, but the fact remains that I join with the other authors of this book in assuming that event data can become in the future an important means of capturing aspects of foreign policy.

Being asked to write the foreword for a volume in which one is a contributor and is affectively tied with the editors (particularly one of them) creates a certain awkwardness. One hesitates to praise the effort too lavishly for fear that the reader will disregard the entire statement as an exercise devoid of sound judgment. Yet it would be wrong for me to shrink from expressing my genuine enthusiasm for the significance of the assault this collection begins against one of the problems I believe to be a fundamental roadblock facing those who wish to think about foreign policy in terms of comparisons, generalizations, and testable theories. Together with the other recent developments that are heightening attention to policy and its attributes, I believe we are assembling the conceptual and empirical means to overcome this critical hindrance. By so doing, the stage is being set for major theoretical advances in foreign policy research.

Charles F. Hermann
Columbus, Ohio

Preface

How can students of foreign policy observe what they want to study? What concepts represent qualities of foreign policy behavior worthy of examination? How can foreign policy behavior be measured so that scholars and policymakers can perceive trends and make useful comparisons? How can researchers bring foreign policy data to bear in the testing of their theories? These are the concerns of this book. In the chapters that follow we present the results of our research on the conceptualization and measurement of nine aspects of foreign policy behavior with the goal of moving toward answers to these questions.

We first perceived the need for this book when, as participants in the Comparative Research on the Events of Nations (CREON) Project, we began trying to explain nations' foreign policy activities. In seeking measures of the kinds of foreign policy behaviors we judged to be important to examine, we discovered a paradox. The traditional theoretical and policy-analysis literature is rich in concepts identifying characteristics of foreign policy and foreign policy behavior, but it has not moved to translate these concepts into operationalized measures. The scientific literature, on the other hand, is characterized by impressive rigor but lacks conceptual richness. Instead, the practitioners of the scientific study of foreign policy have made a premature convergence on a few characteristics of policy and have focused their research only on these characteristics. Consequently, students of foreign policy have at their disposal an inadequate repertoire of concepts that are rigorously developed and operationalized. This condition, we believe, inhibits the development of the field.

In an attempt to begin to eliminate this paradox, the contributors to this book have developed *both* conceptualizations and measures for a series of aspects of foreign policy behavior that seem particularly relevant to the study of foreign policy. Because we are of the opinion that event data allow us to measure a larger set of governmental behaviors than would alternatives such as aggregate data and voting records, the particular measures we report are assessed using the CREON event data set. We have tried, however, to develop the concepts we are measuring in enough richness that they can be operationalized with different types of data. The mandate to each contributor was to indicate why a particular aspect of foreign policy behavior was important to study (what does it tell us about a nation's foreign policy activity?), to develop what we meant by that type of behavior, to show how the behavior could be measured using the CREON event data, and to examine the incidence of the behavior in the CREON Project sample of 38 nations. Frequent discussions among the contributors have focused on sharpening the conceptual development and the operationalizations of these foreign policy behavior measures.

Our general interest in this book is in assessing aspects of foreign policy *behavior,* not aspects of foreign policy. It is our belief that by examining foreign policy behavior we avoid the problems of explicating the goals and the purposes of governments that are usually associated with studying foreign policy. Moreover, a focus on foreign policy behavior provides us with a discrete, definable unit of observation that can be aggregated in many ways. Like the individual vote in voting studies, the foreign policy behavior enables us to have a basic unit of analysis. We have used the political level decision recorded in a foreign policy event to indicate a foreign policy behavior. We can foresee, however, how the foreign policy behavior measures described in this book could be used to develop representations of foreign policy and have suggested some initial linkages.

We begin the book with a more detailed presentation of our reasons for undertaking to develop a set of measures of foreign policy behavior. We also describe the particular event data we have used to operationalize the behavior measures so that all readers have some common understanding of the data displayed throughout the book. Then follow nine chapters that define a particular foreign policy behavior measure. Each of these chapters reports data for the measure for 38 nations. The aspects of foreign policy behavior that are measured indicate activities at different points in the decision-making process. Thus, the behavior measures describe the context at the beginning of the decision-making process, activity during decision making, outputs of the decision-making process, and other governments' reactions to the decisions. We conclude by suggesting ways of combining the measures to look at higher-order properties of behavior with consideration of how we can use foreign policy behavior to assess foreign policy.

This volume has been several years in preparation. As is the case with any such long-term undertaking, many individuals and groups have made invaluable contributions. The authors of the chapters in this book deserve our first vote of thanks. Besides preparing their chapters, all added enormously to the stimulating and supportive environment of the CREON Project. Both kinds of help were crucial to completion of this book.

Since the initial collective effort that gave rise to this volume, the contributors have taken separate paths. Charles F. Hermann is Director of the Mershon Center at the Ohio State University. Roger A. Coate is in the Department of Government and International Studies at the University of South Carolina. Maurice A. East is in the Department of Political Science at the University of Kentucky and is affiliated with the Patterson School of Diplomacy and International Commerce. Gerald L. Hutchins taught for a year at the University of Kentucky and is now with the Urban Institute of the University of Louisville. Dean Swanson served as a research associate at the Centre for Foreign Policy Studies at Dalhousie University before joining the U.S. Department of Commerce, Bureau of Oceans and Fisheries, as an international relations analyst. Stephen A. Salmore is affiliated with the Eagleton Institute and Department of Political Science at Rutgers University. Barbara G. Salmore teaches in the Department of Political Science at Drew University.

In addition to authoring and co-authoring several chapters in the book, Charles Hermann gave even more. In many respects, he is the progenitor of this book. Chuck made the persuasive case for developing measures of foreign policy behavior, guided our collective work in creating these measures, and carefully read and critiqued many of the chapters.

We would also like to express our appreciation to another Chuck. Charles Kegley made room for us on a panel he chaired at the 1974 Southern Political Science Association meetings, so that we could present the initial drafts of papers that subsequently became many of the chapters in this book. The feedback we received from Chuck and from other panel members (Edward Azar, Richard Skinner, Eugene Wittkopf, Michael O'Leary, and Jonathan Wilkenfeld) was most helpful. Moreover, Chuck read an earlier version of this book, as did James Rosenau. Both gave us useful suggestions for which we are grateful.

The work that this book represents could not have been completed without the efforts of many people at the Mershon Center. Carole Dale patiently typed and retyped draft chapters and compiled the manuscript. She was aided by Isabelle Davis and Joan Kafer. William Dixon and William Harper wrote programs to produce the results. A group of quite skilled coders—Beverly Gatliff, Petra and Danny Donofrio—carried out the sometimes tedious task of producing the data, usually cheerfully. Joanne Callahan did the bulk of the keypunching and critiqued and typed the early drafts of her husband's chapters.

Institutions also provided support. DePaul University gave Pat Callahan course reductions that allowed time for writing several of the chapters. The National Science Foundation has granted funding (GS-SOC76-83872) for much of the CREON research. The Instruction and Research Computer Center of The Ohio State University helped with funds for the many computer runs.

Finally, the Mershon Center, under the directorship of Richard C. Snyder, furnished the space, labor force, and resources needed for us to finish this book. In addition, Richard Snyder gave us constant encouragement for this project. His stimulating ideas concerning the analysis of foreign policy decision making provided much of the original impetus for attempting to characterize the nature of foreign policy decisions. In gratitude for his support, tangible and intangible, manifest and subtle, we dedicate this book to him.

Patrick Callahan
Linda P. Brady
Margaret G. Hermann

PART I

Ways of Describing
Foreign Policy Behavior

Editors' Introduction

The foreign policy activities of national governments impinge daily on people's lives. Sometimes they affect many people, as when nations fight wars. Sometimes the effects are subtle, seen only by the few searching for them—for example, when the air is charged with radioactive waste from nuclear weapons tests. At times the effects are beneficial, as in the international trade of manufactured goods, services, and commodities. Too frequently, however, the consequences are tragic, as in the loss of domestic jobs because of the aggressive trading policies of some nations. Because foreign policy activities have the potential for affecting the realization of human goals and values, we must try to understand what they involve. The long, rich tradition of scholarship devoted to foreign policy analysis, including recent efforts to apply quantitative or scientific methods of inquiry to the study of foreign policy behavior, reflects this need.

The contributors to this book also share a commitment to increased understanding of nations' foreign policy activities. We offer this volume to begin filling a gap we perceive in present foreign policy analysis and research. That gap concerns the types of foreign policy behavior being examined. We believe that too little attention has been given to how we might best think about, observe, and measure a diverse set of characteristics of foreign policy behavior. As a consequence, description and measurement of foreign policy activities are less rich than they could be. This book represents an initial attempt to capture the wide variety of behaviors that can characterize the foreign policy activities of nations.

The three chapters that constitute the first section of the book present the background for the volume that is necessary to an understanding of its contents. These chapters indicate why we perceive a need for the careful exposition of a range of aspects of foreign policy behavior and how we have tried to work toward filling this need. The emphasis in these three chapters is on the proposal of criteria that seem essential to developing an adequate set of concepts to describe foreign policy behavior. The criteria have implications for how we move to describe and measure the aspects of foreign policy behavior that we explicate in the next sections of the book.

In Chapter 1, Linda Brady examines the various approaches to describing the foreign policy activities of nations that are found in the literature. She suggests the advantages and disadvantages of the several types of quantitative and nonquantitative approaches one finds in such a literature review. Brady's examination yields four criteria that seem important for those interested in learning more about foreign policy behavior to use in developing their measures. An explication of these criteria indicates a strategy for research that becomes the framework for the development of the foreign policy behavior measures described in this book.

The foreign policy activities that are described in the book represent what one group of researchers believes are important dimensions to understand in examining nations' external behavior. All the contributors to this volume at one time were affiliated with the Comparative Research on the Events of Nations (CREON) Project, which has a particular set of aims and data base. In Chapter 2, Patrick Callahan suggests some of the implications of the CREON Project's interests and data base for the nature of the foreign policy behavior measures that are discussed in the book. He also describes the nature of the data set—an event data set—that is used throughout this volume as a basis for assessing the foreign policy behavior measures that are presented. This information will prove helpful to the reader in evaluating the quality of these behavior measures.

The CREON event data set, described in the second chapter, is used by Stephen and Barbara Salmore in Chapter 3 to demonstrate empirically one of the funda-mental ideas presented in the first chapter. Much previous research on the measure-ment of foreign policy has relied on inductive data reduction techniques, such as factor analysis, to reduce data sets to a small group of underlying dimensions. And, indeed, recent factor analytic studies of event data have shown considerable convergence in the dimensions underlying a wide variety of event data sets drawn from different sources over different periods of time. The Salmores suggest, however, that the convergence is an artifact of the characteristics of behavior that interested the researchers when constructing their original coding schemes. The convergence represents not the true qualities of all foreign policy behavior but a convergence of interests on the part of these foreign policy analysts. In effect, the analysts' images of nations' foreign policy activities affected the kinds of behavior patterns they found. Their implicit a priori conceptions of what foreign policy behaviors were important colored the kinds of information they sought and found. The Salmores' research led us to seek to define and conceptualize in an *explicit* manner the kinds of foreign policy behavior we were interested in measuring from the very beginning of the project. In so doing we tried to represent in our concepts and measures the wide variety of activities in which nations engage.

A Proposal

Suppose researchers wanted to investigate the nature of Chinese foreign policy after the deaths of Mao Tse-tung and Chou En-Lai. In anything other than the most cursory discussion, they would probably focus on a variety of characteristics of the policy. Among the aspects of policy that might be examined are changes in national goals, shifts in the nature of the resources (military, economic, diplomatic) used to implement policies, shifts in priorities given to problems and to the countries to which policies are addressed, changes in the levels of conflict and commitment in behavior, and variations in the degree of success or failure in achieving goals. In other words, the researchers would not attempt to characterize foreign policy as an undifferentiated whole; they would, instead, use a series of categories on which to build the description of policy and then classify policy along a variety of dimensions.

Relying on a series of categories to describe a diverse set of concepts is necessary to help structure the process of observing the complexities of foreign policy activities. This process is somewhat akin to describing the weather. The meteorologist describes the weather according to a number of dimensions: temperature, humidity, barometric pressure, wind direction and velocity, and precipitation probability, to cite a few examples. We learn little about the weather by knowing only one of these dimensions. Similarly with foreign policies, describing these phenomena without anchoring them to a set of dimensions makes discussion and understanding difficult.

We are not the first to suggest using a set of dimensions to describe nations' foreign policy activities. The foreign policy literature reveals a number of ways to characterize the foreign policy behavior of governments. Some are nonquantitative,

AUTHOR'S NOTE: Work on this volume was completed before the author joined the U.S. Department of Defense. Thus, the views expressed in this chapter are her own and should not be attributed to the Department of Defense or any other government agency.

others are quantitative. Among the nonquantitative approaches are idiographic description, implicit conceptualization, and explicit conceptualization. The quantitative approaches include ad hoc operationalization, inductive typologizing, and single dimension development. Let us see how these approaches characterize foreign policy activities and examine their strengths and weaknesses.

NONQUANTITATIVE APPROACHES TO DESCRIBING NATIONS' FOREIGN POLICY ACTIVITIES

Idiographic Description

The distinguishing feature of idiographic description is that it uses terms having little capacity for general application. Rather than describing characteristics of policy that can apply to more than one actor or to more than one point in time, the terms describe the content of policy in very particularistic detail. The description is fixed in time and space and characterizes a unique issue and set of participants. The nature of idiographic description is illustrated in the following quotation:

> The first hot shot in the Cold War came in Eastern Asia, not in Western Europe. At 4 a.m. on Sunday, June 25, 1950, the Kremlin, acting in the face of the United Nations and its Supervisory Commission in Korea, pulled the strings that controlled the puppet "People's Republic" of North Korea. A formidable force of Russian model rapid tanks rolled down over the free Republic of Korea, followed by an initial hundred thousand well-prepared ground troops armed from Russian arsenals [Bemis, 1965: 936-937].

Idiographic descriptions are extremely common in discussions of foreign policy and usually do one of two things: (1) catalogue a series of actions sharing some common element (for example, a common issue or common participants), or (2) explicate the meaning of some foreign policy pronouncement, such as the Truman Doctrine (Crabb, 1976), or such documents as the Panama Canal Treaties (Lowenthal and Baldwin, 1977).

Idiographic descriptions have considerable merit. They contain a great richness of substantive detail. They can be understood by a wide audience. And, when juxtaposed across time or across actors, these descriptions provide the basis for drawing more general conclusions. Thus, they make a useful contribution to knowledge, especially from the perspective of policymakers.

On the other hand, because idiographic descriptions are so particularistic, they lack a set of predetermined schemes for guiding the search for information. The researcher must make numerous judgments about what incidents, and what aspects of those incidents, should be emphasized. Such judgments often vary with individual values and assumptions. Moreover, the use of proper nouns as descriptive terms greatly limits the range of comparisons that can be made and thus complicates the task of comparison. In emphasizing the uniqueness of individual actions, idiographic description renders such actions incommensurable.

Implicit Conceptualization

Many foreign policy analysts employ implicitly conceptualized classification schemes in their description of governments' foreign policy behavior. In contrast to idiographic description, such schemes characterize foreign policy in terms that imply underlying dimensions that are general rather than particular, thereby enabling comparison across time and actors. For example, an analyst recently commented that the "Soviet leadership has adopted a more flexible and more moderate foreign policy" (Leonhard, 1973: 59). This statement compares Soviet foreign policy in 1973 with previous policy in terms of two theoretically based characteristics—flexibility and moderation. Comparisons of Soviet policy and the policies of other nations on these two ideas would also be possible. In implicit conceptualization the description is based on concepts; however, the author leaves the meaning of these concepts undefined. The concepts are *not* developed and used explicitly.

In addition to enabling comparison across time and actors, implicit conceptualizations have provided us with an extensive list of potential dimensions for describing foreign policy. For example, Wilkinson (1969), in discussing comparative foreign relations, mentions at least 19 concepts that could form the basis for classification schemes. Among his 19 concepts are external orientation, foreign policy autonomy, realistic policy, forcibility of policy, defensiveness, and flexibility. North (1974), in his description of Chinese foreign policy, employs 13 terms that imply classification dimensions—for example, hostility, aggressiveness, expansionism, commitment, and degree of involvement. A major problem with the concepts arising from implicit conceptualizations is that the meanings of those dimensions are not explained. Only if researchers share an implicit consensus on their definitions are they useful. But in many instances the terms are used in one way by one researcher and in another way by the next.

Explicit Conceptualization

A rather extensive foreign policy literature focuses on examining the meanings of certain foreign policy activities. The concepts are explicitly and rigorously developed. Indeed, the primary purpose for writing about the particular aspect of foreign policy is to give meaning to it. Among the concepts that have been explicitly defined are nonalignment, neutrality, and power-balancing (see, for example, Crabb, 1976; K. Holsti, 1977; Spiro, 1966). One of the most widely discussed concepts in recent foreign policy writings has been détente (Pipes, 1976). Another concept that has been given special attention is the distinction between "high" and "low" politics (Keohane and Nye, 1977).

Armed with explicit conceptualizations, a researcher can determine whether a country at a particular time is pursuing a certain policy. For instance, a clear definition of détente would allow us to determine when and if the United States and the Soviet Union undertook such a policy, and when and if they abandoned it. However, because those who develop explicit conceptualizations of types of policy do not attempt to make the concepts operational, it is often difficult to identify the range of variation in the concept. Meaningful comparisons become difficult, if not impossible. Continuing with our détente example, without some way of ascertaining variation we cannot determine the degree to which the United States followed a policy of détente during each of the Nixon years, nor can we compare the degree to which the United States pursued détente with the degree to which the Soviet Union pursued détente. The comparative utility of explicit conceptualization

TABLE 1.1
Aspects of Foreign Policy Behavior Tapped by Propositions
in the McGowan-Shapiro (1973) Survey of Comparative
Foreign Policy Research

Dimensions	No. of Propositions
Conflict-cooperation	37
Level of activity/amount of interaction	20
Success	12
Output — foreign policy/undifferentiated	11
Properties of decision making	10
Alliance behavior	8
UN voting dimensions	8
Support for international institutions	7
Change-related dimensions	3
Internal setting	3
Goals	1
Distribution of Foreign aid	1
Demand behavior	1
Total	122

is also limited by the frequent use of particular rather than general terms in the definition. Détente is an example here, too, since it is often defined in such a way that the Soviet Union is the target of the policy.

QUANTITATIVE APPROACHES TO DESCRIBING NATIONS' FOREIGN POLICY ACTIVITIES

Within the last two decades there has been a growing effort to apply quantitative methods to the characterization of foreign policy. Although these efforts have been quite diverse, three approaches seem to appear most often: ad hoc operationalization, inductive typologizing, and single dimension development.

Ad Hoc Operationalization

Ad hoc operationalization is illustrated by East's (1973) study of the relationship between state size and foreign policy behavior. From the theoretical literature, East derived a number of propositions that related small size to a variety of characteristics of foreign policy behavior. The propositions were tested using event data from the CREON Project. This research is classified as involving ad hoc operationalization because of the transition from theoretical concepts to operational indicators. Consider East's treatment of the concept of "low cost" behavior:

> It has been argued above that because of the lack of resources, small states are more likely to employ various techniques of statecraft which will minimize the cost of carrying out their foreign policy. Several studies have noted, for example, the tendency of small states to utilize international organizations

(IGO's) to a larger extent than large states. . . . Another economical means of conducting foreign policy is to direct one's influence attempts at groups of states and at IGO's rather than at individual nations [East, 1973: 565-566].

Rather than explain the meaning of low cost behavior, East examined the empirical indicators of the phenomenon. That is, use of international organizations and attempts to influence groups of states were thought to imply low cost behavior.

Ad hoc operationalization has been used to examine a diverse number of foreign policy activities. The McGowan and Shapiro (1973) survey of comparative foreign policy research reveals 13 broad classes of concepts that have been tapped through ad hoc operationalization. These 13 aspects of foreign policy and the number of propositions involving indicators of the concepts in this survey are reported in Table 1.1.

Because the links between indicators and concepts are left undefined in ad hoc operationalization, it is often difficult to compare studies unless similar indicators have been used. Although we may have ten studies concerned with conflict and cooperation, only two of the studies may have used the same indicators. As a result, cumulation of knowledge becomes a problem. Moreover, ad hoc operationalization is data-dependent. The researcher's task is made difficult when data do not exist, are available for some time periods but not for others, or can be obtained for some governments but not for others.

Inductive Typologizing

Inductive typologizing rests primarily on a methodological foundation. Rather than attempting to develop a priori a set of concepts to guide the observation of foreign policy, researchers using inductive typologizing gather a large body of data and then apply powerful statistical procedures such as factor analysis and canonical analysis to isolate empirical patterns in the data. Each pattern describes a set of highly correlated variables which presumably tap the same underlying phenomenon. Quantitative international politics literature is replete with studies that measure foreign policy phenomena through statistical data reduction techniques. Let us discuss three important types of studies in this tradition: factor analyses of United Nations roll call data, the measurement of foreign policy in the Dimensionality of Nations (DON) Project, and the inductive manipulation of event data.

The analysis of UN roll call votes was a prominent feature of the first wave of quantitative studies of international politics. Alker and Russett (1965) first demonstrated the value of factor analysis as a tool in the study of UN voting. Their study revealed that most of the variance in national positions could be summarized along a few dimensions: Cold War, self-determination, supranationalism, and Palestine-related issues. Later studies (Alker, 1969; Russett, 1967) confirmed the main results of the earlier work while indicating some differences of detail. These studies created tools for characterizing foreign policy. By calculating factor scores, one could determine how a state fit a pattern of behavior, and, by comparing factor scores, one could determine the position of each nation relative to the others in the study. These measures of foreign policy could then be used as dependent variables in further analyses designed to explain foreign policy (see Alker, 1969; Moore, 1975; Vincent, 1971).

The studies in the DON Project differed from the studies of UN voting primarily in the kinds of data employed in the analysis. In addition to UN roll call voting data, Rummel and his colleagues incorporated transaction data (such as trade and tourist traffic), structural variables (for example, number of international organization memberships), and event data. These different inputs to the inductive step were reflected in the different factors that resulted. One of the primary studies (Rummel, 1966b) isolated seven factors: participation, conflict, aid, ideology, popularity, South American pattern, and migration. Ten considerably different dimensions were revealed by factoring data organized by dyads (Rummel, 1969). These dimensions were used to characterize foreign policy, which in turn was related to the logic of social field theory. (See Hilton, 1973, for a critical review of the history and major findings of the DON Project.)

In recent years, researchers have given considerable attention to the analysis of foreign policy event data. A significant element of this research has been the multiple attempts to ascertain the number of dimensions that underlie event data sets. Some studies, such as those by Wilkenfeld (1969, 1975), used factor analysis to specify the dependent variables for their empirical research. Others were more concerned with a general description of the dimensions of behavior. In a representative example of this research, Kegley (1973) used a Guttman circumplex structure for factor analysis and found two general dimensions of foreign policy behavior that he labeled "conflict-cooperation" and "participation." Kegley et al. (1974) have surveyed these studies and report considerable convergence in their findings: Behavior is highly structured around a few dimensions, of which participation and affect are the most fundamental. (In Chapter 3 of this volume, Salmore and Salmore retreat somewhat from this conclusion.)

Although much effort has been directed toward the development of inductive typologies, this approach has several drawbacks. In the process of typologizing we fail to produce sound, rigorous conceptualizations. Indeed, concepts enter in only at the end of research, when the analyst turns to the task of naming the factors. That step answers the question, "What concept represents this factor?" but it does so without attempting to define the concepts. As a result, naming factors is a very tentative and uncertain process, something that users of factor analysis readily admit. The connection between the conceptual name of the factor and the factor itself may be quite tenuous. Some researchers are so conscious of this problem that they refuse to attach names to their factors. Although methodologically sound, such a decision breaks any connection between conceptualization and data reduction.

Problems also arise when the researcher wants to move beyond the present study to other data. The foreign policy property (factor) is defined in terms of the data used in the study—it is a function of the specific variables and a set of weights (factor loadings) which are determined by the configuration of the data. Similar variables for a different year or a different set of actors may yield a different configuration of data, which would produce different values for the factor loadings. Both solutions would be equally valid within the criteria provided by the technique. In other words, the results for one set of data do not provide a means of measuring the same dimensions in another set of data comprised of similar variables. This problem is compounded when (1) the data contain dissimilar variables from one year to the next, as is the case with UN roll call votes where issues change, or (2) one wants to use present results to guide research with an entirely different kind of data (for example, moving from event data to aggregate data).

Single Dimension Development

A limited but significant body of literature has focused on the development of scales that represent a single characteristic of foreign policy behavior. Such studies identify a characteristic of foreign policy that is of some intrinsic interest, conceptualize the characteristic, and then make it operational. Among concepts treated in this way are alignment (Teune and Synnestvedt, 1965) and commitment (Martin, 1977). The concepts, however, that have received the most attention are cooperation and conflict. Among the most extensive efforts to develop scales of conflict and cooperation have been those undertaken by the Stanford group (Moses et al., 1967; Zinnes, 1968; North et al., 1969; O. Holsti, 1972), Azar and his colleagues (Azar et al., 1972a), and Gamson and Modigliani (1971).

The fruits of single dimension development have strengths and weaknesses strikingly different from the results of the other research approaches we have described. Unlike researchers using the other approaches, those focusing on single dimension development have paid considerable attention to developing their concepts, by way of both formal definition and operationalization. Such studies have been fairly clear about what is meant by the concepts. Moreover, concepts developed this way are usable for a variety of comparative analyses. The conflict-cooperation scales mentioned above may be applied in principle to any foreign policy action by any actor at any time.

On the other hand, by focusing on only one dimension at a time, this approach has often lost sight of the richness and complexity of foreign policy. The researchers resemble weather forecasters who announce 100 percent probability of rain without noting that the temperature is below freezing or that the wind velocity is 30 miles per hour gusting to 60 miles per hour. The forecasters' listeners dress for rain and find themselves in a blizzard. Similarly, the emphasis on a single dimension may distort the nature of foreign policy.

To summarize, in this section of the chapter we have surveyed briefly six prevalent approaches to describing the foreign policy activity of governments. We have presented both the strengths and weaknesses of these approaches. Table 1.2 recapitulates these strengths and weaknesses.

CRITERIA FOR DEVELOPING A SET OF DIMENSIONS TO DESCRIBE FOREIGN POLICY ACTIVITIES

If our purpose is to understand foreign policy, are there some lessons to be learned from previous attempts at describing foreign policy activities? It seems to the authors of the present book that the researcher starting out to examine the nature of foreign policy behavior needs to keep four criteria in mind in deciding what aspects of foreign policy to study: (1) concepts should be rigorously developed; (2) concepts should facilitate comparison across studies, across governments, across time; (3) knowledge about the behavior of one actor or of a set of actors on the measures of the concepts should provide useful information for policymaking and/or theory development; and (4) the focus should be on a set of concepts that collectively constitutes a diverse repertoire of activities, thus portraying the com-

TABLE 1.2
Summary of Strengths and Weaknesses of
Six Types of Foreign Policy Description

Type of Description	Strengths	Weaknesses
Nonquantitative:		
Idiographic Description	Richness of substantive detail; appeal to a wide audience	Particularistic and highly judgmental; emphasizes unique, making comparison difficult
Implicit Conceptualization	Concepts are general, not particular; rich, varied repertoire	Concepts not well-developed; lack of agreement among researchers on meaning of concept
Explicit Conceptualization	Concepts rigorously developed; can make limited comparisons	Focus only on conceptualization, not operationalization; concepts often particularistic rather than general
Quantitative:		
Ad Hoc Operationalization	Diversity in concepts explored; attempt at operationalization	Links between concepts and operationalizations undefined; data-dependent; comparison among studies is difficult
Inductive Typologizing	Determine underlying dimensions of foreign policy based on a large array of activities	Concepts poorly developed; data-dependent
Single Dimension Development	Well-developed concepts; sophisticated measurement efforts (e.g., interval scale)	Fail to capture complexity or richness of foreign policy

plexity of foreign policy. Applying these four criteria will help researchers to avoid many of the pitfalls we have observed in previous types of description and to build on their assets. Let us develop these criteria in more detail.

Rigorous Development of Concepts

Rigorous development of concepts requires that terms be carefully defined. It is especially crucial that terms central to the concept be clearly specified, differentiating the concept as defined from other aspects of foreign policy that appear similar to it. Moreover, it is important to indicate how the definition being proposed for the concept is like, or different from, other definitions offered for the concept.

Careful definition of concepts serves two purposes. First, it facilitates the clear communication of ideas. Discourse using terms that are not carefully defined—that evoke the rule of WYKWIM (Well, You Know What I Mean)—may transmit some core of meaning, but the communication will remain fuzzy. More importantly, when researchers use fuzzy concepts, they tend to apply the terms inconsistently across time. Because the terms have fluid meanings, their meanings are likely to change without the researchers knowing it. Careful definition of concepts, therefore, should increase the consistency of researchers' descriptions of foreign policy both within their own research and across studies.

It should be noted that merely making a concept operational does not guarantee that the concept will be clear. Although creating a measurement device ought to provide an inducement for conceptual clarification, as we have already noted not all operationalizations are based on clearly defined concepts (on this point, see Babbie, 1975: 84). The result is an inability to translate operational indicators back into verbal concepts without losing the richness of those concepts. An operationalization is inadequate unless based on a clearly defined concept.

Concepts Facilitate Comparison

The second criterion—that concepts facilitate comparison—deserves somewhat more extensive discussion. The contributors to this volume share a commitment to the comparative study of foreign policy. We will not restate the case for comparative analysis, which has been made in great detail elsewhere (for example, see Rosenau, 1968a; McGowan and Shapiro, 1973; Przeworski and Teune, 1970). Suffice it to say we believe that the comparative method is vital to the development of empirically supported generalizations.

But what if the reader does not take an active interest in the task of developing empirically verified generalizations or does not choose to contribute directly to the comparative study of foreign policy? After all, many scholars for excellent reasons choose to focus on the behavior of a single nation at a specific point in time. Why should they care whether the concepts they use facilitate comparison?

We believe there are three reasons why such scholars should attempt to describe foreign policy by using concepts that enable comparison, even if only implicitly. First, the comparative method is not restricted to cross-national applications. Comparisons can also be made across time. Scholars who analyze foreign policy using such terms as "change," "consistency," and "flexibility" are making across-time comparisons for a single nation. They should be sensitive to the implicit comparability of their concepts. Second, even when research is limited to a single nation at a specific point in time, comparison may be a useful process. For example, the researcher may draw comparisons among the nation's policies toward different geographical regions or among its policies concerning different problems in the external environment. Such analyses are crucial for the investigation of such broader concepts as imperialism. In all cases, comparison is necessary for the establishment of a frame of reference for determining both the unique and the common aspects of policy. Third, a symbiotic relationship exists between the comparative study of foreign policy and the analysis of the foreign policy of a single nation. The latter draws on a body of assumptions and relationships for the background necessary to illuminate the important aspects of the nation being observed; the comparative study of foreign policy seeks to contribute to the development of that fund of assumptions and relationships. Moreover, the student who uses the comparative method draws on the experience of individual nations to illuminate the nature of foreign policy. Scholars who focus on single nations can provide the comparativist with useful data if, in the description of foreign policy, they employ concepts that are amenable to comparison.

Concepts Provide Useful Information
for Policy and for Theory

The third criterion for developing a set of dimensions of foreign policy activities is that knowledge about the behavior of one actor or of a set of actors on each dimension should provide useful information for policy *and* for theory. As C. Hermann (1971a: 59) has argued, "scholars who seek to include foreign policy as a central construct in theories about politics must offer theoretically relevant ways of identifying kinds of policies." At least three kinds of knowledge are of interest to students of foreign policy: (1) knowledge about the effects of a range of independent variables on foreign policy behavior, (2) knowledge about the effects of foreign policy, and (3) knowledge about the linkages between characteristics of foreign policy behavior.

No doubt many foreign policy concepts have been used in the generation of the first kind of knowledge. Most appear in factor analytic studies that indicate the proportion of the variance in the behavior dimension(s) explained by a limited set of independent variables—in other words, how much variation in foreign policy behavior is explained by the independent variables. Generally these studies produce a small number of dependent variables which collectively exhibit a maximum relationship to the group of independent variables. The value of this kind of knowledge for developing empirically verified generalizations concerning the nature of foreign policy cannot be denied. Because parsimony is one of our objectives in the development of theories of foreign policy, the focus on a limited set of independent and dependent variables clearly has merit. But what is chiefly at issue is the tendency of many researchers to emphasize this first kind of knowledge to the exclusion of other kinds of knowledge about foreign policy. Put differently, the criterion of useful information may be satisfied in other ways.

The second kind of knowledge—about effects of foreign policy—is useful to policymakers. Unlike the first kind of knowledge, which cannot be created without reference to a set (however limited) of independent variables, the second type of knowledge focuses only on foreign policy activities. Whereas the first kind of knowledge is explanatory, the second is more often descriptive of trends in national foreign policy behavior. Information about success and failure in foreign policy or about conflictful or cooperative tendencies in foreign policy behavior illustrates this kind of knowledge. Whether the concepts are tied in a theoretical sense to a set of independent variables is irrelevant to an assessment of their usefulness to the policymaker.

A third kind of knowledge of interest to students of foreign policy involves the linkages among characteristics of foreign policy behavior. Schelling's (1960) essay on the use of commitment as a strategy in bargaining situations provides a classic example of this kind of knowledge. Schelling links the making of a commitment and the effective communication of its irreversibility to success in bargaining situations. By committing himself, the actor shifts the burden for the outcome of the situation to the other party. Thus, Schelling argues that commitment is theoretically tied to success in bargaining behavior. Like the second kind of knowledge about foreign policy behavior that we have identified, this third kind of knowledge is independent of any set of independent variables. It tells us about the relationships among characteristics of foreign policy behavior.

It is the contention of the authors of this volume that adequate conceptualizations of foreign policy behavior should provide useful information for policy and/or theory. Admittedly, this criterion is a stringent one. Identifying criteria for assessing policy relevance is, in itself, a difficult task. What constitutes policy-relevant information to one observer may represent theoretical abstraction to another. (For an analysis of this problem see Tanter and Ullman, 1972, particularly the contributions by Bobrow and Whiting.) At the same time, this criterion is at the heart of our intellectual endeavor and serves as the standard against which the contribution of any proposed set of concepts is judged. A set of concepts describing foreign policy activities—no matter how elaborate or rigorous—remains intellectually barren if it fails to provide us with useful knowledge for theory-building or policymaking.

Concepts Cover a Diverse Repertoire of Activities

The set of concepts under study should collectively constitute a diverse repertoire of foreign policy activities. So goes the fourth criterion. The justification for this criterion rests on the complexity of foreign policy. Because the phenomenon, as well as the interests of its students, is multifaceted, its characterization should reflect these complexities.

Although many will accept the validity of this assumption without further demonstration, it would be useful to consider in a little more detail the multidimensional nature of foreign policy. If we think of the process of foreign policymaking as if it were a system, there appear to be four broad classes of foreign policy characteristics.

First, there are characteristics of the *predecisional context* that confronts the acting unit. These characteristics are roughly analogous to the inputs to the system. Predecisional context characteristics tell us what gives rise to the decision activity. One element of the predecisional context is the nature of the stimulus. From examination of the stimulus we can ascertain at least two characteristics of foreign policy. The first concerns whether a specific stimulus existed prior to the action— that is, whether the action was preceded by some concrete stimulus or behavior or by a more amorphous condition. Such characteristics allow us to describe foreign policy as being initiative or reactive in nature. Second, we can learn about the substantive nature of the problem posed by the environment from the stimulus. For example, we can describe foreign policy in terms of the amount of attention paid to a problem or a set of problems.

A second class of foreign policy characteristics concerns the *process* by which foreign policy is made. This class of characteristics is roughly analogous to the "black box" of the simple system. Examples of these characteristics are found in discussions of the structure of the decision-making unit (see Snyder et al., 1962: 96) and the psychological state of the decision makers, such as C. Hermann's (1969) typology of situations (see also Brady, 1974; Brewer, 1972). National goals also fall into this group of characteristics. Following Deutsch (1968), we may consider a goal a characteristic of the decision-making unit (the government or political system), especially if we restrict our vision to those goals of more than a temporary, ad hoc nature. Goals act as a particularly strong component of memory, establishing the relevance and salience of pieces of information and the range of the acceptable alternatives.

A third general class of foreign policy characteristics focuses on the *output* of the decision-making process. Among the common schemes that have characterized output are conflict-cooperation, resources used in the action (for example, military, economic, and cultural), the influence of behavior on the level of activity in the international system (participation, active versus passive policies, neutrality).

The fourth class of policy dimensions, analogous to feedback in the simple system, is labeled *outcome properties*. These concern the effects of policy. The most commonly employed scheme based on outcomes evaluates the degree to which policy has been successful. Among the specific attempts to develop this dimension are Hanrieder's (1967) concept of "compatibility"—whether the goals are feasible given the array of hurdles and opportunities in the environment—and Rosenau's (1970) concern with whether policy is adaptive or maladaptive.

Cross-cutting this framework for classifying policy characteristics by stage of the policy process is another that distinguishes foreign policy activities by whether they tap the *substance* of policy or the *style* of diplomacy and decision making. Researchers who study the substance of policy generally are concerned with the purposes that drive the national decision makers. They employ goals as a central concept, are careful to identify the entity or condition to be affected by the policy, and frequently describe the strategies that are used to achieve those goals. Researchers who study the style of foreign policy describe behavioral regularities, often without direct reference to the purposes of policy. Examples of research questions about style are: Does behavior tend to be conflictful or cooperative? Does the nation tend to act quickly after receipt of a stimulus, or does it tend to move slowly? Does the actor tend to overrespond or underrespond to problems? Does the actor tend to act in concert with others or alone?

The distinction between style and substance is subtle. Although both may be described by behavioral regularities, descriptions of style always imply behavior regularities. Characteristics of style may also be incorporated in substantive descriptions of foreign policy. For example, a policy of neutrality implies acting alone, and the policy of "trilateralism" requires, for example, that the United States act in concert with Japan and Western European nations. The distinction is that descriptions of policy substance always relate explicitly to national purposes, whereas questions of style do not consciously address national purposes. To illustrate the distinction, if we observe that the Albanians tend to be belligerent (to behave in a hostile fashion), we are describing style, but to say that the Albanians are belligerent in order to promote ideological orthodoxy is a description of the substance of policy.

By now it should be clear that foreign policy may be described in an almost infinite number of ways. That observation is hardly original. A few years ago, C. Hermann (1971a) was able to distill nine underlying dimensions from the discussions found in eleven important works on foreign policy. To return to the main point, the complex, multifaceted nature of foreign policy means that no one concept will provide an adequate basis for describing foreign policy. A single dimension may adequately describe one aspect of policy so that a scholar primarily interested in this facet can do valuable research on the dimension. One should not construe the results of this research, however, as broadly indicative of the more general phenomenon of foreign policy. And given the prior assumption that the usefulness of the description of policy will be partly determined by the set of categories brought to the task of description, it follows that researchers need to examine a diverse repertoire of concepts for describing foreign policy behavior.

WHAT NEEDS TO BE DONE?

The discussion of the four criteria on the preceding pages implies an agenda for research. The goal is to create a set of concepts describing foreign policy that will allow cumulative research by analysts using traditional and quantitative approaches as well as the development of a solid theoretical understanding of the nature of foreign policy and its processes.

To begin with, some subsets of the implicitly conceptualized properties scattered throughout the literature need to be developed into *rigorous concepts*. The subsets chosen should have implications for foreign policy theory and foreign policy-making. At least, a case can be made for their relative importance. Following the lead of researchers who have developed single dimensions, we should make an effort to explain each concept individually. Such an effort should rest on a priori development of the concept rather than on inductive statistical procedures. The concepts that result should permit *comparison* across time, across governments, and across studies. Empirical research would follow that would allow the determination of the *theoretical utility and policy relevance* of each concept. Concepts that proved to be resistant to use and barren of substantive insights for theory and policy could be culled and attention focused on what appear to be fruitful concepts.

This volume represents the efforts of one group, the Comparative Research on the Events of Nations (CREON) Project, to carry out the agenda we have just described. Over the course of the past several years we have been developing and making operational concepts for a diverse array of foreign policy activities that we will be testing in empirical research. In presenting these studies, we believe we demonstrate that the agenda is feasible, that a diverse set of concepts describing foreign policy behavior can be developed and used in empirical research. Each of the chapters expands the repertoire of concepts amenable to empirical research. By reporting them here, we hope to make possible their adaptation and use by others. At the very least, the members of the CREON Project will be conducting empirical research on foreign policy behavior in the future; this volume supplements that future research by making explicit our data generating operations for the dependent variable.

The process of developing more rigorous concepts for scientific analysis is an ongoing process. In a sense, this book provides a snapshot of the state of one effort to assess foreign policy behavior. If we look from the static presentation here to the more dynamic process in the field of foreign policy analysis generally, there are two additional purposes that this book might serve. The description of how we went about the job of developing our set of concepts to describe policy might serve as a model for others undertaking this kind of task. Moreover, we hope that the chapters will stimulate debate and discourse among the members of the profession concerning what we should observe about foreign policy. In a sense, therefore, the chapters are discussion papers designed to stimulate the cumulative growth of the field.

This chapter has presented the need for rigorously developing a diverse set of concepts to describe foreign policy. It has also advocated a particular methodology. But we feel that, ultimately, the value of our position must be borne out by the results of our efforts. In that sense, this volume must make the case that this chapter has argued. In order to judge the value of the remainder of the volume, however, the reader must understand in greater detail the nature of the CREON Project, of the data that we have used in this volume, and of the procedures by which we chose and developed the concepts introduced in subsequent chapters. The next chapter provides this background.

The CREON Project

This book reports on one set of sustained efforts to devise measures of foreign policy behavior, namely, those of the Comparative Research on the Events of Nations (CREON) Project. This chapter describes the CREON Project and the primary characteristics of the CREON data.[1] All of the chapters that follow present analyses of foreign policy behavior using the CREON data. The reader will find these analyses much easier to understand once armed with some fundamental knowledge of the nature of the data. This chapter, which draws together the relevant information, provides the necessary background to the reader. The second, and perhaps more interesting, purpose of the chapter is to show how the organizational context in which the behavior measures were developed shaped these efforts. That the attempts to develop measures of foreign policy behavior took place within the context of the CREON Project is a fact with some significance. It affected which measures were developed and how they were developed. By describing the relationship between organizational and intellectual process, the chapter should provide the reader with a broader perspective from which to evaluate the fruits of the CREON Project's effort.

THE CREON BACKGROUND

Four characteristics make the CREON Project distinctive from other quantitative international politics projects.[2] Each characteristic had a major role in structuring the conceptualization and measurement efforts that emerged from the project. First, CREON has been continuously interested in developing measures of multiple properties of foreign policy behavior. CREON has sought to measure not just the nature of the foreign policy output, but also characteristics of the predecisional context, of the decision-making process, and of the outcome properties of behavior. The dedication to multiple properties of behavior is related to the fact that CREON is a foreign policy research project. As was argued in Chapter 1, .multiple classification schemes and dimensions are required for foreign policy analysis. This is not always the case for research that maps the interaction patterns in the international system (McClelland and Hoggard, 1969) or a regional subsystem (Azar et al., 1972a), or for research focusing on the problems of war and peace (Rummel, 1972; Singer and Small, 1972; Small and Singer, 1979).

The urge to measure many aspects of foreign policy behavior was reinforced by a second characteristic of the project. Because the principal investigators were trained in several disciplines, they brought to the project a variety of assumptions about the most powerful sources of foreign policy behavior. (Readers interested in a thorough development of these theoretical perspectives should consult East et al., 1978.) The intellectual heterogeneity of the project reinforced the drive toward multiple classifications of foreign policy behavior. For example, as a result of her training as a psychologist, Margaret Hermann was very interested in whether foreign policy behavior is passive or assertive. The independence/interdependence of action measure (Chapter 11) was created partly in response to this interest.

A third characteristic of the project is implicit in the previous two. CREON was motivated by the desire to develop multivariate theories of foreign policy. Originally, CREON adopted the paradigm proposed in the Rosenau (1966) pretheory: Empirical testing would establish the relative potency of different variable clusters for explaining foreign policy. Over time, the goal was redefined. Now the purpose is to explore the interrelationships of independent variables with each other and with the dependent variables in order to provide a more complete statement of the processes that produce foreign policy behavior. Under either paradigm, though, the dimensions of foreign policy behavior must be applicable, at least in principle, to each of the theoretical perspectives adopted by the principal investigators. Thus, there was a need to arrive at some consensus about the appropriate measures of foreign policy. Each researcher was not able to determine for him or herself which dimensions were interesting and then operationalize them in an idiosyncratic manner.

A fourth characteristic of the project was the assumption that foreign event data should provide the empirical base for the analysis. The most salient alternatives were aggregate data and voting records in the United Nations General Assembly. Event data were deemed superior because they could be used to measure a larger set of governmental behaviors for a more comprehensive set of actors than could either of the alternatives.

THE CREON DATA

To construct an event data set, events are abstracted from the flow of international politics to provide an analytically bounded unit capable of comparison. For CREON, that unit represented the trace of a decision and was defined as "a minimally aggregated action resulting from a decision by the political authorities of a state, who have the power to commit the resources of the national government" (C. Hermann et al., 1973: 19). An event is comprised of four basic elements: an actor, an action, one or more direct targets, and one or more indirect objects.

Three elements in the CREON definition of an event deserve further comment. The first is the direct target-indirect object distinction. The direct targets are those entities (not necessarily nations) that are the physical recipients of the action. The indirect objects are those entities that the actor intends to influence by his action.

To illustrate, consider this example: The President, in an address to a joint session of Congress, accuses the Soviet Union of seeking to destabilize the strategic balance of terror. The Congress would be the direct target, and the Soviet Union would be the indirect object.

The decision to record the event as having multiple direct targets and indirect objects can be compared with the common practice of recording events in dyadic form: actor, action, one recipient. Dyadic form is especially convenient for mapping interaction patterns and the structure of international relations. However, some distortion is introduced into the data when one action having three recipients (targets and objects) is disaggregated to produce three dyadic events. The distortion does not flaw research on interaction patterns, since such research is primarily concerned with the flow of behavior through bilateral channels. But the dyadic form does lose information that is highly significant for some foreign policy concerns. For instance, the researcher may wish to compare nations in terms of their concentration on bilateral relationships versus more complex behavior patterns. The dyadic form does not allow one to make this distinction.

The requirement that the event represent "minimally aggregated action" is the second component of the event definition requiring comment. Very often an activity such as a speech, a press conference, or a communique will contain a variety of actions. For example, President Kennedy's speech of October 22, 1962 contained a number of distinguishable actions: It announced the naval quarantine of Cuba; it asserted U.S. intentions to retaliate against any nuclear attack from Cuba with a nuclear attack on the Soviet Union; it declared U.S. intentions to maintain close surveillance of Cuba; it announced the reinforcement of the Guantanamo naval base; it called for a meeting of the OAS; it called for a meeting of the UN Security Council; and it called upon Premier Khrushchev to order the removal of the missiles from Cuba. Minimal aggregation means that each such unique action would be recorded as a separate event in the CREON data set because each would be the result of a different political-level decision. More specifically, in the coding process it was assumed that a different political decision had occurred and a new event was identified with a change in (1) the individual or group making or announcing the decision, (2) the time frame for the action, (3) the level of commitment,[3] or (4) the kinds of resources used.

Minimal aggregation serves the following purposes. First, it facilitates the collection of event data by providing an unambiguous rule for identifying the unit of analysis, thereby reducing the amount of inference required of the coders and improving the quality of the data. Second, minimal aggregation guarantees comparability of events because each represents a similar phenomenon, namely, a political-level decision. Third, data recorded in minimally aggregated form do not encourage premature closure of research, which can occur when the data collection presupposes the kinds of hypotheses to be tested. Rather, minimal aggregation allows maximum flexibility in creating a unit of analysis appropriate to different kinds of investigations. A researcher interested in the minimally aggregated level can use the data as CREON has recorded it. A researcher who is interested in a more holistic conception of action can reaggregate to reproduce the action. In the example of the Cuban missile crisis, this researcher could characterize the whole of Kennedy's speech. A researcher who is interested in a broad conception of policy can draw together information from events that are widely scattered throughout the data file. The Cuban policy of the United States could be regenerated from data for a number of years. (The process of recreating policy from event data is analyzed in Chapter 14.) When the data are recorded in minimally aggregated form, the researcher can always put together the pieces to form a larger picture. But if the data are recorded in a more highly aggregated fashion, some details are lost to those using the data set. Despite the undeniable benefits of recording the data in minimally aggregated form, the decision had important effects on the validity of some of the measures reported in this volume. That problem is discussed in greater detail in a later section of this chapter, where we consider a variety of validity questions.

The third notable component in CREON's definition of an event is the stipulation that the event represent a *political* decision. Thus, governmental activity that crossed national boundaries but did not require specific authorization from political-level decision makers was excluded from the CREON event data set. Such instances involved the implementation of earlier political-level decisions.[4] For example, a political decision was required to initiate the Egyptian attrition strategy in the war against Israel in 1973. The first military engagement taken as part of that strategy would be recorded in the CREON data as the political-level decision. But subsequent shelling activities would be presumed to have been determined by field commanders carrying out a prior political decision and would be excluded from the data set.[5] As a result, the CREON data contain fewer decision-implementing actions, especially military activities, than do other event data sets. This is entirely appropriate, given CREON's primary concern with foreign policy behavior, but it may result in different patterns across almost all the variables than would be found in another data set.

To summarize the previous discussion, we have presented CREON's definition of an event and highlighted three aspects of that definition—the distinction between direct targets and indirect objects, the requirements that an event be minimally aggregated, and the limitation of data to political-level decisions. Each of these unique characteristics derives from the CREON focus on foreign policy, and each has significant implications for the operationalization of the properties of foreign policy behavior.

Before we consider the process of measure creation in CREON, some other basic characteristics of the data need to be described. Events are usually abstracted from the narrative in some source material. The source used by CREON was an uncollapsed version of *Deadline Data on World Affairs,* a global chronology which draws its news items from multiple sources. The source of the data affects the validity of the measures as they are operationalized using the data set; if the source contains serious bias or distortion, the measures will provide a misleading image of foreign policy. The source validity implications of the use of *Deadline Data* are discussed in some detail later in the chapter. Suffice it to say here that we believe that for our purposes—global, cross-national comparison for the development of theory of foreign policy—*Deadline Data* is a reasonably valid source of data.

The CREON data contain foreign policy events for 38 national entities for 30 months over a ten-year period.[6] The CREON actors and the total number of events coded for each are listed in Table 2.1. The nations were chosen at different stages in the project and represent a diverse mix in terms of the basic attributes of nations

TABLE 2.1
Actors in the CREON Data Set and
Total Number of Events for Each

CREON Nation	Number of Events	CREON Nation	Number of Events
Belgium	381	Lebanon	150
Canada	388	Mexico	191
Chile	209	New Zealand	201
China (PRC)	505	Norway	225
Costa Rica	164	Philippines	199
Cuba	326	Poland	233
Czechoslovakia	206	Soviet Union	1006
East Germany	202	Spain	171
Egypt	454	Switzerland	74
France	855	Thailand	163
Ghana	273	Tunisia	276
Guinea	209	Turkey	317
Iceland	159	Uganda	146
India	496	United States	1916
Israel	348	Uruguay	138
Italy	425	Venezuela	208
Ivory Coast	148	West Germany	646
Japan	271	Yugoslavia	257
Kenya	96	Zambia	78

(size, level of development, degree of political accountability) and geographic location. The time frame was established by drawing one-quarter from each year during the 1959-1968 decade. The years and quarters appear in Table 2.2. The sampling scheme used by CREON carries a number of implications for the data. The sample of nations reflects the variability of the community of nations, although no microstates are included. However, because the sample was not randomly selected, we cannot say how representative it is. The time sample poses more serious problems. By selecting quarters from each year, CREON lacks a continuous time-series of data, which has frustrated efforts to create measures based on the sequencing of behavior and the flow of actions and reactions in the international system.

Perhaps the most important characteristic of the CREON data is the rich selection of variables,[7] which provides extensive information for building additional measures of foreign policy behavior. A few examples will serve to illustrate this claim. CREON attempted to characterize the nature of the stimulus that gave rise to the event: Was the stimulus a prior behavior of another entity? Was it an explicit elicitation of a response? Was the actor in the CREON event pleased or displeased by the stimulus? Answers to these questions proved valuable in the

TABLE 2.2
Time Sample of CREON Data

Year	Months	Year	Months
1959	October, November, December	1964	July, August, September
1960	April, May, June	1965	January, February, March
1961	January, February, March	1966	July, August, September
1962	October, November, December	1967	April, May, June
1963	April, May, June	1968	October, November, December

development of our performance measure, the acceptance/rejection ratio (Chapter 12), by providing clues about the feedback from the environment, and in the development of the measure of independence/interdependence of action (Chapter 11). CREON also attempted to characterize a nation's foreign policy goals. Did the event explicitly establish some foreign policy goal? If so, did the goal necessarily require a long time to achieve, or was it possible that a few actions would bring it to fruition? Answers to these questions made possible the creation of measures of a nation's style of statecraft based on its articulation of goals (Chapter 6). The nature of the internal decision-making process was tapped by a number of variables. Information from these variables on the hierarchical level of the decisionmaker was used in the creation of the commitment scale (Chapter 8).

DEVELOPMENT OF MEASURES OF
FOREIGN POLICY BEHAVIOR

Since the data set was originally defined and gathered, CREON has progressed through three stages of activity in the creation of measures of foreign policy behavior. Stage I concerned the creation of ordinal measures that tap some single dimension of foreign policy behavior. Stage II involved the creation of additional nominal categories to incorporate into the data important kinds of information that were not adequately captured in the original data-gathering efforts. Stage III is an ongoing process of creation using the measures developed in Stages I and II.

Stage I: Scales of Foreign Policy Behavior

CREON has had a continuous interest in creating scales of foreign policy behavior. Original thoughts tended to focus on three—affect, specificity, and commitment—and the original data set included a number of variables that seemed to tap aspects of these concepts. (For a list of these variables, see C. Hermann et al., 1973: 48.) Efforts to develop scales for these three types of behaviors began at The Ohio State University during the 1973-1974 school year. Dean Swanson, Gerald Hutchins, and William Oiler worked on scales of specificity, affect, and commitment, respectively, during an informal seminar directed by Charles Hermann.

The main thrust of Stage I was the CREON Summer Seminar of 1974. The purpose of the seminar was to develop a set of behavior measures to be used by all the members of the project in their empirical research during the subsequent year. The participants in the seminar were Charles and Margaret Hermann, Maurice East, Linda Brady, and four Ohio State University graduate students: Swanson, Hutchins, Patrick Callahan, and Roger Coate.

TABLE 2.3
Concepts Chosen for Examination
During CREON Summer Seminar, 1974

Affect	Skills/resources	Substantive problem areas
Commitment	External consequentiality	Situation generation
Specificity	Acceptance/rejection ratios	Degree of activity
Independence of action	Scope/dispersion of action	Force/reward
Goal properties	Procedural issue areas	Over/under response

The first sessions of the seminar concentrated on identifying possible measures of foreign policy behavior. Each participant wrote a memorandum listing measures of interest and, if necessary, a brief explication of the meaning of the measure. That brainstorming exercise produced a list of roughly 40 distinguishable candidates for further conceptualization and development. The following few sessions were devoted to narrowing the list of candidates to a manageable set. Eventually, consensus was reached on the 15 concepts, listed in Table 2.3, that would be given further attention during the seminar.

A number of considerations shaped the choice of the 15 from among the 40. Affect, commitment, and specificity were included without any serious disagreement or even any extended discussion. In part, that was because the members of the project were impressed with the intellectual merits of these concepts, but also coming into play was the effect of "sunken" costs—the measures had already been under development for a year and there was a sense that such effort should not be wasted. Still other measures in Table 2.3 represented "umbrella" concepts under which a number of the original ideas were grouped because of some perceived commonality of substance. For example, "goal properties" was a covering label for a number of ideas: a typology of the goal's substance, the time-frame for goal achievement (short-term versus long-term), the mix of long-term and short-term goals, the number of goals, and change in goals. (A concern with foreign policy goals was the prevalent characteristic of the original lists of measures. Nearly all the seminar participants suggested some aspect of goals as a measure. Although this was partly due to the prominence of goals in foreign policy analysis, it was also clear that much of the interest in goals was because the CREON data contained information on the goals associated with each event.)

Another determinant of the set of measures in Table 2.3 was the intrinsic importance of each measure. A recurrent question was: "In what ways does this concept relate to important problems?" Usually the reply to that question was based on whether the concept or some closely related term was prominent in the scholarly or policy literature. The principal investigators were also concerned that the measures be applicable to their theoretical perspectives.

Furthermore, it appeared important to seminar members that the set of measures originally proposed reflect a variety of characteristics of foreign policy. Thus, the tendency to use force or rewards was characteristic of foreign policy output, whereas procedural issue areas would measure the decision-making process and external consequentiality would measure the impact or outcome of the output. Although no adequate scheme existed for classifying the components of policy, there was a sense that the measures included for further development should represent a mix of the components or characteristics of foreign policy. Finally, we should explicitly note that one criterion has not been mentioned so far—namely, accessibility in the CREON data. Two concepts included in Table 2.3 for further examination—situation generation and over/under response—were eventually dropped because operationalization problems proved too difficult to handle within the time demands of the project.

After the 15 concepts were identified, the seminar focused its attention on the development of each. Following three weeks of intense analysis and discussion, the seminar met to choose the measures that would serve as the set of common dependent variables in research for the coming year. The particular criteria used were (1) clarity of conceptualization; (2) relationship to the theoretical perspectives; (3) appeal to a wider academic and policymaking audience; (4) accessibility in the CREON data; and (5) personal interest. Seven concepts were included in the final set of measures: affect, commitment, professed orientation to change (a property of national goals), independence/interdependence of action, acceptance/rejection ratios, external consequentiality, and skills/resources. With the exception of skills/resources, the operationalizations of these variables were further redefined, and the variables were used in analyses leading to papers presented at the 1975 American Political Science Association meetings (Salmore and Salmore, 1975; East, 1975; Brady, 1975; M. Hermann, 1980).

Since the 1974 CREON Summer Seminar, some participants have continued Stage I efforts. Swanson continued his work on specificity, producing a dissertation developing the measure and using it in empirical analysis (1976). Hutchins did considerable work on the affect measure in the production of his dissertation (1977). East and an associate (East and Winters, 1975, 1976) developed specific scope of action variables which permitted its readmission into the behavior measures considered in this book. Further examination revealed that the professed orientation to change measure did not really assess change orientation. It has been dropped from further analysis, and Brady has returned to a more general consideration of national goal properties (Chapter 6). Problems arising with both the conceptualization and measurement of external consequentiality has led to its reconsideration and, hence, absence.

Of what significance was the process of developing these measures? Three answers suggest themselves. First, the measures reported in subsequent chapters are much more collective products than their single authorship implies.[8] Indeed, it would be impossible in most cases to allocate the credit owed to particular individuals. Second, the measures are responsive to the characteristics of the CREON data. The variables in the original data set shaped the way many of the measures were conceptualized. Because the measures were being operationalized simultaneously with conceptualization, the variables in the original data naturally biased attention toward giving added significance to those aspects of a concept (loosely understood) that were accessible in the data. This psychological process was reinforced by the necessity to produce measures that could be used in empirical research within a few months. It was practical to adapt conceptualization to make it compatible with the data. On the other hand, it should be noted that in all cases the idea for the behavior property came before the efforts to operationalize. The CREON Summer Seminar was able to give a priori conceptualization a prominent place in the process of developing measures of foreign policy behavior. The point here is that the conceptualization is not untainted by the effects of the data. The third answer to the question is that the measures are all very different in their level of development. Some have been worked on much longer than others. Thus, some authors are able to report more information, such as validity tests, than other authors. The meanings of some concepts initially were much more ambiguous than others, or the variables to be used to create the measure were not as apparent. In either case, the development of the measure required much effort in the conceptualization phase prior to operationalization. As a result, some conceptualizations are not as dependent on the specifics of the CREON data as is the case with other variables. These differences will be reflected in later chapters.

Stage II: Nominal Properties

Stage I not only produced measures for immediate research application, it also revealed some directions for development beyond the measures created in Stage I. Specifically, measures were needed for the skills and resources used in the event, the substantive concern of the action, and the procedures of decision making. The creation of these new variables constituted Stage II of the CREON measurement effort.

The perception of the importance of these variables preceded the beginning of the summer seminar. A six-category skills/resources measure was in the original data set. The original data also contained a set of 11 dichotomous variables describing the membership and structure of the internal decision unit (IDU). (For a more complete description of the IDU variables, see C. Hermann et al., 1973: 95-97). A set of 12 ad hoc behavior categories (such as foreign assistance activity, world or regional organization activity, and military behavior) was initially intended to serve, among other functions, as surrogate indicators of substantive issue or problem areas. (For a more complete description of the ad hoc variables, see C. Hermann et al., 1973: 70-73).

During the summer seminar, all three concepts—skills/resources, decision-making procedures, and substantive problem areas—were identified as behavior properties that should be examined in empirical analysis. However, the efforts to measure these concepts in the original data did not seem adequate. The skills/resources variable was heavily skewed toward diplomatic skills; 85 percent of all events fell into that category. Although diplomatic skills and resources are undoubtedly prevalent in international politics, that proportion seemed unreasonably high. After some reflection, it became clear that the original coding scheme overemphasized announcement of action, which involves diplomatic skills, rather than predecisional activities or implementation, both of which would presumably entail a broader set of skills and resources. After unsuccessfully experimenting with recombining other information in the data set, we decided that a new variable should be coded. The new variable, instrumentalities, would be based on a broader and more sophisticated conceptualization of how skills and resources can be brought to bear during the course of foreign policy action.

Different problems plagued the development of the substantive problem areas variable. For several reasons the ad hoc behavior variables did not provide an adequate indicator of substantive problem areas. Most of the 12 variables were not primarily tests of problems or issues. Nor did the 12 taken together constitute an exhaustive scheme for classifying issues. Moreover, the ad hoc variables were so general that what are ordinarily seen as distinct issues could be grouped under the same heading. For example, under the heading "Military Behavior" would fall U.S. military activities in Vietnam, British withdrawal from the Persian Gulf, Warsaw Pact force maneuvers, arms sales to Chile, granting technical assistance and training to Ghanaian soldiers in Britain, and participation of a naval force in a ceremonial activity.

The development of a new issue areas/problem areas variable proved most difficult. As detailed in Chapter 4, devising issue area classification schemes has been problematic for foreign policy researchers for some time. Within CREON, the solution to the problem was hindered by the existence of alternative visions of the nature of a useful scheme. One faction wanted a scheme emphasizing intuitively meaningful substantive categories, such as international trade, fishing rights, and Middle East conflict. This type of scheme would provide a rich link to the policy sciences but was criticized on three grounds by another faction in the project: (1) such a scheme would not be theoretically based; (2) therefore, it could not provide an exhaustive set of categories; and (3) its applicability would be restricted to a particular historical period. As described in Chapter 4, a variable was created which resolved the conflict by incorporating both a set of general, exhaustive dimensions and a set of contemporary issues.

Similar problems arose during the early efforts to measure the structure and process of decision making. As the general concept evolved, it became clear that the internal decision unit variables in CREON provided an unsatisfactory empirical base for describing decision structures and processes. Too little data were revealed by these categories. Moreover, an adequate characterization of the decision structure and process must go beyond identifying the bureaucratic participants and determining whether they were joined in an ad hoc or formal group. Other important dimensions of the phenomenon were inaccessible in the original CREON data. Unfortunately, a new coding system has not yet been completed for adding this variable, in satisfactory form, to the data set.

Unlike Stage I measures, which were created by a computer-driven recombination of information already in the data, Stage II measures required the generation of new coding rules and an additional pass through the data to append the variables to the data set. The Stage II variables do not represent single conceptual dimensions having ordinal or interval scale properties, as do the Stage I measures. Rather, they are nominal classification schemes that contain multiple dimensions and can give rise to even more. Thus, the chapters on the Stage II measures are considerably different from the chapters presenting the Stage I measures. Because the Stage II measures were created through new coding, reliability questions are more important for the Stage II measures than for the Stage I measures, which required no new coding. Conversely, because the Stage II measures do not represent unidimensional concepts, they pose different kinds of validity problems than do the Stage I measures.

Stage II illustrates the continual interplay of conceptualization and data analysis, as well as the evolutionary development of our understanding of foreign policy. The CREON Project had an early interest in the phenomena represented by the measures created during Stage II. That interest was demonstrated by the inclusion in the original data set of variables tapping each of those phenomena. Data analysis revealed, however, that these initial efforts did not provide adequate representation of the phenomena, so new conceptualizations were devised.

Stage III: Higher-Order Measures

The most recent measurement efforts in CREON have attempted to move beyond the single-event, single-dimension operationalization of foreign policy behavior. The purpose of the efforts has been to characterize foreign policy behavior by drawing together information from a number of events and, in some instances, across a variety of behavior dimensions.

The justification for such efforts is twofold. First, the recording of foreign policy behavior as events is essentially a matter of operational convenience. The event constitutes a bounded, comparable unit of observation that can be recorded by nonexpert coders with a minimum of inference. The analytic distinctiveness of individual events is not a reflection of reality; it is imposed on reality by the observer. In the real world, events are connected and interdependent. Behavior today may be molded by learning induced by responses to yesterday's behavior. Two events may represent an evolving line of policy. Discrete events may be joined as parts of a larger action-reaction process. Such assumptions should not be controversial; they certainly are not original with this chapter. The problem for foreign policy researchers is to find ways to represent the interconnections among events. To date there has been no coherent, concentrated attack on that problem.

The second justification for the Stage III efforts is that the individual behavior dimensions are likely to be interrelated in varying ways. When decision makers act, their behavior is characterized by multiple individual dimensions such as commitment, affect, independence/interdependence, and specificity. The actor makes decisions that simultaneously produce values on all these dimensions. Moreover, the actor may consciously think in terms of these dimensions. Therefore, we expect that there will be patterns of behavior across the behavior dimensions. For example, behaviors that are high on commitment may tend to be high on affect and low on independence/interdependence of action. Similarly, nations that in general act in a highly specific manner may also tend to be relatively low on affect and have a constrained repertoire of instrumentalities. Such patterns may appear across the whole range of behaviors or may be brought into relief only by imposing controls for recipients (targets and objects), substantive problem areas, or time.

It should be clear that the development of measures in Stage III could occur only after the completion of the measurement efforts in Stages I and II. These earlier measures provide the building blocks for the construction of measures in Stage III. In the chapters that follow, we will refer to the Stage I and Stage II measures, which create values for individual events on single dimensions, as first-order measures and the Stage III measures as higher-order measures.

The concept of higher-order measure can be illustrated with an example derived from current research efforts within the CREON Project. Clustering analysis, currently being executed by East at the University of Kentucky, groups nations according to the similarity of their behavior profiles across a variety of behavior properties. Thus, information is combined across events and across behavior dimensions to produce a new nominal scale measure. Chapter 13 discusses measurement strategies for the creation of higher-order measures and provides a number of additional examples drawn from research within CREON.

VALIDITY

An important aspect of measurement is validity. Measures are indicators of underlying theoretical concepts and are developed to allow empirical research on these concepts. Research can advance our understanding only if the measures are valid—that is, if they adequately represent the concepts they are supposed to assess.

Validity is a complex, multidimensional problem. The validity of the products in this book can be evaluated at two different levels. Each of the chapters in this volume takes some concept, develops a conceptual definition, and articulates a logic for observing that concept in empirical data. One may evaluate whether the results of this process seem logically coherent and persuasive. If so, then the chapter provides a sound basis for further development of the measure no matter what body of data is going to be used. For example, if specificity is developed in a conceptually sound fashion, then other researchers can apply that conceptual development to measuring specificity in any kind of data.

The second level of validity evaluation concerns the values of the measures as they are brought to fruition in the CREON data. Do the measures actually measure what they purport to measure? An answer to this question depends on answers to many subsidiary questions. Is the event an appropriate unit of analysis? Is the data set riddled with debilitating biases and inaccuracies? Does the measure hold up under empirical tests of its validity? A measure may be deemed valid on the first level of evaluation but not on the second and still have made a contribution to the discipline. However, if a measure is conceptually unsound, it is of no apparent use even if it appears to pass tests at the second level. Thus, the first level of evaluation is logically prior to and more fundamental than the second. For this reason, the chapters that follow all devote considerable attention to the conceptual development of the measure being described. Readers should consider the sections on conceptual development as arguments for the validity of the measure and judge accordingly.

Nonetheless, validity cannot be determined a priori, because there are many avenues by which a measure can come to represent extraneous influences rather than the concept to be assessed. Let us explore the extraneous influences that could affect all of the measures.

Reliability

Reliability refers to the ability of some measurement schemes to produce the same score for a case over a set of distinct measurement attempts. For the CREON Project, the most important type of reliability was intercoder reliability—whether different persons applying the same set of rules would give the same score to the same event. If so, the data do not represent idiosyncratic perceptions of the individual coders. The researcher can assume that the values represent what the coding rules say they should represent.

CREON tested the level of intercoder reliability using a Krippendorff agreement coefficient, which generalizes Scott's pi "to apply to variables incorporating multilevel decisions (decision trees) and involving multiple coders whose numbers vary across time" (C. Hermann et al., 1973: 23). The values of this coefficient, which range from 0.0 to 1.0, indicate the proportion of agreement among coders greater than that attributable to pure chance. Thus, a value of 0.0 indicates that the coding was purely random and a value of 1.0 indicates perfect agreement among coders on the proper value to be given each of a set of events on a variable.

Reliability questions are handled in two ways in the following chapters, depending on how the measure was generated. The Stage II measures were all coded by hand, and the intercoder reliability scores are presented as part of the documentation of the variable. None of the Stage I variables required new coding. They were all generated by computer, using variables in the original CREON data set. For that reason there are no overall reliability scores attached to the final measures. The reliability scores of the items going into each measure are reported either in the chapter or in the Technical Appendix at the end of the book.

We realize that reporting the reliabilities of the component items is not the same as indicating a reliability for the composite measure. Few of the CREON variables are perfectly reliable—that is, have a coefficient of 1.0. Most are partially unreliable (reliability coefficients of .72 or higher). When measures are generated by recombining information recorded in more than one variable, there is likely to be some cumulative impact of the partial unreliability of each of the component variables. The nature of that impact is unknown. At first it might seem that the reliabilities of the component items suggest limits on the degree of unreliability. Measures created out of low reliability items are unlikely to represent what they purport to represent. But this suggestion is not necessarily true because the intercoder reliability of a whole coding scheme may mask relevant information.

Consider a variable consisting of five categories. The coding rules provide guides for assigning any case to one of these categories. The rules for distinguishing some of the categories (one through three, perhaps) may be clearly written and easy to apply in particular coding decisions, whereas the other rules may be obscure and difficult to apply. (Most persons with actual coding experience will testify to the truth of this claim.) The result would be that one could be extremely confident about the accuracy of a coding decision if the case were coded one, two, or three but should probably be wary of a case coded four or five. The accepted procedure of reporting a single reliability score for a variable, however, hides the more differentiated nature of reliability. Commitment, independence/interdependence of action, specificity, and the acceptance/rejection ratios were all created by using selected categories of variables rather than the entire variable. An assessment of the quality of the measure depends, therefore, on the reliability with which the relevant distinctions can be made, not on the reliability of the variable as a whole. Because the reporting of more detailed reliability information would have required a significant drain on resources as well as the creation of appropriate measures, we have not broken down reliability. However, in several cases where we knew coders had a difficult time with a specific code, we avoided using it in developing the composite measures.

Events as the Unit of Analysis

As indicated earlier, CREON records the foreign policy behavior of nations as minimally aggregated events. That procedure has a number of technical benefits —for example, minimizing coder inference in the definition of the unit of observation and ensuring maximum flexibility in later applications of the data to diverse research problems. Nevertheless, minimal aggregation affects the validity of some of the measures that may conceptually assume a more aggregated unit of analysis. Commitment (Chapter 8) provides an excellent illustration of this point. Commitment measures the extent to which an action creates constraints on the actor's future activity by allocating resources and by creating expectations in others. As the measure is presented in Chapter 8, each minimally aggregated event is assigned a commitment score. One could reasonably argue, however, that constraints actually result from the configuration of events that constitute the whole activity (speech, resolution, array of decisions), not the level of commitment in each of the individual events. Similar problems may arise with efforts to measure affect (Chapter 9) and specificity (Chapter 10).

It should be noted that these validity problems do not result from inadequate conceptualization of the behavior property. The conceptualizations of the scales could be applied to other units of observation, although some minor modifications might be required. To the extent that there is a problem, it is because of the minimally aggregated form of the data. The proper solution is to reaggregate the data—that is, to build representations of more inclusive activities out of the minimally aggregated events—rather than to reject the measures in their totality. The means by which the data could be reaggregated are not entirely obvious. Simple arithmetic or algebraic computations probably will not suffice. Instead, procedures will have to trace the interactive effects of the minimally aggregated events constituting a larger activity.

In this volume we have not presented analyses based on reaggregated events. That does not mean we have been insensitive to the problems discussed above. Rather, we have given priority to the development of behavior measures because (1) we could not do both simultaneously, (2) development of acceptable methods of data reaggregation is a taxing problem, and (3) it is not clear how seriously compromised our results are using minimally aggregated events as the unit of analysis. We believe that the measures reported in this volume can produce research advances in their present state, even if they are imperfect.

Source Validity

The picture of the world provided by event data depends on the picture implicit in the data's source. The more closely the source approximates reality (and reality can never be completely known), the more valid the results using that source. For that reason, event data researchers have devoted considerable attention to the representativeness of their sources. (Recent research on the "source validity problem" is presented in Munton, 1978.)

Source validity cannot be evaluated without considering the purposes of the research. A source that provides an excellent basis for describing the foreign policy behavior of a particular nation may be quite inadequate for all the other nations. Similarly, a source providing an accurate comparison of a set of geographically diverse nations may produce an inferior description of the behavior of a subset when, for example, compared to the coverage in a specialized regional source. In this context we should remember that the purpose of CREON is cross-national, global comparison.

The assumption that source validity can be a problem for event data comes from the belief that news media give greater emphasis to certain kinds of news stories: those involving conflict, identifiable individuals, elite persons and nations, and that which is unexpected (Galtung and Ruge, 1965; Ostgaard, 1965). To the extent that these assumptions are accurate, they imply a predictable pattern of bias in news reporting that should be consistent across news agencies. In addition, it has also been assumed that news is more likely to be reported if it deals with subjects that are culturally proximate and familiar and if the substance of the news is consonant with deeply held beliefs and ideological preconceptions. These two forces may produce different patterns of bias across news agencies because what is proximate and familiar will vary across locations and what is consonant with beliefs will vary across ideologies. These assumptions suggest the proposition that the more widely varied the sources from which *Deadline Data* (CREON's source) abstracted its stories, the less the impact of any single set of biases, and the more valid the data.

Deadline Data abstracts commentary and analysis on some of its news stories as part of its narrative, identifying the source of the commentary. Gatliff (1974) examined the sources of commentary in order to assess the relative frequency with which *Deadline Data* draws news from a variety of sources. The results are reported in Table 2.4. A total of 64 original sources were identified. Of the events *having an identified source,* the majority were reported in the United States press (62 percent); a large number (36 percent) came from the press of other Western nations, including Japan and Israel; and relatively few (less than 1 percent each) came from sources in the Third World or Communist nations.

These figures suggest some tentative conclusions. First, the CREON data probably represent many editorial perspectives and interests. Second, the predominance of Western sources suggests the possibility of a Western bias to the CREON data. That danger can be overestimated, however. The Western sources represent many nations and many viewpoints; they are not homogeneous. Third, the Communist and Third World countries tend to be underrepresented. The resulting bias may be somewhat mitigated, however, by the fact that the Soviet Union and China are elite nations and will be attended to by most news sources, by the fact that the Eastern European nations are proximate and familiar to the Western European nations, and by the fact that some Third World nations are of great interest to their former colonial masters which are Western nations. All of these factors suggest that the nations in those regions will be provided better coverage than the figures would seem to imply.

TABLE 2.4
Number of CREON Events Abstracted
from Sources Used by *Deadline Data*

Deadline Data Sources	Freq.[a]	Percent	Deadline Data Sources	Freq.[a]	Percent
New York Times	2208	37.6	Hsinhua News Agency	7	0.1
Times, London	736	12.5	Paris Ed., New York Times	7	0.1
Christian Science Monitor	423	7.2	New China News Agency	6	0.1
Economist	419	7.1	Africa Report	5	0.1
Monde	373	6.3	Bulletin of EEC	5	0.1
New York Herald Tribune	266	4.5	The Reporter	5	0.1
Washington Post	248	4.2	Tass News Agency	5	0.1
Guardian	199	3.4	Chicago Daily News	4	0.1
Los Angeles Times	133	2.3	Nouvel Observateur	4	0.1
Baltimore Sun	120	2.0	Review of Int'l. Affairs	4	0.1
Neue Zurcher Zeitung	86	1.5	Canadian Press	3	0.1
Welt	85	1.4	New York World Telegram	3	0.1
Int'l. Financial News Survey	55	0.9	Philadelphia Enquirer	3	0.1
Frankfurter Allemeigne	41	0.7	Spiegel	3	0.1
Observer	41	0.7	Foreign Commerce Weekly	2	0.0
US News and World Report	37	0.6	Havana Radio	2	0.0
Financial Times	31	0.5	Korea Herald	2	0.0
World Today	29	0.5	Pravda	2	0.0
European Community	28	0.5	TANYUNG News Agency	2	0.0
East Europe	27	0.5	US State Dept. News Release	1	0.0
World Business	23	0.4	Agence France Presse	1	0.0
People's Daily	23	0.4	African Recorder	1	0.0
Figaro	22	0.4	France Soir	1	0.0
West Africa	21	0.4	Izvestia	1	0.0
Pakistan Times	20	0.3	Jeune Afrique	1	0.0
Asian Recorder	20	0.3	Jerusalem Post Weekly	1	0.0
International Commerce	17	0.3	L'Unite Africaine	1	0.0
Swiss Review of World Affairs	12	0.2	New Statesman	1	0.0
Weltwoche	12	0.2	Newark Star-Ledger	1	0.0
Associated Press	11	0.2	Peking Review	1	0.0
Carriere della Sera	8	0.1	Times, India	·1	0.0
Reuters News Agency	8	0.1	United Press International	1	0.0
			TOTAL	5878	100.0

[a] Only those events in the CREON data set for which a source was indicated in *Deadline Data* are counted here.

Gatliff's study revealed that *The New York Times,* which produced 38 percent of the events, was the most frequent source used by *Deadline Data.* This is a useful piece of data because much attention has been paid to the value of *The New York Times* as a source of event data. Some researchers (Azar et al., 1972b; Burrowes, 1974; Hoggard, 1975; Smith, 1969) find that, compared to regional sources, the *Times* is biased toward reporting conflict and the behavior of Western nations. The precise extent of the *Times*'s bias is unknown, because differences in reporting could result from the biases of both the *Times* and the regional source. Others (Hazelwood and West, 1974; McClelland, 1972a) dispute the significance of the *Times*'s bias. Although they acknowledge that it is inferior to regional sources for studying regional interactions, they argue that it is still the best available source for studying global patterns. Because CREON is concerned with making global comparisons, the largely *Times*-based source may be the most adequate single source. The inclusion in *Deadline Data* of events from other sources helps to lessen even further the dangers of source bias.

Another perspective on the validity problem involves *Deadline Data*'s mission. It is designed for use by scholars and government officials. Thus, the criteria for news selection will differ from those used by newspapers. Compared to other news sources, it should give less emphasis to human interest or sensational stories.

Before we draw any conclusions about the source validity problems of the CREON data, note should be taken of studies that have assessed the value of *Deadline Data* relative to other sources (Azar et al., 1972b; Burrowes, 1974; Doran et al., 1973; Hoggard, 1967). These studies have returned negative verdicts on *Deadline Data.* However, they are not directly relevant to an evaluation of the CREON data for the following reasons: (1) they compared *Deadline Data* to a regional source; (2) they included years before *Deadline Data* began to be published and which are therefore covered scantily; (3) they did not search for events under all appropriate headings used by *Deadline Data*; (4) they studied internal conflict rather than foreign policy; or (5) they used a library edition of *Deadline Data.* The last point is especially significant. The editors of *Deadline Data* make a conscious effort to update their files, by adding new data as the time frame of the chronology expands, while maintaining a constant size for the files. In order to meet this goal, the library file is constantly reedited, with older entries deleted or compressed onto a single card. One stark example is Laos. The 1975 library copy of *Deadline Data* contained one card that replaced 192 cards from the original file. It is little wonder, then, that researchers using a library copy of *Deadline Data* would find it an inadequate source. CREON uses an uncollapsed file—the complete, backdated chronology—which contains over twice the number of events in the library copy (C. Hermann et al., 1973).

Our conclusion, then, is that the source validity problem inherent in the CREON data is probably slight. The data may be used in empirical analysis with fairly high confidence in all but the most subtle distinctions.

External Tests of Validity

The discussion of reliability and source problems underscores an important quality of validity: Although the logical coherence of the development of a measure from a concept is a necessary condition for the measure's validity, it is not a sufficient one. Even if the community of scholar-experts were to agree that the measurement scheme *ought* to tap the concept in question, this would not establish that it *does*. Rather, one must go beyond a priori assessment and attempt to determine if the measure works empirically.

Although the degree of validity testing varies considerably across the measures reported in this volume, two kinds of data on which to make a preliminary assessment of validity are common across all chapters. First, each chapter reports a set of sample events grouped according to the scale values on the measure. Although the sample is too small to draw any definitive conclusions, it does allow the reader to judge whether the ranking appears to be wildly incongruent with the definition of the concept being measured. Second, each chapter arrays the CREON data across the values of the scale and across nations. The reader may examine these arrays to see if they have anomalous qualities. If they do not, that provides some support for the validity of the measures.

We are aware that these are weak tests of validity. Nevertheless, they provide a starting point. The assessment of the plausibility of an array of data would seem to be a natural first test of validity. Moreover, such a test can prove important. For example, in a recent discussion about the value of quantitative approaches to diplomatic history, one of the primary considerations was whether quantitative indicators of power and status provided national rankings that seemed reasonable to the informed historian (Alexandroff et al., 1977; Schroeder, 1977; Small, 1977). Arguments about the plausibility of the data arrays were used by both the critics and the defenders of quantitative historical analysis. In a similar fashion, in a recent review of two quantitative analyses of international politics, Singer (1977) evaluated the plausibility of the data as a validity check.

Such validation tests must be considered preliminary. They allow only highly impressionistic assessments. More rigorous external tests of validity must follow. A massive literature has been developed detailing alternative rigorous validation tests (for example, see Mosteller, 1968; Shively, 1974; and Campbell and Fiske, 1959).

The most commonly applied validation tests check for *criterion validity*—that is, the measure is compared with some external criterion. One type of criterion validity test involves comparing the scores of a series of cases on the measure with the scores assigned those cases by a panel of expert judges. If the scores are highly correlated, then one may conclude that the measure is producing scores consistent with the common view of the meaning of the concept. In Chapter 10 Swanson reports one such validation test for the specificity scale.

A second type of criterion validity test is *concurrent validation*. Here, the researcher correlates the scores derived from the measure with the scores derived from some other, presumably valid, indicator of the same concept. If they are not highly correlated, we would have some doubts about the validity of the scale. An example of this is Holsti and North's (1966) study of the correlation between their content analysis measure of decision makers' perceptions of hostility and the fluctuations in economic indicators prior to the outbreak of World War I.

Predictive validity is a third type of criterion validation. Here one seeks to determine if a measurement scheme enables one to predict accurately something that should be predictable given a valid measure of the concept. The credibility of sample surveys of public opinion rests partly on the pollsters' success at predicting election results, a predictive validity test. Similarly, the validity of the Survey Research Center/Center for Political Studies' measure of a respondent's party identification is buttressed by the high correlation between that measure and reported voting behavior. In predictive validation testing, if the predictions fail, one must reassess the validity of the measure.

A final approach to validation is *construct validity*. This involves embedding a concept in a network of theoretical statements relating multiple variables. From this network hypotheses are derived stating which relationships among variables are expected to be positive, which are expected to be negative, and which are expected to approach zero. Tests are conducted; if the hypotheses are borne out, then confidence in the validity of the measure is enhanced.

These different types of validity tests are potentially powerful devices in the toolbox of foreign policy researchers. One of the serious gaps in the CREON measurement effort to date has been the paucity of such tests. (In the Epilogue, after the measures have all been described, suggestions for validation studies of specific measures are put forward as one direction for future research.) At this point, though, it may be helpful to consider some of the impediments to validation research, impediments that partially explain the deficiency in this area.

Tests of concurrent validity require that alternative indicators of the same concept be available and that the researcher be confident that these indicators also have high degrees of validity. Such conditions cannot be met for many of the measures in this volume. Most of the chapters constitute the first attempts to measure a specific concept, so no alternative indicator exists. Other chapters concern concepts that previously have been developed into measures by others, but the conceptual development underlying the CREON measure differs so substantially from that underlying its precursor that it remains an open question whether the two measures really concern the same concept.

Predictive and construct validation tests presume that the variable being measured can be related in some cause-effect fashion to other variables. This should be the case for all variables, for as Brady argued in Chapter One, one criterion of a good variable is that it should have theoretical (or policy) importance. Nevertheless, there is a large jump from the hunches that we currently rely on about the theoretical significance of a concept to the kinds of precise statements about relationships that one must make before attempting to conduct predictive or construct validation tests. Before the results of such tests can be considered conclusive evidence of the invalidity or validity of a measure, the researcher must be confident both that the hypotheses or predictions are true at the conceptual level and that the measures of the other variables are valid. Otherwise, in principle, the failure of a prediction or hypothesis may be attributed to a variety of factors other than the invalidity of the particular measure. It is our judgment that the comparative study of foreign policy has not yet reached the stage of maturity where the body of extensively tested and supported theory and measurement is adequate enough to avoid such indeterminacy.

Summary

Except when the evaluations are clearly negative, the validity of a measure is a matter of degree. Measures are more or less valid. Moreover, faith in the validity of a measure must always be somewhat tentative, because additional tests of validity can always be devised. No test is able to prove conclusively that a measure is valid. Within the boundaries of these assumptions, what can we say about the validity of the measures reported in this book? Clearly, we cannot say much with confidence; we have conducted too few validation tests to allow anything but tentative suggestions. Nevertheless, the evidence available to us, however meager, points in the same general direction. We are led to believe that the measures are more rather than less valid. We have worked hard to make them conceptually sound and reasonably operationalized. The data base does not appear to suffer from serious source validity problems. Moreover, the initial empirical tests of validity, though modest, do lend credence to our belief in the basic validity of the measures.

More significantly, it is clear that validation of these measures cannot progress very far independent of parallel progress in the comparative study of foreign policy, progress that this volume is intended to promote. It is our belief that reporting our efforts now will stimulate the development of the field, thereby encouraging better validation processes than if we withheld reporting on these behavior measures pending further validation tests on our own.

IN CONCLUSION

This volume draws together the efforts of members of the CREON Project to conceptualize and to operationalize aspects of nations' foreign policy behavior. In this chapter we have described the primary characteristics of the CREON Project and data set. We have provided some history on the development of the measures presented in this book and indicated something about the validity of the measures. Before moving to the discussion of individual behavior measures, we describe one of the first attempts by members of the CREON Project to assess foreign policy behavior. This attempt demonstrates in a dramatic fashion why we have moved from relying on inductive techniques to emphasizing the development of concepts in identifying new dimensions of foreign policy.

NOTES

1. For an extended discussion of the CREON Project and data set, see C. Hermann et al. (1973) and East et al. (1978).

2. For overview descriptions of other projects in quantitative international relations, see Hoole and Zinnes (1976) and Burgess and Lawton (1972). For descriptions of specific projects, see Leng (1975), Singer and Small (1972), Small and Singer (1979), Azar (1971), and Sherwin (1973).

3. This rule was stated before the development of the commitment scale discussed in Chapter 8, and should not be confused with that scale.

4. Rules used by CREON for distinguishing political-level decisions during military conflicts are recorded in Hermann and Swanson (1972). Other relevant documentation regarding the

distinction of political decisions from other actions can be found in C. Hermann (1971a, 1971b).

5. This criterion might be juxtaposed with that used in the World Event Interaction Survey (WEIS). WEIS considers all governmental actions reported in public sources as events, because the public reporting is presumed to indicate that the action is an influence attempt. This procedure makes the boundary between relevant and irrelevant governmental actions largely dependent on the ebb and flow of editorial opinion and judgment within the news gathering and reporting agencies. That news organizations deem an action important and thus worthy of being reported may be a valid way to mark out those events for inclusion if one is interested in mapping the interactions between pairs of nations. Such an interest makes no distinction between the levels of government at which the actions occur. CREON's concern with foreign policy decisions, on the other hand, mandates a distinction between the political-level authorities, who can make such decisions, and those at other bureaucratic levels, who cannot.

6. All analyses in the following chapters are based on the most recent version of the CREON data—Version 6.00.

7. Space does not permit a thorough presentation of the variables in the data set. The Technical Appendix presents the variables that were used in the development of the measures used. Readers interested in all the variables should consult C. Hermann et al. (1973).

8. This point does not apply to the specificity measure as much as to the others, because Swanson was working on this measure prior to the summer seminar and because of the extensive later work in his dissertation.

3

STEPHEN A. SALMORE
BARBARA G. SALMORE

Defining the Limits of the
Inductive Approach

Progress in the comparative study of foreign policy has been hampered by the lack of attention paid to the conceptualization and operationalization of dimensions of foreign policy behavior. This concern has been evident for some time. As Rosenau et al. (1973: 126) noted, the Inter-University Comparative Foreign Policy group (ICFP), which began meetings in 1969, found:

> The issue most constraining to subsequent research proved to be our inability to make progress in solving the problem of identifying, classifying, and operationalizing types of foreign policy behavior—the dependent variable to be subjected to inquiry.

McClelland (1972a: 27), a major figure in the pioneering work on the scientific study of foreign policy, also observed:

> There exist different kinds of foreign policy output and ... it is essential to discover which linked domestic or intrapolity processes are associated regularly with which types of foreign policy outputs. ... Once types of foreign policy output are known, the foreign policy analyst can begin to trace back the linked processes to their domestic origin and to establish explanations (i.e., build models and express theories) of foreign policy formulation.

AUTHORS' NOTE: An earlier version of this chapter, co-authored with Fred Butler and Scott Taylor, was presented at the Workshop on Foreign Policy Behavior: Events Data Approaches, Annual Convention of the Southern Political Science Association, New Orleans, November 7-9, 1974.

McClelland went on to complain that "virtually no work on this taxonomy has been undertaken to date."

Quantitative efforts to describe and classify foreign policy behavior in the past several years have been confined almost exclusively to inductive strategies made possible by the generation of foreign policy event data. Unlike most traditional foreign policy analyses, which offer largely ad hoc and qualitative concept-ualizations of selected foreign policy dimensions (as described in C. Hermann, 1971a, and Kegley, 1973), these empirical, event-based typologies "seek to de-lineate types of foreign policy behavior by statistically testing for the degree to which the constructed classes of external conduct manifest empirically distinct variations" (Kegley et al., 1974: 312).

Because inductive data reduction techniques, particularly factor analysis, have been so prevalent in the efforts to create measures of foreign policy, it is impera-tive that researchers attend to the implications of using these methods. This chapter takes up that task. Specifically, we address the question of whether inductive data reduction techniques such as factor analysis can reveal the universe of empirically useful dimensions of foreign policy. To anticipate our conclusions, we find that such techniques do not have this capability, since they are influenced by researchers' preconceptions of what constitute important di-mensions of foreign policy behavior.

BACKGROUND

Kegley et al. (1974) reviewed seven typologies that were inductively derived from event data. The purpose of their investigation was to assess the extent to which these typologies converged, "and thereby provide a basis for determining the dimensionality of the structure of interstate behavior and its basic classes of action" (p. 315). Because factor analysis was the major data reduction technique in all seven of the studies, and because descriptions of the variables used were also available for all of the studies, it was possible to determine whether similar patterning of foreign policy behaviors emerged in all of the studies. Such a comparison was performed even though the various studies represented different time periods, included different actors, and were generated by different coders. The principal substantive finding which emerged from this exercise was that all seven studies produced a small number of highly structured dimensions of foreign policy behavior. In addition, six of the seven studies produced factor-analytic dimensions that could reasonably be labeled "cooperative" behavior, "conflict-ful" behavior, and "participatory" or "diplomatic" behavior (actions that keep nations in contact with each other and keep the international system in motion).

Closer inspection of the one persistently "deviant case" among the seven studies revealed that it was the only one of the seven based on a fundamentally different coding scheme. Authors of six of the studies had utilized variants of the event coding schemes developed by Rummel (1966b) in the Dimensionality of Nations (DON) Project and by McClelland and Hoggard (1969) in the World Event Interaction Survey (WEIS) Project. The seventh study, however, was based on one of the several foreign event coding schemes, largely unrelated to WEIS, developed by the Comparative Research on the Events of Nations (CREON) Project (C. Hermann et al., 1973). Kegley et al. (1974: 323) thus concluded:

The *a priori,* postulational coding system that is used to order the raw data is extremely important in determining the final empirical typology. . . .

Future typological research should set as a high priority the utilization of diverse *a priori* coding systems.

In this chapter, we attempt to sharpen our understanding of the impact of the initial coding scheme on the results of inductive typologizing efforts. Different factor analyses of foreign policy behavior may produce different results because the researchers' preconceptions about foreign policy behavior are translated into the variables they seek to explore. The CREON data set is particularly useful for ascertaining the impact of these different preconceptions because it contains multiple variable subsets while permitting controls for nations, time periods, data sources, and coders.

METHOD

From the CREON data set one may extract six different variable subsets that may be separately factor analyzed to derive empirically based measures of foreign policy. The CREON data contain at least three different classifications of foreign policy behavior for which all events are coded. As we shall explain, these can be further manipulated to produce six behavior data sets for further analysis. The three basic schemes are:

(1) *Revised WEIS.* A "WEIS-like" scheme that adopts the amendments to the original WEIS scheme suggested by Corson (1970), in addition to a few other categories added by the CREON researchers.

(2) *Sequential Action Scheme (SAS).* A branching scheme that attempts to capture the assumptions underlying the WEIS scheme. These include distinctions between verbal and deed behavior, elicited and unelicited behavior, contingent and noncontingent nature of desires and intentions, as well as indications of level of commitment and affect.

(3) *CREON Variables.* A number of variables that attempt to classify several important properties of foreign policy behavior other than the action itself. These include such properties as the setting and context of the event and the nature of the recipient. These variables are neither mutually exclusive nor exhaustive.

Full documentation on these schemes can be found in C. Hermann et al. (1973).

The Kegley et al. (1974) paper noted two differences between WEIS and CREON event data sets which merit some discussion before the six behavior subsets are identified and described. First, an event in the WEIS coding scheme includes a single actor and a single target. An event in the CREON data, on the other hand, involves an actor and multiple targets as well as one or more indirect objects (see Chapter 2 for an explication of these terms). The CREON data set can be made equivalent to WEIS by separating out the individual targets and objects and having each figure in a separate event for the actor. (Henceforth, we will refer to an event with a single actor but multiple targets/objects as a "monadic event" and an event with a single actor and target as a "dyadic event.")

The second difference between the two data sets revolves around the fact that analyses using WEIS categories must be based on the absolute number of (frequency of) events in any given action category. Because of technical problems it is impossible to analyze the WEIS data in terms of percentages. With mutually exclusive categories, percentages cannot be examined because the resulting correlation matrix would be indeterminate. Because the sum of each nation's percentages would equal 100, any one item in the data matrix would be a linear combination of the remaining items, and the correlation matrix could not be inverted. With the exception of the revised WEIS and SAS schemes, the CREON data set does not have any logical interdependencies that militate against analyses based on percentages (Coate, 1974) and therefore can be examined in both percentage and frequency terms.

These characteristics of the CREON data set make it possible to identify six separate variable subsets that may be analyzed to produce empirical dimensions of foreign policy behavior:

(1) Revised WEIS (WEIS)
(2) Sequential Action Scheme (SAS)
(3) CREON variables, monadic absolute (frequencies)
(4) CREON variables, monadic percentages
(5) CREON variables, dyadic absolute (frequencies)
(6) CREON variables, dyadic percentages

The WEIS scheme, as we have explained, can only be analyzed dyadically. Part of the SAS scheme, the affect component, also can only be analyzed dyadically, because affect can vary among the multiple targets and objects present in the same event. Some variables in the SAS scheme are amenable to either dyadic or monadic analysis. These have been included in the CREON variables.

A factor analysis of each of these six data sets was performed using a principal factor method of extraction.[1] Because there were 35 nations in the CREON data set when these analyses were performed, it was necessary to reduce the number of variables in each subset to less than 35.[2] In all cases, 26 or fewer variables were used. This reduction was accomplished by combining variables according to the following criteria. First, only variables with very small Ns were considered as candidates for combining. Second, on the basis of a hierarchical clustering analysis, only those variables which appeared to have similar profiles were considered as candidates. Finally, variables were combined only when they made some theoretical sense in combination.

Communalities were estimated by the largest off-diagonal correlation. Originally, all factors with eigenvalues greater than 1 were orthogonally rotated to a varimax solution. However, because the point of the exercise was to explain any similarities between factors derived from these different data sets, we thought it appropriate to use a less stringent criterion. Therefore, we rotated those factors with values less than 1 but greater than .6 which yielded an "interpretable" factor after rotation. A summary of the six factor analyses is presented in Appendix 3.1 at the end of this chapter. Factor scores were obtained for each factor derived from the six factor analyses. An intercorrelation matrix of all the factor scores was then calculated. This matrix appears in Appendix 3.2.

RESULTS

Revised WEIS

The factor analysis of the WEIS variables resulted in a pattern of rotated and unrotated loadings similar to that reported in previous studies. Salmore and Munton (1974), using original WEIS data, found three factors explaining 65.7 percent of the total variance. The first two unrotated factors were characterized as an inverse commitment dimension (or general measure of activity) and a conflict-cooperation dimension, respectively. The third unrotated factor, although similar to the second, seemed to tap military behavior. In the present analysis, using the CREON revised WEIS categories, three factors were extracted which explained 84.6 percent of the total variance. As in the Salmore and Munton study, the first unrotated factor corresponds closely to inverse commitment or general level of activity, whereas the second factor has a cooperation-conflict character. The third unrotated factor, although weak, shows moderately high, negative loadings for military force variables and positive loadings for such variables as agree, negotiate, and carry out agreement.

When orthogonally rotated, three fairly discrete factors can be identified. Table 3.1 presents the variable loadings on these factors. The first factor (F1.1) characterized by high loadings on agree, negotiate, increase relationship, carry out agreement, reward, and positive proposal clearly represents a positive behavior dimension. The second factor (F1.2) shows high loadings on negative intention, force, demonstrate, deny, and negative deeds, with very low scores on agree, negative desire, and carry out agreement, suggesting a negative deeds dimension. The third factor (F1.3) is distinguished by high loadings on such behavior categories as negative desire, accuse, threaten, and warn, with very low loadings for agree, reward, and negotiate. This factor seems to be a negative verbal behavior dimension. Kegley et al. (1974: 16) argued that WEIS-based factor analyses yield three factors which can be characterized as representing participation, affect, and war. The results just presented generally support these findings. The first, or positive behavior, factor shows high loadings on participatory kinds of behaviors. The second and third factors deal with negative deeds and negative verbal behavior. The negative verbal behavior factor is similar to the affect factor identified by Kegley et al., while the negative deeds factor includes, among other related kinds of behavior, both warring and warlike actions.

Sequential Action Scheme (SAS)

The Sequential Action Scheme (SAS) employs a decision tree to characterize foreign policy behavior. Five of the branches were used in this exercise:

(1) The nature of verbal behavior (statements of evaluation, desire, or intention) or of physical deeds (symbolic, significant, military nonconflict, or military conflict).

TABLE 3.1
Factor Loadings for Revised WEIS Categories

Revised WEIS Categories	Factors $F1.1^a$	F1.2	F1.3
Agree	.93	.16	.09
Negotiate	.93	.20	.06
Increase relationship	.80	.40	.33
Carry out agreement	.79	.06	.28
Reward	.78	.45	.07
Positive proposal	.72	.47	.43
Consult	.69	.44	.44
Positive comment	.68	.68	.23
Reject	.68	.38	.55
Approve	.65	.48	.18
Negative intention	.41	.86	.27
Force	.21	.84	.15
Demonstrate	.45	.79	.31
Deny	.47	.79	.33
Negative deed	.59	.70	.28
Offer	.44	.69	.42
Yield	-.07	.66	.31
Negative comment	.62	.63	.42
Promise	.48	.61	.48
Positive request	.41	.56	.34
Negative desire	.22	.08	.94
Accuse	.03	.27	.89
Threaten	.18	.44	.83
Warn	.24	.38	.81
Negative proposal	.31	.21	.64

[a] The notation indicates the first variable subset, first dimension extracted.

(2) If the behavior was verbal, an elaboration of the nature of the statement (e.g., contingent verbal policy).
(3) Whether the action was desired (positive) or undesired (negative) by the recipient.
(4) Whether the action was elicited or unelicited.
(5) Whether the actor acted alone or together with another party.

From among the 108 possible combinations of the variables, 26 combinations were distilled for use in the analysis, each having an N of over 249 events in the sample. The final variables are presented in Table 3.2, as are the factor analysis results on these variables.

TABLE 3.2
Factor Loadings for SAS Variables

SAS Variables	Factors			
	F2.1	F2.2	F2.3	F2.4
Unelicited, negative, specific evaluation of other's policy	.91	.29	.22	.02
Unelicited, negative statement of desire concerning future verbal policy or future deed	.89	.20	.06	.34
Negative, contingent statement of intention	.89	.36	.12	−.02
Negative evaluation of own policy	.76	.58	.18	.13
Acts alone, unelicited, positive statement of desire concerning future verbal policy or future deed	.70	.50	.31	.31
Negative statement of desire or intention concerning general policy	.67	.49	.46	.25
Negative symbolic, significant, or military nonconflict deed	.66	.81	.26	.13
Unelicited, positive, specific evaluation of other's policy	.61	.60	.40	.28
Unelicited, positive, symbolic deed	.57	.38	.49	.38
Acts alone, positive statement of desire or intention concerning general policy	.56	.53	.55	.18
Positive, military conflict deed	.28	.91	.20	.91
Negative, military conflict deed	.34	.87	.14	.11
Negative, noncontingent statement of intention	.59	.70	.31	.15
Positive, contingent statement of intention	.65	.67	.21	.08
Positive, military nonconflict deed	.55	.65	.32	.34
Positive, noncontingent statement of intention	.45	.62	.54	.28
Elicited, negative, specific evaluation of other's policy	.53	.61	.11	.40
Positive evaluation of own policy	.55	.60	.44	.34
Unelicited, positive significant deed	.24	.09	.80	.30
Elicited, positive significant deed	.11	.31	.80	.34
Acts together, positive statement of desire or intention about general policy	.08	.17	.77	.43
Positive or negative statement about procedural matter	.54	.33	.64	.34
Elicited, positive, specific evaluation of other's policy	.06	.12	.22	.88
Acts together, unelicited, positive statement of desire concerning future verbal policy or future deed	.15	.16	.31	.79
Elicited, positive, symbolic deed	.08	.14	.25	.74
Elicited, positive statement of desire concerning future verbal policy or future deed	.43	.21	.42	.69

The factor analysis produced four factors explaining 89.8 percent of the total variance. The four factors were rotated to an orthogonal solution. The first rotated factor (F2.1) is characterized by negative, primarily unelicited verbal behavior. The second factor (F2.2) showed high loadings for both of the military conflict clusters, as well as for both categories containing noncontingent behavior. This factor seems to represent a high commitment, military behavior dimension. All clusters loading highly on the third factor (F2.3) involved positive behavior. The two highest loadings were for significant deeds; the rest were for lower commitment, verbal behavior. The fourth factor (F2.4), clearly similar to the third, showed high loadings for positive behavior and, in three of the four variable clusters defining the factor, by elicited behavior.

The correlations between the SAS factors and the WEIS factors are important to note. (These correlations are found in Appendix 3.2.) SAS Factors 3 and 4

TABLE 3.3
Factor Loadings for CREON Variables,
Monadic Absolute Data

CREON Variables	Factors		
	F3.1	F3.2	F3.3
Acts with others	.89	.12	.44
Elicited behavior	.87	.41	.24
Bargaining behavior	.87	.35	.34
Multiple targets	.86	.43	.23
World organization behavior	.82	.28	.12
Regional organization behavior	.79	.15	.40
Deed behavior	.74	.59	.25
Foreign assistance behavior	.71	.62	.16
Treaty behavior	.59	.57	.46
Domestic target	.25	.92	.27
Unilateral alteration behavior	.41	.88	.24
Multiple objects	.47	.83	.27
Propaganda/cultural behavior	.05	.83	.32
Military behavior	.60	.79	.10
Penetrative behavior	.61	.74	-.05
Comment behavior	.64	.74	.22
Protocol behavior	.54	.62	.41
Economic transaction behavior	.54	.25	.74
Border behavior	.23	.35	.53

(F2.3, F2.4), clearly related to each other in a cooperative behavior dimension, are correlated with WEIS Factor 1 (F1.1) (positive behavior) at levels of .75 and .56, respectively. SAS Factor 2 (F2.2), characterized by military behavior, correlates .93 with WEIS Factor 2 (F1.2), the negative deeds dimension. Rounding out the interrelationships, SAS Factor 1 (F2.1), representing negative verbal behavior, correlates .96 with WEIS Factor 3 (F1.3), also characterized by highly negative verbal behavior.

CREON Variables, Monadic Absolute Data

Table 3.3 presents the rotated factor-analytic solution for 19 CREON variables in frequency form from the monadic deck. Three factors emerge which together explain 90.3 percent of the total variation in the data.

An examination of the first factor (F3.1) reveals its general character. Of the 19 variables, 14 load above .50, and 41.9 percent of the total variance is explained by this dimension. The variables loading most heavily primarily involve multilateral behavior. The first six items all pertain to action in multilateral settings, and all six load above .75 on this factor. Other items that load high seem to involve high commitment acts.

The second factor (F3.2) also seems to be a general dimension of activity. Some 36.5 percent of the total variance in the data is explained by this factor, and 11 of the 19 variables load above .50. Although there is considerable overlap with the first factor, the major difference centers on the high loadings on items that involve unilateral action settings. All of the items loading above .80 on this factor tend to describe initiatory action by nations. Of interest here is the fact that actions involving multiple objects fall on a different dimension from those involving multiple targets. The latter load most heavily on the factor that seems to tap multilateral behavior, while the former load on the more unilateral dimension. Thus, it appears that, when nations take unilateral actions, they tend to be making indirect influence attempts rather than direct ones. On the other hand, the relatively weak loading of the multiple objects category on the first factor indicates that action in multilateral settings tends to involve more direct influence attempts. These two findings lend support to the position of the CREON investigators that the use of direct and indirect influence attempts merits the attention of researchers.

The third factor (F3.3) describes a much more specific dimension than the first two. This factor seems to be characterized primarily by economic behavior. It explains 11.9 percent of the total variance, and only two items load above .50.

Comparison of the results of this analysis with the results of the first two factor analyses suggests that somewhat different patterns have been tapped. Factor 1 from this monadic absolute analysis (F3.1) is rather highly correlated (.83) with Factor 1 of the WEIS factor analysis (F1.1); its highest correlation with an SAS factor—Factor 4 (F2.4)—is .67. (The correlations discussed here are found in Appendix 3.2.) Factor 2 of this monadic absolute analysis (F3.2) is correlated .80 with Factor 1 (F2.1) of the SAS analysis. Its largest correlation with a factor from the WEIS analysis is .68 with F1.3. The third factor is largely uncorrelated with any of the factors derived from the WEIS and SAS variable subsets; the largest correlations are −.47 with F1.2 from WEIS and −.53 with F2.2 from SAS.

CREON Variables, Dyadic Absolute Data

Table 3.4 presents the rotated factor-analytic solution for 20 CREON variables in frequency form from the dyadic deck. The items included are nearly the same as those in the previous table: only undesired behavior, a dyadic variable, has been added. Together, the three factors which emerge explain 90.4 percent of the total variation in the data.

An examination of this table reveals the striking similarity between the dyadic data and the monadic data. The first factor (F4.1) is a general dimension which seems to be characterized by high commitment actions taken in multilateral settings. Of the 20 items, 15 load highly on this factor. It explains 46.3 percent of the total variance.

The second factor (F4.2) is also a general dimension of activity in the international system, and, similar to our results for the monadic data, it is characterized by unilateral actions. Of the 20 items, 12 load highly on this factor, which explains 36.2 percent of the total variance. A glance at the loadings of the multiple targets category and of the multiple objects category in this table, however, indicates that the relationships are less clear here than in the monadic

TABLE 3.4
Factor Loadings for CREON Variables,
Dyadic Absolute Data

CREON Variables	F4.1	Factors F4.2	F4.3
Acts with others	.93	.09	.32
Bargaining behavior	.91	.31	.25
Elicited behavior	.90	.31	.19
Multiple targets	.83	.47	.17
Deed behavior	.82	.52	.13
Regional organization behavior	.81	.14	.37
World organization behavior	.81	.34	.08
Foreign assistance behavior	.71	.61	.19
Multiple objects	.71	.68	.18
Penetrative behavior	.69	.65	-.14
Treaty behavior	.69	.57	.29
Protocol behavior	.66	.60	.24
Economic transaction behavior	.62	.23	.57
Domestic target	.27	.91	.21
Undesired behavior	.43	.88	.18
Propaganda/cultural behavior	.06	.88	.27
Unilateral alteration behavior	.44	.88	.20
Military behavior	.62	.77	.06
Comment behavior	.65	.74	.17
Border behavior	.28	.35	.64

data. The multiple objects category loads on both dimensions in the dyadic data.

The third factor (F4.3) describes a more specific dimension of foreign policy behavior, economic behavior, and it explains 7.9 percent of the total variance. As in the monadic data, only economic transactions and border behavior load above .50 on this dimension.

For the frequency data the correlations between the three monadic dimensions and their counterparts in the dyadic data provide a clear picture of similarity between the two data sets. The correlation between F3.1 and F4.1 is .99; for F3.2 and F4.2, it is also .99; and between F3.3 and F4.3, it is .96. (Correlations among factors are reported in Appendix 3.2.) The solution does not mirror as accurately the results of the factor analyses on WEIS and SAS variables. Factor F4.1 is closely related to Factor F1.1 of the WEIS solution (r = .85); it is related .67 to F2.4 of the SAS factors. Factor F4.2 has a moderately high correlation with one factor emerging from each of the WEIS (F1.3, r = .75) and SAS (F2.1, r = .85) solutions. The third dimension from the absolute dyadic variables is not well matched in either WEIS or SAS, the highest correlations being .50 and −.50 with F2.2 and F2.3 of the SAS factor analysis.

TABLE 3.5
Factor Loadings for CREON Variables,
Monadic Percent Data

CREON Variables	F5.1	F5.2	F5.3	F5.4	F5.5
			Factors		
Propaganda/cultural behavior	.93	−.06	.03	−.07	−.10
Unilateral alteration behavior	.89	.27	.25	.07	.08
Bargaining behavior	−.86	−.14	−.38	−.09	−.16
Acts with others	−.85	−.15	−.43	−.10	−.16
Comment behavior	.83	.09	.26	.02	.01
Domestic target	.80	.35	.32	.10	.05
Multiple targets	−.75	−.57	−.16	.02	−.24
Multiple objects	.75	.51	.15	−.01	.28
World organization behavior	−.64	−.49	−.18	−.47	.14
Elicited behavior	−.63	−.37	−.23	−.52	.14
Protocol behavior	.27	.77	.10	−.13	−.31
Treaty behavior	.10	.65	.11	.06	.10
Economic transaction behavior	.04	.57	−.26	.28	.38
Penetrative behavior	.39	.03	.82	.10	−.10
Military behavior	.49	.18	.76	.05	.06
Deed behavior	.02	−.02	.04	.79	.37
Regional organization behavior	−.46	.07	−.25	.62	−.29
Border behavior	.29	.03	.23	.57	.21
Foreign assistance behavior	.07	.03	−.00	.11	.50

CREON Variables, Monadic Percent Data

The results of the factor analysis of the monadic data that are in the form of percentages are presented in Table 3.5. Here five factors emerge which·explain 78.2 percent of the variation in the data.

As in our results for the monadic frequency data, the first factor (F5.1) seems to tap a general activity dimension. Of the 19 items, 10 load at .50 or above, and the factor explains 37.6 percent of the total variance. This dimension combines low commitment acts with both *multilateral* and *unilateral* action settings. It is interesting to note the high positive loadings for the items measuring unilateral behavior on the one hand, and the high negative loadings for the items measuring multilateral behavior on the other. The data in percentage form highlight the important fact that decision makers seem to choose either unilateral actions or multilateral actions, but not both. That is, nations which choose to devote a large percentage of their actions to multilateral settings tend not to act unilaterally, and vice versa.

The remaining factors describe much more specific dimensions of behavior, with none explaining more than 12 percent of the total variance in the data. The

TABLE 3.6
Correlations Between Monadic Percent Data Factors
and Factors from WEIS, SAS, Monadic Absolute
Data, and Dyadic Absolute Data

| | | *Monadic Percent Data* | | | | |
		F5.1	*F5.2*	*F5.3*	*F5.4*	*F5.5*
WEIS	F1.1	-.34	.36	.19	.24	.03
	F1.2	.26	-.21	.52	.00	.06
	F1.3	.64	.21	.09	-.09	-.07
SAS	F2.1	.65	.11	.24	-.06	-.07
	F2.2	.03	-.13	.45	-.01	.09
	F2.3	-.08	.35	-.04	.62	-.02
	F2.4	-.45	.07	.26	-.33	.01
Monadic Absolute Data	F3.1	-.50	.14	.35	.07	.00
	F3.2	.73	-.03	.41	-.07	.01
	F3.3	.28	.47	-.08	.36	.07
Dyadic Absolute Data	F4.1	-.44	.21	.34	.06	.02
	F4.2	.75	-.02	.37	-.07	-.03
	F4.3	.29	.31	-.05	.43	.07

second factor seems to be characterized primarily by status-oriented behavior or economic transactions involving either multiple targets or multiple objects. The third factor is clearly a military factor, with only military and penetrative behavior loading above .50. The fourth factor is characterized primarily by high-commitment acts. Deed behavior loads above .50 only on this dimension. Moreover, both border behavior and regional organization behavior frequently include high commitment.[3] The fifth factor has no items loading over .50, but foreign assistance behavior is close. It is the only variable which has any significance for this factor.

The relationships between this analysis and the previous four analyses are summarized in Table 3.6. The correlations, abstracted from Appendix 3.2, show that very different dimensions underlie this variable subset when compared to the dimensions that underlie the previously analyzed subsets. Only Factor F5.1 is correlated .6 or higher with a factor emerging from each of the other subsets. Factor F5.4 is correlated .62 with Factor F2.3 derived from the SAS variables and F5.3 is correlated .52 with F1.2 from the WEIS variables. Factors F5.2 and F5.5 are very distinct from any of the dimensions emerging from the previous analyses.

CREON Variables, Dyadic Percent Data

The results of the factor analysis of the dyadic data that are in the form of percentages are presented in Table 3.7. Five factors emerge which explain 72.6 percent of the variation in the data.

TABLE 3.7
Factor Loadings for CREON Variables,
Dyadic Percent Data

			Factors		
CREON Variables	F6.1	F6.2	F6.3	F6.4	F6.5
Bargaining behavior	-.96	-.02	-.10	.06	-.20
Acts with others	-.95	.03	-.06	.06	-.26
Undesired behavior	.94	-.10	-.06	-.10	.12
Unilateral alteration behavior	.92	.02	.26	-.04	.03
Domestic target	.90	-.03	.28	.08	.05
Propaganda/cultural behavior	.89	-.16	.08	-.21	-.20
Comment behavior	.85	.00	.30	.10	.14
Military behavior	.71	-.12	.30	.10	.54
Elicited behavior	-.70	-.35	-.43	.00	-.20
World organization behavior	-.67	-.37	.58	.00	.11
Deed behavior	-.15	.79	-.29	.11	.02
Multiple objects	.89	-.67	.03	-.43	-.13
Regional organization behavior	.45	.61	.27	-.03	-.02
Border behavior	.47	.52	-.03	.02	.12
Economic transaction behavior	.07	.50	.04	.04	-.28
Foreign assistance behavior	.13	.40	-.20	.34	-.10
Protocol behavior	.29	-.09	.76	.14	.01
Treaty behavior	.05	-.07	.28	-.10	.07
Multible targets	.19	.20	.01	.80	.00
Penetrative behavior	.46	-.06	.21	-.03	.65

The first factor (F6.1) taps virtually the same general activity dimension as the first factor in the monadic percent data (r = .92). Half the items load above .50, and there is a mixture of positive and negative loadings. The results also reflect the choice between either unilateral or multilateral forms of behavior.

The second factor appears to be a commitment dimension similar to the fourth factor in the monadic percent data (r = .93). Deed behavior loads highest on this dimension. The other items which load high tend to be characterized by high levels of commitment.

Of the remaining three factors, none explains more than 10 percent of the total variance. The third factor involves primarily social-oriented or "status acknowledging" (protocol) behavior and is similar to the second factor in the monadic percent data, F5.2 (r = .77). The fourth factor has no counterpart in the monadic data. The only item which loads on this factor is multiple targets behavior. Its emergence as a distinct dimension is probably a function of how the dyadic data weight events involving multiple targets. The fifth factor, similar to the third factor in the monadic percent data (r = .89), is clearly a military dimension with only military and penetrative behavior loading above .50.

TABLE 3.8
Correlations Between Dyadic Percent Data Factors
and Factors from WEIS, SAS, Monadic Absolute
Data, and Dyadic Absolute Data

| | | Dyadic Percent Data Factors | | | | |
		F6.1	F6.2	F6.3	F6.4	F6.5
WEIS	F1.1	-.26	.24	.34	-.03	.36
	F1.2	.31	-.07	.15	-.02	.56
	F1.3	.65	-.17	.14	-.09	-.01
SAS	F2.1	.67	-.16	.07	-.11	.17
	F2.2	.08	-.05	-.09	.05	.55
	F2.3	-.03	.58	.41	.00	.11
	F2.4	-.41	-.29	.00	-.17	.31
Monadic Absolute Data	F3.1	-.43	.07	.16	-.06	.58
	F3.2	.76	-.18	-.03	-.04	.34
	F3.3	.36	.33	.34	-.13	-.18
Dyadic Absolute Data	F4.1	-.37	.07	.21	.00	.55
	F4.2	.76	-.19	-.02	-.07	.30
	F4.3	.37	.39	.23	-.19	-.15

In Table 3.8, the results for this factor analysis are compared with the results of the first four analyses. The first dyadic percent data factor (F6.1) has moderately strong correlations with one factor in each of the other variable subsets: .65 with F1.3, .67 with F2.1, .76 with F3.2, and .76 with F4.2. The second factor (F6.2) is correlated moderately with only the second SAS dimension (F2.2). The third and fourth factors have no counterparts in the other four variables subsets. The fifth factor is moderately correlated with one factor in each of the other subsets. Overall, the results seem to indicate that the dimensional basis of the dyadic percent data like that of the monadic percent data is very different from the basis of the other variable subsets.

CONCLUSIONS

The results of the six factor analyses confirm one of the major findings of Kegley et al. (1974). Most of the variation in each of the data sets could be explained by a small number of dimensions. In the case of the four data sets comprised of absolute frequencies of events, the percentage of variance explained ranged from 85 to 92 percent. For the two subsets comprised of data in percentage (relative frequency) form, the factor analyses accounted for a somewhat smaller 73 percent and 78 percent. In no case were there more than five factors, even after relaxing the usual criteria.

Comparing the results of the six factor analyses by way of intercorrelating factor scores reveals that the different variable subsets generate different dimensions of behavior. Not only do the analyses produce different numbers of dimensions, ranging from three to five, but in many cases the dimensions derived from one variable subset are not correlated with the dimensions derived from other variable subsets. In only a few cases are the dimensions of one subset highly correlated with the dimensions of another subset. One implication of this finding is that Kegley et al. (1974) were correct in warning that the a priori assumptions embodied in the WEIS-like coding schemes reflect a concern with participation and affect, or qualities of the behavior itself. The CREON variables are designed to tap to a much greater extent qualities relating to setting and context. The results of factor analyses using these different coding schemes reflect these underlying assumptions.

Our findings cast much doubt on the validity of inductive data reduction techniques for identifying new, theoretically interesting dimensions of foreign policy behavior. The techniques appear merely to recast and reorder what the investigator already assumes the dimensions to be. Therefore, at this point, it is probably more useful to adopt a different strategy in the measurement of foreign policy behavior—to decide what we think are important behaviors to measure and then to try to measure them. Inductive data reduction techniques such as factor analysis can be used to further refine and clarify the original assumptions from which the proposed measures were derived.

It is useful to return for a moment to the more fundamental question: how the conceptualization and measurement of foreign policy behavior can be advanced. The CREON, WEIS, and other coding schemes for foreign event data attempt to identify and describe a number of different facets of an elemental unit, the event. The factor-analytic strategies we have described allow us to ask how similar these facets are. Are they measuring the same thing? Are they related? Such inductive techniques as factor analysis are of great assistance in answering these kinds of questions. However, once we ask how these different facets may be combined to form more complex constructs, theoretical and deductive concerns become paramount. Factor analysis and related inductive strategies may be used as "validity checks" to determine whether coding schemes encompass the variations in the data intended by the creators, but they cannot add information beyond the configuration produced by implicit theoretical assumptions.

Forward progress in the delineation of foreign policy behavior thus depends on an effort to move beyond the rather simple dimensions already identified in this and other studies, and to conceptualize richer and more complex properties of foreign policy. That is the task undertaken in succeeding chapters of this volume.

APPENDIX 3.1
Summary Results for Six Factor Analysis

Variable Subset	Factor	Eigenvalue	% Total Variance	
WEIS	F1.1	17.72	68.2	32.9
	F1.2	2.60	10.0	30.1
	F1.3	1.66	6.4	21.6
			84.6	84.6
SAS	F2.1	18.31	70.4	30.9
	F2.2	2.97	11.4	25.5
	F2.3	1.07	4.1	17.8
	F2.4	.99	3.8	15.6
			89.7	89.8
Monadic	F3.1	14.55	76.6	41.9
Absolute	F3.2	1.84	9.7	36.5
Data	F3.3	.75	3.9	11.9
			90.2	90.3
Dyadic	F4.1	15.36	76.8	46.3
Absolute	F4.2	2.03	10.1	36.2
Data	F4.3	.70	3.5	7.9
			90.4	90.4
Monadic	F5.1	9.62	50.6	37.6
Percent	F5.2	2.06	10.9	13.6
Data	F5.3	1.50	7.9	11.3
	F5.4	.98	5.2	10.3
	F5.5	.71	3.7	5.4
			78.3	78.2
Dyadic	F6.1	9.05	45.2	40.6
Percent	F6.2	2.77	13.8	12.4
Data	F6.3	1.21	6.1	8.9
	F6.4	.86	4.3	5.4
	F6.5	.63	3.2	5.4
			72.6	72.7

Intercorrelations Among Factor Scores for Factors from Six Factor Analyses

Variable Subset	Factor	WEIS			SAS				Monadic Absolute Data		
		F1.1	F1.2	F1.3	F2.1	F2.2	F2.3	F2.4	F3.1	F3.2	F3.3
WEIS	F1.1	1.00	-.04	.00	.06	.11	.75	.56	.83	-.09	.43
	F1.2	-.04	1.00	-.02	.18	.93	-.11	-.05	.34	.67	-.47
	F1.3	.00	-.02	1.00	.96	-.20	-.02	-.06	-.19	.68	.46
SAS	F2.1	.06	.18	.96	1.00	-.02	-.01	-.01	-.06	.80	.38
	F2.2	.11	.93	-.20	-.02	1.00	-.02	.00	.49	.51	-.53
	F2.3	.75	-.11	-.02	-.01	-.02	1.00	-.06	.44	-.09	.52
	F2.4	.56	-.05	-.06	-.01	.00	-.06	1.00	.67	-.21	.07
Monadic Absolute Data	F3.1	.83	.34	-.19	-.06	.49	.44	.67	1.00	-.02	-.07
	F3.2	-.09	.67	.68	.80	.51	-.09	-.21	-.02	1.00	-.01
	F3.3	.43	-.47	.46	.38	-.53	.52	.07	-.07	-.01	1.00
Dyadic Absolute Data	F4.1	.85	.34	-.12	.01	.47	.46	.67	.99	.03	-.01
	F4.2	-.11	.59	.75	.85	.42	-.09	-.23	-.07	.99	.04
	F4.3	.37	-.41	.34	.29	-.50	.50	.04	-.10	-.05	.96
Monadic Percent Data	F5.1	-.34	.26	.64	.65	.03	-.08	-.45	-.50	.73	.28
	F5.2	.36	-.21	.21	.11	-.13	.35	.07	.14	-.03	.47
	F5.3	.19	.52	.09	.24	.45	-.04	.26	.35	.41	-.08
	F5.4	.24	.00	-.09	-.06	-.01	.62	-.33	.07	-.07	.36
	F5.5	.03	.06	-.07	-.07	.09	-.02	.01	.00	.01	.07
Dyadic Percent Data	F6.1	-.26	.31	.65	.67	.08	-.03	-.41	-.43	.76	.36
	F6.2	.24	-.07	-.17	-.16	-.05	.58	-.29	.07	-.18	.33
	F6.3	.34	-.15	.14	.07	-.09	.41	.00	.16	-.03	.34
	F6.4	-.03	-.02	-.09	-.11	.05	.00	-.17	-.06	-.04	-.13
	F6.5	.36	.56	-.01	.17	.55	.11	.31	.58	.34	-.18

(Continued)

APPENDIX 3.2 Continued

Variable Subset	Factor	Dyadic Absolute Data			Monadic Percent Data					Dyadic Percent Data				
		F4.1	F4.2	F4.3	F5.1	F5.2	F5.3	F5.4	F5.5	F6.1	F6.2	F6.3	F6.4	F6.5
WEIS	F1.1	.85	-.11	.37	-.34	.36	.19	.24	.03	-.26	.24	.34	-.03	.36
	F1.2	.34	.59	-.41	.26	-.21	.52	.00	.06	.31	-.07	-.15	-.02	.56
	F1.3	-.12	.75	.34	.64	.21	.09	-.09	-.07	.65	-.17	.14	-.09	-.01
SAS	F2.1	.01	.85	.29	.65	.11	.24	-.06	-.07	.67	-.16	.07	-.11	.17
	F2.2	.47	.42	-.50	.03	-.13	.45	-.01	.09	.08	-.05	-.09	.05	.55
	F2.3	.46	-.09	.50	-.08	.35	-.04	.62	-.02	-.03	.58	.41	.00	.11
	F2.4	.67	-.23	.04	-.45	.07	.26	-.33	.01	-.41	-.29	.00	-.17	.31
Monadic Absolute Data	F3.1	.99	-.07	-.10	-.50	.14	.35	.07	.00	-.43	.07	.16	-.06	.58
	F3.2	.03	.99	-.05	.73	-.03	.41	-.07	.01	.76	-.18	-.03	-.04	.34
	F3.3	-.01	.04	.96	.28	.47	-.08	.36	.07	.36	.33	.34	-.13	-.18
Dyadic Absolute Data	F4.1	1.00	-.01	-.06	-.44	.21	.34	.06	.02	-.37	.07	.21	.00	.55
	F4.2	-.01	1.00	-.02	.75	-.02	.37	-.07	-.03	.76	-.19	-.02	-.07	.30
	F4.3	-.06	-.02	1.00	.29	.31	-.05	.43	.07	.37	.39	.23	-.19	-.15
Monadic Percent Data	F5.1	-.44	.75	.29	1.00	-.06	-.06	.00	-.03	.92	-.09	.00	-.06	-.21
	F5.2	.21	-.02	.31	-.06	1.00	.02	-.03	.01	.06	.04	.77	.08	-.11
	F5.3	.34	.37	-.05	-.06	.02	1.00	-.01	.01	.19	-.17	-.04	-.02	.89
	F5.4	.06	-.07	.43	.00	-.03	-.01	1.00	-.01	.08	.93	.07	-.12	.16
	F5.5	.02	-.03	.07	-.03	-.01	-.01	-.01	1.00	.19	.20	-.54	.37	-.13
Dyadic Percent Data	F6.1	-.37	.76	.37	.92	.06	.19	.08	.19	1.00	.00	-.05	.04	-.05
	F6.2	.07	-.19	.39	-.09	.04	-.17	.93	.20	.00	1.00	-.01	-.07	-.01
	F6.3	.21	-.02	.23	.00	.77	-.04	.07	-.54	-.05	-.01	1.00	-.03	-.03
	F6.4	.00	-.07	-.19	-.06	.08	-.02	-.12	.37	.04	-.07	-.03	1.00	-.07
	F6.5	.55	.30	-.15	-.21	-.11	.89	.16	-.13	-.05	-.01	-.03	-.07	1.00

NOTES

1. The dyadic subsets were aggregated to the nation level to provide a common unit of analysis with the data subsets derived from the monadic deck. The particular version of the CREON data used in this analysis was 5.02 and is available through the Inter-University Consortium for Political and Social Research (ICPSR). This version has an N of 35 instead of 38 nations as in Version 6.00 used in developing the measures reported in the rest of this book. The present study preceded the development of the measures described here and, in effect, helped to determine the deductive approach the authors have taken in defining dimensions of foreign policy behavior.

2. Factor analysis is inappropriately used if the number of variables is *not less* than the number of cases (nations).

3. This is true for the following reasons: Border behavior events most often tend to deal with hostile actions (frequently deeds) taken as a result of disputes about borders; activities of regional organizations (for example, NATO, EEC, and the OAS) often have high-commitment economic or military aspects.

PART II

Properties of the Predecisional Context

Editors' Introduction

Students of foreign policy disagree on the relative emphasis to be given external versus internal sources of foreign policy. The "realist" school, headed by such prominent thinkers as Morgenthau, Kissinger, Aron, and Kennan, focus primary attention on the external environment of the state, the challenges it poses to national interests, and the constraints it places on national action. Others emphasize internal determinants. These include the individuals Waltz called "second image theorists" as well as such recent advocates of bureaucratic politics analysis as Neustadt, Allison, and Halperin. The broad literature dealing with the penetration of political systems (for example, Rosenau's idea of "linkage politics" and the various dependencia theories) calls into question the validity of this distinction in principle.

The chapters in this book assume that the international environment is critical, if not sufficient, for understanding foreign policy. By definition, foreign policy behavior is directed toward the external environment or specific components thereof. Ostensibly, such behavior is intended to alter undesirable external conditions or to buttress desired ones that are under duress. To make this assumption neither rules out nor necessitates the further assumption that the actions are ultimately in the national interest as defined by an observer. Nor does it preclude the likelihood that governments are moved to action through an intensely political process of bargaining and maneuver between different bureaucratic actors, some of whom are motivated primarily by internal concerns, or the possibility that foreign entities may enter the domestic political system during the decision-making process. It does reject, however, the possibility that the action can be undertaken solely in response to internal conditions of the country. A winning bureaucratic coalition cannot be created unless there is some external need to legitimize action and to serve as grounds for mobilizing others into action.

Thus, foreign policy activity reflects to a great extent the nature of the external environment of the country, which partially establishes the context for action. Predecisional context properties of behavior seek to record the characteristics of the environment that give rise to and establish the context for decisions. Such characteristics may relate either to the transitory qualities of a situation or to the longer-term structural components of the system.

A fair number of candidate concepts come to mind in thinking about predecisional context properties. C. Hermann's (1969) classification of eight types of situations based on the presence or absence of threat, anticipation of the situation (or surprise), and length of decision time available for a response is one prominent example. Whether the decision situation was triggered by an external stimulus is another example. M. Hermann's measure of independence/interdependence of action (Chapter 11) incorporates this situational element, and thus with some justification could have been considered a context property measure. Measures of reciprocity (reviewed by Callahan in Chapter 13) and the over/under response measure considered in the early phases of the CREON measurement effort (see Chapter 2) are two examples which incorporate information about the behavior, if any, that preceded and presumably stimulated the foreign policy behavior being observed.

The two chapters in this section present measures that do not distinguish between transitory and more stable aspects of the environment. Both concern the allocation of a nation's attention, and attention may be to things passing or permanent. In Chapter 4, C. Hermann and Coate develop a classification scheme for substantive problems. For any nation, the international environment contains an enormous number of problematic characteristics, in the sense that a gap exists between what the nation's officials would like and what is. Because decision-making machinery can act on only a few problems at a time, or else it overloads, nations must be selective about the problems warranting their attention and action. "Important" problems will receive attention before "trivial" ones. The substance of the problem is, therefore, a crucial aspect of the predecisional context in determining if and how a nation will act.

Hermann and Coate's measurement scheme was part of the Stage II measurement efforts within CREON—that is, the creation of additional nominal classification systems. It is a cousin to others' efforts to create foreign policy issue area schemes, but with three innovations: (1) the concentration on problems rather than issues signals a paradigmatic shift from viewing foreign policy activity as influence attempts to viewing it as problem-solving efforts; (2) the classification scheme is hierarchical in nature, based on broad, theoretically derived, universally applicable classes of problems and then differentiated into specific problems that occurred during the CREON decade; and (3) it allows problems to be multidimensional and fall into more than one of the substantive problem areas.

Nations allocate their attention to geographical entities as well as to specific problems. This is attested to most strongly in the existence of geographic bureaus in foreign ministries. Who is involved in a particular aspect of the external environment may be as important as what is involved. It is therefore appropriate to consider which other entities are involved as an important part of the predecisional context. Other entities are best examined by looking at the targets and objects of a nation's action. By now, classification of targets and objects follows well-established conventions. What does need further consideration is how to use such information to derive interesting measures of the distribution of a nation's attention. East and M. Hermann propose such "scope of action" measures in Chapter 5. Unlike the substantive problem area scheme, these measures are part of Stage III efforts to create higher-order properties of behavior. Hence, Chapter 5 also serves as an illustration of some of the kinds of strategies that Callahan suggests in Chapter 13.

All of the chapters reporting on a measure of foreign policy behavior follow a similar format. The format represents an attempt in these chapters to deal with the criteria for developing measures of foreign policy behavior outlined in Chapter 1. The authors begin by indicating the significance of their particular dimension for improving our knowledge about nations' foreign policy behavior. They continue by developing the conceptualization of the dimension. The discussion of conceptualization is followed by a discussion of the general operationalization of the concept and the way it was operationalized using the CREON event data set. Finally, data are presented for each of the 38 nations in the CREON sample, allowing readers to compare and contrast nations' behavior on the measure and to assess the face validity of the measure.

CHARLES F. HERMANN
ROGER A. COATE

Substantive Problem Areas

When we asked college students to construct a classification scheme for the foreign policy stories in a daily newspaper, a large proportion of them created broad categories. They devised such groupings as military assistance, human rights, alliance problems, arms control, and war-related issues. Classifying foreign policy behavior according to its substance seems like such a natural procedure that we would expect most individuals—be they policymakers, scholars, journalists, or members of the attentive public—to propose some variation of these content categories if they were given similar assignments. Of course, depending on the person's familiarity with the subject, the categories might be more or less differentiated. Someone well acquainted with national security and military policy might distinguish between a number of different types of war and military actions short of war. The basic point, however, is that expert and novice alike can be expected to think about foreign policy classification frequently in terms of various substantive issues or problems. With the possible exception of geographical categories, perhaps, no other way of categorizing foreign policy activities is more natural or obvious to most people than grouping them by substance.

In addition to the seemingly natural plausibility of classifying foreign policy behavior by its substance, another reason for advancing such a typology rests on the centrality of the concept of problem in policy analysis. As we shall suggest in this chapter, it may be very useful to view governments as problem solvers or, at least, as entities that attempt to cope with problems. Such an orientation, however, clearly requires a typology of kinds of problems—in this instance, a classification of foreign policy problems.

Given these observations, one might expect numerous classifications of foreign policy behavior based on substance. Such expectations are not realized. Although numerous separate categories of foreign policy activity have been identified and individually examined, there have been few systematic classifications of such behavior by content. The few that have emerged tend to be useful only for organizational purposes—that is, "pigeonholing" specific activities into one grouping or another. They have *not* tended to be classifications whose categories had theoretical import and revealed additional information about a foreign policy behavior once it was identified as an instance of a given grouping.

In this chapter we shall attempt to explore why such a common way of thinking about foreign policy activity has proved so frustrating as a research tool. After reviewing related efforts, we shall offer a conceptualization and classification scheme that those associated with this volume believe warrants further examination. We refer to this way of characterizing foreign policy behaviors as substantive problem areas, but it is closely associated with what are more generally known as foreign policy issue areas.

WHAT SOME OTHERS HAVE DONE

By far the most frequent examination of substantive issues in foreign policy research has occurred in works devoted to only one subject or issue, whether it be foreign assistance (for example, Montgomery, 1967), military deterrence (see George and Smoke, 1974), energy (see Szyliowicz and O'Neill, 1975), or any one of numerous other categories of foreign policy activity. With respect to the task of constructing a classification scheme of substantive issue areas, however, this vast literature is of little help. The authors have not needed to address the question of what defining properties both distinguish and relate the examined kind of policy to some other classes of foreign policy. In brief, because they have concentrated on only one domain of policy, they have not developed or used a classification based on the substance of various kinds of policy.

The recent origins of the concept of issue areas and the concern with comparing different kinds of issues might be traced to inquiries about public policy within the United States, such as Dahl's (1963) study of urban policies in New Haven, Connecticut. In examining three issue areas (political nominations, urban redevelopment, and public education), Dahl discerned fairly distinctive political systems for the different areas of policy, each with its own procedures and participants. In fact, only about three percent of the individuals were actively involved in leadership roles in more than one issue area. The Dahl study demonstrated that the procedures associated with different issues varied and thus provided a justification for classifying policies by their substance.

Although it may exaggerate the impact of this study of local American politics on foreign policy researchers, the subsequent work of such researchers does seem to emphasize two different orientations that are nicely revealed in Dahl's *Who Governs*. One approach to issue areas keys the classification scheme to the characteristics of the process and the nature of the participants associated with a given issue area. (Dahl stressed the distinctiveness of the procedures associated with each kind of issue.) An alternative approach classifies issue areas according to substantive characteristics. (Dahl used substantive designations such as education and redevelopment.) In foreign policy studies of issue areas the procedural and substantive approaches to classification appear to have moved in different directions.

An early example of a procedural issue area scheme was offered by Huntington (1961), who classified military policies as either strategic or structural. The two kinds of policy are distinguished by the process of decision making. Structural decisions are handled by a domestic legislative process, whereas strategic programs have executive participants who may or may not use an executive process as well. A more elaborate procedural issue area classification has been proposed by Lowi (1967) which involves distributive, redistributive, regulatory, and crisis categories. The four categories of issue areas are associated with three separate subsystems (elite, coalition, pluralist), each with distinctive political structures and processes. Zimmerman (1973) superimposes Lowi's scheme onto Wolfers's (1962) concept of a continuum between the poles of power and indifference. The resulting typology, Zimmerman argues, should enable researchers to determine the political process associated with each issue area.[1]

These examples of procedural issue area classifications share a quality normally regarded as critical in any effort to devise a meaningful classification in science. To varying degrees they all have theoretical import. More specifically, they offer categories that purport to provide additional knowledge beyond that used as their defining characteristics. If we are able to locate a given policy in one of Huntington's, Lowi's, or Zimmerman's categories, then we presumably acquire additional information about the political structure, process, and participants associated with that policy. This would be an extremely valuable accomplishment if the relationships hypothesized to hold for policies in various cells of the typologies could be confirmed. Therein lies the problem that appears to beset the procedural issue area schemes. They have proved very difficult to operationalize—that is, to specify the categories in a mutually exclusive and exhaustive manner so that all foreign policies could be unambiguously located in the typology. Interestingly, this latter difficulty has not been so severe for those who have elected the alternative approach of classifying issue areas by differences in substance.

The individuals who have focused on the substantive issue area approach have developed classifications based on the content distinctions between various domains of policy rather than the processes involved in them. For example, Brecher (1972, 1977) uses four broad categories—military-security, political-diplomatic, economic-developmental, and cultural-status. Rosenau (1966) also proposes four categories consisting of territory, status, human resources, and nonhuman resources. He offers a definition of the basic concept of issue areas:

> An issue area is conceived to consist of (1) a cluster of values, the allocation or potential allocation of which (2) leads the affected or potentially affected actors to differ so greatly over (a) the way in which the values should be allocated or (b) the horizontal levels at which the allocations should be authorized that (3) they engage in distinctive behavior designed to mobilize support for the attainment of their particular values [1966: 81].

With the exception of several pilot applications, such as that of Wittkopf and his associates (1974), Rosenau's fourfold classification of issue areas has so far failed to generate much empirical research.[2] His definition of issue area, however, appears to have influenced O'Leary, Coplin, and their colleagues and students at Syracuse University, who have contributed perhaps more than any others to developing both the conceptual and empirical elements of substantive issue area classification. As did Rosenau, O'Leary (1976: 320-321) defines issues as "disputed value allocations (actual or potential)," and notes that "resolving the issue—allocating the values—is what motivates state behavior." Developing the concept further, O'Leary has stipulated that an "area," or the boundaries of an issue, must be determined by a common or specified value outcome. "To speak of an 'issue area' as, for example, a 'military issue area' without specifying what value outcomes are in dispute is merely to label a category whose content is vague" (O'Leary, 1976: 321). Guided by these conceptual insights, O'Leary has developed a series of some 40 issue area categories with such headings as fishing rights, financial problems, and hijacking. He has established coding rules for identifying these issue areas in event data (O'Leary and Shapiro, 1972a, 1972b; Dean et al., 1972).

As with the discussion of the procedural issue area efforts, our review of the development of substantive issue area schemes invites their evaluation against such criteria as (a) exhaustive categorization, (b) mutually exclusive categories, and (c) theoretical importance. With respect to an exhaustive set of categories, we find systems such as Brecher's that attempt to fulfill the condition and others, such as the set advanced by O'Leary and his colleagues, that make no effort to be comprehensive. Conversely, O'Leary's decision rules are designed to permit mutually exclusive classification, whereas others, such as that proposed by Rosenau, appear to have encountered some difficulty with this criterion.[3] Despite individual differences, it seems to us that in general the substantive issue area classification schemes have had more success in realizing these two criteria than those following the procedural issue area approach. It is with respect to the criterion of theoretical importance that we judge most of the substantive issue area classifications to be weak. None of them specifies what additional information or insights an analyst might acquire once he or she has determined that a particular policy can be assigned to a given set or category. Thus, it appears that the procedural and substantive issue area approaches tend to get caught on the opposite horns of a dilemma. The substantive classifications generate differentiations that are more easily observed (and, hence, measured in the sense of producing mutually exclusive and exhaustive categories), whereas the procedural classifications have more clearly indicated their theoretical significance. This observation conforms to Froman's (1968: 52) conclusion "that problems of measurement are most severe with categories that show the greatest theoretical power."

O'Leary and his associates, however, may be succeeding in a demonstration of how a substantive issue area scheme can be given theoretical significance even if the categories do not in themselves impart new information. An integral part of the PRINCE framework (see Coplin et al., 1973), their issue areas become, in effect, the unit of analysis. The issues are compared and evaluated according to a series of dimensions that represent the relationship of actors to any issue (that is, the *salience* of the issue for an actor, the actor's *position* on the issue, the actor's *power* with respect to the issue, and the *affect* the actor displays on the issue). The issues selected by O'Leary are rendered comparable not so much by their shared quality of being value outcomes as by the ability of the PRINCE associates to locate each issue on such properties as salience and affect. This procedure is one that we shall also employ in our substantive problem area classification in an attempt to escape the dilemma that has plagued issue area classifications.

THE CONCEPT OF
SUBSTANTIVE PROBLEM AREA

The present effort is in the tradition of what we have called "substantive issue areas," in that the organizing scheme involves aspects of the substance or content of governmental actions. However, rather than a focus on issues as they have been used in the literature described in the last section, we propose a classification based on the concept of problem. We will be concerned not only with the problem, but also the context in which it occurs. Thus, our classification is a typology, in that it locates every action on multiple dimensions. Some dimensions seek to characterize the problem and others, the context in which the problem occurs.

The orienting idea of the problem deserves fuller exploration. For the purpose of this classification scheme, foreign policy actors are problem managers because they attempt to deal with problems by resolving them, minimizing them, avoiding them, or otherwise coping with them. A problem is a discrepancy between what exists or is expected to exist in the future and some preferred state or condition. The preferred state or condition can be characterized as a goal which, in turn, can be understood in terms of basic values. Having a discrepancy between an actual or anticipated state and a goal means that the actor experiences (or will experience) some deprivation with regard to that basic value. Deprivations can range from losses to narrow self-interest concerns to losses to altruistic aspirations depending on the goals of the entity experiencing the problem. Governments seek to reduce such deprivations and promote rewards or indulgences for themselves and those whose approval they seek. A problem can be regarded as a "foreign policy" problem when the source of the deprivation, those experiencing it, or those whose support is deemed necessary for dealing with it are outside the political jurisdiction of the national government. In each case the involvement of external entities may or may not be actual or perceived.

The concept of allocation of values as advanced by Rosenau (1966) and O'Leary (1976) is not rejected but supplemented by our idea that actors in the foreign policy arena attend to issues when difficulties arise with respect to value allocations. Rosenau (1966: 81) stipulates that for an issue area to exist actors must differ over the actual or potential value allocation. Conflict between actors can be, and often is, the source of value deprivation. By the present formulation of a problem, however, we suggest that no other actor need be a consciously participating party for a problem or value deprivation to occur. The deprivation triggering the problem may be one actor's perception of the world (for example, a perceived status discrepancy), an inadvertent effect of others' behaviors (such as the consequences for the Fourth World of the petroleum-exporting nations' raising oil prices), or the effects of nature (for example, the exhaustion of a natural resource or a natural disaster).

We suggest that problems—including foreign policy problems—are subjective. What constitutes a problem for one actor may not be interpreted as a problem (or may be viewed as a different kind of problem) by others. Moreover, problems are transitory. They have a life cycle of emergence, peak(s), disappearance, and sometimes recurrence. When a nation has abundant energy, energy is not a problem, but when energy is in short supply or far more costly than before, the problem emerges. As we see in the next section, these interpretations have important implications for a classification.

Before detailing the substantive problem area classification scheme, it is appropriate to acknowledge the influence of Lasswell's (1971, 1975) policy sciences orientation on the conceptualization advanced here. Of the three key elements involved in defining a policy sciences viewpoint—it is contextual, problem-oriented, and multimethod—the first two constitute the foundation for this classification. We also have borrowed from Lasswell the idea of viewing problems in terms of value deprivations or foregone value indulgences. It will be evident in our discussion of basic values when the typology is outlined below that Lasswell's set of value outcomes has influenced our own related cluster of value categories.

MAJOR FEATURES OF THE
SUBSTANTIVE PROBLEM AREAS CLASSIFICATION

As we noted previously, the present classification of substantive problem areas is multidimensional. It consists of six different sets of categories or dimensions which collectively ask: Who gets what, where, from whom? The six dimensions can be divided into two broad categories, with one being the "gets what" component that consists of the categorization of basic values and associated problem areas. The other broad category contains the context dimensions that involve who, where, and from whom. In summary, the six dimensions as listed in the coding manual (C. Hermann, 1974) are:

Basic Values	
Type of Deprivation or Problem	value/problem categories
Contemporary Examples of Problems	
Whose Basic Value Is Jeopardized	
Where Is Problem Encountered	context categories
Source of Deprivation	

Several general aspects of the six dimensions should be noted. First, a distinction can be made between those dimensions that tap more transitory qualities and those that concern more durable properties. As we commented in the previous section, problems are subjective and transitory. Therefore, the particular categorization of problems can be expected to change from one time or one kind of analysis to another. In our classification system the two least permanent dimensions are (a) type of deprivation or problem and (b) contemporary examples of problems. Four other dimensions present categories which are expected to be more durable through both time and types of analysis. They are (a) the basic values, (b) whose basic value is jeopardized, (c) where the problem is encountered, and (d) the source of the deprivation. Our intention is to enhance the theoretical utility of the scheme by the introduction of more durable dimensions.

A second general feature of the six dimensions is that the coding of some dimensions is dependent on the categories selected in one or more other dimensions. In classifying a particular foreign policy event, the coder follows a partial decision tree when, for some of the six properties, the category chosen in one dimension determines the subset of categories from which a choice is made in another dimension. This arrangement serves the practical purpose of limiting the number of categories from which a coder must choose at any one point. As we will see later, it also serves to tie the more transitory dimensions to some of the more durable ones.

The following overview cannot produce the complete decision rules in the coding manual for each of the six dimensions. It can, however, present their essential features. They are introduced in the order in which an analyst would code them.

Basic Values

As with all the other behavior measures reported in this book, the operationalization was performed on descriptions of foreign policy activities that had been separated into discrete national governmental actions designated collectively as event data. For the substantive problem area classification the coder first determines what was the specific foreign policy problem, as characterized in the event, to which the government was responding. Once the particular problem is identified, the coder determines what basic value(s) outcome the problem jeopardized. The value classification scheme was influenced by Lasswell (for example, see his 1971 study), who for some time used a short list of eight basic values (power, enlightenment, wealth, well-being, skill, affection, respect, and rectitude). According to Lasswell, the myriad of terms used to describe the value outcomes pursued by humankind can be located in this set of summary categories. At the time the substantive problem area classification was under construction, we were much attracted to the use of a short summary set of value categories, but were not persuaded that all eight of Lasswell's categories would be represented with any regularity in the foreign policy actions of national governments. Accordingly, we subdivided well-being (into physical safety and welfare), combined several others (power with respect, enlightenment with skills, and relegated affection and rectitude to a remainder category).[4] The value categories used in the classification scheme are as follows:

Security/Military-Physical Safety: The desire to enjoy physical safety free from organized violence to persons, property, or national institutions.

Economic Wealth: The desire to enjoy physical goods and services and to maintain and promote the institutions and arrangements (e.g., currency) pertaining thereto.

Respect/Status: The desire to enjoy treatment by others in accordance with both the accepted norms of human interaction and one's own expectations.

Well-Being/Welfare: The desire to enjoy life free from the destructive acts of nature, the unintended acts of humankind, and discrimination based on involuntary or voluntary membership in a class or group.

Enlightenment: The desire to enjoy, transmit, and preserve knowledge and skills and to maintain and promote the institutions and arrangements pertaining thereto.

The basic values categories also include both an "other" category and a category that is used when the information in the event is insufficient for classification.

Whose Value Is Jeopardized?

This context dimension determines, from the perspective of the actor in the event, what entity or collectivity is being deprived (or could be deprived in the future) of one or more of its basic values. The seven primary categories in this part of the scheme can be grouped into three clusters. The first set of categories indicates that the "victim" is part of the actor's collective entity (that is, the government or the entire society, or individuals or groups within the actor's country). The second cluster of categories distinguishes among entities external to the actor (that is, external governments or societies, individuals or groups within foreign countries, regional or global organizations). The third set of categories identifies the jeopardized entity as a combination of the actor nation and some external entities.

Location of the Problem

This context variable refers to the location in physical space on the globe (if applicable) or the relational space in which the change that precipitates the problem occurs. Many foreign policy problems occur in some definable geographical space. To classify such locations the scheme introduces five categories: within the actor's political boundaries, within another political unit's boundaries, within a geographical region, within common space (for example, high seas, Antarctica), or throughout the globe. Three additional categories seek to give some locational orientation to the problem even when it cannot meaningfully be assigned to geographical space. These three focus on (1) symbolic relationships or ideas, (2) intergovernmental organizations, and (3) nongovernmental transnational organizations.

Source of Deprivation

The final context variable concerns the human or nonhuman agent(s) that appears in the account of the event to be the primary, immediate source of the deprivation. In other words, who seems to have created the problem? Although the source may not be determinable from the event (or, for that matter, from more complete accounts of the situation), when the information is discernible, it is classified into one of nine categories. We have found it useful to group the categories into three broader clusters. In the first cluster are the categories that identify national governments or ruling groups as the immediate source of the problem: government(s) of the deprived nation(s), government(s) or nation(s) external to the deprived nation(s), intergovernmental organizations, and the government of the deprived nation(s) jointly with other government(s). The second cluster contains private or nongovernmental sources of deprivation: individuals or groups within the deprived nation(s), individuals or groups external to the deprived nation(s), and nongovernmental transnational organizations. The third cluster contains one category for acts of nature and another one for societal conditions (for example, level of industrialization).

Type of Deprivation or Problem

We now return to the classification of the nature of the problem itself. Unlike the dimensions reviewed so far, the remaining two that deal with the substance

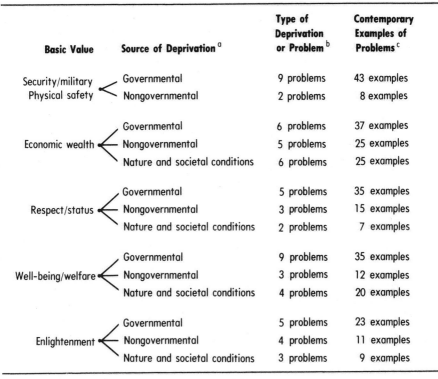

Basic Value	Source of Deprivation [a]	Type of Deprivation or Problem [b]	Contemporary Examples of Problems [c]
Security/military Physical safety	Governmental	9 problems	43 examples
	Nongovernmental	2 problems	8 examples
Economic wealth	Governmental	6 problems	37 examples
	Nongovernmental	5 problems	25 examples
	Nature and societal conditions	6 problems	25 examples
Respect/status	Governmental	5 problems	35 examples
	Nongovernmental	3 problems	15 examples
	Nature and societal conditions	2 problems	7 examples
Well-being/welfare	Governmental	9 problems	35 examples
	Nongovernmental	3 problems	12 examples
	Nature and societal conditions	4 problems	20 examples
Enlightenment	Governmental	5 problems	23 examples
	Nongovernmental	4 problems	11 examples
	Nature and societal conditions	3 problems	9 examples

Figure 4.1 In the substantive problem area classification, the 66 types of deprivations or problems are differentiated by the basic values and the sources of deprivation. Each type of deprivation or problem is further subdivided into a series of contemporary examples of problems which currently total 306.

a. As explained in the text, the context dimension entitled "source of deprivation" is originally classified into one of nine substantive categories. For purposes of organizing "types of deprivation or problem," the sources are collapsed into the three broader groupings shown in this figure. By definition, one of these groupings (nature and societal conditions) is not logically possible as a "source of deprivation" for the security/military-physical safety basic value.
b. The 66 types of deprivations or problems are listed in Appendix 4.1.
c. The 306 contemporary examples are listed in Appendix 4.2.

of the problem depend on other prior coding decisions. The primary reason for this interdependence is to strengthen the comparability and stability of problem classifications. In a manner similar to that of the PRINCE investigators (Coplin et al., 1973), we attempt to relate transitory problem categories to other dimensions with greater durability and some theoretical promise. The two prior dimensions on which substance decisions are dependent consist of basic values and source of deprivation. Figure 4.1 shows that the type of deprivation (third column) branches out from the basic value jeopardized (first column) and the source of the deprivation (second column). As indicated by the decision tree in Figure 4.1, there are 14 broad groupings of types of deprivations or problems listed in the third column. Each of the broad groupings has between two and nine specific types of deprivations or problems within it. The present substantive problem area classification has a total of 66 types of deprivations or problems. These 66 are enumerated in Appendix 4.1 (at the end of this chapter) under the 14 headings established by combining the basic value and source of deprivation categories.

Contemporary Examples of Problems

Each of the 66 types of deprivations or problems is further differentiated into more specific contemporary examples of problems. At the present time there are 306 different examples of contemporary problems in the substantive problem area classification. These 306 are identified under the appropriate type of deprivation in Appendix 4.2. The contemporary example categories are the most concrete and also the most likely to vary from time to time and among actors. Moreover, the relevant example categories will probably vary depending on the purposes of the research. With these characteristics in mind, we have made no attempt to be exhaustive. Furthermore, we anticipate that contemporary example categories can be added, deleted, or recombined given the requirements of a particular research project so long as they fulfill two conditions: (a) that they be mutually exclusive of one another and (b) that they fall within the general boundaries established for the types of deprivations or problems.

To illustrate the nature of the contemporary example categories, consider those listed as jeopardizing the basic value of well-being when the source of deprivation is nature or the conditions of society and the general type of problem is the existence of disease epidemics. Together with an "other" category, six types of disease epidemics are listed as contemporary examples (malaria, typhoid, smallpox, tuberculosis, viral influenza, and cholera). It is likely that someone particularly concerned with problems of disease in international affairs may find some alternative configuration more useful. For example, the investigator may wish to classify diseases into those produced by microorganisms or environmental, genetic, or nutritional factors. Such a modification or any comparable one can be readily accommodated. Once the general type of problem is isolated, the reorganization is a manageable task. Furthermore, if the more general classification is left intact, the theoretical insights that may be generated by it will not be disrupted. In short, the flexible subclassification of contemporary examples is intended to provide a link between the highly particularistic requirements of some kinds of research, such as policy studies, and the more general classifications necessary for theoretical work.

CODING EVENTS FOR
SUBSTANTIVE PROBLEM AREAS

Before we turn to the possible uses of the classification, let us consider the actual coding procedures and related issues of reliability and validity. The reader can form some initial judgment about face validity as well as the coding procedures by examining a sample of the actual coding of a few foreign policy events. Table 4.1 displays five events from the CREON data set and relates the value assigned to each substantive problem area dimension. We will review the steps involved in coding one of these events.

Consider the first event listed in Table 4.1. It is an announcement on May 13, 1960 by Premier Fidel Castro. In an address on Cuban television, he reports that ships of the U.S. Navy have been violating Cuban territorial waters. In efforts to deter these intrusions, he reports that a few days earlier a Cuban patrol boat

TABLE 4.1
Coding with Substantive Problem Area Classification for Five CREON Events

Event One

13 May 1960: Cuban Premier Fidel Castro announces in a television speech that a Cuban warship has fired at a U. S. submarine in Cuban territorial waters. He relates that U. S. naval vessels have been violating Cuban territorial waters.

Coding of Sample Event One: Basic Value = Security/Military-Physical Safety; Whose Basic Value Is Jeopardized = Acting Government or Its Entire Society; Where Is Problem Encountered = Within Actor Nation's Political Boundaries; Source of Deprivation = Foreign Government or Undifferentiated Foreign Nation; Type of Deprivation = Isolated Military Incident; Contemporary Example = Naval Encounters

Event Two

26 July 1966: Switzerland, in a joint communique with the Group of Ten Financial Ministers, agrees that the deliberate creation of additional reserve assets may be necessary in the future to supplement presently adequate reserves of the International Monetary Fund.

Coding of Sample Event Two: Basic Value = Economic Wealth; Whose Basic Value Is Jeopardized = Alliance, Regional, or Global Organization; Where Is Problem Encountered = Intergovernmental Organization; Source of Deprivation = Governments of Deprived Nations; Type of Deprivation = Fiscal or Monetary Arrangements; Contemporary Example = Currency Arrangements

Event Three

4 April 1960: Delegates from the Yugoslav Federal Commission for Nuclear Energy Reach an understanding with U. S. representatives on further cooperation concerning peaceful applications of nuclear energy.

Coding of Sample Event Three: Basic Value = Enlightenment/Skills; Whose Basic Value Is Jeopardized = Actor and Other Nation Temporarily Grouped Together; Where Is Problem Encountered = Intangible Relationship; Source of Deprivation = Entire Society of Deprived Nations; Type of Deprivation = State of Cumulated Knowledge; Contemporary Example = Knowledge Not Yet Developed

Event Four

23 June 1960: Indian Army Chief of Staff, upon completion of inspection tour of Sikkim and Bhutan, states that there are heavy concentrations of Chinese troops along India's border with the People's Republic of China.

Coding of Sample Event Four: Basic Value = Security/Military-Physical Safety; Whose Basic Value Is Jeopardized = Acting Government or Its Entire Society; Where Is Problem Encountered = Bounded within Region; Source of Deprivation = Foreign Government or Undifferentiated Foreign Nation; Type of Deprivation = Nonwar Use of Military Force Applied to Foreigners; Contemporary Example = Demonstrations or Shows of Force

Event Five

7 April 1960: Tunisian delegate to the Emergency Conference of Independent African States supports recommendation to boycott goods from South Africa and France to protest French nuclear tests in the Sahara Desert, French involvement in Algeria, and apartheid in South Africa.

Coding of Sample Event Five: (Note: Because the coder determined that three basic values were involved in this event, all five other dimensions of the coding scheme are coded separately for each basic value.) Basic Value (concerning French nuclear test in Sahara) A = Security/Military-Physical Safety; Whose Basic Value Is Jeopardized A = Actor and Other Nations Temporarily Grouped Together; Where Is Problem Encountered A = Bounded Within Region; Source of Deprivation A = Foreign Government or Undifferentiated Foreign Nation; Type of Deprivation A = Arms Control and Disarmament; Contemporary Example A = Strategic Nuclear Weapons. Basic Value (concerning South African apartheid) B = Well-Being/Welfare; Whose Basic Value Is Jeopardized B = Citizens or Groups in Nation Other than Actor's; Where Is Problem Encoun-

(Continued)

TABLE 4.1   Continued

---

tered B = Within Other Political Unit's Boundaries; Source of Deprivation B (from perspective of those deprived) = Government of Deprived Nation; Type of Deprivation B = Constraints & Discrimination Against Minorities and Subgroups; Contemporary Example B = Racial Discrimination. Basic Value (concerning French actions in Algeria) C = Respect/Status; Whose Basic Value Is Jeopardized C = Citizens or Groups in Nation Other Than Actor's; Where Is Problem Encountered C = Within Other Political Unit's Boundaries; Source of Deprivation C (from perspective of those deprived) = Government of Deprived Nation; Type of Deprivation C = Repudiate or Reject Some Entity or Its Plan; Contemporary Example C = Deny Colonies' Independence.

---

fired at an American submarine, the *USS Sea Poacher*, which Castro asserted was operating in Cuban waters.

The coder or analyst begins by determining the apparent immediate problem with which the actor (Castro) is dealing in the event. One might speculate about the underlying problem facing Castro of consolidating his power or the necessity of convincing the general Cuban public of the hostility of the United States. The immediate overt problem characterized in the event, however, is the alleged violation of Cuban territorial waters by American warships.[5] Once the analyst makes this determination, he or she can start to code the substantive problem area dimensions. First, the coder must select one or more of the basic values. In this illustrative event the coder reasoned that U.S. ships were seen as jeopardizing the physical safety of Cuba. (Notice that it is not necessary to determine how severely the value is jeopardized or whether the harm is actual or potential.) The second dimension concerns whose value is jeopardized. From the seven possible categories the analyst selected the one identifying "the acting government or its society." Although other events will reveal that the United States government contends the incident occurred on the high seas, from the perspective of the account in this event the encounter took place in Cuban territorial waters. Therefore, from among the eight categories establishing the location of the problem, the coder chose "inside the actor nation's political jurisdiction." Nine categories are available for identifying the source of the deprivation—the fourth dimension of the classification to be coded. Castro makes clear in this event that it is the United States; hence, the appropriate category is "foreign government." Having determined that the value of physical safety has been jeopardized by a foreign government, the coder has been directed to nine of the potential 66 types of problems and from those nine has selected the category, "isolated military incidents." In the present coding system that type of problem contains six contemporary examples, of which one is "naval encounters"—the one used in this event. The other events in Table 4.1—and, indeed, in the entire CREON data set—have been coded in a similar fashion.

Notice that the coder never has to make a choice at any point in the coding scheme between more than a few categories. This procedure has a practical advantage with respect to intercoder reliabilities. By nesting the classification of problems—that is, by making choice of problem dependent on prior coding decisions on basic values and sources of deprivation—the coder's range of categories is reduced from 66 to no more than nine. Similarly, the contemporary example dimensions are reduced from an unwieldy 306 categories to an average of five.

As indicated by the fifth event in Table 4.1, an event may entail responses to more than one problem, and the one or several problems may affect more than one basic value. Thus, Tunisia's proposal for an African boycott of French and South African products was a response to three problems—the Algerian War, French nuclear testing in the Sahara, and apartheid in South Africa. Among the approximately 12,000 foreign policy events coded for substantive problem areas, 1,138 events involved two basic values and 85 events involved three basic values. Each time a separate basic value is coded for an event, all five of the other dimensions of the classification scheme are coded. For every basic value, however, there can be only one category selected in each of the other five dimensions.

The following are the intercoder reliabilities for the various dimensions of the substantive problem area classification:

Basic Value	.94
Whose Basic Value Is Jeopardized	.81
Where Is Problem Encountered	.83
Source of Deprivation	.77
Type of Deprivation	.81

The coefficients reported here are coefficients of agreement as determined by the Krippendorff (1971) formula. (For a description of this procedure for calculating intercoder agreement, see Chapter 2.) The reliabilities are based on coding decisions regarding 42 events. The reliability tests were conducted every week during the coding process, which involved 20 weeks and up to three coders.[6] The coefficient of agreement for the overall classification scheme—taking into account all of the choice points—was .81.

APPLYING THE CLASSIFICATION

At the outset of this chapter we suggested that a classification by content was a natural way to think about differentiating foreign policy. Furthermore, the review of efforts to develop procedural or substantive classifications would suggest that others have believed that a set of issue area categories would contribute to the study of foreign policy. In this concluding section we can only allude to some of the promising applications. We will concentrate on uses that involve comparing different substantive issues rather than selecting from the classification a single kind of issue that could then be studied in isolation. We also will emphasize applications of the problem dimensions rather than the contextual ones, although the latter have many uses both separately and in combination with the problem dimensions. (For an example, see Brady's chapter on goals.)

One Nation's Involvement with Problem Areas

Three measures can be constructed to indicate a national government's involvement with particular problem areas. The first of these might be labeled a dispersion or range of concern indicator. If we assume that we have a reasonably adequate listing of the broad types of deprivations or problems in the world at a given time, how many does a particular nation address? This indicator would be the number of different problem areas dealt with by a given government divided by the base of all problem areas which were active in the world at that time. Such information helps us to explore questions about the conditions that lead some nations to range more widely in international affairs than others. A variation in this indicator would be to list the types of problems that are attended to widely.

A second indicator identifies the dominant actor or actors on a particular problem. This simple computation divides the number of events for one nation on a particular issue by all the events of all actors concerned with that issue. In terms of the amount of international activity, what nation or nations dominate an issue and why? Do some governments seem to be among the most active on a broad range of problems, and how do they differ from those which are dominant on only one or two problems?

Salience might be the name applied to a third indicator which constitutes a variation on the second. Because national governments appear to differ significantly in the total amount of their foreign policy activity, a nation might have fewer events pertaining to a given problem than another nation. Even so, the state with fewer events might be devoting a higher proportion of its total foreign policy effort to that issue than is its more generally active counterpart. We can estimate the salience or importance of an issue for a national government by creating a proportion consisting of the number of the nation's events pertaining to a given issue divided by the total foreign policy events for that nation.

In order to work with these problem area indicators, it is first necessary to develop an applicable list of types of problems. We have focused on those problem areas for which there were more than 25 events across the 38 CREON nations during the selected annual quarters for the decade 1959-1968. According to Appendix 4.1, there are 40 such problem areas. We have assumed that these problem areas were the topics of concern to the CREON nations during the decade. Drawing on this list of problems, we can create the three indicators described above and record the performance of the CREON nations with respect to each one. The results appear in Appendix 4.3.

The salience column of Appendix 4.3 (column 2) shows the number of different problem areas which a given nation considered in more than five percent of its events. In other words, salience indicates the problem areas that a nation paid most attention to during the decade 1959-1968. The four most salient problem areas for each CREON nation are listed in column 3 of Appendix 4.3. Generally, these four issues accounted for between one-third and one-half of a nation's events. Several of the problem areas appear repeatedly in the CREON nations' most salient problems. Twenty (53 percent) of the CREON countries were highly concerned with economic assistance (loans, grants, sales or purchases, dues to organizations) during this period. In particular, economic assistance problems were important for the developing countries. For 16 (42 percent) of the countries another economic problem area, trade agreements, was highly salient. Trade agreements involve dealings within common markets, preferential trading agreements, and interactions among cartels of producers and consumer governments.

The nations most concerned with trade agreements were both producing and consumer countries—developed and developing. Nineteen (50 percent) of the countries were concerned with repudiating or rejecting another entity's policies. For the most part the nations most concerned with this problem area were those with heated negative encounters with a traditional adversary (for example, Egypt and Israel) during this decade. For six of the eight CREON nations located on the African continent, discrimination was a highly salient problem during the 1960s.

Appendix 4.3 also indicates which nations dominated the activities in the various problem areas. In contrast to salience, dominance indicates the problem areas in which one CREON nation has more events than the other CREON nations. Columns 4 and 5 of Appendix 4.3 list the three nations with the highest percentages of events in each problem area. Given the large number of events that the United States has in the data set, it is not surprising to find that the United States dominates 32 of the 40 problem areas. Indeed, the six CREON nations with the largest number of events in the data set are also those nations dominating the most problem areas (France, India, Soviet Union, United States, West Germany). More interesting, perhaps, than the number of problem areas a nation dominates are the specific problem areas that a nation dominates. An examination of Appendix 4.3 suggests that the more developed countries dominate problem areas concerned with security/military and economic wealth issues, whereas the developing countries dominate the problem areas concerned with well-being/welfare and enlightenment. Whether well-being/welfare and enlightenment are of the gravest concern to the developing countries, it may be that they are of less concern to the more developed nations.

The last column in Appendix 4.3 contains a measure of dispersion (or the proportion of total problem areas which concern a nation or government). According to these figures, France and the United States have events in all 40 problem areas. Switzerland has events in the smallest number of problem areas, focusing more on economic than other types of problems. For the most part, the CREON countries deal with diverse problems, having events in a majority of the problem areas. The following are problem areas in which all 38 CREON nations had events: trade agreements, fiscal/monetary arrangements, economic assistance, end agreement, repudiate/reject a policy, advance proposals, need diplomatic communication, and constraints on education and research activities. All the CREON countries at some time during the 1960s were concerned or faced with an economic wealth or respect/status problem.

Combining Problem Areas with Other Behavioral Properties

One strategy for explaining the involvement of actors with various foreign policy problems is to develop a special explanation for each problem area. Thus, we might have one model for arms control, another for human rights, a third for labor migration, and so on. Given the subjective and transitory nature of problem areas, such a strategy appears discouraging and designed to leave analysts always working to explain the last decade's problem areas even as new ones have emerged in the world's arena.

An alternative strategy might be to look for some underlying properties of foreign policy actions that are characteristic of every foreign policy event no matter what the problem area. Many of the behavior measures discussed elsewhere in this book could be among the candidates considered for these common properties. This alternative strategy would follow a two-step process. First, we would need to develop reasonably satisfactory explanations for the more or less enduring properties that characterize any foreign policy event (for example, commitment, affect, specificity, interdependence of action). Of course, that would be no easy task, but once such explanations were in place we would be ready for the second step. These more or less stable properties could be used to determine the profiles of current problem areas. In other words, we would attempt to determine whether a particular type of problem area tended to be distinct from other problem areas with respect to the pattern of values for the basic properties associated with it. Wars as a type of problem area, for example, might be found to be high in negative affect and in commitment but more independent than interdependent. Assuming that distinctive profiles or "fingerprints" of these enduring properties could be found for each problem area, we could draw on the "stock" explanations associated with these recurring properties as the basis for an account of the particular problem area.

Is it reasonable to assume that substantive problem areas form distinctive "profiles" with respect to a common set of other properties with which they might be combined? This strikes us as a question worthy of inquiry.[7] As a preliminary demonstration, we cross-tabulated the types of deprivations or problems with three of the behavior measures—potential basic properties—described elsewhere in this volume (commitment, affect, and independence/interdependence of action). For each of the 40 types of deprivations or problems in Appendix 4.1 that had more than 25 events, we isolated the events that pertained to a given problem from all the others. Then for each of the three types of behavior we compared the distribution of values found in events concerned with a given type of problem with the distribution of values for events not concerned with that problem (all other events). Gamma tests were run to compare the value distributions of events related to a problem with those that were not. Table 4.2 displays the twelve problem areas that had at least one of the three behavior measures with a gamma value of .45 or better. If one compares the problem areas by attending only to those gamma values of .45 or more, the problem areas do appear distinctive. For example, "Domestic Use of Military Force" has a strong negative gamma on commitment and a high positive gamma on independence of action. "Nonwar Use of Military Force" is characterized by a high negative value for affect, while "Foreign Isolated Military Incidents" has a high negative value on independence of action. These three military/security problems show different patterns of activity associated with them. As noted by the underlined values in Table 4.2, few of the problem areas have similar patterns with respect to the configuration of high gammas for these three behavior properties. Of course, this test is crude and can be regarded only as a suggestion that distinctive profiles for a common set of underlying behavioral characteristics may be identifiable for substantive problem areas.

TABLE 4.2
Configuration of Gamma Values for Three Behavior Properties
on Selected Types of Problems

Problem	Commitment	Independence/ Interdependence of Action	Affect
Domestic Use of Military Force	−.52	.45	−.20
Nonwar Use of Military Force	−.11	−.41	−.50
Foreign Isolated Military Incidents	−.03	−.60	−.24
Commodity Transactions	.67	.30	.40
General Domestic Economic Conditions	.14	.01	.55
Natural Resources Problems	.56	.18	.88
Reduce or Break off Diplomatic Contact (End Agreement)	−.17	−.48	−.13
Need for Diplomatic Communication	−.49	.26	.27
Constraints on Political and Legal Well-Being	−.29	.24	−.58
Constraints on Minority or Subgroup	−.48	.51	−.54
Constraints on Education and Research Activity	−.15	.76	.44
Economic Incapacity to Support Knowledge Facilities or Products	.49	−.02	.66

NOTE: The operationalizations and conceptualizations of the three behavior properties appearing in this table are described in other chapters in this volume.

Changes in Problem Emphases over Time

Do nations change the problem areas they are interested in over time, or do the problems tend to remain the same across a decade? Although we do not have sufficient events in the CREON data set for enough of the types of deprivation or problem areas to examine variations for each nation, it is possible to check for a general change in problem focus by looking at the basic values. Table 4.3 indicates the percentage of a nation's events that involve each of the five basic values coded in the substantive problem area classification for three-year periods during the 1960s—1960-1962, 1963-1965, 1966-1968.

As Table 4.3 shows, there is fluctuation in the foci of attention among the CREON nations. Most of the dramatic changes occur among the security/ military, economic, and respect/status problems. For several of the nations, all three basic values were emphasized at one point during the decade. For example, the Israeli government started out the decade focusing on respect/status issues, changed to security/military and economic issues in the middle of the decade, and in 1966-68 with the 1967 war moved to a predominantly security/military focus. For other countries, the shifts are generally between security/military and economic issues. Ghana and Uruguay demonstrate dramatically the shift from a security/military to an economic focus across the decade. Both start out with

TABLE 4.3
Percentage of Events by Basic Values for CREON Nations in Three Time Periods During 1960s

CREON Nation	1960-62						1963-65						1966-68					
	N^a	Military	Economic	Respect/Status	Well-Being	Enlightenment	N^a	Military	Economic	Respect/Status	Well-Being	Enlightenment	N^a	Military	Economic	Respect/Status	Well-Being	Enlightenment
Belgium	139	.16	.45	.28	.06	.05	115	.11	.61	.25	.00	.03	147	.20	.40	.34	.03	.03
Canada	124	.29	.23	.36	.07	.04	125	.27	.47	.22	.02	.02	163	.30	.28	.32	.04	.06
Chile	72	.21	.26	.29	.18	.06	61	.11	.64	.18	.05	.02	79	.05	.46	.30	.09	.10
China (PRC)	179	.57	.09	.32	.01	.01	227	.48	.07	.42	.02	.01	101	.63	.04	.29	.03	.01
Costa Rica	44	.27	.23	.25	.16	.09	71	.25	.48	.15	.08	.03	51	.12	.39	.29	.10	.10
Cuba	178	.35	.18	.38	.06	.03	104	.34	.25	.36	.02	.03	55	.42	.11	.36	.07	.04
Czechoslovakia	63	.27	.25	.35	.10	.03	59	.30	.39	.24	.00	.07	83	.30	.14	.45	.04	.07
East Germany	31	.26	.32	.36	.00	.06	62	.23	.27	.39	.08	.03	110	.25	.08	.60	.04	.03
Egypt	159	.36	.13	.38	.10	.03	171	.29	.24	.34	.08	.05	135	.52	.16	.30	.01	.01
France	260	.23	.32	.36	.04	.05	319	.24	.35	.32	.02	.04	299	.29	.31	.28	.03	.08
Ghana	144	.36	.10	.33	.17	.03	97	.17	.31	.32	.19	.01	54	.07	.37	.28	.18	.09
Guinea	106	.28	.12	.35	.18	.07	78	.14	.33	.36	.13	.04	45	.18	.20	.40	.11	.11
Iceland	44	.21	.27	.36	.11	.05	41	.17	.58	.17	.02	.05	66	.21	.35	.33	.05	.06
India	210	.58	.10	.24	.06	.01	158	.40	.31	.20	.05	.04	128	.34	.28	.23	.09	.06
Israel	68	.16	.19	.41	.13	.10	98	.41	.32	.23	.02	.02	185	.63	.12	.17	.05	.02
Italy	155	.15	.43	.30	.06	.06	109	.08	.60	.27	.02	.03	172	.23	.35	.31	.04	.06
Ivory Coast	44	.18	.25	.39	.14	.06	82	.29	.28	.29	.13	.00	44	.04	.43	.34	.09	.09
Japan	82	.19	.39	.26	.10	.06	95	.09	.59	.27	.01	.03	92	.20	.36	.30	.08	.06
Kenya	b						59	.17	.36	.17	.30	.00	51	.14	.29	.33	.08	.10
Lebanon	45	.20	.22	.42	.11	.04	59	.20	.42	.34	.00	.03	51	.35	.23	.25	.14	.08
Mexico	64	.28	.22	.28	.12	.09	67	.16	.58	.21	.00	.04	66	.06	.41	.31	.08	.11
New Zealand	67	.24	.15	.48	.10	.03	68	.29	.53	.12	.06	.00	64	.23	.28	.36	.11	.05
Norway	73	.25	.30	.33	.08	.04	67	.28	.49	.18	.01	.03	75	.27	.24	.39	.08	.05
Philippines	53	.40	.11	.30	.13	.06	62	.34	.48	.13	.03	.02	87	.28	.25	.28	.05	.11
Poland	78	.29	.26	.32	.09	.04	70	.31	.37	.26	.04	.01	82	.43	.08	.35	.08	.08
Soviet Union	340	.46	.07	.41	.03	.03	338	.51	.11	.31	.02	.04	336	.53	.08	.29	.05	.04
Spain	62	.27	.19	.32	.16	.05	45	.13	.56	.29	.00	.02	67	.16	.28	.39	.09	.07
Switzerland	22	.14	.59	.23	.00	.04	20	.00	.80	.15	.05	.00	34	.00	.65	.35	.00	.00
Thailand	50	.34	.14	.32	.12	.08	46	.37	.52	.09	.00	.02	68	.31	.22	.32	.09	.06
Tunisia	104	.36	.13	.31	.17	.03	116	.17	.29	.40	.10	.04	66	.15	.30	.36	.08	.11
Turkey	70	.26	.19	.41	.11	.03	121	.31	.31	.26	.03	.08	114	.38	.18	.25	.11	.08
Uganda	28	.18	.21	.32	.21	.07	93	.19	.31	.31	.18	.01	47	.04	.36	.34	.15	.11
United States	704	.54	.12	.27	.05	.02	684	.48	.20	.29	.02	.01	557	.43	.18	.29	.07	.03
Uruguay	41	.27	.19	.32	.17	.05	43	.14	.56	.26	.04	.00	54	.06	.44	.28	.13	.09
Venezuela	72	.33	.24	.28	.11	.04	56	.14	.55	.23	.04	.04	85	.21	.38	.26	.08	.07
West Germany	192	.16	.42	.35	.03	.04	204	.10	.40	.47	.01	.01	278	.27	.32	.34	.02	.03
Yugoslavia	85	.24	.09	.54	.09	.04	94	.07	.44	.35	.03	.11	84	.24	.20	.42	.08	.06
Zambia	b						7	.00	.86	.14	.00	.00	86	.09	.29	.29	.24	.08
Totals	4252	.35	.20	.33	.08	.04	4391	.30	.34	.29	.04	.03	436	.32	.25	.31	.06	.06

[a] The Ns here are the number of events in the CREON data set that a nation has during the specific time period.

[b] Kenya and Zambia were not independent during this time period and thus have no events in the data set.

about one-third of their events concerned with security/military problems and less than one-fifth of their events concerned with economic issues. By the end of the decade these percentages are reversed.

Across the decade we note that for both developing and developed countries there is an increase in economic concerns during the middle part of the decade (1963-65). For 23 of the 38 nations (61 percent), there was a 15 percent or more increase in events concerned with economic issues during this three-year period over the first third of the decade (1960-62). Moreover, for many (17) of these same nations, there is a similar decrease in economic events during the last part of the decade.

An examination of nations approximately half of whose events focus on a particular type of issue reveals an emphasis on security/military issues for China (PRC), the Soviet Union, and the United States throughout the decade. Caught in the Sino-Indian border conflict early in the decade, India has over half its events classified as security/military from 1960 to 1962, but this percentage decreases to one-third by the end of the decade. For Egypt and Israel, the percentage of events concerned with security/military affairs increases to over half of their events during the period involving the 1967 war. With regard to economic issues, Switzerland, of all the CREON countries, appears the most consistently concerned with economic problems. Three-fifths or more of the Swiss government's events fall in the economic category. Table 4.3 suggests that nations tend to spend about one-third of their time dealing with respect/status issues. Of the CREON nations 27 in 1960-62, 18 in 1963-65, and 30 in 1966-68 focused about one-third of their events on respect/status issues.

Although most of the CREON countries attended to well-being and enlightenment issues only about five to ten percent of the time, we note in Table 4.3 that the developing nations, particularly those in Africa, focused more on these issues than did others. Well-being and enlightenment issues appear important to countries just getting "on their feet." At least it may be important for the leaders of these countries to pay lip service to these problems to keep or to consolidate their power.

The patterning of events for the industrialized nations on the security/ military, economic, and respect/status issues provides us with a set of contradictions. While the Soviet Union and the United States focused throughout the decade on security/military and respect/status affairs, Belgium, France, Japan, and West Germany focused more of the time on economic issues. Respect/status issues were also relevant to these countries, but security/military affairs received less attention. In the case of Belgium, Japan, and West Germany, security/ military issues ranked a poor third behind economic and respect/status concerns. While the two superpowers concentrated on armaments and arms control, Belgium, France, Japan, and West Germany were building economically.

SUMMARY

This chapter has addressed a dilemma. Classifying foreign policy activity by the content of such actions seems obvious. Efforts to develop issue area classifications have, however, foundered either on the problem of empirical measurement or on the weakness of theoretical insight. We believe the dilemma need not be insurmountable. As a possible candidate procedure for overcoming these difficulties, we have proposed a classification that combines some more stable characteristics of problems (the underlying basic values involved) and context (who is deprived, location of problem, source of deprivation) with a two-tier set of more transitory problem characteristics. As with so many scholarly papers, we conclude with the need for further research to determine whether the proposed system can indeed reduce the noted dilemma.

APPENDIX 4.1
Types of Deprivations or Problems and Associated Basic Values and Sources of Deprivation Codes

This appendix lists the 66 types of problems contained in the classification scheme. For easy reference, these types of problems are numbered consecutively from 1 to 66. However, these are not the identification numbers used in the coding manual (C. Hermann, 1974). The frequency with which a particular type of problem occurs in the data set appears in parentheses following the description of that type of problem.

If Basic Value is coded *security/military-physical safety* and the Source of Deprivation is in the *governmental* cluster of categories, then the Type of Deprivation is selected from categories 1-9.

(1)   Domestic use of military-police force against own nationals or other military activities within own country (119)
(2)   Nonwar use of military force applied to (directed toward) foreigners (i.e., people not members of the country which military serves) (489)
(3)   War and large-scale combat actions (includes military assistance during war) (877)
(4)   Isolated military incidents (noncontinuous actions involving military force outside of the country of at least one party whose military units are engaged) (457)
(5)   Conflict negotiation or military settlement (395)
(6)   Arms control and disarmament (692)
(7)   Military alliances (all aspects other than actual engagement in combat) (327)
(8)   Nonalliance force maintenance and preparedness (144)
(9)   Verbal threats, statements of doctrine, and general activities (primarily verbal) pertaining to use of force (588)

If Basic Value is coded *security/military-physical safety* and the Source of Deprivation is in the *nongovernmental* cluster of categories, then the Type of Deprivation is selected from categories 10-11.

(10)   Domestic violence (confined to one country with vast majority of participants being nationals of country in which conflict occurs) (328)
(11)   External violence (primarily participants in violence are acting outside their own country) (19)

If Basic Value is coded *economic wealth* and the Source of Deprivation is in the *governmental* cluster of categories, then the Type of Deprivation is selected from categories 12-17.

(12)   Substantive categories of commerce, industry, and international trade (commodity transactions) (101)
(13)   Trade agreements and associations between international entities (700)
(14)   Fiscal or monetary arrangements proposed or existing between two or more international actors (519)
(15)   Financial conditions within one entity (143)
(16)   Regulation and protective actions (691)
(17)   Economic assistance to other entities (714)

If Basic Value is coded *economic wealth* and the Source of Deprivation is in the *nongovernmental* cluster of categories, then the Type of Deprivation is selected from categories 18-22.

(18)   Business firms owned by and/or operated primarily within one nation (11)

(19) Multinational corporations—business firms owned by and/or operated in two or more countries to a substantial degree (9)

(20) Interest groups and associations (organizations of persons having shared interest in some economic activity cooperating to promote their interests through lobbying, promotional activities, and direct political and economic action) (1)

(21) Activities of individuals or loose, temporary collections of individuals (19)

(22) Banks and related financial institutions (1)

If Basic Value is coded *economic wealth* and the Source of Deprivation is in the *nature of societal conditions* cluster of categories, then the Type of Deprivation is selected from categories 23-28.

(23) General condition of a society's economy (336)

(24) Natural resource problems (difficulties pertaining to the natural resources found in the society or under its control) (108)

(25) Agricultural problems (66)

(26) Labor problems (3)

(27) Industrial problems (146)

(28) Transportation and distribution problems (73)

If the Basic Value is coded *respect/status* and the Source of Deprivation is in the *governmental* cluster of categories, then the Type of Deprivation is selected from categories 29-33.

(29) Acknowledge (at least tacitly) errors (or inadequacies under present conditions) in past policies, statements, or activities (including yielding under political or military pressure) or inability to fulfill policies and goals; admit one has been wrong (154)

(30) Engage in termination or violation of some currently existing agreement or activity (672)

(31) Repudiate or reject some entity or its plans, policies, or actions (1341)

(32) Advance proposal, resolution, or request that could create embarrassment, create an unfavorable political situation, or otherwise create problem for recipient (1030)

(33) Need for diplomatic and political communication with other nations (participatory actions designed to maintain exchanges and contracts between nations which in and of themselves are not reported as involving specific substantive topics; includes actions designed to avoid further problems by failure to follow expected norms) (1040)

If the Basic Value is coded *respect/status* and the Source of Deprivation is in the *nongovernmental* cluster of categories, then the Type of Deprivation is selected from categories 34-36.

(34) Individual or group opposition to governmental actions or policies (93)

(35) Misconduct, impropriety, or accidents by individuals or groups creates an "incident" (embarrassing incidents) and possible (real or potential) shame to country with which they are affiliated (47)

(36) Challenges and/or defeats in competition (4)

If the Basic Value is coded *respect/status* and the Source of Deprivation is in the *nature or societal conditions* cluster of categories, then the Type of Deprivation is selected from categories 37-38.

(37) Widespread public rejection of actual or proposed international commitment or of those individuals widely associated with that commitment (or election of those opposed to it) (1)

(38) Existence or potential emergence of conditions which reduce entity's standing vis-a-vis other nations or other international actors (4)

If the Basic Value is coded *well-being/welfare* and the Source of Deprivation is in the *governmental* cluster of categories, then the Type of Deprivation is selected from categories 39-47.

(39) Constraints on political and legal well-being (263)

(40) Constraints on economic well-being (38)

(41) Constraints on health care (68)

(42) Constraints on travel and mobility (23)

(43)   Constraints on shelter and housing (1)
(44)   Constraints on religious beliefs and practices (22)
(45)   Constraints on criminal activities and treatment of criminals (4)
(46)   Constraints on minorities or subgroups; discrimination (271)
(47)   Damage to victims of war (46)

If the Basic Value is coded *well-being/welfare* and the Source of Deprivation is in the *nongovernmental* cluster of categories, then the Type of Deprivation is selected from categories 48-50.

(48)   Engaging in criminal acts (8)
(49)   Nongovernmental discrimination against minority or subgroup (3)
(50)   Private withholding or withdrawal of service and/or assistance (0)

If the Basic Value is coded *well-being/welfare* and the Source of Deprivation is in the *nature or societal conditions* cluster of categories, then the Type of Deprivation is selected from categories 51-54.

(51)   Existence of hunger, malnutrition, famine (35)
(52)   Existence of poverty; inadequate resources to provide the necessities of life—food, shelter, clothing (46)
(53)   Existence of disease; epidemics (3)
(54)   Natural disasters (47)

If the Basic Value is coded *enlightenment* and the Source of Deprivation is in the *governmental* cluster of categories, then the Type of Deprivation is selected from categories 55-59.

(55)   Censorship or discrediting of foreign information (information may be either about foreign events or about domestic events reported by foreigners) (10)
(56)   Restrictions on personal interaction with foreign persons or groups (69)
(57)   Regulation on exchange of knowledge products with foreigners (physical products pertaining to knowledge including artwork, inventions, or any physical commodity other than news media such as newspapers or magazines) (9)
(58)   Constraints on citizen advocacy of foreign ideas (2)
(59)   Constraints on or failure to support educational and research activities (388)

If the Basic Value is coded *enlightenment* and the Source of Deprivation is in the *nongovernmental* cluster of categories, then the Type of Deprivation is selected from categories 60-63.

(60)   Private acts of physical abuse or violence against foreign ideas, those expressing them, or those using foreign knowledge products, associating with foreigners, or sharing domestic knowledge with foreigners (0)
(61)   Private nonviolent acts against foreign ideas or their advocates (0)
(62)   Private statements of repudiation of foreign ideas or their advocates (0)
(63)   Private groups or individuals refuse to share their knowledge or expertise with others (0)

If the Basic Value is coded *enlightenment* and the Source of Deprivation is in the *nature or societal conditions* cluster of categories, then the Type of Deprivation is selected from categories 64-66.

(64)   State of cumulated knowledge (49)
(65)   Economic capability (unable to support the cost of knowledge facilities or products) (110)
(66)   Religious or ideological prohibitions (cultural, ethical, or ideological norms make ideas or products reprehensible or unbelievable) (2)

APPENDIX 4.2

Contemporary Examples of Foreign Policy Problems
Organized by Types of Deprivations

This appendix lists the 306 "Contemporary Problems" currently coded in the CREON Substantive Problem Area Classification. They are listed under the appropriate "Type of Deprivation" category which must first be coded. As indicated in Figure 4.1 and Appendix 4.1 of this chapter, the "Type of Deprivation" category is in turn dependent on prior coding decisions on "Basic Values" and "Source of Deprivation." Further information on the coding procedure appears in C. Hermann (1974).

(1) Domestic use of military police force against own nationals or other military activities within their own country

    01 = riot/demonstration/strike control
    02 = defense of key governmental officials and installations
    03 = counterinsurgency
    04 = coup d'etat
    05 = civic action projects

(2) Nonwar use of military force applied to (directed toward) foreigners (i.e., people not members of the country which military serves)

    01 = military occupation of foreign territory
    02 = demonstrations or shows of force
    03 = military assistance or training
    04 = foreign bases, installations, rights of military personnel abroad
    05 = overflight or port of call privileges
    06 = prisoners of war, espionage agents, spies, imprisonment of foreigners

(3) War and large-scale combat actions (includes military assistance during war)

    01 = civil war
    02 = border war

(4) Isolated military incidents (noncontinuous actions involving military force outside of the country of at least one party whose military units are engaged)

    01 = guerrilla raids
    02 = air strikes
    03 = naval encounters
    04 = border encounters
    05 = military treaty or agreement violations
    06 = espionage or spying on by military units or activities

(5) Conflict negotiation or military settlement

    01 = cease-fires/peace agreements/surrender arrangements
    02 = prisoner, spy negotiations or exchanges
    03 = peacekeeping forces
    04 = boundary or border determinations/negotiations
    05 = international organization resolutions concerning cessation of violence or means of peacekeeping

(6) Arms control and disarmament

    01 = strategic nuclear weapons
    02 = proliferation of nuclear weapons
    03 = chemical/biological weapons
    04 = conventional arms
    05 = complete or general disarmament
    06 = inspection and verification

(7)   Military alliances (all aspects other than actual engagement in combat)

    01 = alliance formation, membership changes, conditions for joint action
    02 = alliance financing
    03 = control and organizational aspects
    04 = military needs
    05 = negotiation between alliances

(8)   Nonalliance force maintenance and preparedness

    01 = manpower, draft, recruitment
    02 = financing
    03 = adequacy of existing weapons
    04 = concealment of military activities, maneuvers, weapons deployments

(9)   Verbal threats, doctrines, and general activities (primarily verbal) pertaining to use of force

    01 = military warnings, threat to use force, ultimatum
    02 = deterrence strategy
    03 = pledges, guarantees of military protection and support
    04 = subversion or ideological advocacy with possible overtones of resort to force

(10)   Domestic violence (confined to one country with vast majority of participants being nationals of country in which conflict occurs)

    01 = domestic-oriented violent riots, strikes, protest demonstrations
    02 = intergroup violence—conflict between religions, tribes, racial groups
    03 = terrorism/kidnapping/hijacking/bombing/sabotage—attacks on victims chosen more or less at random or because of their representation of some broader class
    04 = antigovernment violence—armed rebellion, coups and attempted coups, revolution, assassination, guerrilla warfare
    05 = hostility to foreigners within country—attacks on occupying troops, foreign officials, foreign nongovernmental visitors, colonial administrators

(11)   External violence (primarily participants in violence acting outside their own country)

    01 = foreign terrorist activities
    02 = participation in foreign wars—individuals or groups on their own join and/or lead combat activities in wars in which their own country is not formally involved
    03 = foreign private organizations engage or support violent actions—business firms, ethnic organizations pay for or promote violence outside their country of origin

(12)   Substantive categories of commerce, industry, and international trade

    01 = arms
    02 = automobiles and other road vehicles
    03 = coal and coke
    04 = grains
    05 = fish or other sea products
    06 = oil, gas, and petroleum
    07 = iron ore
    08 = precious metals and stones
    09 = textiles
    10 = fertilizers
    11 = complete facilities or plants
    12 = electronic parts and equipment
    13 = uranium and other radioactive elements
    14 = other natural resources
    15 = other agricultural products
    16 = other manufactured goods

(13)   Trade agreements and associations between international entities

   01 = common markets, custom unions
   02 = preferential trading agreements, "most favored nation" status
   03 = cartels of producer governments
   04 = cartels of consumer governments
   05 = arrangements between consumers and producers of a given commodity

(14)   Fiscal or monetary arrangements proposed or existing between two or more international actors

   01 = international banks, credit arrangements, international fiscal assistance agencies
   02 = currency arrangements—means of fixing relative value of currencies; mechanisms for revaluation

(15)   Financial conditions of one entity

   01 = budget deficits, shortage of working capital
   02 = taxation problems
   03 = unfavorable balance of payments

(16)   Regulations and protective actions

   01 = nationalization of privately owned businesses
   02 = export licenses
   03 = embargoes
   04 = import tariffs and duties
   05 = import quotas
   06 = subsidies to domestic products
   07 = fishing rights

(17)   Economic assistance to other entities

   01 = loans, credits
   02 = sales or purchases
   03 = aid or grants
   04 = dues or contributions to organizations or collective efforts

(18)   Business firms owned by and/or operated primarily within one nation

   01 = foreign sales
   02 = governmental control and regulation
   03 = investment activities of
   04 = productivity
   05 = domestic marketing and price activities
   06 = labor issues
   07 = financial condition

(19)   Multinational corporations—business firms owned by and/or operated to a substantial degree in two or more countries

   01 = relations with national governments
   02 = effects on market and commodity price
   03 = investment activities of
   04 = productivity
   05 = labor issues
   06 = financial condition

(20)   Interest groups and associations (organizations of persons having shared interest in some economic activity cooperating to promote their interests through lobbying, promotional activities, and direct political and economic action)

   01 = trade unions
   02 = agricultural associations

　　　　03 = manufacturing and commercial associations
　　　　04 = humanitarian and service groups

(21)　Activities of individuals or loose, temporary collections of individuals

　　　　01 = private investors
　　　　02 = consumer activity—temporary boycotts, protests, demonstrations
　　　　03 = workers activity— "wildcat" strikes, demonstrations, absenteeism
　　　　04 = violation of fishing limits

(22)　Banks and related financial institutions

　　　　01 = lending rates; loan policies
　　　　02 = international activities of
　　　　03 = relations with government
　　　　04 = assets and investors

(23)　General condition of a society's economy

　　　　01 = existence and rate of inflation
　　　　02 = existence or possibility of recession or depression
　　　　03 = difficulties in fulfilling economic plans and goals
　　　　04 = rate and direction of all goods and services produced

(24)　Natural resource problems (difficulties pertaining to the natural resources found in the society or under its control)

　　　　01 = nonexistence or depletion of natural resources
　　　　02 = lack of development of natural resources
　　　　03 = ability to control price, rate of consumption, and consumers

(25)　Agricultural problems

　　　　01 = excessive dependency on single crop
　　　　02 = ownership of arable land and collectivization problems
　　　　03 = crop failures
　　　　04 = market difficulties
　　　　05 = shortages of agricultural materials

(26)　Labor problems

　　　　01 = shortage of skilled labor
　　　　02 = high unemployment
　　　　03 = labor/management disputes; exploitation
　　　　04 = foreign labor or aliens, migrant workers

(27)　Industrial problems

　　　　01 = foreign ownership or control
　　　　02 = shortage of capital
　　　　03 = lack of modernization; uncompetitive
　　　　04 = shortages or reduced quality of nonlabor or semifinished materials
　　　　05 = market difficulties

(28)　Transportation and distribution problems

　　　　01 = difficulties in railroad system
　　　　02 = difficulties in merchant marine
　　　　03 = difficulties in air transportation
　　　　04 = difficulties in highway/trucking system

(29) Acknowledgement (at least tacitly) of errors (or inadequacies under present conditions) in past policy, statements, or activities (including yielding under political or military pressure) or inability to fulfill policies and goals; admission that one has been wrong

01 = diplomatic apology
02 = provide material compensation, restoration, reparations
03 = agree to compromise settlement or to seek settlement on less than original terms; make concessions
04 = admit political corruption
05 = grant colony or subnational territory greater autonomy or independence
06 = surrender to other existing entities all or part of territory and/or population
07 = yield selective sovereignty by granting existing entities rights or privileges on own territory or control over citizens under certain conditions
08 = concede inability to reach agreement with other entities or to correct or gain adequate redress from wrong doing by another entity

(30) Engaging in termination or violation of some existing agreement or activity presently engaged in

01 = break off or cancel negotiations, talks, visits
02 = violate, cancel, reduce, or modify treaty or formal agreement
03 = break, reduce, or temporarily disrupt diplomatic relations
04 = expel diplomats or other official representatives or abuse or violate diplomatic protocol
05 = withdraw from alliance, union, federation, common market
06 = terminate or reduce assistance or contribution—financial, technical, military, etc.
07 = default on payment for goods and services, repayment of loans, etc.
08 = expel private citizens from own country

(31) Repudiating or rejecting some entity or its plans, policies, or actions

01 = verbally denounce or protest action, statement or plans, form of government, ideology, leaders, etc., of another entity(ies)
02 = refuse to accept communication or to receive diplomat or other representative
03 = reject proposal, plan, request, or offer including votes against resolution favored by deprived entity
04 = oppose or reject entity for membership or affiliation with organization, alliance, etc.
05 = refuse visas for citizens of deprived country or deny or complicate their immigration into entity creating deprivation
06 = deny colonies or other subnational regions independence or greater autonomy

(32) Advancing proposal, resolution, or request that could create embarrassment, create an unfavorable political situation, or otherwise create problem for recipient

01 = seek new or expanded financial or other assistance
02 = propose collaboration on specific mutual projects
03 = establish or expand diplomatic representation
04 = create or expand treaty or agreement or organization
05 = admit entity to an existing organization or upgrade its present affiliation
06 = form permanent organization, alliance, or consultative agreement
07 = joint initiative or position vis-à-vis third parties
08 = suggest state visit or other travel

(33) Need for diplomatic and political communication with other nations (participatory actions designed to maintain exchanges and contracts between nations and which, in and

of themselves, are not reported as involving specific substantive topics, includes actions designed to avoid further problems by failure to follow expected norms)

01 = state visits, international ceremonies
02 = joint communiques
03 = general statements of praise or acknowledgment
04 = annual or interim reports in an international organization designed to summarize past behavior and activities

(34)   Opposition to actions and/or policies

01 = verbally denounce or repudiate deprived entity(ies)
02 = physical demonstrations, protests against deprived entity(ies)
03 = prohibit or expel membership or participation in organization or put on "probation"
04 = withhold benefits—goods, services, convention sites, etc.

(35)   Misconduct, impropriety, or accidents by individuals or groups creates an "incident" and possible (real or potential) shame to country with which they are affiliated

01 = tourists
02 = businesses or corporations
03 = missionaries or religious representatives
04 = fugitives, criminals, terrorists
05 = students, educators, cultural exchange personnel
06 = crashes, wrecks, accidents

(36)   Challenges and/or defeats in competition

01 = sports
02 = scientific endeavors, technological feats
03 = business sales
04 = trade fairs, exhibitions
05 = cultural and artistic achievements

(37)   Widespread public rejection of actual or proposed international commitment or those individuals widely associated with that commitment (or election of those opposed to it)

01 = defeat in national referendum, election, or other voting occasion
02 = results of poll or survey indicating widespread opposition or dissatisfaction
03 = campaigns, rallies, marches in opposition to external activity or commitment

(38)   Existence or potential emergence of conditions which reduce entity's standing vis-à-vis other nation or other international actors

01 = domestic economic conditions
02 = domestic political instability
03 = domestic social problems
04 = domestic health conditions

(39)   Constraints on political and legal well being

01 = abolish or impose limitations on political parties or opposition groups
02 = abolish or suspend constitution of laws; "emergency powers"
03 = alteration or abuse of judicial procedures
04 = restrict opportunities for individual political participation (e.g., voting, holding office, advocating political preferences)
05 = unlawful seizure of government, overthrow, dismissal, or elimination of "legal" officeholders
06 = unlawful arrest or incarceration or "disappearance"
07 = governmental corruption, scandal, acceptance of bribes

(40) Constraints on economic well being

01 = abuse of taxation power
02 = limitations on employment opportunities or promotion
03 = inadequate protection against life's accidents or "disrupting experiences" (e.g., governmental insurance for unemployment, disability, retirement)
04 = governmental economic mismanagement, bankruptcy, economic fraud, regulation of inflation, depression
05 = arrangements or mismanagement between governments causing economic hardships; balance of payments deficit; revaluation of currency

(41) Constraints on health care

01 = regulation affecting access to or quality of medical services
02 = adequacy of pollution control and protection of environment
03 = involvement in population problems, birth control, abortion, family planning

(42) Constraints on travel and mobility

01 = imposition of curfews
02 = restrictions on domestic travel
03 = adequacy of public transportation system
04 = complicate process for travel; refuse immigration of citizens who desire to leave country
05 = restrictions on temporary visits across borders

(43) Constraints on shelter and housing

01 = adequacy and availability of living units
02 = restrictions on ownership

(44) Constraints on religious beliefs and practices

01 = prohibitions on certain religions, religious movements and organizations
02 = restrictions on public expression of certain religious beliefs or practices

(45) Constraints on criminal activities and treatment of criminals

01 = adequacy of police protection
02 = treatment of prisoners and nature of punishment
03 = drug abuse and traffic in drugs and narcotics

(46) Constraints on minorities or subgroups; discrimination

01 = racial discrimination
02 = ethnic or nationality discrimination
03 = sex-based discrimination

(47) Damage to victims of war

01 = civil war
02 = border war
03 = isolated terrorist attacks
04 = sieges, embargoes, blockades
05 = world wars

(48) Engaging in criminal acts

01 = crimes by legal corporations
02 = crimes by "organized crime syndicates"
03 = crimes by political parties and politically motivated groups
04 = acts of violence against humans by other than corporations, syndicates, or political parties

05 = destruction or theft of property by other than corporations, syndicates, or political parties

06 = monetary or financial crimes by other than corporations, syndicates, or political parties

(49) Nongovernmental discrimination against minority or subgroup

01 = racial discrimination against minority or subgroup
02 = ethnic or nationality discrimination
03 = sex-based discrimination

(50) Private withholding or withdrawal of service and/or assistance

01 = failure to provide financial grants, loans, gifts, etc.
02 = strikes, work slowdowns, massive absenteeism
03 = boycotts, blacklists, etc.

(51) Existence of hunger, malnutrition, famine

01 = attributable primarily to crop failure
02 = attributable primarily to drought
03 = attributable primarily to chronic imbalance between population and agricultural production
04 = attributable primarily to inequality in distribution of food stuffs

(52) Existence of poverty; inadequate resources to provide the necessities of life–food, shelter, clothing

01 = urban slums; squalor
02 = society-wide poverty associated with nation's low level of economic development

(53) Existence of disease; epidemics

01 = malaria
02 = typhoid
03 = smallpox
04 = tuberculosis
05 = viral influenza
06 = cholera

(54) Natural disasters

01 = hurricane, tornado, cyclone, typhoon
02 = flood
03 = earthquake
04 = fire
05 = drought
06 = insect and crop, feed and animal diseases
07 = volcanoes
08 = radioactive fallout

(55) Censorship or discrediting of foreign information (information may be either about foreign events or about domestic events reported by foreigners)

01 = foreign journalists censored
02 = prohibit internal distribution of information from foreign sources
03 = restriction on citizens from disseminating their work abroad
04 = regulate domestic media
05 = deny truth of knowledge from foreign sources
06 = restrict foreigners from speaking in country

(56)   Restrictions on personal interaction with foreign persons or groups

      01 = cultural exchanges
      02 = travel restrictions
      03 = participation in international nongovernmental conferences
      04 = refuse collaboration on joint knowledge explorations
      05 = restrict or expel foreign missionaries, educators, technicians

(57)   Regulation on exchange of knowledge products with foreigners (physical products pertaining to knowledge including art work, inventions, or any physical commodity other than a news medium such as newspaper or magazine)

      01 = technical assistance
      02 = sell or purchase restrictions on knowledge products
      03 = reject international conventions on copyrights and exchange of materials
      04 = seize or prohibit foreign books, other materials
      05 = black market activity in knowledge products

(58)   Constraints on citizen advocacy of foreign ideas

      01 = denouncement, arrest, trial and/or imprisonment for expressions of foreign ideas against the state; actions which government regards as "heresy"

(59)   Constraints on or failure to support educational and research activities

      01 = agricultural programs
      02 = art programs
      03 = medical programs
      04 = science and technology
      05 = finance and economics
      06 = trades and commerce
      07 = law

(60)   Private acts of physical abuse or violence against foreign ideas, those expressing them, or those using foreign knowledge products or associated with foreigners—or sharing domestic knowledge with foreigners

      01 = destruction of books and libraries, communication facilities maintained by or contributed to country by foreigners
      02 = mob or group action against fellow citizens associated with foreign ideas or transmitting ideas to foreigners
      03 = private violent action against individuals for knowledge dissemination with foreigners

(61)   Private nonviolent acts against foreign ideas or their advocates or transmission of domestic knowledge to foreigners

      01 = nongovernment discrimination against those citizens identified with foreign ideas or transmitting ideas to foreigners
      02 = economic boycotts, blacklists against foreign knowledge products, facilities or their users; or against those transmitting knowledge to foreigners
      03 = demonstrations, strikes, protests against foreign knowledge products, facilities, or their users or against those transmitting knowledge to foreigners
      04 = deny or revoke membership or affiliation in some organization

(62)   Private statements of repudiation of foreign ideas or their advocates

      01 = private denouncements of foreign ideas, knowledge products, etc.
      02 = private reprimand to fellow citizens for their association with foreign ideas or transmitting knowledge to foreigners

(63) Private groups or individuals refuse to share their knowledge, expertise with others

01 = protest against policies of government and/or people
02 = experts avoid country for better economic incentives elsewhere

(64) State of cumulated knowledge

01 = knowledge capability lost from disaster, war, purge, etc.
02 = knowledge capability not yet developed

(65) Economic capability (unable to bear the cost of support knowledge facilities or products)

01 = basic education
02 = advanced or technical training
03 = research
04 = cultural enrichment

(66) Religious or ideological prohibitions (cultural, ethical, or ideological norms make ideas or products reprehensible or unbelievable)

01 = religious constraints
02 = political ideological constraints
03 = cultural experience constraints

APPENDIX 4.3

Indicators of Problem Area Salience, and Dispersion for CREON Nations During Decade 1959-1968

CREON Nation	Number of Problem Areas Salient for Nation[a]	Four Most Salient Problem Areas[b]	Number of Problem Areas Which Nation Dominates[c]	Problem Areas Dominated[d]	Proportion of Total Problem Areas Which Nation Addresses (Dispersion)[e]
Belgium	7	Regulations and Protective Actions (16%) Trade Agreements (9%) Fiscal Monetary Arrangements (7%) Advance Proposals (14%)	3	Regulations and Protective Actions (10%) Economic Assistance (4%) Transportation Distribution (4%)	.90
Canada	7	War (6%) Trade Agreements (8%) Advance Proposals (8%) Need Diplomatic Communication (7%)	2	Economic Assistance (4%) Nongovernmental Opposition to Policies (9%)	.90
Chile	9	Trade Agreements (9%) Economic Assistance (8%) Repudiate/Reject Policy (8%) Advance Proposals (9%)	2	Health Care (6%) Natural Disasters (13%)	.80
China (PRC)	8	War (20%) Verbal Threats (9%) End Agreements (11%) Repudiate/Reject Policy (11%)	6	Domestic Use of Military (6%) War (12%) Verbal Threats (8%) Commodity Transactions (10%) End Agreements (9%) Economic Well-Being (13%)	.75
Costa Rica	6	Verbal Threats (8%) Fiscal/Monetary Arrangements (6%) Economic Assistance (10%) Need for Diplomatic Communication (8%)	1	Natural Disasters (11%)	.85
Cuba	7	Foreign Isolated Military Incidents (9%) Verbal Threats (9%) Regulations and Protective Actions (8%) End Agreements (16%)	4	Foreign Isolated Military Incidents (9%) Agriculture (12%) End Agreements (9%) State of Knowledge (10%)	.85
Czechoslovakia	6	Arms Control (7%) Repudiate/Reject Policy (12%) Trade Agreements (9%) Need Diplomatic Communication (8%)	0		.80
East Germany	5	Verbal Threats (6%) Trade Agreements (10%) Repudiate/Reject Policy (23%) Need Diplomatic Communication (10%)	1	Embarrassing Incidents (13%)	.70
Egypt	5	War (8%) Verbal Threats (7%) Repudiate/Reject Policy (13%) Need Diplomatic Communication (8%)	2	Domestic Violence (7%) Industry (5%)	.88
France	6	Trade Agreements (7%) Regulations and Protective Actions (10%) Advance Proposals (11%) Need Diplomatic Communication (10%)	18	Nonwar Use of Military Force (7%) Arms Control (5%) Trade Agreements (10%) Fiscal/Monetary Arrangements (9%) Financial Conditions (10%) Regulations and Protective Actions (13%) Economic Assistance (6%) General Domestic Economic Conditions (6%)	1.00

APPENDIX 4.3 (Continued)

CREON Nation	Number of Problem Areas Salient for Nation[a]	Four Most Salient Problem Areas[b]	Number of Problem Areas Which Nation Dominates[c]	Problem Areas Dominated[d]	Proportion of Total Problem Areas Which Nation Addresses (Dispersion)[e]
France				Industry (7%) Transportation and Distribution (4%) Acknowledge Error (10%) Advance Proposals (10%) Need Diplomatic Communication (9%) Poverty (17%) Restriction on Personal Interactions (14%) Constraints on Education and Research Activities (7%) State of Knowledge (10%) Inability to Support Knowledge Facilities (14%)	
Ghana	5	Economic Assistance (6%) Repudiate/Reject Policy (14%) Advance Proposals (10%) Discrimination (11%)	3	Domestic Use of Military Force (6%) Constraints on Political/Legal Well-Being (5%) Discrimination (13%)	.85
Guinea	6	War (7%) Repudiate/Reject Policy (15%) Advance Proposals (7%) Discrimination (10%)	2	Discrimination (9%) Inability to Support Knowledge Facilities (6%)	.80
Iceland	9	Arms Control (6%) Economic Assistance (12%) Advance Proposals (9%) Need Diplomatic Communication (10%)	0		.75
India	5	War (9%) Conflict Negotiation/ Settlement (11%) Force Maintenance (6%) Need Diplomatic Communication (8%)	10	Conflict Negotiation/ Settlement (14%) Force Maintenance (21%) Domestic Violence (7%) General Domestic Economic Conditions (6%) Natural Resources Problems (11%) Agriculture (8%) Industry (5%) Constraints on Political/Legal Well-Being (5%) Hunger (9%) State of Knowledge (10%)	.95
Israel	7	Foreign Isolated Military Incidents (16%) Conflict Negotiation/ Settlement (11%) Verbal Threats (6%) Repudiate/Reject Policy (8%)	3	Conflict Negotiation/ Settlement (11%) Agriculture (8%) Victims of War (11%)	.92
Italy	8	Arms Control (6%) Regulations and Protective Actions (14%) Advance Proposals (11%) Trade Agreements (9%)	2	Trade Agreements (6%) Constraints on Education and Research Activities (5%)	.92
Ivory Coast	7	Trade Agreements (6%) Economic Assistance (10%) Repudiate/Reject Policy (13%) Discrimination (8%)	0		.70
Japan	8	Trade Agreements (9%) Regulations and Protective Actions (10%) Economic Assistance (8%) Repudiate/Reject Policy (10%)	2	Nongovernmental Opposition to Policies (8%) Victims of War (7%)	.88

APPENDIX 4.3 (Continued)

CREON Nation	Number of Problem Areas Salient for Nation[a]	Four Most Salient Problem Areas[b]	Number of Problem Areas Which Nation Dominates[c]	Problem Areas Dominated[d]	Proportion of Total Problem Areas Which Nation Addresses (Dispersion)[e]
Kenya	8	Fiscal/Monetary Arrangements (8%) Economic Assistance (8%) Repudiate/Reject Policy (9%) Constraints on Political/Legal Well-Being (8%) Discrimination (11%)	0		.70
Lebanon	6	Verbal Threats (6%) Economic Assistance (10%) Repudiate/Reject Policy (10%) Advance Proposals (10%)	0		.72
Mexico	7	Arms Control (8%) Trade Agreements (9%) Economic Assistance (10%) Need Diplomatic Communication (11%)	0		.78
New Zealand	9	War (6%) Regulations and Protective Actions (8%) Economic Assistance (7%) Advance Proposals (10%)	0		.72
Norway	8	Military Alliances (7%) Regulations and Protective Actions (9%) Economic Assistance (10%) Need Diplomatic Communication (9%)	0		.78
Philippines	6	War (8%) Verbal Threats (6%) Economic Assistance (9%) Repudiate/Reject Policy (8%)	1	Health Care (6%)	.88
Poland	9	Arms Control (9%) Verbal Threats (7%) Trade Agreements (12%) Need Diplomatic Communications (9%)	0		.75
Soviet Union	8	War (10%) Foreign Isolated Military Incidents (8%) Arms Control (10%) Repudiate/Reject Policy (14%)	18	Domestic Use of Military Force (9%) Nonwar Use of Military Force (12%) Foreign Isolated Military Incidents (20%) Conflict Negotiation/ Settlement (12%) Arms Control (15%) Force Maintenance (15%) Verbal Threats (10%) Commodity Transactions (14%) Natural Resources Problems (7%) Acknowledge Error (10%) End Agreements (11%) Repudiate/Reject Policy (11%) Need Diplomatic Communication (7%) Constraints on Political/Legal Well Being (6%) Victims of War (6%) Restrictions on Personal Interactions (12%) Constraints on Education and Research Activities (7%) State of Knowledge (12%)	.92

APPENDIX 4.3 (Continued)

CREON Nation	Number of Problem Areas Salient for Nation[a]	Four Most Salient Problem Areas[b]	Number of Problem Areas Which Nation Dominates[c]	Problem Areas Dominated[d]	Proportion of Total Problem Areas Which Nation Addresses (Dispersion)[e]
Spain	7	Nonwar Use of Military Force (7%) Economic Assistance (10%) Repudiate/Reject Policy (10%) Advance Proposals (12%)	0		.82
Switzerland	5	Trade Agreements (15%) Fiscal/Monetary Arrangements (24%) Regulations and Protective Actions (19%) Advance Proposals (11%)	0		.32
Thailand	6	Verbal Threats (5%) Economic Assistance (11%) Repudiate/Reject Policy (8%) Need Diplomatic Communication (12%)	0		.72
Tunisia	6	War (7%) Repudiate/Reject Policy (16%) Need Diplomatic Communication (7%) Discrimination (8%)	2	Transportation and Distribution (4%) Discrimination (9%)	.90
Turkey	6	Military Alliances (9%) Economic Assistance (6%) Repudiate/Reject Policy (9%) Need Diplomatic Communication (9%)	5	Military Alliances (10%) Transportation and Distribution (4%) Hunger (9%) Natural Disasters (19%) Restrictions on Personal Interactions (12%)	.90
Uganda	6	Fiscal/Monetary Arrangements (7%) Economic Assistance (10%) Repudiate/Reject Policy (15%) Discrimination (10%)	0		.70
United States	7	Nonwar Use of Military Force (7%) War (12%) Arms Control (7%) Repudiate/Reject Policy (8%)	32	See note f	1.00
Uruguay	7	Trade Agreements (87%) Regulations and Protective Actions (8%) Economic Assistance (10%) Repudiate/Reject Policy (11%)	0		.78
Venezuela	8	Foreign Isolated Military Incidents (5%) Trade Agreements (9%) Economic Assistance (8%) Repudiate/Reject Policy (8%)	0		.88
West Germany	8	Military Alliances (6%) Trade Agreements (9%) Regulations and Protective Actions (10%) Repudiate/Reject Policy (11%)	12	Military Alliances (14%) Force Maintenance (15%) Trade Agreements (9%) Fiscal/Monetary Arrangements (9%) Financial Conditions (12%) Regulations and Protective Actions (12%) General Domestic Economic Conditions (5%) Industry (5%) Repudiate/Reject	.88

APPENDIX 4.3 (Continued)

CREON Nation	Number of Problem Areas Salient for Nation[a]	Four Most Salient Problem Areas[b]	Number of Problem Areas Which Nation Dominates[c]	Problem Areas Dominated[d]	Proportion of Total Problem Areas Which Nation Addresses (Dispersion)[e]
West Germany				Policy (6%) Nongovernmental Opposition to Policies (9%) Constraints on Economic Well-Being (11%) Poverty (13%)	
Yugoslavia	8	Trade Agreements (6%) Economic Assistance (6%) End Agreements (7%) Repudiate/Reject Policy (12%) Need Diplomatic Communication (18%)	0		.85
Zambia	10	Economic Assistance (5%) Repudiate/Reject Policy (9%) Advance Proposals (8%) Constraints on Political/Legal Well-Being (13%)	1	Transportation and Distribution (6%)	.60

[a] A salient problem area is one which involves more than 5% of a nation's events across the decade 1959—1968.

[b] The percentage of events in a problem area is listed in parentheses after the problem area. The problem areas are listed in the order they appear in Appendix 4.1. Where more than four problem areas are indicated, there were ties among several for salience.

[c] Figures here represent the number of problem areas in which a nation has among the highest three percentages of events concerned with that issue across all 38 nations. The percentages used in determining these figures were calculated by dividing the number of events in a problem area for a nation by the total number of events in that problem area across all the CREON countries.

[d] The percentage listed here following the problem area indicates the proportion of the total number of events in the problem area across all 38 nations that involved the dominant nation. The problem areas are listed in the order they appear in Appendix 4.1.

[e] The figures in this column represent what proportion of the 40 problem areas with 25 or more events in the CREON data set a nation was concerned with during the decade 1959—1968.

[f] The following are the eight problem areas in which the United States was not dominant during the decade: Domestic Use of Military Force, Conflict Negotiation/Settlement, Trade Agreements, Regulations and Protective Actions, Discrimination, Victims of War, Natural Disasters, and Constraints on Education and Research Activities. The United States accounted for 25% or more of the events in the following problem areas: Nonwar Use of Military Force, War, Military Alliances, Domestic Violence, Nongovernmental Opposition to Policies, Embarrassing Incidents, Hunger, and Poverty.

NOTES

1. One of the editors of this volume (Callahan) believes that we have misinterpreted the authors cited in this paragraph as illustrative of the procedural orientation to issue areas. He suggests that Huntington, Lowi, and Zimmerman have actually used substantive features to classify policies and then related these features in a causal way with the procedures associated with each category. We would admit there is some ambiguity on this point—particularly in Zimmerman—but we believe that our editor has mistaken the authors' substantive examples of each procedural category for the categories themselves. Certainly we believe the authors' purpose in each case was to create what we have here called a "procedural issue area classification." For example, in the opening paragraph of his research note, after posing several questions about the process by which foreign policy is made, Zimmerman (1973: 1204) observes: "This note attempts to further our efforts to answer these questions by suggesting a general paradigm for the study of the foreign policy process." The reader, as always, is left to make a final judgment.

2. Rosenau (1967a) made another attempt to construct a typology of issue areas and hoped it would become the framework for a series of essays that would distinguish foreign from domestic issue areas. In the introduction to the resulting collection he edited, Rosenau (1967b: 7) acknowledges: "this volume reflects failure of the issue area concept to spark imaginations or organize thoughts to a significant degree." Whether his evaluation is too harsh is something readers of that volume must decide for themselves. Several more limited attempts have enjoyed some success in distinguishing foreign policy issue areas in general from various domestic issue areas using roll call votes in the U.S. Congress (Cimbala, 1969; Clausen, 1973).

3. Wittkopf and Ferris (1974: 11) report in their pilot application of the Rosenau issue area scheme that "in practice we frequently found it difficult to place each discrete code into one and only one issue area."

4. In retrospect, the decision to reorganize the Lasswell value categories may have been somewhat hasty, particularly our combination of several of the values so that they cannot easily be separated. For an attempt to use the original eight values in comparative foreign policy analysis, see Callahan (1977).

5. It should be emphasized that we can never know with any degree of confidence what characterization of a problem actually was held by policymakers and motivated their behaviors. Our intention is to infer the characterization of the problem as it is publicly reported.

6. We want to thank Petra Donofrio, Beverly Gatliff, and Gerald Hutchins for their aid in coding the CREON events using the substantive problem area classification.

7. We gratefully acknowledge the assistance of Larry Fuell in performing the preliminary analysis described in the following paragraphs and in working with us generally on the substantive problem area classification.

5

MAURICE A. EAST
MARGARET G. HERMANN

Scope of Action

Targets in Foreign Policy Behavior

In this chapter we are going to focus on one aspect of foreign policy behavior that is often neglected. Who is the target or recipient of the activity? Specifically we are interested in the scope of a government's actions or the distribution of an acting nation's foreign policy behavior across various recipients or categories of recipients in the international arena.

Scope of action is a useful concept for answering several types of questions about a government's foreign policy activity. Thus, we can learn through scope of action where a government's foreign policy activity is concentrated. Is such activity evenly distributed across possible recipients in the international system, or is it centered on one or two other actors or types of actors? Are different types of recipients of varying importance to different types of actors? What proportion of its activity is a government willing to devote to a given target?

We are interested in developing in this chapter a measure that assesses where governments are directing their foreign policy actions. It seems reasonable to assume that the foreign policy behavior of states is not random but that governments deliberately direct their foreign policy actions toward specific targets. In trying to cope with the foreign (and, at times, domestic) policy problems facing them, policymakers act to influence *certain* other governments. In fact, problems are often identified by specific regions of the world (for example, the Middle East conflict). The relevance of targets is evidenced in the way many foreign offices are organized—by nations or geographical regions. The more important targets often have desks or foreign service officers devoted to monitoring and dealing with their behavior.

AUTHORS' NOTE: Appreciation is due Barbara Winters and William Dixon for their help with this chapter—Barbara in the early stages of the consideration of scope of action and Bill with the data analysis presented in the chapter.

Although the study of targeting in foreign policy behavior has generally been neglected, several studies have recognized that states behave differently toward different targets. Rummel (1967) was one of the first international relations scholars to demonstrate the importance of analyzing a government's international behavior, not just in aggregate, but in relation to the particular target of the behavior. Rummel was not, however, interested in exploring who the target was or how and why nations select some entities in the international system to the neglect of others. More recently, studies by Harf (1974), C. Hermann and Salmore (1971), Rosenau and Hoggard (1974), and Wittkopf (1972) have examined targets as a means of explaining aspects of foreign policy. In this research targets or aspects of the target were used as independent variables rather than as aspects of the action itself which is our concern in this chapter.

Two studies are of more direct relevance to the examination of targeting as a part of foreign policy behavior. Kegley (1974) examined the raw number of targets addressed in the WEIS (World Event Interaction Survey) data, concluding that targeting is highly selective. Winters (1975) looked at the status and regional distributions of foreign policy recipients on a systemic level and noted that high-status states and nations in the American-Western European region were the most popular targets of behavior.

Why is it important in studying foreign policy behavior to look at targets or a government's scope of action? Our response to this question builds on social interaction and social exchange theory in sociology. As Blau (1968: 452) notes about the basic assumptions of social exchange theory:

> The basic assumptions of the theory of social exchange are that men enter into new social associations because they expect doing so to be rewarding and that they continue relations with old associates and expand their interaction with them because they actually find doing so to be rewarding.

In a similar manner, we assume that states interact with other entities because there is some expectation of benefits or rewards. Such benefits can range from simple economic gain to increased power, strategic or tactical advantage, greater prestige, or the attainment of specific foreign policy objectives. The expected rewards may also be conceived of in terms of "negative rewards"—that is, the reduction of threat. Thus, the selection of targets can be tied to the widely accepted model of foreign policy behavior in which a nation-state's actions are assumed to emanate from a set of specific foreign policy goals and objectives. Targets are chosen because it is assumed that interactions with these targets will be rewarding in terms of facilitating the achievement of the actor state's foreign policy goals or objectives.

By examining a government's scope of action, we also learn which other governments or international actors are the targets of influence. What other actors is a government trying to influence in the international system? In some sense, we begin to build a sociometric map for the acting government of the international actors on which it is trying to have an impact. We map the foci of attention of each acting government, noting how dispersed or concentrated they are and, if attention is focused, what types of international actors are the center of attention. Some governments may be pleased to build relationships with a few other governments— or perhaps only act in international organizations, while for other governments the world is for the taking—all other governments are targets for relationships. In effect, by ascertaining scope of action we can begin to determine the leadership patterns among nations. We can assess nations' spheres of influence.

Theoretically, all other nations and international organizations can form the targets of a government's activity. Geographic location, available resources, and traditions, however, can impose limits on who among the potential targets will become actual targets. By classifying targets and examining an acting government's scope of action across the various types of targets, we can begin developing a rationale for why nations choose certain targets over others. Then an interesting question arises: Under what conditions will a change in targets or a nation's scope of action occur? When do governments break out of more traditional acting patterns to include others? With some mapping of government's targets we can perceive where changes are happening, and by typing targets we can gain an initial clue about what may have led to the change.

In the rest of this chapter we will develop the conceptualization of scope of action and a way of operationalizing this concept. We will then examine scope of action using the CREON events data set to illustrate how targets can be studied as an aspect of foreign policy behavior.

CONCEPTUALIZATION

Scope of action, as we define it here, refers to the distribution of a government's foreign policy activity across potential targets or recipients in the international arena. We will be interested in two aspects of scope of action: the selection ratio and the concentration ratio. The selection ratio indicates the extent of a government's scope of action. Of all possible targets or recipients, what number does a particular government choose to include in its foreign policy activity? In other words, how focused or dispersed is a government's foreign policy behavior among recipients in the international system? Are there certain fairly predictable targets that the government addresses repeatedly, or does the government interact with most other potential recipients (governments and international organizations) in the world?

The concentration ratio, on the other hand, focuses on what percentage of a government's foreign policy activity is directed toward a particular recipient. The concentration ratio suggests the relative importance attributed to a specific recipient. Whereas with the selection ratio we are interested in dispersion of actual targets across possible targets, with the concentration ratio we are interested in dispersion of events across targets.

In addition to examining the selection ratio and concentration ratio for individual targets or recipients, we can classify targets and examine the dispersion of foreign policy activity toward these classes or types of targets. Thus, we might divide recipients according to geographical region of the world and examine the selection and concentration ratios for a particular government toward each region of the world. In this way we can begin to assess governments' spheres of activity and influence.

In any discussion of recipients, particularly in relation to the selection ratio, it is important to take into account potential as well as actual targets. We can say very little about dispersion unless we know the population within which the dispersion can occur. This may seem an obvious point, but it is interesting how often researchers have overlooked this need. By examining who it is that a government does *not* choose to address and contrasting such information with data on the international actors whom the government does address, we can get a more accurate picture of that government's biases in attention—of its field of attention.

OPERATIONALIZATION

In operationalizing the selection ratio measure of scope of action, we need to determine the number of potential targets toward which a government could address its foreign policy activity, as well as the number of targets it actually does address. The selection ratio becomes the proportion of the possible targets that are, indeed, addressed by a government. In ascertaining what are potential recipients for the denominator of the selection ratio, it is important to count international organizations in addition to nations, since international organizations have been shown to be an important forum for foreign policy activity, particularly for smaller states (see East, 1973; C. Hermann et al., 1973).

A question arises at this point. Does one count as an actual target any recipient of one event, or should there be some evidence of continued activity—say, at least, 10 to 15 events? The issue here is whether some sustained interaction is necessary for a government to be considered as "selecting" that recipient or focusing attention on the recipient. In reporting on the selection ratio, a researcher might profitably record several selection ratios based on different cutoff points. In other words, one selection ratio might reflect all the actual targets no matter how many events were addressed to each recipient. Another selection ratio might include as actual targets only those recipients that were the objects of 10 to 15 foreign policy behaviors on the part of the acting government. It would seem less likely that the recipient is a fluke or random occurrence if the interaction occurs more than once during a specific period of time.

There are several ways of operationalizing the concentration ratio. The first measure is, in effect, a measure of salience. What percentage of a government's foreign policy events is directed toward each of its targets? The higher the percentage of a government's events that are directed toward a particular external entity, the more concentrated is the acting government's foreign policy behavior on that entity and the more salient the particular target is to the acting government.

A second approach to concentration focuses on the total distribution of events among targets for a specific acting government. After determining what proportion of the acting government's foreign policy behavior is directed toward each target, the proportions are squared and summed to indicate the degree to which the acting government's activity is focused or dispersed across targets. This concentration index can vary from 1.0 (activity directed toward only one target) to 0 (activity equally distributed across targets.[1] Here we are assessing degree of concentration across all targets that were addressed, whereas in the first concentration ratio we were trying to ascertain which specific nations or international organizations were favored targets. To distinguish these two indices, let us call the focus on the whole distribution the "concentration index" and the focus on specific targets the "index of salience."

OPERATIONALIZING SCOPE OF ACTION
WITH THE CREON DATA

Selection Ratio

The selection ratio is the number of actual targets toward which foreign policy activity is addressed divided by the total number of possible targets. In the CREON event data set an event includes an actor, action, and one or more recipients. Because many of the events had multiple targets, we transformed the basic CREON data set into a dyadic data set in which each event has only one actor and one target. In effect, what we did was to split events with multiple targets into one event per target. Using the dyadic deck, we counted the number of different targets toward which each of the 38 nations in the CREON sample directed their foreign policy behavior.[2]

To ascertain the number of potential targets available to the CREON nations during the 1959-1968 decade, the following rule was used: To be considered a potential target, a nation or international organization had to receive one foreign policy action from at least one of the CREON nations during the ten-year period. Using this criterion, we identified 228 possible or potential targets. Table 5.1 presents the selection ratios for the 38 CREON countries across the decade, and it includes both the number of different targets actually addressed and the selection ratios. We have used several different cutoffs in determining the selection ratios. Three different selection ratios are presented: one event addressed to a target, five or more events, and ten or more events. Of interest is the change in the selection ratio as the requirement for amount of sustained activity increases.

An examination of the selection ratios shows that only four of the CREON countries (Canada, France, the Soviet Union, and the United States) address one action or more to half of the possible targets. The majority of the nations in Table 5.1 address their foreign policy activity toward one-quarter to one-third of the potential targets. Increasing the amount of activity that must be targeted to a recipient before it is counted in the selection ratio dramatically *decreases* the number of different targets addressed. Whereas the mean selection ratio is .31 for one or more events, it is .08 for five or more events and .04 for ten or more events. Sustained interaction is focused on only a few targets.

What can we learn about the recipients selected by the CREON countries? By grouping the recipients by geographical region, we can learn whether there is any regional bias in where the CREON nations addressed their foreign policy actions during the 1960s. Table 5.2 displays the selection ratios toward recipients in six geographical regions: the Atlantic Community, Latin America, Eastern Europe, Africa, the Middle East, and Asia.[3] The six regions follow standard geographical lines, with the possible exception of the combination of North American and Western European countries into one category called Atlantic Community recipients and the separation of the Eastern European countries. These decisions were made because these groups of countries participate in several common regional organizations that differ from one another in political orientation. The selection ratios in Table 5.2 are based on one or more events being directed toward a recipient.

TABLE 5.1
Selection Ratios for 38 CREON Countries

CREON Nation	Based on 1 or More Events	Based on 5 or More Events	Based on 10 or More Events
Belgium	.37 (84)	.10 (22)	.03 (7)
Canada	.46 (104)	.11 (24)	.06 (14)
Chile	.31 (70)	.05 (12)	.03 (6)
China (PRC)	.31 (70)	.11 (25)	.06 (14)
Costa Rica	.26 (59)	.04 (8)	.01 (3)
Cuba	.30 (69)	.06 (13)	.03 (6)
Czechoslovakia	.28 (64)	.06 (13)	.01 (3)
East Germany	.14 (32)	.05 (12)	.02 (5)
Egypt	.32 (72)	.10 (22)	.07 (15)
France	.60 (137)	.24 (55)	.13 (30)
Ghana	.36 (81)	.09 (21)	.04 (9)
Guinea	.29 (67)	.05 (11)	.00 (0)
Iceland	.28 (64)	.02 (5)	.01 (3)
India	.37 (85)	.12 (27)	.06 (14)
Israel	.28 (64)	.08 (18)	.04 (10)
Italy	.39 (88)	.10 (23)	.04 (10)
Ivory Coast	.25 (58)	.03 (7)	.01 (3)
Japan	.33 (75)	.08 (18)	.02 (4)
Kenya	.24 (54)	.03 (6)	.01 (3)
Lebanon	.21 (47)	.04 (9)	.01 (3)
Mexico	.30 (68)	.04 (9)	.02 (5)
New Zealand	.29 (65)	.06 (13)	.01 (2)
Norway	.32 (73)	.05 (12)	.02 (4)
Philippines	.29 (65)	.06 (14)	.03 (6)
Poland	.26 (60)	.08 (18)	.00 (0)
Soviet Union	.46 (106)	.22 (50)	.16 (36)
Spain	.24 (54)	.04 (8)	.01 (3)
Switzerland	.09 (21)	.02 (4)	.00 (0)
Thailand	.25 (58)	.04 (10)	.02 (5)
Tunisia	.30 (68)	.08 (18)	.04 (10)
Turkey	.31 (71)	.09 (21)	.03 (6)
Uganada	.24 (54)	.03 (7)	.01 (3)
United States	.65 (149)	.32 (72)	.20 (45)
Uruguay	.29 (65)	.04 (9)	.01 (2)
Venezuela	.33 (76)	.06 (14)	.02 (4)
West Germany	.36 (82)	.14 (32)	.05 (12)
Yugoslavia	.27 (61)	.07 (15)	.02 (4)
Zambia	.14 (33)	.02 (4)	.01 (3)

NOTE: The selection ratios are based on the proportion of possible recipients a nation addresses. Each column defines the number of events a nation must address to a recipient before that recipient is considered an "actual" recipient in determining the selection ratio. The numbers in parentheses after the selection ratios are the actual number of recipients addressed with that number of events.

Table 5.2 indicates that the CREON countries interacted with more recipients in their own region than in other regions. For 31 of the countries (82 percent), the largest selection ratios occur for the regions in which that country is located. The seven deviant nations are China (PRC), Guinea, Ivory Coast, Japan, Spain, the United States, and Zambia. These seven countries show more highly dispersed activity in at least one region other than their own. For China (PRC) this region is

TABLE 5.2
Selection Ratios by Region for the 38 CREON Nations

CREON Nation	Atlantic Community Recipients (N = 33)	Latin American Recipients (N = 35)	Eastern European Recipients (N = 16)	African Recipients (N = 48)	Middle Eastern Recipients (N = 14)	Asian Recipients (N = 32)
Belgium	.78 (25)	.09 (3)	.44 (7)	.31 (15)	.37 (7)	.22 (7)
Canada	.59 (19)	.37 (13)	.56 (9)	.40 (19)	.37 (7)	.44 (14)
Chile	.33 (11)	.59 (20)	.19 (3)	.17 (8)	.32 (6)	.19 (6)
China (PRC)	.27 (9)	.03 (1)	.69 (11)	.17 (8)	.32 (6)	.68 (21)
Costa Rica	.27 (9)	.50 (17)	.19 (3)	.12 (6)	.32 (6)	.12 (4)
Cuba	.33 (11)	.59 (20)	.50 (8)	.12 (6)	.32 (6)	.16 (5)
Czechoslovakia	.42 (14)	.11 (4)	.60 (9)	.12 (6)	.42 (8)	.28 (9)
East Germany	.21 (7)	.03 (1)	.60 (9)	.02 (1)	.21 (4)	.16 (5)
Egypt	.39 (13)	.00 (0)	.38 (6)	.35 (17)	.83 (15)	.12 (4)
France	.84 (27)	.60 (21)	.56 (9)	.52 (25)	.63 (12)	.41 (13)
Ghana	.45 (13)	.11 (4)	.19 (3)	.53 (25)	.47 (9)	.22 (7)
Guinea	.33 (11)	.03 (1)	.31 (5)	.49 (23)	.53 (10)	.12 (4)
Iceland	.62 (20)	.06 (2)	.31 (5)	.19 (9)	.37 (7)	.12 (4)
India	.48 (16)	.09 (3)	.50 (8)	.27 (13)	.37 (7)	.58 (18)
Israel	.39 (13)	.11 (4)	.25 (4)	.17 (8)	.61 (11)	.19 (6)
Italy	.72 (23)	.09 (3)	.38 (6)	.35 (17)	.42 (8)	.34 (11)
Ivory Coast	.27 (9)	.03 (1)	.19 (3)	.38 (18)	.42 (8)	.25 (8)
Japan	.48 (16)	.11 (4)	.25 (4)	.25 (12)	.53 (10)	.35 (11)
Kenya	.33 (11)	.03 (1)	.25 (4)	.40 (19)	.26 (5)	.16 (5)
Lebanon	.30 (10)	.03 (1)	.19 (3)	.19 (9)	.56 (10)	.09 (3)
Mexico	.30 (10)	.53 (18)	.19 (3)	.21 (10)	.32 (6)	.16 (5)
New Zealand	.39 (13)	.06 (2)	.19 (3)	.23 (11)	.32 (6)	.45 (14)
Norway	.62 (20)	.11 (4)	.44 (7)	.19 (9)	.42 (8)	.19 (6)
Philippines	.27 (9)	.11 (4)	.19 (3)	.19 (9)	.37 (7)	.45 (14)
Poland	.42 (14)	.03 (1)	.60 (9).	.17 (8)	.32 (6)	.25 (8)
Soviet Union	.58 (19)	.29 (10)	.87 (13)	.27 (13)	.53 (10)	.47 (15)
Spain	.31 (10)	.09 (3)	.19 (3)	.19 (9)	.37 (7)	.12 (4)
Switzerland	.34 (11)	.03 (1)	.19 (3)	.00 (0)	.00 (0)	.03 (1)
Thailand	.24 (8)	.03 (1)	.29 (3)	.17 (8)	.32 (6)	.45 (14)
Tunisia	.39 (13)	.03 (1)	.25 (4)	.36 (17)	.53 (10)	.19 (6)
Turkey	.61 (20)	.06 (2)	.38 (6)	.17 (8)	.44 (8)	.19 (6)
Uganda	.24 (8)	.03 (1)	.19 (3)	.38 (18)	.32 (6)	.19 (6)
United States	.62 (20)	.86 (30)	.62 (10)	.35 (17)	.79 (15)	.56 (18)
Uruguay	.33 (11)	.47 (16)	.19 (3)	.17 (8)	.37 (7)	.12 (4)
Venezuela	.30 (10)	.65 (22)	.19 (3)	.21 (10)	.42 (8)	.19 (6)
West Germany	.81 (26)	.14 (5)	.56 (9)	.23 (11)	.37 (7)	.22 (7)
Yugoslavia	.39 (13)	.06 (2)	.44 (7)	.17 (8)	.33 (6)	.25 (8)
Zambia	.24 (8)	.03 (1)	.12 (2)	.15 (7)	.21 (4)	.19 (6)

NOTE: The specific nations and organizations included in each of these clusters are listed in footnote 3. The numbers in parentheses are the actual number of recipients addressed in that cluster of nations. When one of the CREON countries was a part of the cluster, the N for that cluster was reduced by one in calculating the selection ratio.

Eastern Europe; for Guinea, the Ivory Coast, and Spain, it is the Middle East; for Japan, it is the Atlantic Community and the Middle East; for the United States, it is Latin America and the Middle East; and for Zambia, it is the Atlantic Community, the Middle East, and Asia.

France and the United States show the most consistent dispersion across the various geographical regions. Both countries address over 50 percent of the possible recipients in each area but one. Switzerland shows the least dispersion of activity outside its own region—for two of the regions it addressed none of the nations or international organizations.

We have focused on only one way of grouping the recipients here. Others include by available resources and by adversaries/friends. Table 5.2 suggests that by categorizing recipients, we can begin to refine the scope of action variables specifying in more detail where a government focuses its attention in the international system.

Concentration Ratios

We have proposed two concentration ratios which are designated the index of salience and the concentration index. The index of salience indicates what percentage of a government's events is directed toward a specific target. Table 5.3 lists the three most salient targets in the 1960s for each of the CREON countries. Moreover, the table indicates the three most salient targets in each of the geographical regions we considered earlier in discussing the selection ratio. In determining the index of salience for each regional cluster, only those events addressed to the recipients in that cluster were considered in determining the percentages. Where more than three nations are listed, a tie occurred between the third and fourth recipients in the percentage of events each received.

The United States, Great Britain, and the Soviet Union are among the most salient recipients over all the targets for the CREON countries. The United States is among the three most salient recipients for 23 of the countries (61 percent); Great Britain for 20 of the countries (53 percent); and the Soviet Union for 17 of the countries (45 percent). Certain countries seem particularly salient in specific regions. Thus, Cuba and Guyana stand out among the Latin American recipients. South Africa and the Congo Kinshasa stand out among African recipients; Israel and Egypt among the Middle Eastern recipients; and China, Taiwan, North Vietnam, and South Vietnam among Asian recipients. For the most part these are "hot spots" in the regions during the 1960s. Each at some point during the decade drew the attention of the world to itself, generally through a military (or threatened military) crisis.

For most of the CREON countries, one other nation in their geographic region is among the most salient across recipients. The recipients that are salient outside a CREON country's geographical area are usually of a similar ideological persuasion or are adversaries. Among the regional organizations that were most salient for the CREON countries during this decade, we note the OAS (Organization of American States) and the EEC (European Economic Community).

Table 5.4 augments the previous table by indicating the salience of all recipients in each region to the CREON countries during 1960s. Table 5.4 suggests how much activity a CREON government addressed toward targets in the various regions. We note that one-third of all the events were addressed to the Atlantic Community nations—the largest percentage for any of the geographical areas. Latin American and African nations received the smallest amount of attention from the CREON countries during this decade.

(text continued on page 129)

TABLE 5.3

Most Salient Targets for 38 CREON Countries During 1960s

CREON Nation	Over All Recipients	Atlantic Community Recipients	Latin American Recipients	Eastern European Recipients	African Recipients	Middle Eastern Recipients	Asian Recipients
Belgium	Great Britain (.14) United States (.09) Soviet Union (.05)	Great Britain (.24) United States (.15) France (.07)	Peru (.60) Cuba (.20) Guyana (.20)	Soviet Union (.63) Warsaw Pact (.15) Czechoslovakia (.07)	Congo Kinshasa (.35) South Africa (.15) Nigeria (.10)	Turkey (.32) Israel (.21) Egypt (.16)	China (PRC) (.27) Japan (.20) India (.13)
Canada	United States (.12) Great Britain (.07) Soviet Union (.07)	United States (.38) Great Britain (.23) NATO (.13)	Cuba (.29) Peru (.17) Central American Common Market (.08) IADB (.08)	Soviet Union (.73) East Germany (.07) Warsaw Pact (.07)	Rhodesia (.06) Uganda (.06) Ghana (.06)	Israel (.32) Egypt (.23) Jordan (.19)	South Vietnam (.28) North Vietnam (.20) China (PRC) (.14)
Chile	United States (.10) Great Britain (.08) Cuba (.06)	United States (.36) Great Britain (.29) Portugal (.14)	Cuba (.20) Alliance for Progress (.18) OAS (.17)	Soviet Union (.83) Hungary (.08) Albania (.08)	South Africa (.33) Congo Kinshasa (.28) Uganda (.11)	Algeria (.25) Israel (.25) Egypt (.12)	China (PRC) (.36) South Vietnam (.18) Taiwan (.18)
China (PRC)	United States (.23) Soviet Union (.13) South Vietnam (.09)	United States (.80) Great Britain (.10) France (.04)	Cuba (1.00)	Soviet Union (.75) Yugoslavia (.07) Albania (.05)	Congo Kinshasa (.35) Ghana (.17) French Guinea (.17)	Egypt (.40) Israel (.20) Jordan (.17)	South Vietnam (.20) India (.19) North Vietnam (.16)
Costa Rica	United States (.12) Cuba (.09) OAS (.07)	United States (.56) Great Britain (.20) Portugal (.08)	Cuba (.21) OAS (.18) Central American Common Market (.07) Alliance for Progress (.07)	Soviet Union (.80) Hungary (.10) Albania (.10)	South Africa (.50) Uganda (.10) Tanzania (.10)	Israel (.38) Egypt (.12) Jordan (.12)	China (PRC) (.43) Taiwan (.29) Indonesia (.14)
Cuba	United States (.38) Soviet Union (.11) OAS (.04)	United States (.84) Great Britain (.07) France (.02) Portugal (.02)	OAS (.21) Venezuela (.17) Chile (.06)	Soviet Union (.75) Poland (.05) Czechoslovakia (.05) Rumania (.05)	South Africa (.45) Tanzania (.18) Uganda (.09)	Israel (.26) Egypt (.22) Syria (.22)	China (PRC) (.53) North Vietnam (.24) Taiwan (.12)
Czechoslovakia	Soviet Unit (.13) China (PRC) (.10) West Germany (.07)	West Germany (.31) United States (.15) Great Britain (.13)	Cuba (.50) Guyana (.17) Argentina (.17) Brazil (.17)	Soviet Union (.55) East Germany (.11) Poland (.06)	South Africa (.55) Nigeria (.09) Uganda (.09)	Egypt (.21) Israel (.21) Turkey (.16)	China (PRC) (.45) Mongolia (.13) North Vietnam (.11)
East Germany	West Germany (.36) Soviet Union (.07) China (PRC) (.06)	West Germany (.70) United States (.11) NATO (.06)	Cuba (1.00)	Soviet Union (.27) Czechoslovakia (.16) World Party Congress (.16)	Tanzania (1.00)	Egypt (.47) Israel (.27) Syria (.13)	China (PRC) (.68) North Vietnam (.11) South Vietnam (.11)

(Continued)

TABLE 5.3 Continued

CREON Nation	Over All Recipients	Atlantic Community Recipients	Latin American Recipients	Eastern European Recipients	African Recipients	Middle Eastern Recipients	Asian Recipients
Egypt	Israel (.18) Great Britain (.11) United States (.09)	Great Britain (.34) United States (.26) France (.13)	(No Events)	Soviet Union (.54) East Germany (.31) Poland (.05) Czechoslovakia (.05)	Congo Kinshasa (.48) South Africa (.31) OAU (.06)	Israel (.47) Yemen (.12) Jordan (.10)	China (PRC) (.57) India (.30) Indonesia (.10)
France	United States (.12) Great Britain (.07) Soviet Union (.07)	United States (.28) Great Britain (.18) EEC (.10)	Cuba (.16) Peru (.14) OAS (.14)	Soviet Union (.75) East Germany (.14) Warsaw Pact (.03)	Congo Kinshasa (.16) South Africa (.13) Nigeria (.07)	Israel (.21) Jordan (.16) Egypt (.16)	South Vietnam (.24) Laos (.21) North Vietnam (.17)
Ghana	Congo Kinshasa (.11) South Africa (.09) Great Britain (.09)	Great Britain (.31) Portugal (.13) France (.12)	Cuba (.25) Haiti (.25) Dominican Republic (.25) Guyana (.25)	Soviet Union (.85) Hungary (.08) Albania (.08)	Congo Kinshasa (.31) South Africa (.25) Togo (.05)	Egypt (.26) Israel (.22) Tunisia (.09)	China (PRC) (.46) India (.23) Taiwan (.08)
Guinea	South Africa (.15) Congo Kinshasa (.07) Great Britain (.06)	Great Britain (.24) United States (.22) France (.22)	Guyana (1.00)	Soviet Union (.67) Yugoslavia (.08) East Germany (.08)*	South Africa (.27) Congo Kinshasa (.21) Ghana (.05)	Egypt (.29) Israel (.25) Algeria (.11)	China (PRC) (.44) Taiwan (.22) Indonesia (.22)
Iceland	Great Britain (.15) Soviet Union (.09) United States (.07)	Great Britain (.34) United States (.17) France (.08)	Cuba (.50) Guyana (.50)	Soviet Union (.74) Warsaw Pact (.11) Hungary (.05)*	South Africa (.43) Nigeria (.07) Uganda (.07)*	Israel (.23) Turkey (.15)* Egypt (.15)*	China (PRC) (.50) Taiwan (.25)* Indonesia (.12)*
India	China (PRC) (.18) United States (.12) Soviet Union (.07)	United States (.41) Great Britain (.23) Belgium (.09)	Cuba (.33) Guyana (.33) Brazil (.33)	Soviet Union (.83) East Germany (.07) Czechoslovakia (.02)*	Congo Kinshasa (.58) South Africa (.20)* Ghana (.02)*	Israel (.26) Egypt (.26) Jordan (.19) Syria (.19)	China (PRC) (.49) Pakistan (.15) South Vietnam (.10)
Israel	Syria (.18) Egypt (.18) Jordan (.12)	United States (.41) West Germany (.18) Great Britain (.16)	Argentina (.85) Guyana (.05) IADB (.05) Pan American Union (.05)	Soviet Union (.90) Hungary (.03) Albania (.03) Bulgaria (.03)	Congo Kinshasa (.31) South Africa (.31)* Cameroon (.06)*	Syria (.33) Egypt (.32) Jordan (.23)	China (PRC) (.45) Taiwan (.18)* Japan (.09)*
Italy	Great Britain (.13) United States (.09) Soviet Union (.07)	Great Britain (.24) United States (.17) EEC (.08)	Cuba (.43) Peru (.43) Guyana (.14)	Soviet Union (.80) East Germany (.03)* Hungary (.03)*	South Africa (.24) Nigeria (.15) EEC African States Assoc. (.12)	Turkey (.32) Israel (.20)* Egypt (.12)*	China (PRC) (.28) India (.10)* Laos (.10)*
Ivory Coast	Great Britain (.08) U.N. Security Council (.07) South Africa (.06)	Great Britain (.29) Portugal (.19) EEC (.12)	Guyana (1.00)	Soviet Union (.60) Hungary (.20) Albania (.20)	South Africa (.24) Congo Kinshasa (.19)* Ghana (.07)*	Turkey (.31) Egypt (.15) Syria (.15)	China (PRC) (.17) Cambodia (.17) Indonesia (.17) South Vietnam (.17)

TABLE 5.3 Continued

CREON Nation	Over All Recipients	Atlantic Community Recipients	Latin American Recipients	Eastern European Recipients	African Recipients	Middle Eastern Recipients	Asian Recipients
Japan	United States (.15) Soviet Union (.07) China (PRC) (.06)	United States (.43) Great Britain (.16) France (.09)	Peru (.50) Brazil (.17) Guyana (.17) IADB (.17)	Soviet Union (.88) East Germany (.04) Hungary (.04) Albania (.04)	South Africa (.35) Ghana (.10) Central Bank of West Africa (.10)	Israel (.20) Egypt (.14) Syria (.14)	China (PRC) (.34) South Vietnam (.15) India (.09)
Kenya	Great Britain (.13) South Africa (.09) Congo Kinshasa (.08)	Great Britain (.50) Belgium (.12) United States (.09)	Guyana (1.00)	Soviet Union (.40) East Germany (.20) Albania (.20) Bulgaria (.20)	South Africa (.19) Congo Kinshasa (.17) OAU (.16)	Egypt (.43) Tunisia (.14)* Syria (.14)*	China (PRC) (.60) Taiwan (.10)* Indonesia (.10)*
Lebanon	Israel (.12) United States (.11) Great Britain (.08)	United States (.36) Great Britain (.28) Portugal (.11)	Guyana (1.00)	Soviet Union (.80) Hungary (.10) Albania (.10)	South Africa (.38) French Guinea (.08)* Cameroon (.08)*	Israel (.35) Syria (.17) Egypt (.13)	China (PRC) (.57) Taiwan (.29) New Zealand (.14)
Mexico	United States (.09) Cuba (.09) OAS (.07)	United States (.39) Great Britain (.24) Portugal (.10)	Cuba (.27) OAS (.20) Venezuela (.08)	Soviet Union (.85) Hungary (.08) Albania (.08)	South Africa (.44) Liberia (.06)* Cameroon (.16)*	Israel (.29) Algeria (.14)* Egypt (.14)*	China (PRC) (.44) Taiwan (.22)* India (.11)*
New Zealand	Great Britain (.11) South Vietnam (.05) North Vietnam (.04) South Africa (.04) China (PRC) (.04)	Great Britain (.38) United States (.15) EEC (.15)	Cuba (.50) Guyana (.50)	Soviet Union (.75) Hungary (.12) Albania (.12)	South Africa (.33) Rhodesia (.26) Nigeria (.07) Uganda (.07)	Israel (.33) Syria (.22)* Algeria (.11)*	South Vietnam (.17) North Vietnam (.16) China (PRC) (.16)
Norway	Soviet Union (.12) Great Britain (.08) United States (.07)	Great Britain (.19) United States (.17) EEC (.11)	Cuba (.25) Haiti (.25) Dominican Republic (.25) Guyana (.25)	Soviet Union (.74) Finland (.09) Warsaw Pact (.06)	South Africa (.39) Congo Kinshasa (.17) Uganda (.11)	Egypt (.20) Israel (.20) Turkey (.20)	China (PRC) (.27) Indonesia (.27) Malaysia (.20)
Philippines	United States (.13) South Vietnam (.11) North Vietnam (.07)	United States (.53) Great Britain (.22) Portugal (.10)	Cuba (.25) Haiti (.25) Dominican Republic (.25) Guyana (.25)	Soviet Union (.85) Hungary (.08) Albania (.08)	South Africa (.44) Congo Kinshasa (.17)* Senegal (.06)*	Egypt (.20) Israel (.20) Kuwait (.20)	South Vietnam (.26) North Vietnam (.16) Laos (.10)

(Continued)

TABLE 5.3 Continued

CREON Nation	Over All Recipients			Atlantic Community Recipients			Latin American Recipients			Eastern European Recipients			African Recipients			Middle Eastern Recipients			Asian Recipients		
Poland	West Germany (.12)	Soviet Union (.09)	East Germany (.08)	West Germany (.35)	United States (.22)	Great Britain (.15)	Guyana (1.00)			Soviet Union (.31)	East Germany (.29)	Bulgaria (.10) / COMECON (.10)	South Africa (.53)	Liberia (.07)*	Cameroon (.07)*	Israel (.47)	Egypt (.18)	Syria (.12) / Jordan (.12)	China (PRC) (.31)	Mongolia (.19)	North Korea (.16) / North Vietnam (.16)
Soviet Union	United States (.19)	Cuba (.06)	China (PRC) (.05)	United States (.48)	Great Britain (.15)	West Germany (.11)	Cuba (.76)	OAS (.06)	Mexico (.05) / Brazil (.05)	East Germany (.27)	Czechoslovakia (.15)	Poland (.12)	Congo Kinshasa (.65)	South Africa (.12)	Liberia (.04) / Ghana (.04)	Israel (.33)	Egypt (.19)	Syria (.15)	China (PRC) (.27)	Laos (.18)	North Vietnam (.17)
Spain	Great Britain (.14)	United States (.07)	Soviet Union (.07)	Great Britain (.44)	United States (.20)	Portugal (.10)	Cuba (.67)	Peru (.25)	Guyana (.08)	Soviet Union (.83)	Hungary (.08)	Albania (.08)	South Africa (.33)	Spanish Guinea (.20)*	Cameroon (.07)*	Morocco (.35)	Israel (.19)	Egypt (.15)	China (PRC) (.50)	Taiwan (.25)	Indonesia (.12) / New Zealand (.12)
Switzerland	Great Britain (.16)	EEC (.16)	United States (.14)	Great Britain (.21)	EEC (.21)	United States (.18)	Peru (1.00)			Czechoslovakia (.43)	Soviet Union (.29)	Finland (.29)	(No Events)			(No Events)			Japan (1.00)		
Thailand	United States (.08)	South Vietnam (.08)	North Vietnam (.08)	United States (.42)	Great Britain (.27)	Portugal (.15)	Guyana (1.00)			Soviet Union (.80)	Hungary (.10)	Albania (.10)	South Africa (.46)	Cameroon (.08)*	Nigeria (.08)*	Israel (.29)	Algeria (.14)*	Egypt (.14)*	South Vietnam (.17)	North Vietnam (.17)	China (PRC) (.15) / Laos (.15)
Tunisia	France (.10)	Congo Kinshasa (.07)	Great Britain (.07)	France (.31)	Great Britain (.21)	United States (.13)	Guyana (1.00)			Soviet Union (.73)	East Germany (.09)	Hungary (.09) / Albania (.09)	Congo Kinshasa (.34)	South Africa (.33)*	Ghana (.03)*	Israel (.26)	Egypt (.22)	Jordan (.19)	China (PRC) (.50)	Taiwan (.14)	Laos (.14)
Turkey	Cyprus (.11)	Soviet Union (.09)	United States (.09)	Cyprus (.21)	United States (.18)	NATO (.14)	Cuba (.67)	Guyana (.33)		Soviet Union (.84)	Warsaw Pact (.05)*	East Germany (.03)*	South Africa (.35)	Congo Kinshasa (.29)*	Cameroon (.06)*	Egypt (.20)	Israel (.20)	Iran (.17) / Syria (.17)	Pakistan (.36)	China (PRC) (.27)	India (.18)
Uganda	Great Britain (.15)	Congo Kinshasa (.09)	South Africa (.09)	Great Britain (.48)	United States (.17)	Portugal (.17)	Guyana (1.00)			Soviet Union (.60)	Hungary (.20)	Albania (.20)	Congo Kinshasa (.23)	South Africa (.23)	East African Community (.08) / OAU (.08)	Egypt (.22)	Israel (.22)	Syria (.22)	China (PRC) (.25)	New Zealand (.25)*	Taiwan (.12)*

TABLE 5.3 Continued

CREON Nation	Over All Recipients	Atlantic Community Recipients	Latin American Recipients	Eastern European Recipients	African Recipients	Middle Eastern Recipients	Asian Recipients
United States	Soviet Union (.13)	NATO (.24)	Cuba (.55)	Soviet Union (.88)	Congo Kinshasa (.57)	Turkey (.21)	South Vietnam (.25)
	Cuba (.08)	West Germany (.17)	OAS (.11)	East Germany (.04)	South Africa (.10)	Israel (.19)	North Vietnam (.24)
	South Vietnam (.07)	Great Britain (.16)	Alliance for Progress (.10)	Yugoslavia (.03)	Uganda (.06)	Egypt (.19)	Laos (.17)
Uruguay	Great Britain (.09)	Great Britain (.38)	Cuba (.25)	Soviet Union (.80)	South Africa (.46)	Israel (.30)	China (PRC) (.50)
	Cuba (.07)	Portugal (.21)	OAS (.15)	Hungary (.10)	Ghana (.08)*	Syria (.20)*	Taiwan (.25)*
	Soviet Union (.06)	United States (.12)	IADB (.12)	Albania (.10)	Cameroon (.08)*	Egypt (.10)*	Indonesia (.12)
							New Zealand (.12)
Venezuela	Cuba (.11)	Great Britain (.38)	Cuba (.28)	Soviet Union (.82)	South Africa (.38)	OPEC (.31)	China (PRC) (.36)
	Great Britain (.08)	United States (.30)	OAS (.15)	Hungary (.09)	Uganda (.12)*	Algeria (.12)*	Taiwan (.18)
	United States (.06)	Portugal (.15)	Dominican Republic (.09)	Albania (.09)	Senegal (.06)*	Egypt (.12)*	South Vietnam (.18)
West Germany	United States (.13)	United States (.22)	Cuba (.46)	Soviet Union (.58)	African States Associated w/EEC (.22)	Israel (.39)	China (PRC) (.28)
	Great Britain (.09)	Great Britain (.16)	Peru (.31)*	East Germany (.26)	Nigeria (.17)	Egypt (.25)	India (.20)
	France (.08)	France (.14)	Chile (.08)*	Warsaw Pact (.06)	Tanzania (.17)	Jordan (.11)	Japan (.16)
						Turkey (.11)	Pakistan (.16)
Yugoslavia	Soviet Union (.15)	United States (.41)	Cuba (.83)	Soviet Union (.65)	Congo Kinshasa (.43)	Israel (.39)	China (PRC) (.48)
	United States (.10)	Great Britain (.23)	Guyana (.17)	Poland (.10)	South Africa (.29)	Egypt (.22)	South Vietnam (.14)
	China (PRC) (.06)	Portugal (.11)		Hungary (.10)	Cameroon (.05)*	Algeria (.11)*	North Vietnam (.10)
Zambia	Rhodesia (.23)	Great Britain (.51)	Guyana (1.00)	Soviet Union (.50)	Rhodesia (.63)	Egypt (.25)	China (PRC) (.44)
	Great Britain (.21)	Commonw'th (.23)		Albania (.50)	South Africa (.16)	Syria (.25)	Taiwan (.11)*
	Commonwealth (.10)	Portugal (.09)			Tanzania (.11)	Jordan (.25)	Japan (.11)*
						Israel (.25)	

NOTE: The numbers in parentheses are the percentage of events directed toward that recipient. An asterisk by a nation's name indicates that there are several other recipients with the same score that are not listed. The abbreviations used in the table stand for the following organizations: NATO = North Atlantic Treaty Organization; OAS = Organization of American States; IADB = Inter-American Development Bank; OAU = Organization of African Unity; EEC = European Economic Community.

TABLE 5.4
Salience Index for Various Types of Recipients for 38 CREON Countries

CREON Nation	Atlantic Community Recipients	Latin American Recipients	Eastern European Recipients	African Recipients	Middle Eastern Recipients	Asian Recipients
Belgium	.57	.01	.07	.11	.05	.04
Canada	.31	.05	.10	.07	.13	.19
Chile	.29	.31	.06	.09	.04	.05
China (PRC)	.28	.01	.17	.03	.03	.43
Costa Rica	.22	.41	.06	.06	.05	.04
Cuba	.46	.20	.15	.03	.05	.04
Czechoslovakia	.25	.03	.24	.05	.09	.22
East Germany	.53	.004	.27	.01	.07	.09
Egypt	.33	.00	.07	.08	.38	.05
France	.41	.04	.09	.06	.11	.15
Ghana	.29	.01	.04	.34	.07	.08
Guinea	.25	.01	.06	.36	.13	.04
Iceland	.44	.01	.13	.09	.09	.05
India	.28	.004	.09	.11	.04	.37
Israel	.17	.04	.06	.03	.54	.02
Italy	.52	.02	.09	.08	.06	.07
Ivory Coast	.27	.01	.03	.27	.08	.15
Japan	.36	.02	.08	.07	.12	.19
Kenya	.27	.01	.04	.46	.06	.08
Lebanon	.31	.01	.07	.08	.35	.05
Mexico	.23	.33	.07	.09	.04	.05
New Zealand	.29	.01	.04	.14	.05	.31
Norway	.42	.02	.15	.08	.11	.07
Philippines	.24	.02	.05	.07	.04	.40
Poland	.36	.003	.30	.05	.06	.11
Soviet Union	.39	.05	.08	.05	.11	.17
Spain	.33	.08	.08	.01	.17	.05
Switzerland	.62	.06	.13	.00	.00	.02
Thailand	.19	.01	.06	.08	.04	.44
Tunisia	.32	.003	.04	.20	.24	.05
Turkey	.52	.01	.11	.05	.09	.07
Uganda	.31	.01	.03	.39	.06	.05
United States	.20	.14	.14	.03	.07	.30
Uruguay	.23	.27	.07	.09	.07	.05
Venezuela	.21	.39	.05	.07	.07	.05
West Germany	.57	.02	.17	.03	.08	.04
Yugoslavia	.25	.003	.23	.10	.08	.13
Zambia	.41	.01	.02	.36	.04	.09
Mean	.33	.07	.11	.00	.11	.17

NOTE: The specific nations and organizations included in each of the regional clusters are listed in footnote 3. The percentages in each row do not total 100 because a certain percentage of the CREON countries' events were directed toward U.N. organizations which are not included in the regional breakdowns.

Table 5.4 again suggests the regional bias in choice of a target we noted with the selection ratio. For 27 of the CREON nations (71 percent), the most salient region is that in which they are located. Those countries where this is not the case include the two superpowers (U.S. and Soviet Union), four Eastern European nations (Czechoslovakia, East Germany, Poland, and Yugoslavia), two African countries (Ivory Coast and Zambia), Cuba, and Japan. With the exception of the U.S., the Atlantic Community nations are more salient to these countries than to nations in their own geographical regions. For the United States, Asian countries are more often targets than Atlantic Community nations. The latter is probably a result of American involvement in the Vietnamese conflict.

Table 5.4 gives us information on which countries are *not* salient or are outside the focus of attention of each CREON country. Thus, for example, for China we note few events directed toward recipients in Latin America, Africa, and the Middle East. For Mexico we observe few events percentage-wise toward countries outside the Atlantic Community of Latin America. Kenya focuses its attention on other African countries and Atlantic Community nations but directs relatively little activity toward nations in other geographical regions.

Let us now turn to the concentration index which indicates across the various types of recipients how concentrated or focused a CREON nation's activity is for each group. The concentration index represents the sum of the squared proportions of activity across a type of recipient. For instance, suppose Egypt directed 15 percent of its foreign policy activity toward the United States, 45 percent toward Israel, and 40 percent toward Great Britain. Using these three figures, the concentration index for Egypt would be: $(15\%)^2 + (45\%)^2 + (40\%)^2$ or .38. Table 5.5 presents the concentration indices for the CREON countries. The concentration index theoretically ranged from 1.0 (activity is directed toward only one target) to .00 (activity is equally distributed across targets). As we observed earlier, the lower limit is influenced by the total number of potential targets. Thus, the lower limits for the types of recipients in Table 5.5 are: all recipients (N of possible targets is 228) = .004, Atlantic Community recipients (N is 33) = .03, Latin American recipients (N is 35) = .03, Eastern European recipients (N is 16) = .06, African recipients (N is 48) = .02, Middle Eastern recipients (N is 19) = .05, Asian recipients (N is 32) = .03. Given the near zero quality of these lower limits, we will assume in examining Table 5.5 a scale of .00 to 1.

The data in Table 5.5 indicate that across all recipients the CREON countries' foreign policy activity is fairly dispersed and not concentrated. The most concentrated behavior is seen for Cuba, East Germany, and Zambia. But on a scale of .00 to 1, even this behavior is not very concentrated. When we look at the behavior toward targets in the various regions of the world, however, a different story emerges. Behavior is fairly focused toward Latin American and Eastern European nations. The means for nations in these two regions are .53 and .55, respectively. Twelve of the CREON countries show the most extreme concentration toward nations in Latin America. Generally, this extreme concentration occurs for CREON

TABLE 5.5

Concentration Index for 38 CREON Nations

CREON Nation	For All Recipients	Atlantic Community Recipients	Latin American Recipients	Eastern European Recipients	African Recipients	Middle Eastern Recipients	Asian Recipients
Belgium	.040	.10	.44	.43	.17	.20	.17
Canada	.039	.22	.14	.55	.14	.23	.16
Chile	.039	.24	.12	.71	.22	.19	.22
China (PRC)	.096	.66	1.00	.57	.21	.25	.14
Costa Rica	.043	.36	.11	.66	.30	.22	.31
Cuba	.167	.71	.10	.57	.27	.20	.36
Czechoslovakia	.044	.15	.33	.33	.34	.16	.25
East Germany	.120	.36	1.00	.15	1.00	.32	.50
Egypt	.068	.22	a	.38	.25	.26	.42
France	.035	.14	.08	.59	.07	.14	.15
Ghana	.040	.16	.25	.73	.17	.16	.29
Guinea	.036	.18	1.00	.47	.13	.18	.31
Iceland	.047	.16	.50	.56	.22	.16	.34
India	.070	.24	.33	.70	.38	.21	.28
Israel	.094	.24	.73	.81	.22	.27	.27
Italy	.040	.11	.39	.65	.11	.19	.14
Ivory Coast	.032	.16	1.00	.44	.12	.17	.15
Japan	.046	.23	.33	.77	.16	.12	.17
Kenya	.049	.28	1.00	.28	.11	.27	.40
Lebanon	.053	.23	1.00	.66	.20	.19	.43
Mexico	.037	.23	.14	.73	.23	.18	.28
New Zealand	.036	.20	.50	.59	.20	.21	.11
Norway	.037	.10	.25	.57	.21	.16	.21
Philippines	.047	.34	.25	.73	.25	.16	.13
Poland	.050	.19	1.00	.22	.32	.29	.19
Soviet Union	.055	.27	.58	.12	.45	.20	.16

TABLE 5.5 Continued

CREON Nation	For All Recipients	Atlantic Community Recipients	Latin American Recipients	Eastern European Recipients	African Recipients	Middle Eastern Recipients	Asian Recipients
Spain	.047	.26	.51	.71	.18	.21	.34
Switzerland	.076	.14	1.00	.35	[a]	[a]	1.00
Thailand	.039	.28	1.00	.66	.25	.18	.12
Tunisia	.041	.18	1.00	.55	.23	.18	.31
Turkey	.048	.13	.56	.71	.23	.16	.25
Uganda	.054	.29	1.00	.44	.14	.19	.19
United States	.044	.13	.32	.78	.35	.15	.17
Uruguay	.033	.22	.12	.66	.25	.18	.34
Venezuela	.038	.26	.13	.69	.19	.17	.22
West Germany	.054	.12	.33	.40	.14	.24	.19
Yugoslavia	.052	.24	.72	.45	.28	.24	.28
Zambia	.117	.33	1.00	.50	.44	.25	.26
Mean	.055	.24	.53	.55	.24	.20	.27

NOTE: The specific nations included in each of these clusters are listed in footnote 3.

[a]This nation addressed no events toward a recipient in this cluster of nations.

countries directing few events toward Latin American nations. What little activity there is they direct toward one country. With regard to Eastern European countries, a tendency to direct more events to the Soviet Union than to the other nations increases the concentration index toward this area.

For two-thirds (26) of the CREON countries the foreign policy activity is the most dispersed (least concentrated) to nations within their own geographical region. There is a tendency for the Atlantic Community nations among the CREON countries to exhibit highly concentrated behavior toward the Eastern European (or, primarily, Warsaw Pact) nations. The Soviet Union, as the perceived adversary, is the recipient of much of the foreign policy activity directed toward these nations. The opposite does not appear to be the case, however. The four Eastern European nations in the CREON sample do not tend to concentrate their behavior toward one as opposed to the others among the Atlantic Community (or NATO) countries. The most concentrated behavior toward the Atlantic Community nations occurs for China and Cuba, which both focus their attention on the United States, as we note in Table 5.3.

SUMMARY

In this chapter we have developed several ways of examining a nation's scope of action or the distribution of a government's foreign policy activity across potential targets or recipients in the international arena. The particular measures that were developed were a selection ratio and indices of salience and concentration. The selection ratio suggests who among the potential targets is chosen as a recipient. The salience and concentration indices indicate how often foreign policy behavior is directed toward specific targets.

The data on the countries in the CREON sample of nations suggest that behavior is not evenly distributed among targets in the international system. The CREON countries focus their attention differentially toward the governments of other nations. The data on geographical region indicate that knowledge about who the target is enhances the differences in the scope of action measures. A next step in examining where nations focus their foreign policy activity could profitably be the development of a typology of targets and/or a typology of the nature of dyadic relationships to which the scope of action measures could be applied.

NOTES

1. The actual base value of the concentration index is influenced by the number of possible targets that a nation can address. The larger the number, the closer the base value is to .00. To ascertain the base value, we divide 1 by the number of potential targets and square the result, then multiply by the number of possible targets. In other words, we ascertain the percentage that would indicate an equal distribution of behavior across targets, square this proportion, and sum this figure across the potential targets.

2. Recipients in the CREON event data set can have several functions. They can participate with the acting government in the foreign policy action (for example, in issuing a joint communique); they can facilitate the action (for instance, in providing the site for a meeting). They can be the direct target of the behavior, or they can be the object that the acting government is trying to influence (indirect object) but not the direct target of the action (for example, the United States in a Chinese note to North Vietnam condemning the United States). In examining scope of action, we have looked only at recipients that were direct targets and

indirect objects. For a more detailed discussion of the coding rules for the various roles recipients can have, see the "Roles of Recipients" variable in the Technical Appendix.

3. The following nations and organizations are included in each of the regional groups: *Atlantic Community*—United States, Canada, Great Britain, NATO (North Atlantic Treaty Organization), Ireland, Netherlands, Belgium, Luxembourg, EEC (European Economic Community), France, Euratom, Switzerland, Spain, ECSC (European Coal and Steel Community), Portugal, Council of Europe, WEU (Western European Union), West Germany, Benelux Customs Union, OECD (Organization for Economic Cooperation and Development), EFTA (European Free Trade Association), British Commonwealth, Austria, European Parliament, Italy, Vatican, Malta, Greece, Cyprus, Sweden, Norway, Denmark, Iceland. *Latin America*—OAS (Organization of American States), Pan American Union, Alliance for Progress, Central American Bank of Integration, LAFTA (Latin American Free Trade Association), Central American Common Market, ODECA (Organization of Central American States), IADB (Inter-American Development Bank), OAS Special Security Council, Conference of Latin American Leaders and the U.S., Inter-American Peace Commission, Cuba, Haiti, Dominican Republic, Jamaica, Trinidad and Tobago, Barbados, Mexico, Guatemala, Honduras, El Salvador, Nicaragua, Costa Rica, Panama, Carefta, Colombia, Venezuela, Guyana, Ecuador, Peru, Brazil, Bolivia, Chile, Argentina, Uruguay. *Eastern Europe*—East Germany, Poland, Hungary, Czechoslovakia, Albania, Yugoslavia, Bulgaria, Rumania, Soviet Union, Finland, 19 Nation Pro-Soviet Party Congress, Warsaw Pact, COMECON (Council of Mutual Economic Assistance), World Congress of Communist Parties, Summit Meeting of European Communist Parties, Rumanian Communist Party Congress. *Africa*—OAU (Organization of African Unity), French Community, Casablanca Powers, Brazzaville Powers, East African Community, Central Bank of West Africa, Spanish Guinea, Cape Colony, Canary Islands, 18 Associated African States of EEC, U.N. Conciliation Commission for the Congro, Gambia, Mali Federation, Mali, Senegal, Dahomey, Mauritania, Niger, Ivory Coast, French Guinea, Upper Volta, Liberia, Sierra Leone, Ghana, Togo, Cameroon, Nigeria, Central African Republic, Chad, Congo Brazzaville, Congo Kinshasa, Uganda, Kenya, Tanzania, Burundi, Rwanda, Somalia, Ethiopia, Zambia, Rhodesia, South Africa, Malagasy (Madasgascar), OCAM (Inter-African and Malagasy Organization), Monrovia Group, Conference of African States, Emergency Conference of African States, Third African Independence Conference, All African People's Conference. *Middle East*—Morocco, Arab League, OPEC (Organization of Petroleum Exporting Countries), Algeria, Tunisia, Libya, Sudan, Iran, Turkey, Iraq, Egypt, Syria, Lebanon, Jordan, Israel, Saudi Arabia, Yemen, People's Republic of Southern Yemen, Kuwait. *Asia*—Afghanistan, Colombo Plan, South Pacific Commission, Association of Southeast Asia, China (PRC), Mongolia, Taiwan, North Korea, South Korea, Japan, India, Bhutan, Sikkum, Pakistan, Burma, Ceylon, Maldive Islands, Nepal, Thailand, Cambodia, Laos, North Vietnam, South Vietnam, Malaysia, Sabah, Singapore, Philippines, Indonesia, Australia, U.N. Economic Commission for Asia, New Zealand, Western Samoa.

PART III

Properties of the Decision-Making Process

Editors' Introduction

One of the important premises of the CREON measurement effort is that, because foreign policy is a multifaceted phenomenon, a variety of measures are needed to capture its varied nature. Chapters 4 and 5 examined ways in which foreign policy behavior could be used to catch a glimpse of the inputs that gave rise to decision-making activity—that is, the predecisional context. The two chapters in this section (Chapters 6 and 7) follow the flow of the simple system model referred to in Chapter 1 by looking at characteristics of the decision-making process.

Although historically the nature of decision making has provoked considerable research interest in its own right, it has also been considered important as an intervening or independent variable affecting the nature of foreign policy outputs. One of the crucial assumptions differentiating the foreign policy approach to international politics from the systems approach seems to be the belief that understanding foreign policy depends on understanding who becomes involved in decision-making activities, with what resources, for what ends, and with what effects.

A considerable body of research exists on decision-making processes. Most of the systematic research relies on surveys of or interviews with foreign policy officials or on simulations. Very little systematic research has been done on data drawn from actual instances of decision making. One prominent exception to this is found in the Stanford studies on the crisis preceding the outbreak of World War I. The dearth of systematic historical research reflects the enormous difficulty in coming up with information about the making of specific decisions. Full information about decisions becomes available only with the opening of diplomatic archives many years after the event. Information closer to the time of the event is usually scattered and unreliable. News accounts may reflect bureaucratic maneuvers and thus give a misleading impression of the overall nature of the decision-making process. Other sources, such as memoirs and interviews with participants, are liable to err through selective or distorted memory and recall. Reconstituting an accurate description of what took place is therefore a painstaking effort of assessing and synthesizing information and inferring conclusions about what actually occurred.

During the course of the CREON measurement effort, there were three attempts to create measures of properties of the decision-making process. The procedural issue areas scheme, briefly alluded to by C. Hermann and Coate in Chapter 4, was an effort to describe directly how a decision was made. It ultimately proved unachievable because of problems in observing the configuration of organizations and relationships in each decision giving rise to an event.

The other two attempts to capture characteristics of the decision-making process were indirect. One concerned the nature of the goals underlying foreign policy behavior. As indicated in Chapter 1, goals are considered elements of the process because they are invoked or clarified during decision making and, in turn, shape the nature of the process as well as the behavior. In Chapter 6, Brady presents two CREON measures of goals. For reasons that she discusses there, efforts to capture the content of goals within the context of the CREON data set proved sterile. Therefore, attention shifted to other characteristics of goals: time frame for goal realization and beneficiaries of action. As she points out, these are characteristics of behavior which are interesting in themselves and not just as proximate predictors of other qualities of behavior.

The two measures of goal properties fit differently into the history of the CREON measurement efforts. Time frame for goal realization is actually not a result of a new measurement effort following the 1974 CREON Summer Seminar. Instead, it rests on a reconceptualization of a variable already in the CREON data set. Beneficiaries, however, is a product of the Stage II measurement efforts. Specifically, it is drawn from one component of the substantive problem area scheme (whose value is jeopardized) described, but not in detail, in Chapter 4. The chapter on goal properties, therefore, not only presents some innovative conceptualizations of properties of events, but also fulfills a basic responsibility to report our data-gathering procedures.

The other attempt to reflect the decision-making process—that is, the instrumentalities measure described by C. Hermann in Chapter 7—also is indirect. Classification of behavior in terms of the instruments (skills and resources) used is common. Hermann's contribution is based on an awareness that specialized resources are used at more phases of the decision-making process than just implementation. He incorporates into the measure a model of the flow of action from decision through announcement to implementation. Coding involves recording at each point the kinds of instruments used in that particular phase. This measure is a nominal coding scheme added to the data as part of the CREON Stage II efforts.

Goal Properties of
Foreign Policy Activities

Of all the concepts which appear in descriptions and explanations of foreign policy, none has been more central than foreign policy goals—whether characterized broadly as the national interest or defined more narrowly as a set of objectives that guide behavior. To the extent that government officials engage in foreign policy behavior for a purpose—to promote or maintain desired conditions or to avoid undesired future situations in the international system—all countries have constructed their foreign policies around goals. By goals decision makers have judged the foreign policies of other nations. And political analysts have used goals as a yardstick to evaluate foreign policy successes and failures. Thus, goals have served both as standards for policy decisions and as criteria for policy evaluation.

Precisely because they have been viewed, by participants and observers alike, as the glue that holds foreign policy together, goals have been the objects of extensive study. The first thing we note about many of these studies is that they focus on the substance or content of goals. Morgenthau (1973), for example, has advanced three goals pursued by nation-states: status quo, imperialism, and prestige. Aron (1966) has argued for the centrality of security, force (power), and glory objectives in foreign policy. One recognizes, on surveying these substantive goal discussions, one common (although often implicit) underlying assumption—namely, that the specified goals are applicable to all nations.

A second characteristic of the literature on goals is the tendency to view goals as independent or intervening variables that explain patterns in foreign policy behavior (Swanson, 1977: 2). Hopkins and Mansbach (1973: 59) make the general point:

AUTHOR'S NOTE: I would like to express my appreciation to several of my colleagues on the CREON Project—in particular, Patrick Callahan, William Dixon, Joe Hagan, and Dean Swanson—for their comments on earlier drafts and for assistance in the preparation of this chapter. The views expressed in this chapter are my own and should not be attributed to the Department of Defense or any other government agency.

"All actors in international politics pursue goals that determine, or at least affect, their behavior." Implicit in this view is the belief that decision makers initiate actions that will bring them closer to their goals and that rational (or, at a minimum, satisficing) behavior characterizes the policy-making process. Either foreign policy actions are linked to clearly defined goals—the rational model—or they are connected to "alternatives or subgoals more feasible of achievement and meeting minimally satisfactory criteria" (Bloomfield, 1974: 20)—the satisficing model. In either case, foreign policy is purposive and can be explained, at least in part, by decision makers' objectives.

Our effort is distinctive from most previous studies because we do not attempt to describe goals in terms of their substance; rather, we use nonsubstantive dimensions of goals to develop alternative characterizations of foreign policy behavior. To anticipate the argument, we believe that *nonsubstantive dimensions* of goals provide theoretically compelling and empirically viable alternatives to substantive goal classifications and that these dimensions can be used to characterize *foreign policy behavior*. These characterizations of foreign policy behavior we will call *goal properties*.

Through the development of goal-based measures of foreign policy behavior, we can examine goals as dependent variables rather than as independent or intervening variables in foreign policy analyses. We have chosen this unorthodox approach because of the serious problems presented by the substantive approach to goals. The next section of this chapter will briefly summarize these problems in order to lay the ground work for further development of goal properties.

PROBLEMS IN IDENTIFYING GOALS

There are two major difficulties in a substantive approach to the study of goals, difficulties that have motivated us to pursue a different course. These are the difficulty in determining what a state's goals are and the difficulty in predicting behaviors from knowledge of goals.

First, there is little consensus on the best approach to the identification of goals. One alternative contends that goals may be inferred from behavior: "a state's goals are simply whatever its government is doing" (Sprout and Sprout, 1971: 113). For example, the Soviet Union's naval presence in the Indian Ocean suggests the Soviet objective of filling a power vacuum in that area. And Cuba's aid to Angolan rebels demonstrates the Cuban objective of exporting revolutionary movements.

A major problem with this alternative is that it provides little indication of whose behavior should be observed. Foreign policy behaviors are the outcome of a political process and, as such, they often represent the desires of organizational, bureaucratic, or individual actors (Halperin, 1974). Because governments are not unitary actors, they may pursue multiple and often conflicting goals, thus increasing the difficulty of inferring national goals from behavior.

More fundamentally, more than one set of goals may appear to be consistent with a particular line of behavior (C. Hermann, 1978: 31). The Soviet Union's decision to place offensive missiles in Cuba is a case in point. Allison (1971) has suggested at least five explanations for Khrushchev's behavior: to create a bargaining chip in dealing with Kennedy in a summit meeting or in a UN confrontation on another issue, to split NATO and set the stage for a Soviet move in Berlin, to provide for Cuban defense against another Bay of Pigs, to reduce the credibility of U.S. commitments and thus demonstrate a power shift in the Cold War struggle, and to bolster Soviet missile power vis-à-vis the United States. Because each objective is consistent with the Soviet decision and because there is not a one-to-one correspondence between behavior and goals, it is difficult to infer goals from behavior.

A second approach to determining what a state's goals are relies not on inferences from behavior but on decision makers' statements of desired future conditions in the international system. Thus, we equate national goals with professed goals: "the state's goals are what those spokesmen determine them to be" (Sprout and Sprout, 1971: 115). To adopt this perspective undoubtedly simplifies the task of goal identification. The observer need only identify the primary governmental spokesmen and peruse their public addresses to determine the state's goals.

But this simplified procedure produces a simplistic result. How willing are we to take professed goals at face value? The expression of desired future conditions is only one reason why decision makers publicly state foreign policy goals. Decision makers often use statements of goals to achieve domestic political and economic objectives as well as foreign policy objectives. For example, arguments by European members of NATO for the standardization of defense technology and production within the alliance clearly have economic as well as political, military, and security foundations. Prime Minister Callaghan of Great Britain estimated that increased standardization would result in more efficient production through longer production runs and would eliminate costly duplication in research and development programs. Competitive research and development with licensed co-production has been promoted as an effective means of involving European industry in the economic benefits of standardization. The professed goal of standardization serves both foreign and domestic interests.

In addition to the difficulty in determining what a state's goals are, a substantive approach to goals presents us with the problem of predicting behaviors from knowledge of goals. Self-preservation, territorial integrity, and ethnic, religious, or linguistic unity are core goals that often are included in substantive goal classifications. Core goals are "goals for which most people are willing to make ultimate sacrifices" (K. Holsti, 1977: 145); they are held in common by decision makers regardless of nation or situation. The advantage of a core goal approach to substantive classification is that it simplifies the task of classification by assuming that diverse nations pursue similar objectives. If all nations pursue similar goals and if goals are linked to subsequent behaviors, then why do nations initiate such diverse behaviors in the international system? Clearly, core goals are too gross to be relevant to particular situations; therefore, they have limited empirical utility in the prediction of foreign policy behaviors (see Hopkins and Mansbach, 1973: 59-60).

Difficulties associated with identifying the national interest and predicting foreign policy behaviors from knowledge of that interest illustrate the problem. The "national interest" is probably the most casually used and popularized concept in international relations. Theorists of the realist school assume that decision makers act according to interest defined as power where the fundamental national interest is national survival (Morgenthau, 1951). The abstract nature and undifferentiated character of the national interest, so defined, complicate the linkage of interest to concrete activities. The researcher who attempts to explain foreign policy behaviors in terms of the national interest is channeled into a tautological argument. Whatever a nation is doing at a particular moment can be explained by the concept of interest defined as power. But this approach does not permit explanations of variations in foreign policy activities, because the national interest—the explanatory variable—remains constant.

Because of these problems with substantive goal classifications, we have pursued a different course. The difficulties in determining what a state's goals are and in predicting behaviors from knowledge of goals, combined with our interest in developing characterizations of foreign policy behavior, have prompted us to focus on goal properties.

CONCEPTUALIZING GOAL PROPERTIES

Goal properties are those dimensions of foreign policy behavior that characterize nonsubstantive aspects of goals—that is, the context within which values are expressed. Although the development of substantive classifications of foreign policy goals has been a major preoccupation of goal-oriented research, it is by no means the only theoretically compelling perspective on goals. We contend that an equally compelling, although to this point generally neglected, research direction is the development of foreign policy behavior measures based on dimensions of goals other than their substance.

Two features distinguish this approach from previous research on foreign policy goals. First, we focus not on substantive classifications but on nonsubstantive properties of goals that describe the context within which values are expressed. Second, we develop measures of foreign policy behavior from these goal properties. Each feature requires further elaboration.

Rather than generate yet another classification of goals based on content, we have developed nonsubstantive dimensions of goals. Among the dimensions examined are characteristics of goals that describe the time frame within which the goal will be fulfilled, whether the goal is an end in itself or a means to another end, the entities that will benefit from realization of the goal, and the agent or agents from which responsive behavior is required in order to achieve the goal. Nonsubstantive properties characterize goals as they (the goals) are expressed along with concrete behaviors. For example, the goal of self-preservation may be either immediate or long range, depending on the context in which the goal is expressed. If the goal is expressed with behavior initiated during a foreign policy crisis, self-preservation often is characterized by an immediate or short-term time frame; whereas if the same goal is expressed in more routine situations, it often is characterized by needing an extended time frame for realization. Thus, knowledge of the goal's content is not sufficient to assign values on nonsubstantive goal properties.

Although the idea of nonsubstantive characteristics of goals is not revolutionary, it has been overshadowed by the attention paid to the content of goals. In general, however, authors who describe the content of foreign policy goals also acknowledge the significance of other characteristics of goals. For instance, Organski (1968: 76, 81) has distinguished between goals that benefit the actor (national) and goals that benefit other entities (humanitarian), between goals that require an extended time frame for realization (long-range) and goals that require less time for realization (intermediate). Wolfers (1962: 73) also has distinguished between goals that benefit the actor (possession) and goals that benefit external entities (milieu). That these characteristics have generated less reflection than have the authors' substantive classifications does not deny their significance.

A second distinctive characteristic of our approach is the use of nonsubstantive properties of goals to develop measures of foreign policy behavior. Rather than define goal properties as independent or intervening variables in the foreign policy process, we have developed measures of foreign policy behavior which allow us to construe goal properties as dependent variables. Our concern with the development of measures of foreign policy behavior has had a dramatic impact on our approach to the conceptualization of goal properties. We assume that to have empirical utility measures of foreign policy behavior should be action- or event-based. Goal properties vary across events and, as a consequence, provide useful starting points for the construction of measures of foreign policy behavior.

Each foreign policy action is assigned a score on each nonsubstantive property of goals; these scores may vary dramatically from one action to the next. Just as variations in other dimensions of foreign policy behavior can be monitored across time, so variations in goal properties can be observed across time. Thus, goal properties provide an effective means of describing variations in foreign policy behavior.

Consider one goal property—time frame for goal realization. The time frame for goal realization describes whether a goal may be realized within a short period of time or over the long term. It is possible to characterize the time frame for realization of a specific goal as expressed in a discrete foreign policy action. When defined as a goal property of foreign policy behavior, time frame is assessed in the context of a specific foreign policy action. As we noted previously, time frame may be long range in one context and short term under other conditions, although the substance or content of the goal may remain constant. Nonsubstantive properties of goals vary as a nation translates goals into policy through actions and as it evaluates the effects of other nations' actions on its goals. Consequently, time frame for goal realization may be adjusted as actions are initiated and as the actor assesses the impact of others' behaviors on the fulfillment of the goal.

For instance, during the first months of his administration, President Carter made overtures toward the Cuban government with the objective of normalizing U.S.-Cuban relations. Following such significant events as the lifting of a U.S. ban on travel to Cuba which had been in force since 1961 and the negotiation of an agreement concerning fishing rights and maritime boundaries, the administration expressed hopes that the objective of improved U.S.-Cuban relations could be achieved in the short term. But increased Cuban military involvement in Angola and the Horn of Africa prompted reconsideration of the time frame for normalization. In his comments concerning Cuban involvement in the African continent, President Carter reassessed the time frame for normalization, adjusting it from short term to long range. Although the content of the goal remained constant, the time frame for fulfillment of the goal varied dramatically from one context to the next.

This example suggests the theoretically compelling nature of goal properties. There are two reasons why it is important to know how and why properties such as time frame for goal realization may vary from event to event. These reasons are grounded in the "contextual" nature of goal properties. Goal properties are contextual because they describe the relationship between a goal and the situation or the actions of others. First, goal properties enable us to assess the status of a goal at a particular moment. How close to goal fulfillment does the action bring decision makers? As the time frame for goal fulfillment is adjusted from long range to short term, the goal becomes more immediate. Conversely, as in the U.S.-Cuban relations example, with the time frame for goal fulfillment adjusted from short term to long range, the goal becomes less immediate.

The second reason concerns the relationship between substantive goals and goal properties. Variations in nonsubstantive properties of goals may precede changes in substantive goals. For instance, the adjustment of a short-term time frame to a long-range time frame for a particular goal may signal the subsequent dropping of that objective and its replacement with an objective more likely achievable in the short term. Thus, nonsubstantive properties of goals provide indicators of where decision makers stand at particular moments with respect to their nation's goals.

DEVELOPING MEASURES OF GOAL PROPERTIES

With goal properties we are focusing on not just one behavior measure but a cluster of behavior measures. In this chapter we describe the conceptual and operational development of two goal properties—time frame for goal realization and beneficiaries—which illustrate the kinds of measures that can be designed.

Time Frame for Goal Realization

Conceptualization. Goals are future-oriented by their nature. However, there is wide variation in the effort required to achieve particular goals. Some goals are relatively specific and may be achieved through a few actions taken over a brief period; other goals are more abstract and may require multiple actions taken over an extended period. Goals that demand an extended period for fulfillment often concern fundamental transformations in conditions or states of affairs in the international system. Goals that may be achieved through a few actions often imply desired conditions that differ only marginally from existing conditions in the international system.

Time frame for goal realization measures the time required for the achievement of a goal as expressed in the context of a concrete foreign policy action. In principle, values on this variable range from immediate achievement to short-term achievement to long-range achievement. Immediate achievement means goal fulfillment is coterminous with action; the behavior represents the achievement of a desired condition. Short-term achievement means that goal fulfillment requires a few actions in addition to the present behavior. Long-range achievement means goals are reached after an extended time and multiple actions in addition to the present behavior. Thus, time frame characterizes the relationship between the actor in the present situation and the desired objective. Variation in time frame can reflect differences in leadership style. Whether a nation consistently pursues short-term or long-range goals may depend on the leadership style of its decision makers. Kissinger (1969: 29) has argued that leadership groups are influenced by "their experiences during their rise to eminence; the structure in which they operate; the values of their society." Bureaucratic-pragmatic leadership groups tend to await developments in the international system rather than to initiate, to focus on immediate issues "only as the pressure of events imposes the need for resolving them" (1969: 30), and to neglect the long range, which is not represented because it lacks a bureaucratic constituency. One might expect these leadership groups to pursue foreign policy goals that are characterized by immediate or short-term time frames for fulfillment. Ideological leadership groups, in contrast, because of their commitment to ideology as the criterion against which to measure success or failure, tend to pursue foreign policy goals that are characterized by long-range time frames for fulfillment.

Variation in time frame for the fulfillment of goals may also result from different situational conditions. Previous research has suggested that crises or other types of high-threat situations focus decision makers' attention on immediate problems (Brady, 1978); one might expect decision makers, when confronted with crisis situations, to initiate foreign policy behaviors which characterize their objectives as immediate or short term. Under more routine conditions, when policy-makers have an extended period in which to make decisions, they are likely to adopt a long-range perspective on the problem, other things being equal, and are likely to initiate foreign policy behaviors which characterize their objectives as long range.

Time frame for goal realization may provide, over the long term, the elements of a performance measure for foreign policy decision makers. Within the context of specified substantive goals, variations in the time frame measure indicate whether decision makers are moving closer to or further away from their objectives. Potentially, the measure may permit us to assess the status of a nation's goals across time.

Operationalization. International event data collected by the CREON Project provide one means of making operational this goal property of foreign policy behavior. For each event the coders attempted to identify one or more goals (see the goals variable in the Technical Appendix)[1] by asking a series of questions: Does the event refer to a desired future condition promoted by the present behavior? Does the actor indicate that his behavior is directed toward the preservation or maintenance of the existing state of affairs? Does the event consist of a verbal statement of the actor's desired policy? If an affirmative response can be given to any of these questions, then a goal is present in the event. Notice that in the initial coding process we do not classify goals according to their substance.

Once the coder has identified a goal, he or she determines whether the goal is first or second order. First-order goals refer to specific, definite future conditions that are achievable in the near future and are often recognizable as a means or as instruments to achieve some future end. Second-order goals, on the other hand, refer to abstract, future conditions that are achievable only in the long-range, distant future, or that are attainable only by numerous actions and often appear as end states or conditions (see Salmore and Brady, 1972: 79).

The goals variable is the basis for our measure of time frame for goal realization. We believe the absence of professed goals in an event may indicate that decision makers have not conceptualized their behavior in terms of an explicit goal. Often behaviors are initiated to fulfill previously made obligations, and such behaviors

TABLE 6.1
Sample CREON Events Coded for Time Frame for Goal Realization

Short Term

1. *Event:* (11-20-62)	Venezuela's delegate to the UN General Assembly votes yes on a resolution calling for early establishment by the UN World Meteorological Organization of a worldwide monitoring network to measure radioactive fallout.
Goals: First Order:	Establishment by UN World Meteorological Organization of a worldwide monitoring network to measure radioactive fallout.
2. *Event:* (07-26-66)	Switzerland agrees with other members of the Group of Ten to provide for the participation of developing countries in discussions on international monetary reform.
Goals: First Order:	Enable developing countries to participate in discussions on international monetary reform.

Long Range

3. *Event:* (05-18-60)	USSR Premier Khrushchev declares that he intends to sign a separate peace treaty with East Germany depriving the United States, Great Britain, and France of their occupation rights in West Berlin.
Goals: Second Order	To deprive the Western Powers of their occupation rights in West Berlin.
4. *Event:* (06-05-60)	Cuba plans to establish diplomatic relations with the People's Republic of China.
Goals: Second Order:	Establish relations with the People's Republic of China.

may not be accompanied by an explicit statement of the actor's goals. For instance, the implementation of a trade agreement may not be accompanied by a statement of objectives. Only those CREON events that were accompanied by a statement indicating the presence of at least one goal form the basis for the time frame measure. If decision makers express first-order goals in the context of a specific event, we believe they express a short-term orientation in their behavior—that is, given the present situation, few additional actions are required to achieve the stated goals. A similar argument applies to long-range orientation. If decision makers express second-order goals in the context of a specific event, they express a long-range orientation in their behavior. That is, given the present situation, multiple additional actions are required to achieve the expressed goals.

Table 6.1 shows several CREON events coded for the time frame for goal realization measure. Although we believe that these events correspond to our intuitive conceptions of short- and long-range time frames, we encourage the reader to examine them to make his or her own assessment of the face validity of this goal property of foreign policy behavior.

Empirical characteristics. The frequency distribution for the time frame for goal realization measure across all events in the CREON data set appears in Table 6.2. Nearly two-thirds of the events are characterized by a short-term time frame for goal realization. This distribution suggests the predominance of short-term foreign policy strategies in the contemporary international system. Simon (1976) argues

TABLE 6.2
Event Distribution for
Time Frame for Goal Realization

Time Frame	Relative Frequency (%)	Absolute Frequency
Short Term	64	4840
Long Range	36	2727
Total	100	7567

NOTE: This distribution includes *only* those CREON events considered by the coders to contain a goal.

that these strategies are compatible with the limited abilities of individuals to process information and to evaluate alternatives. Because individuals experience difficulty in forecasting the consequences of their actions, particularly in the long term, they accept a more immediate perspective on the problem and settle for an alternative that represents a "better" course (the "satisficing" model). The greater the uncertainty associated with a long-term outcome, the greater the reliance on acceptance within the organization as the criterion for choice (see Cyert and March, 1963).

Beyond their comparability with human limitations, short-term foreign policy strategies divert attention from potentially divisive discussions of long-term foreign policy objectives. Short-term strategies tend to be incremental, which makes it possible for decision makers to agree on immediate choices whether or not they agree on ultimate long-term objectives (see Braybrooke and Lindblom, 1963: 134). For these reasons, we are not surprised by the predominance of short-term time frames with respect to the fulfillment of foreign policy goals.

Table 6.3 presents the distribution of events across the time frame categories for the 38 CREON nations. The first point to be noted about this distribution is that decision makers tend to adopt short-term foreign policy strategies more often than long-range strategies. For no nation does the short-term time frame category include less than 53 percent of the events initiated by that nation's decision makers.

Other patterns emerge as well. Egypt and Israel initiated the greatest proportion of events characterized by a short-term time frame. Three-fourths of their events that considered a goal conceived of a short-term goal. These figures may not be surprising when we know that the CREON data include the 1967 war and that much of the literature on crisis decision making has documented a shift by decision makers to more immediate concerns when they are confronted with high-threat situations (C. Hermann, 1972). Uganda, Kenya, and the Ivory Coast form a cluster of African nations with around 70 percent of their events characterized by a short-term time frame for goal realization. This imbalance in favor of short-term goals may be due to the immediate economic and political concerns of these newly independent nations in the 1960s, the optimistic attitudes concerning the achievement of goals which characterized that period, and the subsequent institutionalization of economic and political interaction in organizations such as the Organization of African Unity.

TABLE 6.3
Time Frame for Goal Realization: Distribution by CREON Nations

CREON Nation	Short Term	Long Term
Belgium	64.5 (176)	35.5 (97)
Canada	63.7 (162)	36.3 (92)
Chile	57.2 (79)	42.8 (59)
China (PRC)	62.8 (159)	37.2 (94)
Costa Ric	57.5 (61)	42.5 (45)
Cuba	59.4 (120)	40.6 (82)
Czechoslovakia	a	a
East Germany	59.1 (81)	40.9 (56)
Egypt	75.3 (183)	24.7 (60)
France	56.9 (296)	43.1 (224)
Ghana	66.0 (126)	34.0 (65)
Guinea	66.2 (102)	33.8 (52)
Iceland	66.0 (64)	34.0 (33)
India	60.9 (181)	39.1 (116)
Israel	75.4 (132)	24.6 (43)
Italy	62.1 (180)	37.9 (110)
Ivory Coast	69.2 (72)	30.8 (32)
Japan	55.2 (100)	44.8 (81)
Kenya	73.3 (44)	26.7 (16)
Lebanon	69.0 (58)	31.0 (26)
Mexico	67.2 (90)	32.8 (44)
New Zealand	62.8 (71)	37.2 (42)
Norway	69.6 (103)	30.4 (45)
Philippines	62.4 (83)	37.6 (50)
Poland	a	a
Soviet Union	69.4 (384)	30.6 (169)
Spain	71.4 (65)	28.6 (26)
Switzerland	53.7 (29)	46.3 (25)
Thailand	65.1 (56)	34.9 (30)
Tunisia	65.4 (117)	34.6 (62)
Turkey	69.8 (148)	30.2 (64)
Uganda	73.7 (73)	26.3 (26)
United States	63.2 (709)	36.3 (413)
Uruguay	65.3 (64)	34.7 (34)
Venezuela	61.6 (85)	38.4 (53)
West Germany	56.2 (246)	43.8 (192)
Yugoslavia	71.5 (113)	28.5 (45)
Zambia	53.8 (28)	46.2 (24)

NOTE: The first number in the short-term and long-term columns for each row is the relative frequency of that time frame category for the nation. The second number, in parentheses, is the absolute frequency of that time frame category. The events considered in this distribution were those which contained a goal.

[a]The goals variable is in the process of being coded for this country and thus no data are available at present.

Turning to the long-range category, we observe that France, Japan, Switzerland, West Germany, and Zambia initiated the greatest proportion of their events with a long-range time frame for goal fulfillment. Almost half of the events of these nations that contained a goal considered goals with long-range possibilities for achievement. Several explanations for these findings suggest themselves. In the case of Switzerland, its independence, neutral posture, and participation in various international organizations may have enabled the Swiss government to focus on longer-range objectives. The latter rationale applies as well to France, Japan, and West Germany, which were major actors in such regional international organizations as the Organization for Economic Cooperation and Development (OECD) and/or NATO. Moreover, for these nations development may be accompanied by more time to consider long-range goals. Finally, Zambia's longer-term goal focus may be due to its long-standing concern with the intractable problems of Southern Africa.

These descriptions suggest the face validity of time frame for goal realization. Although further conceptual development and refinement of the measure are necessary, we believe that time frame has potential as a measure of foreign policy behavior.

Beneficiaries

Conceptualization. Because goals represent desired future conditions in the international system, they benefit one or more international actors. Beneficiaries are most often thought of as being internal to the acting nation—the government or the domestic public. It is rare that a decision maker professes goals that do not benefit his society at least indirectly. The most critical of these benefits are national survival, territorial integrity, and protection of the population, which appear in nearly all substantive classifications of goals.

The concept of the national interest also suggests the significance of domestic beneficiaries. Decision makers act on the basis of their estimate of what is best for the country, of what is in the national interest. Whether these estimates represent subjective judgments or detached analyses, policymakers' choices are justified because they benefit the government or the domestic public (Morgenthau, 1951; Lerche, 1961).

But often decision makers engage in foreign policy behaviors that benefit entities external to the acting nation—other nations, groups or mass publics in other societies, or international organizations and alliances. External beneficiaries are central to understanding the formation of international political communities. The integration of political communities requires both citizen loyalty and consensus on issues of citizens in the various countries. Additionally, consensus is a product of substantive agreement on the appropriate solutions to common problems (Jacob and Toscano, 1964). From either perspective, the development of shared loyalties or substantive agreement is linked to the belief that what benefits one benefits all. As mutual relevance increases, the potential for international community increases (see Cobb and Elder, 1970).

The emerging literature concerning political and economic interdependence forecasts new leadership styles and changing conceptions of the national interest. As the need for policy coordination becomes more pronounced, an interpretation of the national interest that includes external beneficiaries becomes more critical for the solution of common problems. This phenomenon may occur more readily within fragmented political regimes such as the United States than in coherent regimes, such as France, which have a tradition of centralized politics (see Keohane and Nye, 1977). As we argued earlier, the presence of multiple bureaucratic actors in fragmented political regimes leads us to expect multiple interpretations of the national interest and multiple definitions of beneficiaries.

Beneficiaries, similar to time frame for goal realization, are identified in the context of a specific event. Entities which are beneficiaries in the context of one event may not be beneficiaries in the context of a subsequent event, although the substance of the goal may remain constant. This event-to-event variation enables us to monitor variations in beneficiaries across time.

The beneficiaries measure describes the relationship between the actor in the present situation and the desired objective, in terms of who benefits if the goal is fulfilled. The value of the beneficiaries measure is its potential as an indicator of national orientation. Variations in the number and range of beneficiaries across time may indicate changing national orientations. How inwardly or outwardly oriented is the government? Is the government interested in what happens to others outside its own boundaries? These are some of the questions that information on beneficiaries can help us to address.

Operationalization. Beneficiaries have been identified through information provided in the CREON substantive problem area coding scheme.[2] For each event, the coder identifies at least one problem or "discrepancy between what is or what is expected in the future and what one prefers. What is preferred involves one or more goals which in turn represent basic values" (C. Hermann, 1974: 1). The coder then asks what desirable conditions or values the problem affects. Response to this question is in terms of one of five substantive value categories: security/military, economic wealth, respect/status, well-being/welfare, and enlightenment. These categories describe, respectively, physical safety; tangible, material wealth; image of self in relation to others; quality of life; and access to and possession of transferable knowledge. Since there may be multiple problems in a single event, a single basic value is coded for each identified problem.[3]

Beneficiaries have been identified by addressing two questions: Whose basic value is being jeopardized? Who will benefit if the problem is solved? For each problem and value the coder identifies the entities that will benefit if the problem is solved. There are six types of beneficiaries: (1) the acting government or its entire society; (2) citizens or groups in the actor's nation; (3) external governments or entire national societies; (4) citizens or groups in nations other than the actor's; (5) the actor and other nations temporarily grouped together; or (6) alliance, regional, or global organizations. Notice that just as a single event may be coded as involving multiple problems and values, so also a single event can have multiple beneficiaries— at least one beneficiary per problem.

Table 6.4 presents sample CREON events that have been coded for each of the beneficiary categories. Although we believe that these events accord with our notions of actor, external entities, and actor and external entities beneficiaries, we encourage the reader to make his or her own judgment concerning the face validity of the beneficiaries measure.

TABLE 6.4
Sample CREON Events Coded for Type of Beneficiary

1.	*Event:* (06-30-60)	India's Minister of Steel, Mines, and Fuel announces that 100 oil experts from the Soviet Union will come to India to help establish an oil production industry.
	Beneficiary:	Acting government/society
2.	*Event:* (06-30-67)	Soviet Union sends a protest note to the United States charging that U.S. planes bombed a Soviet merchant ship in Haiphong Harbor.
	Beneficiary:	Citizens or group in acting nation
3.	*Event:* (10-30-62)	New Zealand's delegate to the UN General Assembly votes against a resolution sponsored by the Soviet Union to remove Taiwan from the United Nations and install the People's Republic of China in its place.
	Beneficiary:	External government/society
4.	*Event:* (06-14-60)	Ghana agrees with sanction adopted by the Third Conference of Independent African States which includes severance of diplomatic relations with South Africa.
	Beneficiary:	Citizens or groups in external society
5.	*Event:* (05-27-60)	Japan signs a one-year trade agreement with Taiwan to export iron and steel products, machinery, ships, rolling stock, textiles, farm and marine products, and to import crude sugar, salt, bananas, and canned pineapple.
	Beneficiary:	Acting nation and others in a temporary grouping
6.	*Event:* (05-09-60)	Prime Minister Diefenbaker agrees with the Conference of Commonwealth Prime Ministers to admit Nigeria to the Commonwealth after it gains independence on 10-01-60.
	Beneficiary:	Alliance, regional, or global organization

Empirical characteristics. Table 6.5 presents the frequency distribution for the beneficiaries measure across the events in the CREON data set. Notice that while 22 percent of the events benefit the acting government and 29 percent of the events benefit external governments, nearly 50 percent benefit the actor *and* others (including international organizations and alliances). These patterns suggest that a broad interpretation of the national interest may be warranted.

Let us examine the distribution of beneficiaries for the 38 CREON nations, as presented in Table 6.6. Those nations that engaged in foreign policy behaviors which benefited themselves primarily (those with 35 percent or more of their problems in the actor beneficiary category) tended to be isolated from the international system or tended to be involved in conflicts during the 1959-1968 period—that is, China (PRC), Cuba, East Germany, India, and Israel. The Soviet Union, China, and the United States, as well as most of the African nations in our sample, engaged in foreign policy behaviors that benefited external entities.

Major actors like the United States, the Soviet Union, and China, given their capabilities and the extent of their participation in the international system, are

TABLE 6.5
Distribution of Events by Type of Beneficiary

Beneficiary	Relative Frequency (%)	Absolute Frequency
Actor:	21.7	2632
Actor Government/Society	20.2	2455
Actor Groups/Citizens	1.5	177
External Entities:	29.0	3515
External Government/Society	21.3	2579
External Groups/Citizens	7.7	936
Actor and External Entities:	49.3	5979
Actor and Others	28.2	3420
International Organizations	21.1	2559
Unidentifiable [a]	0.0	3

[a] The beneficiaries for three problems could not be classified.

likely to engage in behaviors that benefit external entities. But the nature of these benefits probably varies. The United States and the Soviet Union, for example, have provided political and military benefits to external entities through their participation in NATO and the Warsaw Pact Organization, respectively. Both of these nations have adopted foreign aid strategies that, in effect, provide political benefits to themselves while providing economic benefits to recipients.

The emphasis on external entities by the Ivory Coast, Guinea, Ghana, Uganda, Kenya, and Zambia may reflect the increased interaction which occurred among many of the emerging African states during the 1960s. In most instances, the anticolonial postures of these states provided ideological and political benefits to all emerging states. In addition, the development of regional organizations such as the Organization of African Unity tended to benefit all participants.

The results for the combined actor and external beneficiary category are more difficult to interpret. Before looking at the data, one might expect that major actors—or those with extensive capabilities—would engage in foreign policy behaviors that benefit multiple entities, both domestic and foreign. Underlying this expectation is the assumption that, as the range of beneficiaries expands for a particular event, the capabilities of the actor must necessarily expand. But this does not appear to be the case. Those nations that engaged in foreign policy behaviors which benefited both domestic and foreign entities tended to be smaller nations or those that were active in international organizations such as the United Nations, the European Economic Community, and the Organization of African Unity during the decade 1959-1968. Multiple beneficiaries make sense for many of these nations, particularly since the benefits can be transferred in a multilateral forum, thus making more efficient use of scarce resources.

TABLE 6.6
Beneficiaries: Distribution by CREON Nations

CREON Nation	Actor	External	Actor and External
Belgium	06.9 (26) [a]	19.6 (74)	73.5 (277)
Canada	13.5 (52)	33.6 (129)	52.9 (203)
Chile	17.6 (36)	20.5 (42)	62.0 (127)
China (PRC)	37.7 (190)	35.5 (179)	26.8 (135)
Costa Rica	13.1 (21)	18.8 (30)	68.1 (109)
Cuba	64.7 (209)	11.8 (38)	23.5 (76)
Czechoslovakia	18.4 (38)	26.7 (55)	54.9 (113)
East Germany	37.9 (71)	10.7 (20)	51.4 (96)
Egypt	21.5 (97)	29.0 (131)	49.5 (224)
France	12.4 (105)	28.9 (245)	58.8 (500)
Ghana	10.4 (28)	40.9 (110)	48.7 (131)
Guinea	10.2 (21)	41.5 (85)	48.3 (99)
Iceland	12.9 (20)	21.9 (34)	65.2 (101)
India	42.5 (209)	24.2 (119)	33.3 (164)
Israel	57.9 (199)	09.9 (34)	32.2 (111)
Italy	07.0 (29)	20.0 (84)	73.1 (307)
Japan	20.3 (54)	25.6 (68)	54.1 (144)
Kenya	13.7 (13)	44.2 (42)	42.1 (40)
Lebanon	17.9 (26)	24.1 (35)	57.9 (84)
Mexico	15.6 (29)	18.3 (34)	66.1 (123)
New Zealand	06.1 (12)	31.4 (62)	62.4 (123)
Norway	08.6 (19)	25.8 (57)	65.6 (145)
Philippines	14.8 (29)	33.3 (65)	51.8 (101)
Poland	21.0 (49)	21.5 (50)	57.5 (134)
Soviet Union	21.9 (218)	39.4 (394)	38.7 (386)
Spain	27.6 (46)	20.4 (34)	52.1 (87)
Switzerland	09.5 (7)	06.8 (5)	83.8 (62)
Thailand	09.4 (15)	29.0 (46)	61.6 (98)
Tunisia	12.1 (33)	35.9 (98)	52.0 (142)
Turkey	20.5 (64)	25.7 (80)	53.9 (168)
Uganda	09.7 (14)	38.6 (56)	51.7 (75)
United States	25.1 (480)	39.1 (746)	35.8 (684)
Uruguay	11.9 (16)	29.1 (39)	59.0 (79)
Venezuela	24.5 (50)	19.6 (40)	55.9 (114)
West Germany	20.2 (130)	16.2 (104)	63.7 (410)
Yugoslavia	13.4 (34)	28.5 (72)	58.1 (147)
Zambia	32.5 (25)	37.7 (29)	29.9 (23)

[a] The first number here is the relative frequency of the particular beneficiary category for the nation. The second number, in parentheses, is the absolute frequency of the beneficiary category for the nation.

For most of the CREON countries the percentages suggest an orientation with regard to who benefits from a foreign policy action. The nations are either oriented toward themselves, toward others, or have both an internal and external orientation—a "let's share" attitude. With one-half or more of their events falling into one of these categories, the governments suggest their orientations. There are, however, several nations whose events are more evenly divided among the beneficiary categories or, at least, fairly evenly divided between two of the categories. The events for China, the United States, and the Soviet Union are roughly evenly divided among the three types of beneficiaries. The behavior of these governments may suggest a certain pragmatism—"deal with issues concerning goals where and how you can." Three of the African countries—Ghana, Guinea, and Kenya—show almost equal behavior focused on external beneficiaries as on themselves and external beneficiaries. These governments share when they can but are not timid in participating in others' problems—particularly what they perceive as all-African issues—when such issues may prove relevant to them at a later time.

These data reflect the potential of beneficiaries as an indicator of national foreign policy orientations. Changes in the focus and range of beneficiaries extant in the international system have potential as an indicator of fundamental transformations in the international system. For example, variations in the focus and range of beneficiaries may indicate a shift from bipolar to multipolar power structures. In short, beneficiaries provide another perspective on the relationship between foreign policy goals and behavior.

SUMMARY

In this chapter we have outlined an unorthodox approach to the development of goal-based measures of foreign policy behavior. This approach assumes that goal properties which characterize the context within which values are expressed provide theoretically compelling and empirically viable alternatives to substantive or content properties of goals and that these dimensions can be used to characterize foreign policy behavior.

The approach we have outlined has advantages and disadvantages. The advantages are that goal properties are accorded deserved attention and that foreign policy behavior measures are constructed which assess the status of national goals, thus providing potential indicators of foreign policy performance. The primary disadvantage is that the content of the goals is neglected. But, on balance, we believe that goal properties merit consideration as alternative characterizations of foreign policy behavior.

NOTES

1. In the Technical Appendix at the end of this book, the editors have included descriptions of the CREON variables relevant to forming certain of the foreign policy behavior measures that are discussed in this and succeeding chapters. In addition to a description of the variable, a frequency distribution across categories and an intercoder reliability are reported. At the beginning of this appendix, the reader will find a list of the variables with an identifying number to help in finding a specific variable.

2. For a more detailed description of the substantive problem area classification see Chapter 4.

3. We have focused in this analysis on the first problem for each event. Some 90 percent of the events were concerned only with a single problem.

Instruments of Foreign Policy

In 1973 the Arab members of the Organization of Petroleum Exporting Countries (OPEC) engaged in an embargo against the United States and the Netherlands and subsequently raised the price of their product to all countries. Few observers would deny that significant near-term benefits accrued to the members of OPEC as a result of these actions. In retrospect, it might be asked why this effective cartel did not engage in such activities earlier. The answer to such an inquiry usually refers to the internal divisions among the Arab states, the lack of mutual trust, and the absence of the necessary skills to form an effective coalition.

A recurrent stumbling block in arms control negotiations between the United States and the Soviet Union has been verification of agreements. On-site inspection by teams from one side of the territory of the other has long been characterized both as an essential means of assuring compliance (U.S.A.) and as an unacceptable intrusion on national sovereignty that could serve the primary purpose of espionage (USSR). The verification issue stalemated many possible areas of agreement until both sides developed satellite reconnaissance capability that routinely allowed each to photograph completely and with amazing resolution the territory of the other. The satellites are complemented by sophisticated radar and other monitoring devices for weapons testing. The Strategic Arms Limitation Talks (SALT) and agreements emanating from them have depended on these capabilities.

Both of these illustrations concern the formation of new instruments for the conduct of foreign policy. In one case, the instruments primarily involved the forging of new human skills and organizational arrangements (creating a coalition with sufficient internal cohesion to use such economic procedures as embargo, price-setting, and production rates); whereas the other depended on the emergence of new technological resources. Both developments, however, led to altered policies pursued by the countries involved. The two examples reveal several basic

—if sometimes neglected—points. The objectives or needs of national governments and societies may go unfulfilled until the appropriate instruments are devised and applied. Thus, understanding foreign policy behavior requires careful attention to the means or instruments available and used. A second point is that the instruments of foreign policy affect the nature of policy.

This chapter considers the possibility of classifying foreign policy behaviors according to the instruments involved. It considers how instruments might be conceptualized and how they might be used to enhance our understanding of foreign policy activities. As with other chapters in this volume, one possible way of operationalizing instruments using event data is described and the results displayed.

Before proceeding further it may prove instructive to identify four assumptions that underlie this examination of the instruments of foreign policy:

(1) A single foreign policy action may simultaneously involve more than one instrument.
(2) When foreign policymaking is examined as a process involving different stages, various instruments may be involved during different phases of the process.
(3) The specific categorization of foreign policy instruments can be varied to fit the questions of concern to the analyst.
(4) The classification of instruments can be used either as a set of dependent variables (that to be explained) or as a set of independent variables (that which explains something else).

CONCEPTUALIZATION

Instruments constitute the inventory of means or capabilities used by a government or other foreign policy actor in the formation and implementation of its foreign policies. From an analytic point of view, instruments offer a way of classifying various foreign policy activities according to the devices and procedures employed in the pursuit of some substantive issue or problem. Two broad categories of foreign policy instruments can be identified—human skills and physical resources. Skills consist of abilities to perform certain tasks that cannot be satisfactorily performed without a combination of knowledge, practice, and aptitude. Skills relevant to foreign policy vary with the substantive requirements of the issues involved. In today's world applicable skills can range from leading troops in combat to analyzing the consequences of international currency transactions, from negotiating a trade agreement on the most favorable terms to instructing farmers in other countries on the use of new agricultural procedures.

Complementing the skill aspects of instruments are the physical resources. Resources applicable to foreign policy can be natural commodities such as ores, petroleum, or grain. Alternatively, they can be manufactured products formed or altered by humans, such as medicines, computers, and weapons.

In complex societies professions often form around skills that are used repeatedly (examples are the armed services and the foreign service), and industries or organizations of various kinds emerge around valued resources (for example, extraction industries or banks). Often foreign policy instruments will involve a mix of human skills and physical resources. Of course, not all the skills or resources available to a society will be at the disposal of a government or other actor, nor will all the instruments available to a government necessarily be directed to the handling of its external affairs. In this chapter we will be concerned only with the skills and resources that a government or other actor can bring to bear on its foreign policy activities.

Consideration of several of the previously mentioned assumptions may further the conceptualization of instruments. If one treats the process of foreign policy-making as divisible into rough stages or phases, then different instruments can often be found in use at various stages. Suppose we divide the policy process simply into the predecision or preparation phase, the decision and announcement or revelation of decision phase, and the implementation phase. It is relatively easy to recognize the role of instruments in the final or implementation stage of foreign policy activity. Often, however, one can find evidence of their presence at earlier points in the process. The earlier example of satellite reconnaissance can be elaborated to illustrate the point. The scientific and technological skills and resources involved in acquiring information on an adversary's current strategic weapons configuration may be used to develop a specific kind of arms control proposal (the preparation stage). Using political skills, a president may dramatically reveal at a press conference that efforts to reach a new arms limitation agreement will be initiated (decision or announcement stage). The actual conduct of the negotiations then involves individuals and groups using diplomatic skills (the implementation stage).

Not only can multiple instruments be employed at various points in the policy process, but it also seems reasonable to assume that multiple skills and resources may co-occur in any single phase. For example, George et al. (1971) have described the use of coercive diplomacy in the conduct of foreign affairs. Coercive diplomacy entails the use of force as part of a signal of intentions. Almost by definition, the implementation of such a policy involves the nearly simultaneous use of both military and diplomatic instruments. In sum, there is no necessary one-to-one relationship between one instance of policy and one instrument.

Although a variety of terms are used to describe what here has been designated as the concept of instrumentalities, the equivalent terms occupy a central location in virtually every inventory or survey of foreign policy activities. In his basic textbook, K. Holsti (1977) refers to the "instruments of policy" and includes chapters on diplomatic bargaining, propaganda, economic techniques, clandestine actions, and military intervention. The Sprouts (1971) refer to the "instruments of statecraft" and develop a classification based on the distinction between human and nonhuman instruments. Using a concept related to instruments, Wilkinson (1969) devotes a chapter to capabilities which emphasizes economic, military, and political capabilities. When one turns from textbook materials to research efforts, the studies of instruments tend to concentrate on a single type and thus limit the possibility of making comparisons. Among the numerous possible examples of studies of a single broad type of instruments, the following illustrations seem representative: foreign assistance (Montgomery, 1967; Nelson, 1968), propaganda (Barghoorn, 1964; Coombs, 1964), military (Janowitz, 1960; Kahn, 1965), and diplomacy (Campbell, 1971; Bailey, 1968). Yarmolinsky's (1969) examination of the uses and relative effects of the U.S.

Departments of State and Defense is the type of analysis that begins to perform the comparative analysis of instruments. Despite the limited research dealing with skills and resources as a general phenomena, it is not difficult to postulate the significance various modes or instruments have on the output of foreign policy-making as well as other aspects of the decision process.

POSSIBLE SIGNIFICANCE OF
INSTRUMENTS CLASSICICATION AND VARIABLES

It is possible to classify the instruments used by various national governments in many ways. The utility of a particular classification will depend on the nature of the relationship between a given classificatory scheme and the exact questions of interest. Later in this chapter, for example, eight broad categories will be examined: (1) diplomacy, (2) domestic politics, (3) military, (4) intelligence, (5) economics, (6) science/technology, (7) promotion, and (8) natural resources. Regardless of the specific categories, however, some general observations can be made indicating why knowledge about the instruments of foreign policy could be worthwhile.

If certain conditions are fulfilled, knowledge about instruments has value for policymaking. Assume that we develop some understanding about the probable effects of using various instruments to influence others. When a government uses some discretion about what instruments or mix of instruments it uses, then the combination of instruments can be orchestrated for best results. Instruments frequently fall into that class of variables that is readily manipulable by governments and other foreign policy actors. Policymakers often are better able to control which instruments of policy are used than they are to change the nature of the countries residing on their borders or the mineral deposits within their own country. In short, instruments are accessible levers for altering policy. Therefore, understanding what leads a government to rely on certain skills and resources and what consequences follow from a given use pattern could have very practical results.

For policymakers and analysts alike the significance of knowing the nature of foreign policy instruments will depend on the manner in which the classification is shaped to form variables. Let us consider several types of variables that could be created using nominal categories of instruments such as the eight noted above.

In discussing social science research methods, Kaplan has suggested the "law of the instrument" which is well remembered as a result of his characterization of the law through an analogy: "Give a small boy a hammer, and he will find that everything he encounters needs pounding" (Kaplan, 1964: 28). Does a similar phenomenon exist in the conduct of foreign policy? Governments that invest heavily in the development and maintenance of a certain set of skills and resources will tend to apply them widely—perhaps excessively. Wilkinson seems to suggest exactly such an effect with respect to the instruments of foreign policy. He observes that states "whose military means are notably better than their non-military capabilities are subject to a strong pressure to militarize their foreign policies" (Wilkinson, 1969: 44-45). To explore the possibility that governments or other foreign policy actors may tend to emphasize some instrument of policy to the exclusion of others, one might develop an "index of instrument concentration" variable. This variable could be calculated with some measure of inequality such as the Gini Index. In a simple application, a government with a low concentration index would tend to use each category of instruments with approximately equal frequency; whereas high concentration would result in primary dependence on one or two categories with clear subordination of the others. It might be observed that the problems that a government faces could force such a concentration. If, for example, the very security of the nation were threatened by a lingering border dispute with a hostile neighbor, then concentration on military instruments might seem a reasonable expectation. Indeed, the simple index of instrument concentration might reveal something about the external environment of the actor as it has been interpreted by the policymakers.

An additional use of the concentration index might be established if one controlled for substantive problem area. (That measure is discussed in Chapter 4.) Do some actors compared with others have a substantially higher index of instrument concentration when dealing with comparable types of problems? Such a finding might be indicative of certain dispositions of the individuals or collectivities that formulate policy. Do some governments or ministries rely on a small set of standard operating procedures that are relatively invariant regardless of the problem they face? The answers could be important for determining how effectively a government will handle any sudden changes in its environment.

Another variable that could be constructed with a set of instrument categories might be labeled "multiple instrument actions." With such a variable, a value would be determined for each foreign policy action or event based on the number of different kinds of instruments involved in that one action. If instruments were grouped into a set of broad categories (such as the eight suggested at the beginning of this section), the highest value would be achieved if a single action included every possible instrumentality category. Assuming that every action must involve at least one category, the lowest score on this variable would be one.

A number of authors have discussed the general problem of complexity in political decision making (for example, Simon, 1968; Brunner and Brewer, 1971; Steinbruner, 1974). Certainly the policy difficulties they describe characterize the conduct of foreign policy. Usually complexity is defined as a relationship between the demands of the environment and the capabilities of the actor. It is evident that instruments, as an indicator of capacity, could be an integral part of such a definition of complexity. One might use the measure of multiple instrument actions in combination with some estimate of the demands of the environment with which the action is intended to deal. For example, environmental requirements might be estimated by the number of external entities involved or by a judgmental ranking of the degree of uncertainty associated with the problem being addressed relative to other problems. The result would be an indicator of complexity. A government using a restricted range of instruments to deal with a highly demanding problem might give observers reason for caution in expecting successful coping.

The multiple instrument actions measure also may reveal things about internal decision processes. A foreign policy initiative rated as a high multiple instrument action probably will create many more demands for coordination and integrated activities than another action with a low score. Furthermore, a government that repeatedly engages in high multiple instrument actions probably has more organizational integration and consensus among its involved ministries than a government that attempts such feats only occasionally.

Further insights into internal operations might be possible if one could determine in what phase of the decision process various instruments were invoked. As an initial attempt, we can distinguish between instruments involved during the preparation for a decision (that is, predecision period), the announcement of a decision, and the implementation of a decision. If we find a high score for multiple instruments during the preparation stage, it might suggest the seriousness with which the government attended to the problem. Given the conflict -producing processes frequently associated with bureaucratic politics, the use of numerous skills and resources during the preparation stage—indicating possible involvement of multiple agencies—followed by the limitation to one instrument (and probably one agency) during the implementation stage could suggest a number of agencies or ministries whose personnel are disgruntled at having been cut out of the action.

These two variables, an index of instrument concentration and a measure of multiple instrument actions, suggest the possible significance of classifying foreign policy activities by the combination of skills and resources involved. Both of these variables could be employed with the feedback measure, discussed elsewhere in this volume, to determine whether certain instruments or combination of instruments increased the likelihood of acceptance by others of an actor's proposal on a given issue. Of course, the variables discussed and the insights their use might provide are intended to be suggestive rather than exhaustive. Numerous other uses are possible.

In addition to indicating the significance of instruments by proposing how they might be formed into useful measures, we can also enhance our understanding of foreign policy through the exploration of certain questions about the configuration of instruments. Below are five questions, together with brief commentaries, that may indicate fruitful avenues for research on the consequences of using certain instruments in the conduct of foreign policy.

(1) Under what conditions will a government or other foreign policy actor experience pressure to use a set of skills and resources once they have been acquired? Among the issues raised by this question is the possible effect of the magnitude of expenditure invested to acquire the instrument (the need to justify the great cost) and of the bureaucratic vigor of an organization whose mission centers on the use of selected instruments.

(2) Are instruments that are more directly and uniquely susceptible to government control in a given society more frequently used? This question suggests the possibility that ease of access rather than appropriateness for a given problem may influence the use of certain skills and resources.

(3) Are certain types of instrumentalities, which may require less societal complexity to develop and maintain, more likely to dominate the foreign policy activities of less-developed countries? Perhaps this question should be prefaced by another asking whether some instruments are less demanding to develop. It would seem that diplomatic and political instruments are among the least demanding in terms of societal development and that the scientific -technological may be at the other extreme.

(4) Are there significant differences in the time required to mobilize various kinds of skills and resources and the time necessary to employ them in an

effective manner? Since the problems foreign policy actors encounter vary in the immediacy of their time requirements, the issue arises whether a government may face an incongruency between the instruments available to it and the requirements of the problems it faces.

(5) To what extent does an outcome regarded as successful by the initiating policymakers lead in the future to repeated and increased use of the instrument originally employed? The exploration of this issue includes not only the application of the original instrument to similar future problems but also its extension into other types of problems.

DEVELOPING SPECIFIC NOMINAL CATEGORIES

Up to this point the use of instrumentalities for studying foreign policy activities has been discussed without the detailed examination of specific types of skills and resources. This section describes eight possible categories of instrumentalities and reports how they are being applied in one research effort. It should be remembered, of course, that other ways of categorizing instrumentalities are quite possible, including more complex schemes that might subdivide these broad groupings.

Diplomatic instruments are skills and resources used by a government to represent itself and its citizens to foreign governments and other international actors (public and private). This category includes the formulation and administration of nonviolent aspects of foreign policy, particularly (a) the presentation of the government's position on external affairs, (b) the protection of its citizens and their property abroad and the regulation of their dealings with those from outside the country, and (c) the negotiation on behalf of the government with other international actors. Diplomatic resources include the network of embassies, legations, and consulates overseas and their connecting communications network, as well as existing treaties or other agreements that involve commitments with international actors. Individuals with the relevant skills (for example, knowledge of foreign entities, representational and bargaining abilities) almost invariably are members of the diplomatic corps and the foreign ministry or are officials appointed by and directly responsible to the country's highest political authority.

Domestic political instruments refer to those skills and resources that a government uses for programs within the society and ultimately to maintain itself in office when such a determination depends on the support of domestic groups and collectivities. They include the methods to control or obtain support from within the government or party, as well as methods applicable to the entire society. Domestic political instruments can be employed to influence domestic issues as well as those dealing with foreign affairs, but for the present purposes such instruments become salient when it is necessary to win domestic support—or at least control domestic opposition—with regard to a foreign policy matter. One of the most important skills involves practical knowledge in the operation of the domestic political system which, in turn, may require such other skills as legal techniques, budgetary processes, and administrative procedures. Financial and organizational capabilities are among the important resources which include budgets, taxation, political parties, courts and judicial rulings, interest groups, media, and police units.

Military skills and resources are those capabilities applicable to threat, use, or control of organized physical violence against others in the name of the state. Such instruments include the maintenance of military forces, their activities, personnel, equipment, and so forth. This category also includes those skills and resources that characterize the management, planning, and deployment of military personnel and equipment. Examples of such techniques are weapons development; weapons control; increasing or decreasing military capabilities; airlifting, sealifting, and other support operations; threats of force; requests for and administration of military assistance; military planning activity in alliances; joint "war games"; or treaties involving military activity or defense.

Intelligence instruments are skills and resources used in the collection and interpretation of the capabilities, plans, attitudes, and actions of other international actors located, at least in part, outside the political jurisdiction of the national government. Such instruments include the extralegal operations usually performed in a covert manner that are designed to influence other actors but that the initiating government would seek to deny knowledge of, or responsibility for, if detected. A variety of analytic and observational skills are applicable to the intelligence function. These are talents that can be used to maintain surveillance of foreign actors or to interpret numerous indicators of the capabilities or intentions of international actors. Resources include informants, complex encoding and decoding devices, varied reconnaissance equipment, and materials generated by the actors being examined. It should be noted that individuals in other professions (for example, military or diplomatic) may engage in intelligence activities; when they do so, their activities should be classified as involving intelligence instruments. Furthermore, the skills and resources used in clandestine intelligence operations may be borrowed from other instruments, such as the military or propaganda agencies.

Economic instruments are distinguished by activities concerning the allocation and management of the material wealth of nations or their governments or other international groups. Such activities involve the production, distribution, and consumption of goods and services or the procedures for exchanging wealth, including the fiscal matters pertaining to monetary transactions. Examples of the techniques involved are requests for and the administration of loans, credits, and other forms of economic assistance; the negotiation and regulation of trade and economic transfers; the procedures covering tariff arrangements and other trade barriers; the use of economic sanctions and boycotts; the establishment of trade preferences such as most-favored-nation treatment; and the mechanisms for relating the value of one currency relative to others.

Scientific/technological instruments share a common foundation in that body of knowledge produced by the generally accepted methods of science. Scientific skills and resources involve activities pertaining to the basic corpus of theory, empirical results, and the procedures for their continuous investigation and extension. Technological skills and resources concern the application of the existing body of scientific knowledge for practical problem solving rather than for the extension of fundamental knowledge. Individuals trained in the physical, biological, and certain behavioral sciences are part of the cadre of professionals with scientific and technological skills as well as those trained in such applied areas as medicine and engineering. The resources of scientific/technological instruments are widespread in industrialized societies and range from the vast array of scientific apparatus to the seemingly innumerable products of technology. Among the applications of scientific/technological instrumentalities in foreign affairs are such familiar undertakings as the establishment and maintenance of international satellite communications, explorations of the oceans for resource extraction, educational exchange programs, population projects, agricultural and other technical assistance programs, and more exotic enterprises such as joint ventures in space.

Promotive instrumentalities involve propaganda as well as ideological and cultural activities. Foreign policy propaganda means the purposive effort to persuade another entity(ies) to support or adopt particular opinions, attitudes, sets of beliefs, or actions with respect to some international actor and its policies. Ideological activities are undertakings by governments or ruling parties that prescribe a preferred comprehensive program of social and political action that expresses a "desired and correct" mode of operation for the social/political community. Cultural activities include the manifestations in various forms of learned behavior patterns of any specific nationality, race, or people regarded as expressing the traditional or indigenous way of life. Promotive activities are normally directed at human collectivities other than external national governments—general publics, specialized elites, or minority groups in one or more foreign countries. Examples of promotive activities include cultural exchanges, the use of symbols to project positive images of one's social/political/cultural community, the use of symbols to project negative images of an opponent's community, and appeals to people in other countries with common religious, ethnic, or cultural backgrounds.

Natural resources instruments involve the potential or actual use of natural resources, or knowledge thereof, in the conduct of foreign policy activities. Skills and resources used in the development and protection of natural resources as well as their cultivation or extraction are included. No assumption is made concerning the level of expertise involved in these activities (for example, primitive farming could be included). Resources include not only the natural products (for example, fossil fuels, food, ores, timber, water) but also equipment necessary for their acquisition and processing. Skills involve practical knowledge and abilities concerning the nature and use of these natural resources and the methods for their development and use. A potential overlap exists between this category of instruments and those classified as scientific/technological. There is an important distinction, however. The natural resources category makes no necessary presumption of the application of the methods of science. In some parts of the world enormous technological investments have been made to capture and use natural resources, but in other areas the use of natural resources has not necessarily involved modern technology. Thus, the so-called rice bowl in Southeast Asia flourished as a significant natural resource before the introduction of scientific methods of agriculture. The government of a developing country may engage in considerable foreign policy activity using a recognized natural resource as an instrument even before it has the capability to employ that resource—an example is the Mexican Government and its oil reserves.

ANALYZING INSTRUMENTS WITH EVENT DATA

The foreign policy events in the CREON Project were content analyzed for types of instruments using the eight categories reviewed in the previous section. In principle, it was assumed that every event must have at least one of the eight types of instruments. In actuality, some events were not codable because they provided insufficient information to determine what instrument(s) may have been involved. Any event could involve more than one type of instrument. As a result, 22,738 instruments were identified in the 12,710 events for which there was sufficient information to make a judgment about instrumentalities.

Table 7.1 reproduces seven illustrative CREON events and reports the categories of instruments coded for each one. Inspection of the table shows that all the coding of instruments was done in the context of one of the stages of the policy process. A basic three-stage characterization of the process was used similar to the one described earlier in the chapter. Each instrument found to be present in an event was coded as occurring in (a) the preparation stage prior to the decision represented in the event, (b) the announcement stage when the decision was revealed, or (c) the subsequent implementation of the decision. On the basis of preliminary experience we decided to permit up to three separate instruments to be coded in each stage.[1]

Because the operationalization of the stages or phases of the process involved a concept of time to differentiate among the three, some elaboration may be useful. The stages of the policy process were identified as falling into the past (always preparation), the future (always implementation), or the present (either announcement or implementation). The stipulated date(s) on which a given event occurred were treated as the present, and in the majority of cases that time frame was classifiable as the announcement phase of the process. Most events are dated from when they became public knowledge, and announcements are often the mode for the revelation of governmental foreign policy. The form of disclosure frequently is some sort of written or oral communication—for example, a speech, interview, joint communique, document publication, press release, or unauthorized disclosure.

Sometimes, however, an event is revealed by the direct observation of government activity by individuals outside the government—media, private citizens, or external actors. In most of these cases, the observation (and the dating of the event) corresponds to the implementation phase, and both the preparation and the announcement (or decision, if no announcement occurred) are in the past. In either case, any disclosure about the planning or preliminary work necessary for the event is in the past, relative to the time of disclosure.

In short, events are revealed at either the announcement stage or the implementation stage. Any cues about the skills and resources involved at present (the date of the event) were coded as pertaining to one or the other depending on the type of event. If the event was an announcement, any references to prior activity necessary to make ready for the announcement were scrutinized for the identification of instruments used in the preparation. References to necessary future actions were examined for instruments needed for the implementation. If the event occurred as implementation, any past references were first divided into preparation and announcement stages, and the search was then conducted for instruments applicable to each.

Was it possible to instruct individuals to differentiate among the three policy process phases and the eight instrument categories in a consistent and reliable fashion? A sample of 61 events was randomly drawn from the CREON data set and examined by each of four coders. Researchers then computed the Krippendorff (1971) coefficient of agreement (described in Chapter 2 as an extremely useful measure of multiple coder reliability for data such as these). The coefficients of agreement for the three stages and for the eight broad categories of instruments

TABLE 7.1

Illustrative Coding of Instrumentalities Using CREON Events

Event	Coding of Event
1. *April 20, 1963.* In a speech to a domestic audience in Havana, Cuban Premier Fidel Castro asserts that the governments of Cuba and the USSR learned from their sources in the exiled Cuban Revolutionary Council of plans for a second invasion of Cuba supported by the United States.	*Preparation* = intelligence (asserted basis for statement is intelligence gleaned from Cuban Revolutionary Council) *Announcement* = domestic/political/promotive (speech is directed, at least initially, to domestic audience in Havana, but speaker knows it will also be publicly monitored abroad) *Implementation* = none discernible
2. *January 7, 1965.* The government of France signs an agreement with the USSR to sell 250,000 tons of wheat, to be delivered between February and May of that year.	*Preparation* = economic and diplomatic (negotiating agreement entailed economic and diplomatic skills and resources) *Announcement* = diplomatic (signing international agreement is diplomatic instrumentality) *Implementation* = economic and natural resource (delivery of wheat will require economic and natural resource skills and resources)
3. *January 28, 1965.* East Germany endorses an agreement between COMECON and Yugoslavia establishing the basis for cooperation in the fields of foreign trade, currency, and financial relations, and scientific and technical research in the chemical, metallurgical, and engineering industries.	*Preparation* = diplomatic (German Democratic Republic's decision to endorse agreement follows diplomatic interactions with COMECON members and Yugoslavia) *Announcement* = diplomatic (ratification of international agreement entails diplomatic skills) *Implementation* = economic and scientific/technical (areas of cooperation specified require these instrumentalities)
4. *July 25, 1966.* In a joint communique with the NATO Defense Ministers, the Canadian Minister of Defense reaffirms the principle of an annual defense planning review for the ensuing five years and indicates that the next review will begin in January 1967.	*Preparation* = military (military skills were involved in the preparation for this statement) *Announcement* = diplomatic (communique used diplomatic skills) *Implementation* = military (the forthcoming planning review will entail military skills and resources)

(Continued)

TABLE 7.1 Continued

Event	Coding of Event
5. *September 25, 1966.* The government of Venezuela joins with other members of the International Bank for Reconstruction and Development in releasing the joint annual report of the IBRD and IDA which shows 12 new IDA loans totaling $284 million.	*Preparation* = economic and diplomatic (skills and resources of economic and diplomatic nature involved in report preparation and approval) *Announcement* = diplomatic *Implementation* = none discernible (loans entail economic implementation, but this event is annual report)
6. *April 19, 1967.* In a televised address, Cuban Premier Fidel Castro proclaims that Cuba will conduct a Holy War against the forces of United States imperialism throughout Latin America.	*Preparation* = none discernible *Announcement* = promotive and domestic/political (address involves major symbol manipulation to influence both domestic and external audiences) *Implementation* = none discernible (reference to Holy War too vague to code as requiring military)
7. *April 30, 1967.* At a public rally in Lusaka, Zambian President Kaunda states that security officials have been watching the activities of foreigners in Zambia who have been collecting information for the Rhodesian government.	*Preparation* = intelligence *Announcement* = domestic/political and promotive (symbol manipulation designed to influence domestic audience and alert foreign sources of Zambia's vigilance) *Implementation* = none discernible

were both .83. No systematic validity studies have been performed to date to determine whether either the process phases or the actual instrument categories capture the kind of phenomena associated with their intended meaning. The reader can form some personal judgment of the face validity of the instrument and stage categories by examining the coding of the sample of events in Table 7.1. Other indications of face validity also emerge in tabular material presented below.

Instrument Category and Policy Stage Distributions

Table 7.2 gives the frequency breakdowns for each type of instrument in the three policy stages. Cf all identified instruments, half occurred in the implementation stage, 43 percent concerned announcements, and less than seven percent dealt with the preparation phase.[2] The bottom of the table reveals that only about ten percent of all events could be coded for at least one instrument in the preparation phase. This finding is not surprising since preparation is almost never the immediate subject of an event. In giving information about what is happening now, the source often fails to add descriptive information about that earlier stage. Accordingly, one should be extremely cautious in interpreting the relative use of instruments in that stage of the policy process. Similarly, few instances of the use of the intelligence instrument were found in any stage (and most of those found applied to the United States), probably because governments do not normally point out when intelligence skills and resources are used.

Looking at the overall totals in Table 7.2, one notices that diplomatic instruments are by far the most frequently used. Economic and military instruments are a distant second and third, respectively. It might be recalled that McClelland and Hoggard (1969) found that roughly a third of all public international activity concerned participatory maintenance of the international system. Though diplomatic instruments would be frequently involved in other types of activity, they would likely be used almost exclusively in these persistent kinds of actions.

The distribution pattern changes, however, when different phases of the process are separately examined in Table 7.2. Economic instruments dominate the preparation stage among the relatively few events for which information existed. In the announcement phase diplomatic instruments prevail, with both promotive and domestic political instruments being used more often than they are in the other stages. There would appear to be a plausibility to this pattern of usage. Decisions in foreign affairs, and more particularly their announcement, are likely to be undertaken by those individuals and organizations having diplomatic, political, and propaganda skills and resources. By contrast, when it comes to implementation of foreign policy, economic and military instruments join with the prevailing diplomatic skills and resources as the most common types.

Use of Instruments by Countries

Table 7.3 displays the frequency and percentage of instruments in the eight categories for the 38 nations in the CREON Project during the decade 1959-1968.[3] The table permits cross-national comparison of the use of foreign policy instruments. One way to analyze the information in Table 7.3 is through a comparison of the relative activity of national governments using one type of instrument.

TABLE 7.2
Percentage and Frequency Distribution of Instruments by Process Stages

	Preparation		Announcement		Implementation		Totals	
	N	%	N	%	N	%	N	%
Diplomatic	275	18.0	8000	80.8	6150	54.4	14425	63.4
Domestic/Political	5	0.3	394	4.0	59	0.5	458	2.0
Military	117	7.7	363	3.7	1343	11.9	1823	8.0
Intelligence	54	3.5	4	0.0	31	0.3	89	0.4
Economic	1045	68.3	357	3.6	2893	25.6	4295	18.9
Scientific/Technological	25	1.6	10	0.1	490	4.3	525	2.3
Promotive	2	0.1	734	7.4	86	0.8	822	3.6
Natural Resources	6	0.4	35	0.4	260	2.3	301	1.3
Total N Instruments	1529	6.7	9897	43.5	11312	49.7	22738	
Total Classifiable Events	1376		8942		9354		12710	
Missing Events	11324		3768		3356			

TABLE 7.3
Distribution of Instruments in Sample of Events for 38 Nations

CREON Nation	Diplomatic % (N)	Domestic Political % (N)	Military % (N)	Intelligence % (N)	Economic % (N)	Scientific/ Technological % (N)	Promotive % (N)	Natural Resources % (N)
Belgium	58.2 (435)	1.1 (8)	4.6 (34)	.1 (1)	31.6 (236)	2.3 (17)	.3 (2)	1.9 (14)
Canada	58.5 (437)	5.5 (41)	8.7 (65)	.1 (1)	20.7 (155)	2.1 (16)	1.6 (12)	2.7 (20)
Chile	63.5 (271)	.7 (3)	2.8 (12)	.0 (0)	27.9 (119)	3.3 (14)	.2 (1)	1.6 (7)
China (PRC)	63.7 (480)	.9 (7)	9.2 (69)	.0 (0)	5.0 (38)	.4 (3)	19.5 (147)	1.3 (10)
Costa Rica	61.8 (209)	.0 (0)	3.3 (11)	.6 (2)	30.2 (102)	3.0 (10)	.0 (0)	1.2 (4)
Cuba	67.5 (344)	1.0 (5)	6.3 (32)	.6 (3)	12.0 (61)	1.8 (9)	10.0 (51)	1.0 (5)
Czechoslovakia	67.9 (288)	2.4 (10)	7.1 (30)	.5 (2)	12.0 (51)	3.8 (16)	5.4 (23)	.9 (4)
East Germany	57.5 (204)	12.4 (44)	8.5 (30)	.3 (1)	11.5 (41)	2.8 (10)	5.9 (21)	1.1 (4)
Egypt	60.3 (467)	1.2 (9)	11.2 (87)	.0 (0)	15.4 (119)	1.5 (12)	9.3 (72)	1.2 (9)
France	61.4 (915)	1.0 (15)	6.3 (94)	.1 (1)	22.1 (329)	3.4 (51)	4.3 (64)	1.4 (21)
Ghana	72.3 (375)	1.7 (9)	4.0 (21)	.0 (0)	18.5 (96)	2.1 (11)	.4 (2)	1.0 (5)
Guinea	70.7 (275)	.0 (0)	4.1 (16)	.0 (0)	19.0 (74)	3.3 (13)	1.8 (7)	1.0 (4)
Iceland	62.9 (205)	.3 (1)	7.4 (24)	.0 (0)	24.8 (81)	2.1 (7)	.0 (0)	2.5 (8)
India	62.9 (611)	7.1 (69)	11.1 (108)	.0 (0)	13.5 (131)	2.2 (21)	1.9 (18)	1.4 (14)
Israel	54.8 (331)	4.5 (27)	16.1 (97)	.8 (15)	15.6 (94)	2.3 (14)	4.8 (29)	1.2 (7)
Italy	58.2 (477)	2.1 (17)	6.3 (52)	.2 (2)	27.7 (227)	3.0 (25)	.5 (4)	2.0 (16)
Ivory Coast	69.4 (220)	.0 (0)	3.2 (10)	.0 (0)	25.2 (80)	1.9 (6)	.0 (0)	.3 (1)
Japan	59.3 (306)	1.4 (7)	2.3 (12)	.4 (2)	29.8 (154)	2.5 (13)	1.9 (10)	2.3 (12)
Kenya	62.7 (126)	.5 (1)	2.5 (5)	.0 (0)	30.3 (61)	2.0 (4)	.0 (0)	2.0 (4)
Lebanon	63.9 (198)	.6 (2)	6.1 (19)	.0 (0)	24.8 (77)	2.9 (9)	.3 (1)	1.3 (4)
Mexico	66.3 (265)	.8 (3)	3.3 (13)	.0 (0)	26.0 (104)	2.8 (11)	.5 (2)	.5 (2)
New Zealand	71.7 (292)	1.5 (6)	3.4 (14)	.0 (0)	19.7 (80)	1.7 (7)	.0 (0)	2.0 (8)
Norway	65.8 (293)	.2 (1)	7.0 (31)	.0 (0)	23.1 (103)	1.8 (8)	.7 (3)	1.3 (6)
Philippines	68.3 (284)	.0 (0)	5.8 (24)	.2 (1)	20.2 (84)	3.4 (14)	1.0 (4)	1.2 (5)
Poland	70.3 (319)	1.3 (6)	6.8 (31)	.0 (0)	10.4 (47)	2.4 (11)	6.4 (29)	2.4 (11)

(Continued)

TABLE 7.3 Continued

CREON Nation	Diplomatic	Domestic/Political	Military	Intelligence	Economic	Scientific/Technological	Promotive	Natural Resources
Soviet Union	69.5 (1035)	2.9 (43)	9.3 (139)	.3 (5)	5.8 (86)	2.6 (38)	9.1 (136)	.5 (8)
Spain	61.8 (212)	1.5 (5)	4.7 (16)	.0 (0)	27.1 (93)	3.2 (11)	.6 (2)	1.2 (4)
Switzerland	39.0 (55)	1.4 (2)	1.4 (2)	3.5 (5)	51.8 (73)	.7 (1)	.0 (0)	2.1 (3)
Thailand	68.4 (236)	.0 (0)	5.5 (19)	.3 (1)	21.7 (75)	2.0 (7)	1.4 (5)	.6 (2)
Tunisia	69.7 (366)	1.5 (8)	4.4 (23)	.4 (2)	18.9 (99)	2.3 (12)	1.9 (10)	1.0 (5)
Turkey	62.7 (372)	.8 (5)	11.6 (69)	.0 (0)	18.9 (112)	2.4 (14)	2.2 (13)	1.3 (8)
Uganda	70.6 (211)	.0 (0)	2.0 (6)	.0 (0)	24.4 (73)	2.0 (6)	.3 (1)	.7 (2)
United States	61.9 (1785)	2.3 (65)	16.1 (465)	1.7 (48)	11.1 (320)	1.4 (39)	4.3 (124)	1.2 (36)
Uruguay	65.7 (195)	.0 (0)	2.7 (8)	.0 (0)	27.9 (83)	3.0 (9)	.0 (0)	.7 (2)
Venezuela	62.9 (259)	.7 (3)	5.1 (21)	1.0 (4)	26.5 (109)	2.7 (11)	.2 (1)	1.0 (4)
West Germany	57.4 (653)	2.6 (29)	9.0 (103)	.1 (1)	26.6 (302)	1.8 (20)	1.2 (14)	1.3 (15)
Yugoslavia	70.6 (324)	1.5 (7)	1.5 (7)	.0 (0)	18.7 (86)	3.9 (18)	2.4 (11)	1.3 (6)
Zambia	62.5 (95)	.0 (0)	2.6 (4)	1.3 (2)	26.3 (40)	4.6 (7)	2.0 (3)	.7 (1)
Totals	63.4 (14,425)	2.0 (458)	8.0 (1,823)	.4 (89)	18.9 (4,295)	2.3 (525)	3.6 (822)	1.3 (301)

As we might expect from the overall totals, diplomatic instruments constitute the predominant category of skills and resources used by every government and ruling political party. Only for Switzerland are less than half of all its instruments classified as diplomatic. In terms of absolute frequencies—which, of course, are always affected by a country's overall number of events—the United States, USSR, France, West Germany, and India rank highest in the use of diplomatic instruments. India ranks sixth in total number of events in the CREON data (behind China and the other four countries listed above). It may edge out the People's Republic of China in the frequent use of diplomatic instruments, not only because of China's relative isolation (particularly during the Cultural Revolution) but also because of India's active leadership of Third World nations under Prime Minister Nehru.

The second most numerous instruments are economic, and for 14 countries 25 percent or more of all their instruments were classified in that category. Among the 14 are five of the six Latin American countries in the sample (the exception being Cuba) and five of the Western European nations. That Japan ranks among this group is expected, but the presence of Iceland, Lebanon, and the Ivory Coast is perhaps surprising. The countries with the lowest proportion of economic instruments are the United States (which nevertheless has the highest absolute frequency of economic instruments) and members of the Communist Bloc. As we shall see, these countries in the 1960s, unlike most other countries in the world, were relatively more concerned with issues that required other types of instruments.

Israel and the United States were the countries with the highest proportion of instruments in the military category. Except for West Germany, the eight highest-ranking nations in proportion of military instruments were involved for at least part of the decade in active conflict situations: United States (Vietnam and superpower confrontations—for example, the Cuban missile crisis), Israel (1967 War and continuous confrontation with Arab states), Turkey (conflict with Greece over Cyprus), Egypt (war with Israel), India (border war with China), Soviet Union (Czechoslovakia and superpower confrontations), and China (border war with India, tensions over Vietnam and with the Soviet Union).

Another type of cross-national comparison that can be made using Table 7.3 involves ranking for each nation the types of instruments that it uses most frequently. Thus, countries can be compared by the similarity of their rank order of instrument use. Because some instruments appear so seldom, only the top four ranks will be examined in the following examples. In the most common profile, diplomatic instruments rank first, followed by economic, then military; scientific/technological instruments rank fourth. The CREON data revealed relatively few cases of scientific/technological instruments compared with the three major types. Its widespread occurrence as the fourth-ranked kind of instrument may indicate that the absolute number understates its importance. The rank profile of diplomatic, economic, military, and scientific/technological is manifested by 16 of the 38 countries, including such developing countries as Kenya, Mexico, the Philippines, and Tunisia. It also applies to such European countries as Belgium, Italy, Norway, and Spain. If the profile is relaxed to permit the reverse ordering of scientific/technological and military, then the cluster also includes Japan and three more developing countries. Nations that follow this pattern of instruments seem to be concerned with trade and development (whether as donors or recipients) and to be unable to ignore military security, although they have strong allies or relatively weak adversaries that allow them to keep military activity limited.

Other profiles combine promotive instruments with the three most common types of skills and resources. For example, France, Israel, and the United States have the following ordering: 1 = diplomatic, 2 = military, 3 = economic, and 4 = promotive. For the Soviet Union, the order for promotive and economic instruments is reversed. For China, it is diplomatic, promotive, military, and, finally, economic. For Poland and Czechoslovakia, as well as Egypt, the ordering is diplomatic, economic, military, and then promotive. The various ruling Communist parties, as well as the other nations in this general grouping, seem interested in a strong military posture and have a felt need to justify and proselytize for their form of social and political order. It is interesting that for Yugoslavia military instruments drop out of the top four categories noted above and are replaced by scientific/technological skills and resources.

Several other profiles of note begin with the three most common instruments and then add a different fourth rank. Natural resources were important for Iceland and New Zealand. Domestic political instruments were ranked fourth in Canada, India, and West Germany and climbed to second rank in East Germany.

Instrument-Based Variables

Earlier in this chapter two variables were proposed that could be constructed from a classification of instruments. One, the multiple instruments measure, indicated the number of different instruments used in a single event. The other was a measure of the degree of concentration across a number of events on one or a few types of instruments. Using the CREON instrumentality data, both variables were operationalized.

The multiple instruments measure has a range corresponding to the possible total number of different instruments that can be used in a single event. For the present classification, the theoretical range is from 1.0 to 8.0, with the highest value indicating that all eight different instruments were used in a single event.

This initial analysis employs the average number of instrument types present in events. The first column in Table 7.4 displays the means for the multiple instruments measure for all events initiated by each country in the CREON sample. The first observation is that means computed for such large numbers of events yield little variation among nations. All countries fall between Cuba, with an average of 1.21 instruments for all its events, and Switzerland, with an average of 1.57 instruments. Whereas some of the highest means are for industrialized countries (such as Belgium, Czechoslovakia, and West Germany) and the lowest for less-developed countries (for example, Ghana, Guinea, and Uganda), the United States and the Soviet Union also are among the countries with the lowest means. As bloc leaders with a strong need to take note of virtually all foreign activity, they may engage in a number of events that are little more than evaluative comments on many of the activities of other actors. Such comments likely entail only one instrument.

A further undertaking sought to differentiate between classes of events involving more or less use of multiple instruments. Each nation's events were classified as concerned with either high- or low-attention problems. The analysis

TABLE 7.4
Mean Values for Two Variables Based on Instrument Categories for 38 Nations,
1959-1968

| CREON Nation | Multiple Instrument Actions | | | Concentration Index | | |
	All Events	Low-Attention Problems	High-Attention Problems	All Events	Low-Attention Problems	High-Attention Problems
Belgium	1.49	1.36	1.56	.48	.46	.50
Canada	1.45	1.42	1.47	.42	.44	.39
Chile	1.41	1.43	1.40	.51	.59	.43
China (PRC)	1.35	1.34	1.36	.45	.49	.41
Costa Rica	1.39	1.32	1.44	.51	.55	.47
Cuba	1.21	1.27	1.17	.48	.58	.37
Czechoslovakia	1.50	1.45	1.54	.49	.50	.48
East Germany	1.46	1.39	1.50	.36	.37	.35
Egypt	1.41	1.49	1.35	.45	.49	.40
France	1.35	1.35	1.35	.46	.52	.40
Ghana	1.30	1.43	1.19	.63	.77	.49
Guinea	1.32	1.42	1.23	.59	.74	.43
Iceland	1.33	1.27	1.37	.52	.56	.47
India	1.49	1.55	1.44	.48	.52	.43
Israel	1.40	1.47	1.37	.40	.42	.38
Italy	1.45	1.36	1.50	.43	.46	.40
Ivory Coast	1.36	1.40	1.34	.61	.64	.58
Japan	1.38	1.33	1.42	.47	.48	.46
Kenya	1.38	1.50	1.31	.53	.66	.40
Lebanon	1.37	1.47	1.31	.54	.59	.48
Mexico	1.43	1.38	1.47	.55	.55	.55
New Zealand	1.34	1.40	1.31	.60	.66	.54
Norway	1.33	1.36	1.32	.55	.54	.56
Philippines	1.35	1.48	1.26	.58	.67	.49
Poland	1.44	1.32	1.52	.52	.51	.54
Soviet Union	1.26	1.36	1.23	.49	.58	.40
Spain	1.35	1.34	1.35	.52	.55	.48
Switzerland	1.57	1.73	1.50	.42	.48	.37
Thailand	1.34	1.34	1.35	.60	.62	.58
Tunisia	1.34	1.48	1.20	.61	.75	.47
Turkey	1.38	1.38	1.37	.49	.50	.48
Uganda	1.32	1.36	1.28	.62	.68	.56
United States	1.24	1.30	1.19	.46	.52	.39
Uruguay	1.44	1.48	1.42	.55	.62	.48
Venezuela	1.37	1.42	1.31	.52	.60	.44
West Germany	1.48	1.49	1.48	.42	.45	.39
Yugoslavia	1.32	1.24	1.38	.59	.58	.60
Zambia	1.35	1.38	1.34	.54	.51	.57

used the part of the substantive problem area scheme that classified problems according to the type of deprivation (see Chapter 4).[4] If a given substantive problem area contained five percent or more of all the foreign events of a country, that problem was classified as a high-attention problem for the country. Every event—and, accordingly, the instruments present in the event—that addressed such a problem was regarded as dealing with a high-attention problem. The remaining events (and their associated instruments) all dealt with problems that involved less than five percent of a given nation's foreign policy activity during the decade. These events and their instruments were categorized as concerned with low-attention problems. It was anticipated that problems receiving more of a government's attention were more likely to be regarded as important and, therefore, more instruments would be used in each event addressing such problems.

The second and third columns of Table 7.4 present the multiple instrument actions means for low- and high-attention problems. Again, the variations are quite modest. Furthermore, for 22 of the 38 nations, the differences between high- and low-attention problems are in the direction of fewer types of instruments on the average in events involving problems to which high attention was paid. Perhaps more meaningful shifts in the multiple instruments measure are possible only when more specific kinds of foreign policy activity are examined in a less aggregated manner.

The second proposed measure using instruments required the construction of a concentration index. The particular index employed was the rather common one advanced by Hirschman (1945) and Michaely (1962). For that index one must first determine each category's proportion of the total of all instruments used by a government. The concentration index can then be calculated as the sum of the squared proportional shares. If the proportion of each type of instrument is represented as p_i, then the index is as follows:

$$\text{Concentration index} = \sum_i p_i^2$$

With eight categories of instruments, the minimal value is .125, indicating the least concentration and, in effect, equal use of all eight categories. The maximum value (highest concentration) where there is dependence on only one instrument is 1.00.

The fourth column in Table 7.4 gives the mean concentration index values for the foreign policy instruments used in the 38 countries between 1959 and 1968. The nation with the highest dependence on only a few instruments—a mean concentration index of .63—is Ghana, followed closely by Uganda, Ivory Coast, Tunisia, Thailand, and New Zealand. Despite the presence of New Zealand near this extreme of the range, further inspection of the data suggests that less-developed countries tend to emphasize the repeated use of a few instruments when compared with more developed nations. Indeed, the nations with the least concentration, or most balanced use of instruments, are East Germany, Israel, Canada, Switzerland, and Italy. All are nations with diverse skills and resources and foreign policy agendas demanding a careful orchestration of actions to maintain certain roles.

As was done previously with the multiple instruments measure, a check was made to determine whether the mean concentration index would differ between high- and low-attention problems. The results appear in the fifth and sixth columns of Table 7.4. A clear pattern emerges. For 32 of the 38 nations, there is less concentration of instruments in high- as compared with low-attention problems. If attention is regarded as an indicator of the importance of a problem, then governments appear to use a greater variety of instruments when dealing with their most important problems. Because the use of instruments entails costs to a government, it seems plausible that they would be more prepared to expend these resources to influence problems of greater concern to them. Consistent with this interpretation is the relatively greater magnitude of the shift toward greater diversity (less concentration) in the use of instruments for high-attention problems by poorer nations (such as Guinea, Tunisia, Ghana, Kenya, and Cuba). These countries have high instrument concentration indices when all their events are lumped together. It might be concluded that less-developed nations compared with richer ones cannot as readily afford to use a diversity of instruments in conducting most of their foreign policy (hence the high overall concentration indices). As with almost all nations, however, when matters of great importance arise, poor nations employ more of the instruments at their disposal. Consequently, the shift between high- and low-attention problems is more substantial for less-developed nations. Drawing on the earlier data with the multiple instruments measure, however, one sees that the change in the pattern of instrument use for most nations is not in using more instruments in each individual action. Instead, it appears that in high-attention problems governments tend to take more different actions, each involving different types of instruments.

CONCLUSIONS

The last several pages have suggested a possible linkage between the skills and resources used in foreign policy and the overall capabilities of a country. Other factors that might be expected to affect instrument use are the world view of the regime and the nature of the problems in its salient external environment. A number of elements that may alter the way instruments are used seem to invite inquiry.

Left relatively unexplored in this essay are questions that arise from different patterns of instrument usage—that is, the consequences of various styles and mixes of instruments. For example, consider the greater emphasis on promotional instruments in the foreign policy activities of the United States, the Soviet Union, the People's Republic of China, and a few others. Is the development of these instruments a prerequisite for actual or aspiring bloc or world leaders? Are other governments without such extensive use of promotional instruments more or less successful in leadership attempts?

Undoubtedly the reader will wish to pose other questions about both the conditions for and consequences of various types of instruments. All such inquiries suggest the value of examining instruments or the means of statecraft as one way of conceptualizing an aspect of foreign policy activity.

NOTES

1. A preliminary coding of foreign policy instruments that did not use the division into policy stages resulted in the overwhelming classification of all events as involving diplomatic skills and resources. One reason for introducing the process stages and the allowance of up to three different instruments in each stage was to capture more adequately the use of other types of instruments. Although the limit to three instruments per process stage may appear unfortunate given our subsequent interest in multiple instrument actions, the practical effect was inconsequential, as few stages could be reliably determined to have more than three.

2. Nations governed by ruling Communist parties and the United States and Israel tended to have a higher proportion of their instruments in the announcement category. These may be states which devote considerable international effort to ideological pronouncements and other verbal symbol manipulations devoid of any immediate follow-up activities. Those governments with somewhat higher proportions of preparatory-phase instrumentalities were four of the six black African countries in the sample (Ivory Coast, Kenya, Uganda, and Zambia), plus Mexico, Switzerland, Spain, Iceland, Lebanon, and Thailand. One might have expected more discernible information about instruments involved in the preparatory stages from more open political systems that are disposed to reveal policy process information. The data suggest, however, that countries with a strong concern about economic matters were more likely to have events coded for instruments in the preparatory stage.

3. It should be remembered that the CREON data sampled one quarter (3 months) for each of the ten years from 1959 through 1968. Consequently, the totals are based on a sample of reported events for the decade, not all reported events.

4. One category from the list of types of deprivations in the substantive problem area scheme was excluded. That category concerned the need for diplomatic communications. As we have seen in this chapter, all nations engaged in a high volume of activity involving diplomatic instruments. It was felt that the inclusion of such a category would inflate the high-attention problem category in a way that reduced its usefulness as an indicator of problem importance.

PART IV

Output Properties of Foreign
Policy Behavior

Editors' Introduction

Historically, the central focus in the measurement of foreign policy behavior has been with characteristics of output or with what it is that the nation *does* in the foreign policy arena. The WEIS scheme developed by McClelland, and other measurement instruments adapted from it, record output or the nature of an action. Similarly, conflict-cooperation scales deal with the nature of action. As Salmore and Salmore pointed out in Chapter 3, the concentration on characteristics of output is probably the underlying reason for the common finding that affect and participation emerge as the primary dimensions of most event data sets.

The chapters presented in this section share the assumption that characterizing the output of governments is an important task. The previous chapters developed measures using the foreign policy output of nations, but in each case the measure was intended to tap a phenomenon that existed prior to the action. Substantive problem area (Chapter 4) tells us the problem to which an action is addressed. Although discrepant examples could be found, generally the problem predates the decision-making activity that results in action. The action is the window through which we can get a glimpse of the problems that stimulate action. Similarly with goal properties, the action provides evidence about the decision-making group's goals, but the goals presumably antedated the action and, in fact, partly account for the action. In contrast, the chapters in this section are devoted primarily to conceptualizing and measuring properties of output for its own sake.

Measures of output properties are not new to the CREON Project. Most of the variables in the original data set draw on qualities of outputs. The chapters in this section, however, go beyond the original variables in two respects. First, they attempt to create measures of concepts whose theoretical import is attested to by their extensive use in the foreign policy and international relations literature. Many of the original variables were incorporated into the data set not because of their central position in bodies of theory, but because they reliably captured observable differences between events. Second, the chapters attempt to create unidimensional, ordinal measures of properties that are logically attributes, to a greater or lesser degree, of all behaviors. Many of the original variables were dichotomies indicating the presence or absence of some attribute. Often, the distribution was severely skewed, with the preponderance of events lacking the attribute.

Chapter 8 focuses on the concept of commitment. Salmore and Salmore, in Chapter 3, found that the primary factor underlying the Revised WEIS scheme in the CREON data represents "inverse commitment"; a similar finding emerged from Salmore and Munton's (1974) factor analysis of WEIS data. Moreover, the interpretations Salmore and Salmore offer for factors emerging from other variable subsets in CREON emphasize the level of commitment shared by the variables characterizing the factor. Commitment appears to be an important quality of foreign policy behavior. However, as Callahan points out in Chapter 8, the concept of commitment has been woefully underdeveloped, with different theorists employing different definitions. He attempts to overcome this problem by synthesizing a definition compatible with the main alternative definitions extant in the literature. Using this definition, Callahan builds an 11-point scale of commitment.

Although a strong case can be made for striving to measure commitment, an even stronger case can be made for affect. As Brady indicated in the first chapter, affect (in the guise of conflict/cooperation) has been the dominant variable in foreign policy research. Given the relevance of affect to the normative concerns of controlling conflict and promoting peace, and given the importance of affect in peace research, it is only appropriate that affect be conceptualized and operationalized. In Chapter 9, Hermann, Hermann, and Hutchins describe the creation of CREON's affect measure. Especially noteworthy is their solution to a problem caused by CREON's nondyadic event structure: the overloading of the neutral category of the scale. The solution, which involved an additional classification of targets and objects, parallels that used by East and M. Hermann in building the scope of action measures discussed in Chapter 5.

Specificity, developed by Swanson in Chapter 10, deals with the quality of communications acts between nations. Communication, whether intended to or not, helps shape actors' expectations about the future. This concern for the development of expectation is shared with commitment, but the two measures concern different expectations. (Specificity concerns the actor's communication of its own expectations about others' future behavior, whereas commitment concerns the creation in others of expectations about the actor's future behavior.) The amount of detail explicitly presented about the actor's expectations should largely determine the richness and accuracy of those expectations, with significant consequences for subsequent behavior. This is the notion specificity is intended to embody.

The final chapter in this section (Chapter 11), by M. Hermann, develops a measure of the independence/interdependence of a nation's behavior. This measure establishes the way an event links the actor to other members of the international system and may be used to look at the government's drive to maintain autonomous control over its actions. The measure actually is an amalgam of two independent subdimensions: whether the action is an initiative or a reaction, and whether it is taken unilaterally or multilaterally. The initiative-reactive dimension could justify our considering independence/interdependence of action as a measure of the predecisional context, but we think that the overarching concept of independence/interdependence of action necessitates viewing the measure as an output property.

All of these measures are Stage I products of the CREON Project. All were created through a recombination of information already stored in the CREON event data set. For these measures especially, the reader would do well to evaluate separately their conceptualization and operationalization. The quality of the operational measure depended on the availability of appropriate variables in the CREON data. Occasionally, such variables were not available. Where the operationalization is found wanting, the conceptual work can still provide guidance for later, more successful measurement attempts.

Commitment

To avoid commitment to any policy or action means to value one's resources more highly than their use, and to value one's self more highly than anything one might do. In organizations as well as in individuals, the continued refusal of commitment thus represents one particular variety of self-centeredness and of self-overestimation. As it is exactly this self-overestimation which in the long run tends to destroy autonomy and learning capacity, there may be perhaps some good evidence for the truth of the biblical prediction that he who would lose his life shall find it [Deutsch, 1963: 231-232].

Even an awesomely mighty and wealthy nation's government may enter into so many commitments to defend, develop, or control so many different colonies, satellite countries, or weaker allies, that it simply may not have the wherewithal to do so if its power in more than a few of them should be challenged simultaneously by local uprisings, outside attacks, infiltration, or combinations of these. Here again, a government and nation may find themselves overcommitted, vulnerable to any really serious crisis in their prestige that might precipitate a run by their client countries on all their commitments and promises [Deutsch, 1978: 48].

These two statements underline the dilemma of commitment in foreign policy. On the one hand, if nations are to achieve their foreign policy goals, they must be willing to undertake commitments. On the other hand, committing oneself entails risks that would be avoided if commitments were avoided.

A number of bodies of theory develop or build on the problem of tailoring commitments to an appropriate level. One concerns the commitment of resources for the achievement of foreign policy goals. Clearly, the willingness or ability of a nation to commit resources is intimately tied to its capacity to achieve its goals. States that cannot or will not use their resources will fail to fulfill many of their goals and will probably be less adaptable and less viable societies than nations less strongly constrained. Are there any distinctions among nations that enable us to predict and understand differences in their propensity to use resources? Morgen-thau (1973), for example, has asserted that nations with a pacifistic national culture, such as the United States and Great Britain, are generally unwilling to commit resources to create the military power necessary to fulfill political commit-ments. Others have argued that democratic systems suffer a similar defect, at least when compared to nondemocratic systems (Brzezinski and Huntington, 1964). The Sprouts (1971) have suggested that all states will increasingly feel a gap between demands and resources, a situation which will lead to retrenchment in international commitments.

Theorists of deterrence also have been attentive to the necessity for commit-ment. They argue that in order to deter a potential aggressor, a nation must bind itself to the security of another nation. For the commitment to be successful, it must be credible; to be credible, it must appear to be rigid. "The commitment process on which all American overseas deterrence depends—and on which all confidence in the alliance depends—is a process of surrendering and destroying options that we might have been expected to find attractive in an emergency" (Schelling, 1966: 44).

The binding of oneself implied by deterrence commitments leads into one of the problems of commitment—that is, the process through which decision makers become tied to some undertaking. When that happens, policy develops its own momentum; the government loses some of its capacity to direct its own behavior. There are many mechanisms that generate commitment to a policy or goal. Making a tough decision will often trigger psychological mechanisms for reducing cognitive dissonance; self-reinforcing patterns of perceptual distortion may follow (DeRivera, 1968) that make it easier to continue the initial course than to change it. Such psychological processes can be reinforced by the inertial qualities of the bureau-cratic machine. According to Kissinger (1974: 20):

> Once the decision-making apparatus has disgorged a policy, it becomes very difficult to change it. The alternative to the status quo is the prospect of repeating the whole anguishing process of arriving at decisions. This explains to some extent the curious phenomenon that decisions taken with enormous doubt and perhaps with a close division become practically sacrosanct once adopted.

The process of rigidification of policy via commitment has important implica-tions. If a state is to achieve its goals, it must be able to throw off unsuccessful policies and replace them with more appropriate ones. To be unable to do so is to fall prey to the dangers of "self-closure" of a political system, so incisively analyzed by Deutsch (1963). A specific manifestation of this problem of rigidification is implied in Russett's (1962) scheme for explaining the outbreak of war—that decision makers become aware of the imminence of war only after the momentum of their policies makes the war impossible to avert.

This chapter is not intended to provide an exhaustive discussion of the theoret-ical and normative applications of the concept of commitment. It is clear from even this brief review that it is central to the most fundamental concerns of foreign policy and international relations analysis. In order to develop a deeper understanding of these concerns, systematic research on patterns of commitment in foreign policy behavior would be helpful. A precondition for such research is a valid measure of the degree of commitment in a foreign policy action. This chapter sets out to create such a measure. Before we can reach that goal, however, we must first clarify the meaning of the concept.

AMBIGUITIES IN THE CONCEPT OF COMMITMENT

Perhaps it is inevitable that concepts rich in substantive applications are also riddled with ambiguities in ordinary usage. That certainly is the case with commitment. Before a fruitful effort can be made to develop measures of commitment, we must explore three areas of fundamental ambiguity in the use of the concept commitment: the meaning of commitment, the distinction between the substance and the intensity of the commitment, and whether commitment is to be used as an independent or dependent variable.

Meaning of Commitment

Resource commitment. Commitment has tended to have one of four possible meanings in discussions of foreign policy. The first is succinctly defined by Wilkinson (1969: 18): "A commitment is a specific employment of resources in support of a given policy." This interpretation is implicit in the first set of theoretical concerns discussed at the start of the chapter. Although this meaning is not entirely clear (for example, what constitutes a resource?), it provides a generally reliable means for classifying foreign policy behavior. In most cases observers could agree that a specific employment of resources was involved. As a shorthand convenience, we shall refer to this meaning as resource commitment.

Binding commitment. The second common meaning of commitment is the binding or pledging of oneself to some outcome, course of action, or nation. Commitment defined this way is one of the central concerns of the bargaining literature (Schelling, 1960), as well as research on the impact of alliance commitments on war and systemic stability (Singer and Small, 1969). Unlike the first definition of commitment, binding commitment is very problematic at the point of observation. There is no general agreement about when a state becomes bound to some object. George and Smoke (1974) even reject the question. They argue that the "binary view of commitment" is inappropriate; commitment should be examined in terms of degrees rather than as an either-or proposition.

Situationally imposed commitment. The third meaning of commitment is a generalized requirement that a state act in certain situations to achieve or to avoid particular outcomes. The difference between this meaning of commitment and binding commitment is that here the need or requirement for action does not originate within the state. Instead, the requirement to act derives from general aspects of the environment of the decision-making unit. One example of this is suggested by Weinstein's (1969) discussion of situational commitments: a state is committed to act if and only if its national interests are likely to be affected in a situation. Another example is found in George and Smoke's (1974) discussion of the concept of systemic polarity which they claim "can mean the level or worth of the stakes at issue in conflict (and hence, presumably, the degree of motivation or commitment of players in the struggle)" (1974: 47). Presumably, such commitments could also derive from the roles a nation adopts in the world. According to K. Holsti (1970), national roles create expectations in others, which, in turn, create pressure for the nation to act according to the dictates of the role. Thus, it is often asserted that nations considered great powers have certain commitments as a result of the responsibilities of the great power role.

Internal commitment. The last meaning of commitment refers to a psychological state of the decision maker or the political disposition of a government, in which a decision-making unit is committed to the extent that it feels obligated to attempt to bring about some outcome—the stronger the sense of obligation, the stronger the commitment. We refer to this meaning of commitment as internal commitment, because psychological commitment is internal to the decision maker and because the constraining political forces are internal to the nation or government. Internal commitment is central to the second set of theoretical concerns discussed at the start of the chapter—that is, the problems of rigidity that may occur when the decision-making unit becomes tied to some policy. There has been some research in this area. In an examination of the effects of psychological commitment, Poteat (1976) found that as General MacArthur's commitment to victory in Korea increased, the distortions in his estimates of Chinese intentions became more pronounced. As evidence mounted that the Chinese were preparing to cross the Yalu River, MacArthur perceived a decreasing probability of such an occurrence. Sullivan (1972) has examined patterns in the expression of symbolic commitment, a potential indicator of internal commitment, and discovered that expression of symbolic commitment by the United States was correlated with patterns of escalation and deescalation in Vietnam.

Substance Versus Intensity

Whatever the definition of commitment that is adopted for research, we must decide whether to examine the substance of the commitment or the intensity or degree of commitment.

With the exception of resource commitment, the definitions of commitment all imply some content—the outcome, policy, or actor to which the state or decision-maker is committed. This content can be distinguished from the intensity of the commitment—the stronger the feelings of obligation (internal commitment), the more tightly binding the pledge (binding commitment), or the more overwhelming the interests or responsibilities (situationally imposed commitment), the more intense the commitment. Consider the following illustration of this distinction. During the Korean war, the United States' goal changed a number of times: First it was to deny the North Koreans' military victory, next it was to punish them in order to deter future aggression, and later to defeat them and unify the country (see Stoessinger, 1974). Each transition was a change in the substance of the commitment, but as the substance changed, the intensity remained roughly the same. The intensity of commitment can also change while the substance of the commitment remains the same. An example of this phenomenon would be the allegation, as yet unproved, that the Carter administration's commitment to human rights decreased after his first couple of months in office.

For resource commitment the analogue for substance would be the kind of resources used. Thus, one may speak of military commitments or economic commitments, among others. Intensity of commitment would be comparable to the amount of resources used. The distinction for resource commitment between substance and intensity is illustrated by U.S. involvement in Vietnam. When the United States first provided military advisers to South Vietnam, it moved from an economic to a military commitment, a change in the substance of the commitment. When the United States sent more troops to South Vietnam, it increased the intensity of its commitment (the amount of resources) but did not change the substance (kind of resources) of the commitment.

The crucial point is that it is confusing to use such phrases as "increasing commitments." Instead, one must specify whether that means more substantive commitments, broader substantive commitments, or greater intensity of commitment. A further implication is that, when we are developing measures of commitment, we should first specify whether the purpose is to distinguish changes in the substance of commitments or to measure differences in the intensity of the commitments.

Independent or Dependent Variable

The first two areas of ambiguity in the use of commitment relate to its conceptualization. The last area concerns how commitment is used in foreign policy theory and analysis. Commitment can serve as either an independent (or intervening) variable or as the dependent variable.[1]

The difference has implications for how commitment is conceptualized and measured. A researcher treating commitment as a dimension of foreign policy behavior—the dependent variable—will not want to incorporate the situationally imposed or internal meanings of commitment in the measurement of commitment. These types of commitment do not focus on aspects of foreign policy behavior. They could, however, be used as independent variables to explain characteristics of foreign policy behavior, including intensity of resource commitment or intensity of binding commitment. Some researchers might be interested in explaining the level of internal commitment. If so, the other meanings of commitment would be inappropriate guides to measurement, although the other types of commitment might be used as independent variables explaining the level of internal commitment.

To summarize, commitment is not a unidimensional concept (see Shively, 1974). There are different facets to commitment, each having a different conceptual meaning. Within each facet of commitment, differentiations can be made in terms of substance and intensity. And each facet of commitment is amenable to certain kinds of theoretical interests and not amenable to others. Thus, the researcher who wishes to study commitment must first define the substantive interests of the research, then proceed to define commitment.

In the remainder of this chapter, our development of the concept of commitment is based on our desire to measure it as a dimension of foreign policy behavior. Moreover, our attention will focus on the intensity of commitment rather than on the substance of the commitment. Within the boundaries set by these choices, one logical approach would be to develop two scales of commitment: a scale measuring the intensity of resource commitment and a scale measuring the intensity of binding commitment. In this chapter we attempt a more ambitious program. First, we propose a new conceptual definition of commitment synthesized from the four definitions discussed earlier. Then we attempt to develop a scale of commitment based on the synthesis. This chapter is written in the belief that it is better to pursue a more ambitious goal at first. Development of a single scale of commitment would promote economy in our research. More important, as we will detail in the next two sections, there is an interactive effect between resource commitment and binding commitment. Development of a single scale would enable us to incorporate these interactive effects into the scale. Of course, if we should fail to develop a successful synthesis of binding and resource commitment, we can always fall back on the less ambitious goal of developing separate scales.

A DEFINITION OF COMMITMENT

We will use the notion of constraints as a basis for synthesizing an overarching definition of commitment. Implicit in the previously discussed meanings of commitment is the element of constraints on decision making. In each definition, a commitment limits the range of future options. Resource commitment creates constraints by reducing the reserves of scarce resources. Resources used for one undertaking cannot be allocated simultaneously to other projects. Moreover, resources can be reallocated to other tasks only with some difficulty. Binding commitment creates constraints by linking the actor to certain options. Failure to fulfill a binding commitment is costly, because others will be less willing in the future to accept such commitments as a basis for their relationship to the actor. Thus, the actor is constrained not to choose options that would violate the binding commitment. Situationally imposed commitment implies constraints in a number of ways, depending on what aspects of the situation impose the commitment. In some cases, national interest considerations tip the cost-benefit balance toward the choice of one option and the rejection of others. Internal commitment implies psychological or political constraints that lead to the choice of certain options, usually the continuation of present policy.

On the basis of this analysis we can offer the following definitions of commitment as a characteristic of foreign policy behavior.[2]

> Commitment is the creation through foreign policy behavior of constraints on the actor's future behavior, provided that the constraints can be reasonably anticipated to be consequences of the action.

> Intensity of commitment in an action is the extent of constraint on the actor's future behavior produced by the current behavior.

Constraints are central to commitment, but not all constraints are relevant. We are interested in commitment as a characteristic of foreign policy behavior; therefore, we are interested only in constraints that arise as a consequence of foreign policy behavior. Thus, for example, resource constraints deriving from a nation's poverty are irrelevant, as are the constraints emerging from motivations of national interest.

Moreover, we are not concerned with constraints that cannot be anticipated to be consequences of behavior—for example, constraints resulting from accidents or natural disasters.

DEVELOPMENT OF A COMMITMENT SCALE

We want to translate the conceptual definition of commitment into a scale of the intensity of commitment in any foreign policy behavior. Our discussion in the first and second sections of this chapter suggests an important premise for this translation process—namely, that there are two primary mechanisms by which foreign policy behavior can create constraints on future policy options: allocation of scarce resources and generation of expectations in others. Earlier in this section, we argued that allocation of scarce resources creates constraints. Two clarifications of this idea are relevant here. First, allocation of scarce resources is not equivalent to resource commitment because not all resource commitments create constraints. Some resource commitments use such small amounts of resources that their use does not jeopardize the viability of other ongoing or potential enterprises. Second, some actions may affect the availability of resources without actually depleting them. For example, demobilization of forces would not normally be considered an instance of resource commitment. Nevertheless, such an action would limit the resources available in the future and would therefore create constraints. Reallocation of scarce resources through the reduction of a capability will be considered a form of constraint-producing resource allocation.

The expectations of other political actors, both internal and external to one's own political system, also create constraints. Violation of those expectations will make the actor appear erratic. It will undercut the policies of partners, occasionally causing them serious difficulties. Neustadt (1970), for example, has argued that violated expectations are one of four elements triggering crises in American-British relations. Violated expectations produce uncertainty, to which other nations react by adopting an increasingly cautious and defensive diplomatic stance that, in many instances, undermines the actor's capacity to fulfill its foreign policy goals. In this way, the expectations of other nations increase the costs associated with certain policy options, creating constraints against the choice of these options. (For an extended discussion that clearly links commitment to the expectations others have about a state's behavior, see Schelling, 1966). Binding commitments create constraints because they generate expectations. Moral commitments or commitments derived from a national role—subsets of situationally imposed commitment—exist because certain behaviors are expected to follow.

Thus, we argue that the intensity of commitment in a foreign policy behavior is a function of the resources used and the expectations generated by the behavior. Presumably, if one could directly measure resources used and expectations generated, then one could simply add the two components to derive the commitment score. Unfortunately, that is not possible. Research has not produced ways to measure these two components in discrete events, and it is unlikely that the scales would be comparable if such measurement instruments existed.[3] Therefore, some other measurement approach is required.

This task is particularly challenging, because it requires the existence of theory relating the characteristics of foreign policy behavior to the degree of constraints produced. No such theory exists. Ideas are scattered throughout the literature, but they neither constitute a coherent whole nor represent rigorous empirical research. We confront a "Catch-22" situation. Without theory, efforts to develop measures must be tentative, but without measures of the concept, the research required to develop the theory cannot take place. Therefore, at this time the scale must rest on a series of theoretical assumptions.

Underlying Assumptions

Before presenting the commitment scale, some discussion of the basic assumptions is in order. The scale builds on three sets of assumptions. One set relates the allocation of resources to the intensity of commitment. The second set states the general relationship between the expectations generated by an event and the level of commitment in the event. The third set concerns the impact of nonverbal behavior on the expectations generated by the event. In each assumption, the relationship is assumed to hold, other things being equal.

Resource allocation and commitment intensity. The resources allocated in two events can be compared along three different dimensions. The first is the amount of resources.

ASSUMPTION 1: The more of any one resource allocated by a foreign policy action, the greater the constraints on behavior and, in turn, the greater the intensity of the commitment.

The second dimension concerns the kind of resources allocated in the event. No single metric exists against which all resources can be compared. For example, no one can say how many dollars are equivalent to the life of a soldier. It is impossible to compare directly the amounts of resources used when different kinds of resources are used. Therefore, reference is often made to the kinds of resources used in order to estimate the intensity of commitment. For example, greater commitment is attributed to an action when human lives are expended than when nonhuman resources are used. Qualitative comparison of resources probably is a valid exercise when the analysis is limited to research within one cultural tradition. However, it is less useful for cross-national research because there is no universally accepted system of value. A nation with a surplus population and foreign exchange difficulties may contract more constraints through a monetary agreement than a war, whereas a nation with a small population and strong treasury may be affected very differently. Thus, the second asumption is:

ASSUMPTION 2: There is no cross-nationally valid qualitative standard for comparing the constraints produced by different kinds of allocations of resources.

The third dimension refers to the reversibility of the allocation. Some resource allocations are irreversible; the resource is destroyed (for example, a bomb exploded), transformed (concrete turned into a dam), or control is passed to another government (foreign assistance grants). Other resource allocations are moderately reversible, as when the resources are placed under the limited control of another actor, a situation which complicates but does not preclude their reallocation to other tasks. Examples include the provision of technical assistance personnel and the assignment of troops to a peacetime alliance. Another class of moderately reversible resource allocations includes actions in which the actor reduces its capacity to act, provided that the capacity can be increased later. For instance, partial demobilization of forces would qualify as a moderately reversible resource allocation. Still other resource allocations are essentially reversible. The actor maintains control over them, so they can be reallocated at will. However, every reallocation process involves some time, so the resources are unavailable for at least a brief period; there are some constraints incurred by their allocation. The argument can be summarized as:

ASSUMPTION 3: The more reversible the resource allocation, the fewer the constraints produced and the less intense the commitment.

Hilsman (1967: 144) provides support for this assumption by reference to the example of ships showing the flag: "Fleets can be moved around so easily that they do not constitute very much of a commitment, especially in an age of nuclear power."

Generation of expectations and commitment intensity. The next set of assumptions relates the expectations that are generated by an event to the level of commitment in the event. Expectations can be compared in terms of their strength. When expectations are strong, other nations and domestic groups will build policy around the expectations. If their expectations are violated, there will be repercussions and costs for the violation. Thus, the following assumption can be offered:

ASSUMPTION 4: The stronger the expectations generated by an event, the greater the constraints on future policy and the greater the intensity of the commitment.

Strength of expectations is a relatively amorphous concept, but it can be given a more definite meaning. Strength of expectations is a function of two other characteristics of the expectations: the specificity or diffuseness of the expectations in terms of the anticipated behavior, and the certainty that the behavior will occur.

The specificity or diffuseness of the expected behavior refers to the inclusiveness of the set of behaviors consistent with the expectations. The less inclusive the set, the more specific (less diffuse) the expectations. To illustrate, suppose one nation promises to assist in the global struggle for human rights, whereas another promises to break diplomatic relations with any nation that flagrantly violates human rights. The former produces more diffuse expectations than does the latter. Breaking diplomatic relations with violators of human rights is one form of support for human rights, but the former includes a wider variety of actions. There are two implications of specific expectations. First, other actors are more likely to base policy on their expectations when those expectations are relatively specific. Second, when expectations are relatively diffuse, the actor may more persuasively argue that it has in fact fulfilled its obligations by almost any action, thereby deflecting some of the odium of violated expectations. These two arguments suggest the following assumption.

ASSUMPTION 5: The more specific the expectations generated by a behavior, the stronger the expectations and, thus (by Assumption 4), the greater the intensity of the commitment.

The certainty of expectations refers to the degree of confidence of others that the expected behavior will occur. Certainty is roughly analogous to credibility, except that credibility is an attribute of the actor's commitment whereas certainty is an attribute of the expectations of others. A number of variables contribute to the certainty of expectations. Expectations will be more certain if they are compatible with others' perceptions of the actor's national interests. Expectations will also be more certain if the actor has a reputation for fulfilling its commitments. Both of these variables characterize the historical and political context in which the commitment behavior occurs.

Other variables influencing certainty of expectations are derived from the behavior itself. It is important to learn whether the behavior demonstrates commitment by an act of binding commitment or by revealing internal commitment. Binding commitment is significant because, without it, observers are in the position of having to infer the actor's obligations. Obligations are easier to avoid when others have inferred them than when they are explicitly adopted by the acting nation. One can legitimately deny responsibility for the harmful effects of a failure to fulfill expectations when those expectations were not produced by a binding commitment. The acting nation can argue that the failure has no bearing on whether it will fulfill other expectations deriving from binding commitments.

Demonstrations of internal commitment are even more powerful ways of producing highly certain expectations of future behavior. Russett's (1963) research on the determinants of successful deterrence reveals that binding commitment does not create totally certain expectations. "Clearly too, it is not enough simply for the defender to make a formal promise to protect the pawn. . . . In at least six cases an attacker has chosen to ignore an explicit and publicly acknowledged commitment binding the defender to protect the pawn" (Russett, 1963: 100-101). Demonstrations of internal commitment produce highly certain expectations because they reveal the behavioral predispositions of the government, which are fairly strong grounds for anticipating future behavior. Jervis' (1970: 18-19) discussion of an index is relevant here:

In contrast to signals, indices are statements or actions that carry some inherent evidence that the image projected is correct because they are believed to be inextricably linked to the actor's capabilities or intentions.

Demonstrations of internal commitment would be indices. This discussion can be summarized in two assumptions:

ASSUMPTION 6: The more certain the expectations, the stronger those expectations and the more intense the commitment.

ASSUMPTION 7: Actions that demonstrate internal commitment are the most effective means for increasing the certainty of expectations; binding commitments are somewhat weaker means for producing that effect.

Whether the commitment is conditional or unconditional affects the certainty of binding commitments. Conditions on a commitment define the requirements that must be met before the expected behavior will happen. For example, most defense alliances require an action by a nation only if the alliance partner is attacked. Conditions are important because they reduce the certainty of expectations. George and Smoke (1974: 554-555) quote A.J.P. Taylor's discussion of the Locarno Pact of 1925 which "rested on the assumption that the promises given would never have to be made good—otherwise the British Government would not have given them." Another example of this phenomenon is embedded in Kissinger's (1975: 612) argument on why the Sinai Accord was not a major commitment for the United States: "Other provisions refer to contingencies which may never arise and are related—sometimes explicitly—to present circumstances subject to a rapid change." This discussion suggests the next assumption:

ASSUMPTION 8: Conditions placed on a binding commitment reduce the certainty of the expectations generated by the action and, thus (by Assumption 6), reduce the intensity of the commitment.

The joint implications of the assumptions relating to expectations can be illustrated with reference to the United States' commitment to NATO. There probably is no stronger expectation concerning U.S. foreign policy than that the United States would come to the assistance of Western Europe in case of an attack by the Soviet Union. This expectation stems somewhat from the formal treaty of alliance but more importantly from the regular reassertion of the pledge by high government officials and, most importantly, by the repeated demonstration of internal commitment to the alliance, especially the stationing of troops in Europe.

Resource allocation and expectation generation. The final set of assumptions concerns the impact of nonverbal behavior on the expectations generated by the event. Some nonverbal behaviors result in the allocation of resources and have an impact on the intensity of the commitment described by Assumptions 1 and 3. Other significant nonverbal actions do not result in the allocation of resources, except in the most reversible fashion. For example, Egypt's takeover of the Suez Canal was primarily a nonverbal activity, but it did not result in the allocation of many resources. Similarly, the American military withdrawal from Vietnam had the effect of conserving rather than using resources. The relevance of nonverbal behaviors is indicated by Schelling's (1966: 65) dictum that "one cannot incur a genuine commitment by purely verbal means." Nonverbal behavior buttresses stated policy by revealing dedication to the policy goals. This assumes, however, that the nonverbal behavior is somehow significant. It is possible for nonverbal foreign policy actions to contradict rather than support stated policy. For example, the minimal contributions of several Western European nations to the Vietnam war effort denied support for the war, despite stated policy. Assumption 9 follows from this discussion.

ASSUMPTION 9: Significant nonverbal actions tend to produce strong expectations and, thus, to be intensely committing; insignificant, symbolic nonverbal actions tend to generate weak expectations and, thus, to produce low levels of commitment.

Jervis (1970: 19) has raised a related issue: "Actions are not automatically less ambiguous than words. Indeed, without an accompanying message it may be impossible for the perceiving actor to determine what image the other is trying to project." This argument refers back to the distinction between relatively specific versus relatively diffuse expectations. A nonverbal action unaccompanied by a verbal explanation will produce relatively diffuse expectations. However, the expectations may involve a high degree of certainty—others can anticipate some subsequent behavior changes even if they are not able to anticipate what the changes will be. Therefore, although not maximally committing, such actions can produce strong expectations and, in turn, strong constraints.

A similar argument can be made about self-fulfilling nonverbal actions. As developed in this chapter, the commitment dimension refers to the future. But some deeds, such as giving emergency disaster relief, are completed soon after their announcement. This does not mean, however, that the action produces no commitment. Such behaviors do reveal certain tendencies in foreign policy. Expectations are generated to the extent that they can be inferred from these observed tendencies. Such expectations will be very diffuse or, if specific, relatively low in certainty. Nevertheless, expectations are created and serve to constrain foreign policy. Thus, we have Assumption 10:

> ASSUMPTION 10: To the extent that a nonverbal action does not continue into the future and is not accompanied by a verbal statement of policy, expectations are weakened and commitment is less intense. However, commitment is still more intense than if the behavior were merely verbal.

One final point concerns the effect of reversibility of resource allocation on the expectations that are generated. Because resources can be reclaimed under some circumstances, their reversible use indicates lower dedication to policy goals and should, therefore, produce weaker expectations than irreversible resource allocations. This argument reinforces Assumption 3—the more reversible the resource allocation, the lower the constraints produced and the less intense the commitment.

CREON Commitment Scale

The ten assumptions about the process of creating commitments are related to the commitment scale used in the CREON Project. The logic of the scale is summarized in Figure 8.1. The first step in creating the scale was to separate all foreign policy events into four classes ranked according to the intensity of commitment. The first group contained all significant nonverbal behaviors, including those that involved allocations of significant amounts of tangible resources. These events rank highest because they generate strong expectations (Assumption 9) and, in the case of resource allocating events, because the allocation of resources produces constraints (Assumption 1).

The second-ranked group consisted of events that involved some form of pledging by the government. These events were assumed to generate expectations about future behavior, as were the events that fell into the third category—events that generated expectations through implicit indication of intentions. The former are ranked higher on the commitment scale because explicit verbal statements of intentions are more specific about what future behaviors to expect (Assumption 5)

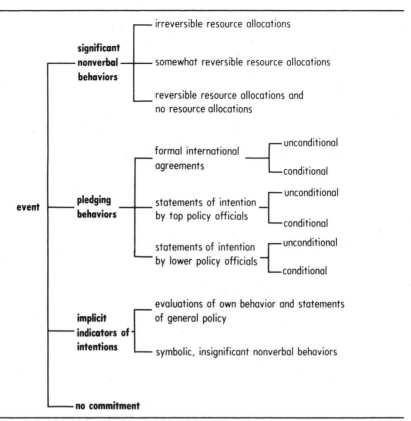

Figure 8.1   Flow diagram for logic of commitment scale used in the CREON Project.

and also because they produce more certain expectations about future behavior (Assumption 6).

The last category included behaviors that did not produce any commitment because they neither used resources nor generated expectations about the nation's future behavior. The action content of this category included events that evaluated the behavior of others or that expressed desires about how others should act. This focus of attention on others' behavior should not result in the stimulation of expectations about one's own behavior.

The second step in the development of the scale was to articulate further each of these main groups. Starting at the highest level, significant nonverbal behaviors were subdivided into three subsets; irreversible resource allocations, partially reversible resource allocations, and reversible resource allocations and no resource allocations. The primary dimension differentiating the subsets is the reversibility of the resource allocation. By Assumption 3 we have posited that the less reversible the resource allocation, the stronger the resource constraints and the stronger the commitment resulting from the action. Thus, the irreversible resource allocations are assigned a higher commitment value than are the partially reversible resource allocations, which, in turn, are more committing than the reversible resource allocations. The third subset in this group includes essentially reversible resource allocation behaviors along with significant nonverbal behaviors that involve no resource allocations. The reasoning for this combination was as follows. The resource constraints placed on policymakers by essentially reversible resource allocations are slight; therefore, the expectations generated by such events are weak relative to the expectations that may be generated by significant nonverbal behaviors that do not involve the allocation of resources. There is no persuasive reason to believe that, in general, the former are either more or less intensely committing than the latter.

There are two stages in the further breakdown of the group of behaviors that consist of acts of pledging or explicitly undertaking some formal commitment. The first stage distinguishes three mechanisms by which the pledge is communicated: a formal, documented international agreement, a statement of intention by a top policymaker, and a statement of intention by a lower-echelon policymaker. These mechanisms are listed in rank order of commitment intensity. Pledges put in formal international agreements indicate clearly that some formal commitment has been made. Such agreements increase the certainty of the expectations generated by the event, thereby increasing the intensity of the commitment (Assumption 6). Since formal international agreements are reasonably precise in their definition of the obligations entailed, the specificity of the expectations also increases and, thus, so does the intensity of the commitment (Assumption 5).

Statements of intention by governmental officials involve pledging behavior and generate expectations. As Kissinger (1975: 613) noted about the Sinai Accords:

> The fact that many provisions are not by any definition standard international commitments does not mean, of course, that the United States is morally or politically free to act as if they did not exist. On the contrary, they are important statements of diplomatic policy and engage the good faith of the United States as long as the circumstances that gave rise to them continue.

Statements of intention are separated into groups on the basis of the hierarchical level of the author of the statement. The reason is that the lower levels of a government are not able to bind the higher levels of government to a course of action. Hilsman (1971: 34) cites Paul Nitze as saying that "the regional assistant secretary is the first person on the ladder who can *commit* the Unites States of America." Statements of intention emanating from the lower levels of the bureaucracy are not as clear a commitment—the certainty of expectations is relatively low and thus commitment is less intense.

The second stage in differentiating types of pledges distinguishes conditional from unconditional pledges. For each pledging mechanism conditional pledges produce less intense commitment than do otherwise similar unconditional pledges (see Assumption 8).[4]

As we have already noted, the third major group of events generates expectations without explicit pledges or statements of intention. This group can be subdivided into two categories: verbal statements that imply certain lines of future behavior and symbolic nonverbal behaviors. Verbal statements that imply future behaviors include a nation's evaluation of its own policies. Positive evaluations imply continuation of the policies while negative evaluations imply change. Such statements would have some effect on the expectations of others. Also included are statements of general policy, which are usually too diffuse to produce very strong expectations but not totally irrelevant.

Symbolic, insignificant nonverbal behavior produces some expectations, but of a very weak nature. As we argued earlier, such actions tend to be ambiguous in their implications and sometimes deny the substance of verbally stated policy.

Operationalization and Validity

The CREON commitment scale was generated by recombining information previously recorded in the CREON data set. A detailed description of these procedures is provided in Appendix 8.1. The process of operationalization forced us to flesh out the meaning of the abstract concepts that constitute the scale, such as symbolic deeds, moderately reversible resource allocations, and binding international agreements. The decisions that were made extended the conceptualization of the measure somewhat, so the reader may want to proceed to the appendix at this time. The scale that was created had eleven levels of intensity of commitment. In this section we will concentrate on validity questions.

For one validity test, 85 events were randomly selected from the CREON data. After the description of the event was read, each was assigned a commitment score. These scores were compared with the scores derived from the operationalizing procedure described in the appendix. The results are reported in Table 8.1. Of the 85 events, 51 (60 percent) were similarly scaled by the two procedures; 30 (35 percent) were scaled higher from the event descriptions than by the operationalization procedure while 4 (5 percent) were scaled lower. These results would seem to indicate that the scale contains some error. The rank-order correlation between the scores, however, turns out to be quite strong; tau-b equals .70. Across all points, the scale derived from the operationalization procedure seems to provide a fairly accurate representation of what results from classifying event descriptions.

Examination of the scores for this sample of events suggests several more specific comments on the validity of the scale. First, behavior in the context of an international organization appears to cause problems. For example, in three events a nation's representative on the board of governors of an international organization accepted the annual report of the organization; these events were coded 3 (evaluation of own policy) using the operationalization procedure. The author, reading the event description, coded them 1 (evaluation of other's policies, thus no commitment) because this seemed a more appropriate rating, even though the events in a sense were evaluations of one's own past behavior as a member of the organization. Similarly, in two other events a vote with the majority to accept a new member into the United Nations was classified as an international agreement (level 8) using the operationalization procedure. Although there is an element of agreement in the events, they seem more appropriately considered no more committing than general policy statements (level 3). Finally, a vote in an international organization ordering the staff of the organization to undertake some activity came out of the operationalization procedure as a 7 (unconditional statement of intention by top policymakers), when it more appropriately is considered a desire, level 1.

Because collective behavior directed toward the governing of the collectivity seems troublesome for the scale, some systematic bias may be introduced into the

TABLE 8.1

Comparison of Scores Based on Event Description
and Operationalization Procedure

		Score Based on Event Description											
		1	2	3	4	5	6	7	8	9	10	11	Total
	1	7	2										9
	2		6				1	1					8
	3	5	2	4									11
Score Based on	4				5								5
Operationalization	5	3		2	1	1							7
Procedure	6	1		1			6						8
	7	1		3				2					6
	8			2			1		4				7
	9						1		2	7		1	11
	10								3		1		4
	11		1								1	8	10
	Total	17	11	12	6	1	8	3	10	7	2	9	85

tau-b = .70

data. Such actions appear to be scaled too high. Therefore, nations that have a higher proportion of their behavior in international organization contexts may have relatively more such events with inflated commitment scores. Small nations use international organizations relatively more than do large nations; hence, the average commitment scores for small nations may be somewhat inflated. On the other hand, pariah states such as China and East Germany have relatively few events in the context of international organizations, so their commitment scores are probably the least affected by this apparent source of error.

A second observation about the validity of the scale focuses on the eighth level, formal international agreements. Of the ten events that seemed to the author to fall in this group, only four were placed there by the operationalization procedure. Moreover, of the seven events that were placed in this level by the operationalization procedure, only four seemed correct. The problem appears to result from the computer routine that generated the scale. It was programmed to place each event in the highest appropriate commitment level. Some of the international agreement events had values on other CREON variables that appeared to be appropriate for a higher level of commitment. Thus, for example, an agreement to provide foreign aid appeared to be a foreign aid event—commitment level 10.

A third area of concern about validity centers on level 3 on the scale. Of the 11 events that fell into this level using the operationalization procedure, only 4 seemed correct; of the 12 events that appeared to belong to this level, only 4 came out on this level. Some of these miscodings involved the problem with international organizations that we have already discussed. Others revealed a subtle distinction between statements of general policy and statements of intention. A great deal of coder judgment is required. The criterion used to code commitment was "Is the event specific enough in its definition of the problem and policy that one can infer future behavior? If there is any doubt, record the lower level of commitment." To illustrate, in a speech on June 4, 1967, Nasser rejected in advance any declaration by the United States, the United Kingdom, or any other maritime nation that the Gulf of Aqaba was an international waterway. This rejection provides some specific indications about future Egyptian behavior. One may translate the statement to say that Egypt intends to follow a certain course concerning the Gulf of Aqaba. Therefore, the event was appropriately coded as an unconditional statement of intention by a top policymaker (level 7). This event can be contrasted with the May 25, 1963 approval by Ghana's President Nkrumah of a declaration of principles, including peaceful settlement of disputes, drawn up at the Addis Ababa Conference. The event was judged to be too vague to be translated into a meaningful statement of intentions, so it was coded 3 (general policy) rather than the 7 applied by the operationalization procedure.

A fourth class of validity problems concerns the proper value to be assigned events in which the actor engages in a negotiation. Compare the following events: (1) Switzerland has begun informal discussions with the United States to curb the use of secret bank accounts by Americans; (2) an Israeli delegate attends the Law of the Sea Conference, which will consider territorial sea and fishing limits. One may reasonably infer from the first event that Switzerland is contemplating a change in policy. The event, therefore, constitutes an implied evaluation of one's own policy and is correctly coded as level 3 on the commitment scale. One may not make a similar inference from the second event, which should have been considered a symbolic deed and recorded as commitment level 2. There were also two instances where meetings which should have been coded 2 were coded 1, thereby underestimating the level of commitment.

A further observation about validity is that the effect of coder reliability on this measure appears to be substantial. Of the 85 events, 17 (20 percent) are assigned to the wrong commitment level because of some apparent coder error. This is not surprising, given the large number of variables that were employed to operationalize this dimension.

At this point it should be noted that the preceding analysis of validity was structured to reveal the maximum level of invalidity. The independent commitment-coding decisions were made in such a way that in ambiguous cases they were in disagreement with the values assigned the cases in the CREON data. Another observer may well have concluded that there were fewer scaling errors in the sample of events. Considering the procedure, we believe that the scale has sufficient validity to warrant use in empirical analysis.

Before progressing to empirical analyses using the commitment scale, we present in Table 8.2 a set of events correctly scaled on commitment. These events provide a basis for the reader to judge whether the scale produces intuitively acceptable results—that is, results that have face validity. We believe that they do, although the results reinforce the point that high commitment is not equivalent to significance.

TABLE 8.2
Sample Events Scaled on Commitment

Commitment Level	Event
1. No commitment	In a note to Togo, Ghana protests the harboring of plotters who attempted to assassinate the Ghanaian president and calls for their repatriation. (December 7, 1962)
	Canadian Foreign Minister declares, in NATO Council final communique, that solution to German problem can be found only in reunification on basis of self-determination. (May 4, 1960)
2. Symbolic, insignificant nonverbal behaviors	Switzerland government orders two Soviet embassy employees to leave immediately because of espionage. (May 11, 1960)
	East Germany establishes a Consulate General in Dar-Es-Salaam, capital city of Tanzania. (February 19, 1965)
3. Verbal evaluations of own policy, or statement of general policy	Venezuela declares the Lake Maracaibo area to be a zone of military operations against Venezuelan saboteurs directed from Cuba. (October 27, 1962)
	U.S. resumes talks in Geneva, with USSR and the United Kingdom, on suspension of nuclear tests. (October 27, 1959)
4. Conditional statements of intention by lower policy officials	Ghanaian U.N. General Assembly delegate votes to adopt a resolution that would suspend South African membership in UNCTAD until it terminates its policy of racial discrimination. (December 13, 1968)
	USSR threatens to transfer the orders for 20 fishing vessels to U.K. yards, if Japan does not accept repayment terms it has offered. (May 11, 1963)
5. Unconditional statements of intention by lower policy officials	Soviet U.N. delegate Federenko tells newsmen that he has informed U.N. Secretary General U Thant that the USSR has accepted the Afro-Asian plan for settling the dispute over voting rights because of its debts to the U.N. (January 18, 1965)
	Switzerland states its readiness to put $200 million rendered under bilateral arrangements behind any one of the 10 major industrial powers in the IMF. (November 23, 1962)
6. Conditional statements of intention by top policy officials	In a message read by Secretary of State Herter to the NATO Council meeting, U.S. President Eisenhower says that, if negotiations with the USSR do not prosper, the U.S. looks to combine NATO forces as insurance against aggression. (May 2, 1960)
	West German Chancellor Erhard declares that West Germany will have to revise its political and economic relations with the UAR if Ulbricht is received there. (February 12, 1965)

TABLE 8.2   Continued

Commitment Level	Event
7. Unconditional statements of intention by top policy officials	At a meeting of the Presidents of American States, Mexico signs a declaration stating that the Latin American common market will be based on the complete convergence of LAFTA and CACM, and will take into account the interests of the Latin American countries not yet affiliated with these systems. (April 14, 1967)
	French President DeGaulle, in joint communique at EEC summit meeting, states that U.K., Denmark, and Ireland membership applications will be studied further by the EEC Council of Ministers and that there will probably be another top-level meeting of the EEC to decide on applications. (May 30, 1967)
8. Formal international agreements	Italian Foreign Minister Fanfani signs agreement on cooperation in agricultural research with USSR Foreign Minister Gromyko. (May 12, 1967)
	Within EEC, West Germany agrees with Turkey on achievement of full customs union. (June 25, 1963)
9. Reversible resource allocations and no resource allocations	Spain agrees to purchase 70 F-5 supersonic tactical fighters from the U.S. at an estimated cost of $50 million. (January 11, 1965)
	Costa Rican Security Minister Trejos announces closing of border with Panama. (December 2, 1968)
10. Partially reversible resource allocations	Tunisia recalls its troops on their way to the front during the Middle East crisis. (June 9, 1967)
	UAR Middle East News Agency announces that UAR is sending 52 experts and technicians to Yemen. (October 9, 1962)
11. Irreversible resource allocations	Two UAR MIGs attack the village of Nahub in the Federation of South Arabia.
	Yugoslavia grants $9.8 million to Tanganyika for purchase of agricultural machinery.

Empirical Application

A frequency distribution of the CREON data along the commitment scale is presented in Table 8.3. One prominent characteristic of the distribution is the concentration of behavior in the lower end of the scale. The lowest point on the scale—behaviors that are deemed to generate no commitment—contains 44 percent of the events. The lowest three categories together contain two-thirds of the events. Comparatively few events fall into the higher commitment categories. The five highest commitment levels contain only one-quarter of the events; the highest three levels contain only 9 percent of the events. The skew of the distribution is especially noteworthy considering that the errors in the scale tend to overestimate the level of commitment.

TABLE 8.3
Distribution of CREON Events on Commitment Scale

Commitment Score	Description	Frequency	Relative Frequencies
11	Irreversible resource allocations	491	3.9
10	Partially reversible resource allocations	40	.3
9	Reversible resource allocations and no resource allocations	570	4.5
8	Formal international agreements	621	4.9
7	Unconditional statements of intention by top policy officials	1224	9.6
6	Conditional statements of intention by top policy officials	134	1.1
5	Unconditional statements of intention by lower policy officials	1064	8.4
4	Conditional statements of intention by lower policy officials	113	0.9
3	Verbal evaluations of own policy or statements of general policy	2283	18.0
2	Symbolic, insignificant nonverbal behaviors	409	3.2
1	No commitment	5761	45.3
TOTAL		12710	100.0

TABLE 8.4
Percentage of Statements Related to Military.
Foreign Assistance, and Economic Transaction Behaviors

| Commitment Level | Type of Foreign Policy Behavior | | |
	Military[1]	Foreign Assistance[2]	Economic Transaction[3]
4. Conditional statements of intention by lower policy officials	47	12	5
5. Unconditional statements of intention by lower policy officials	17	5	3
6. Conditional statements of intention by top policy officials	52	18	1
7. Unconditional statements of intention by top policy officials	26	6	4

[1] Categories 1-2 of CREON variable, Military Behavior (see Technical Appendix).

[2] Categories 1-4 of CREON variable, Foreign Assistance Behavior (see Technical Appendix).

[3] Categories 1-4 of CREON variable, Economic Transaction Behavior (see Technical Appendix).

That behavior tends toward the low commitment end of the scale is a finding deserving of explanation. One possible explanation comes to mind—the "least effort" principle, whereby decision makers choose low-commitment alternatives when they are available. A characteristic of the distribution of the scale seems to confound this conclusion, however. By a ratio of roughly ten to one, unconditional statements of intention occur more frequently than conditional statements of intention. We can offer a possible reason for this apparent paradox. The substance of the problem may influence whether a pledge is made conditionally. Certain subject matters—trade, economic aid, and cultural exchanges—are not treated conditionally. Pledges made concerning more politically sensitive matters—military support, for example—are made with conditions attached. Because diplomatic behavior more frequently deals with less rather than more sensitive problems, it follows that unconditional pledges will occur more frequently than conditional pledges. Data produced by the CREON Project provide some support for this explanation, as revealed in Table 8.4. For both levels of policymakers, conditional statements of intention were more likely to have some military substance and less likely to involve foreign assistance or an economic transaction.

Returning to the distribution of the commitment scale, a second characteristic of the distribution is its marked discontinuities. Four categories—partially reversible resource allocations, symbolic insignificant nonverbal behaviors, and conditional statements of intention by either top or lower officials—have very low frequencies, especially when compared to their neighboring categories. This finding suggests that certain of the distinctions built into the scale, although conceptually sound, do not provide powerful tools for empirical differentiation. Their inclusion in the scale may entail greater costs in loss of economy than they are worth in terms of conceptual and empirical veracity.

TABLE 8.5
Commitment: Distribution by Nations

CREON Nation	1	2-3	4-5	6-8	9-10	11	Mean[1]
Belgium	41 (151)[2]	17 (65)	11 (40)	23 (85)	5 (19)	4 (13)	4.00
Canada	43 (161)	18 (66)	13 (49)	18 (63)	4 (16)	5 (17)	3.76
Chile	49 (98)	24 (49)	5 (9)	18 (37)	3 (6)	2 (3)	3.15
China (PRC)	50 (252)	20 (101)	13 (67)	7 (36)	4 (21)	5 (25)	3.14
Costa Rica	47 (75)	26 (42)	5 (8)	18 (28)	2 (3)	3 (4)	3.17
Cuba	48 (152)	15 (48)	13 (41)	13 (42)	8 (25)	4 (12)	3.54
Czechoslovakia	52 (107)	27 (56)	8 (17)	13 (26)	0 (0)	0 (0)	3.33
East Germany	48 (19)	19 (35)	7 (14)	16 (29)	6 (11)	4 (8)	3.44
Egypt	34 (149)	33 (144)	7 (30)	16 (72)	8 (36)	3 (12)	3.77
France	41 (342)	20 (167)	9 (72)	21 (173)	6 (47)	4 (37)	3.92
Ghana	57 (154)	20 (53)	5 (14)	15 (42)	2 (4)	2 (4)	2.62
Guinea	61 (123)	16 (32)	4 (9)	12 (24)	4 (9)	3 (6)	2.83
Iceland	52 (80)	23 (35)	5 (7)	13 (20)	6 (9)	2 (3)	3.10
India	50 (246)	25 (124)	4 (20)	13 (65)	4 (21)	3 (13)	3.05
Israel	38 (129)	23 (78)	15 (50)	10 (35)	8 (16)	10 (35)	4.04
Italy	44 (182)	16 (67)	9 (39)	21 (86)	6 (25)	4 (15)	3.85
Ivory Coast	54 (77)	19 (27)	7 (10)	17 (24)	3 (4)	1 (2)	3.09
Japan	39 (102)	22 (57)	12 (31)	14 (37)	8 (20)	5 (13)	3.94
Kenya	47 (44)	26 (24)	9 (8)	15 (14)	3 (3)	1 (1)	3.07
Lebanon	39 (56)	26 (38)	9 (13)	20 (29)	4 (6)	1 (2)	3.54
Mexico	46 (85)	24 (44)	12 (22)	16 (30)	1 (1)	2 (4)	3.20
New Zealand	56 (112)	27 (55)	3 (6)	14 (28)	0 (0)	0 (0)	2.82
Norway	50 (109)	23 (50)	7 (16)	16 (36)	1 (3)	3 (6)	3.16
Philippines	46 (89)	28 (55)	7 (13)	12 (23)	5 (10)	3 (5)	3.23
Poland	55 (128)	24 (57)	10 (23)	11 (25)	0 (0)	0 (0)	3.17
Soviet Union	51 (505)	15 (150)	12 (118)	15 (129)	6 (54)	3 (26)	3.27
Spain	48 (79)	27 (48)	9 (15)	8 (13)	4 (7)	2 (3)	2.95
Switzerland	37 (27)	25 (18)	14 (10)	19 (14)	4 (3)	1 (1)	3.69
Thailand	43 (66)	31 (48)	7 (11)	14 (21)	3 (4)	3 (4)	3.23
Tunisia	45 (121)	26 (70)	7 (18)	18 (48)	4 (11)	1 (3)	3.25
Turkey	41 (125)	28 (85)	7 (21)	18 (55)	5 (15)	3 (8)	3.55
Uganda	51 (73)	25 (36)	6 (9)	15 (21)	1 (2)	2 (3)	2.99
United States	37 (700)	23 (425)	11 (202)	17 (310)	5 (90)	8 (144)	4.01
Uruguay	52 (69)	21 (28)	9 (12)	15 (20)	1 (1)	2 (3)	2.97
Venezuela	48 (99)	22 (45)	7 (15)	17 (35)	3 (6)	2 (5)	3.25
West Germany	38 (235)	20 (124)	8 (51)	23 (141)	5 (33)	5 (36)	4.10
Yugoslavia	57 (139)	16 (39)	10 (25)	11 (28)	3 (8)	2 (6)	2.93
Zambia	33 (25)	35 (27)	4 (3)	21 (16)	7 (5)	1 (1)	3.69

[1] The mean level of commitment based on all 11 categories of the commitment scale.

[2] The first number is a relative frequency (number of events at that level of commitment divided by the nation's total number of events); the second number is an absolute frequency (number of events considered to fall at that level of commitment).

It is also useful to compare nations along the commitment dimension. Table 8.5 provides a breakdown of the commitment scores for each nation in the CREON sample. The mean level of commitment for each country is reported in this table, as well as the absolute and relative frequencies of that nation's behavior in the categories in a partially collapsed version of the commitment scale.

Perhaps the most significant aspect of the data in Table 8.5 is the lack of variation across nations in the mean level of commitment. West Germany is highest with 4.10; Ghana is lowest with 2.62. The range (1.5) is quite low, given the range of the scale. This cross-national similarity strongly suggests that some set of forces leads nations to fairly-similar patterns of commitment behavior. All nations employ large amounts of low-commitment behavior in their conduct of foreign policy. All nations also engage in some highly committing behavior. An important research task is to identify the forces that produce such similarity of commitment.

Although the national patterns of commitment are very similar, there is some variation across nations, and we should try to account for it. We cannot provide convincing, empirically validated explanations at this time. However, the pattern of variation provides a basis for exploratory speculation.

The first salient pattern is the tendency for more economically developed nations to fall into the higher ranks in the table. Perhaps financial well-being encourages a tendency toward more intense commitment in foreign policy behavior. This explanation is not completely satisfactory, though. Some relatively rich nations—Norway, New Zealand, and the Soviet Union are the most significant cases—are not ranked highly, and some poor nations—Cuba, Egypt, Turkey, and Zambia—are relatively high.

A second factor appears to be whether the state was a participant in a military conflict during the decade (1959-1968). This may account for the high ranking of Egypt and Israel. However, China and India, which fought a series of border wars during the 1960s, rank quite low on the scale.

A third factor that might be involved in the pattern of commitment is the political or geographic isolation of states. Iceland and Norway are on the periphery of Europe. New Zealand is far removed geographically from all nations except Australia. An especially notable case is China. Politically isolated, its low level of commitment is determined by the very low relative frequency (7 percent) of formal international agreements and statements of intention by high-level policy officials. Other nations having low relative frequencies for these categories of commitment are also social isolates: Israel (10 percent), Spain (8 percent), and Yugoslavia (11 percent).

A related phenomenon is the effect of neutrality and nonalignment. Many of the nations ranking low on the scale are states that conscientiously avoided entanglement in the East-West conflict of the 1960s. Examples are Guinea, Ghana, Iceland, India, and Yugoslavia. Egypt and Switzerland are anomalies for this observation.

A final factor appears to be the age of the nation. Most of the lowest-ranking nations have recently emerged from colonialism. With the exception of Zambia, all the African nations in the sample ranked in the bottom ten. The extreme poverty of these nations may play a part in producing this pattern, but we would also conjecture that two other characteristics of new nations serve to reduce the intensity of commitment in their behavior. First, the memory of recent external domination may produce in elites a strong desire to maintain autonomy over their behavior, including the avoidance of constraints. Second, these nations are located in regions lacking both a history of intraregional interaction and a rich set of regional organizations and linkages. Presumably such a history and organized environment should stimulate self-constraining behavior, so the new nations that lack these forces lack one strong set of positive inducements to more intense commitment.

The arguments just presented are highly conjectural and should be read not as conclusions but as working hypotheses. Space is lacking in this chapter to undertake a thorough empirical investigation of causal forces that affect the intensity of commitment in foreign policy behavior. Clearly, such an analysis will have to be multivariate and will be complex. The previous discussion does, however, suggest some candidates for further analysis.

SUMMARY

The common thread running through various uses of the concept of commitment is constraints. Therefore, commitment as a characteristic of foreign policy behavior is best seen as the creation of constraints on the actor's future behavior, provided that the constraints can be reasonably anticipated to be consequences of the action. The intensity of commitment in an action is the extent of constraint produced by the action. Constraints are created through two fundamental processes: allocation of resources and the generation of expectations in others. Allocating resources generates expectations, so in a real sense expectations are the key to commitment. Based on these premises and a series of additional assumptions, an 11-point ordinal scale of the intensity of commitment in an event was created. Tests for validity reveal some specific problems, but overall the measure's validity appears to be high.

Preliminary analysis using the intensity of commitment scale indicates a definite preponderance of low commitment behavior over high. Although this finding may indicate the operation of a "least effort" principle, other characteristics of the distribution of events appear to be inconsistent with such an interpretation. Across nations, there is a notable consistency in mean level of commitment, suggesting that membership in the international system places some strong, uniform constraints on nations to act to constrain themselves. Variation, therefore, is probably due to contextual factors, especially the nature of the situation and the type of substantive problem being confronted. Cross-national variation appears to be interpretable but is not explained at this time. Viable candidates for explanatory factors include the nation's capacity to act, its social and geographic isolation, its recent experience with bondage relationships, and its recent participation in military conflict.

APPENDIX 8.1
Operationalizing Commitment with CREON Data

Level 1: No Commitment

The lowest point on the commitment scale contains events that do not produce commitment; they neither allocate resources nor generate expectations. They are identified in the first two columns of the Sequential Action Scheme (SAS) employed by CREON (see description in the Technical Appendix at the end of this book). Each of the CREON variables that is included in one of the behavior measures is described in full in the Technical Appendix. As part of this description, intercoder reliabilities and frequencies for each of the categories are presented. Two basic SAS categories are included. Desire statements concern the actor's wishes about the future behavior of other entities. Evaluative statements record the actor's evaluation of current or past events. Excluded are events in which the actor makes some evaluation of his own behavior because these events imply either the continuation or discontinuation of present policies. The following SAS codes fall into the lowest point on the scale:

10	Evaluation: procedural
11	Evaluation: nonspecific
13	Evaluation: specific—other's policy
20	Desire: procedural
21	Desire: general policy
23	Desire: future general policy
25	Desire: future deed

Level 2: Symbolic, Insignificant Nonverbal Behaviors

Symbolic actions constitute the next highest level on the commitment scale. The primary means for identifying such actions in CREON is column 1 of SAS. A code of 4 indicates a symbolic deed, defined as "those deeds involving only minor resource commitment which would be regarded as 'insignificant' given the total income of the actor government; in other words, the necessary resources can be readily absorbed by the actor within its existing budget and without special allocation" (C. Hermann et al., 1973: 77).

A second method for identifying symbolic actions involves specific classes of exchange relationships. When a state receives things from another without any reciprocal exchange, expectations will tend to be generated, but they will also tend to be of an ambiguous nature. Such actions are captured by the following codes of the Transfer with Foreign Entity variable (see description of this variable in the Technical Appendix):

02	Receives grant
04	Receives loan
11	Receives reparation

We also include in this category events in which the actor adopts a position on some matter of procedure or protocol. Although these positions indicate specific intentions with regard to some issue, the issues generally are narrow and trivial. The long-term implications of such behavior tend to be ambiguous. Therefore, it is reasonable to include them among the symbolic actions. They are identified by the following code on the SAS:

30	Intent: procedural

Level 3: Verbal Evaluations of
Own Policy/Statements of General Policy

Events that generate expectations for future behavior through evaluations of one's own behavior or by statements of one's general policy comprise the third level on the scale. Evaluations of one's own behavior are recorded in the SAS using the following codes:

12	Evaluative: specific—own policy
14	Evaluative: specific—own and other's policy

In the CREON data, general policy statements express intentions in "vague or general terms so that it is not clear what specific activities the actor intends to undertake" (C. Hermann et al., 1973: 81). Such events are identified in the SAS by the code:

31   Intent: general policy

Level 4: Conditional Statements of Intention by Lower Officials

The next highest level on the scale contains conditional statements of intention by lower-level governmental officials. Lower-level governmental officials are here construed to mean all officials *except* heads of state, government, or ruling party, cabinet ministers or their equivalents, or ambassadors. In the CREON data, three types of variables partially tap the difference between these two levels of officialdom. First, if a high official announces the decision, then presumably that person participated in the decision. Such an occurrence is captured by the Official Position of Announcer of Action variable, code 2: "political executive (head of government or ruling political party or minister within acting state)" (see description in Technical Appendix). Second, it is reasonable to infer the participation of a top leader if the action is announced by a lower governmental official who clearly indicates that the head of state participated in the decision. This would be indicated by a code of 1 ("yes") on the CREON variable Head of State Present (for description see Technical Appendix) *and* the following codes on the Official Position of Announcer of Action variable:

4   Communications personnel
5   Military personnel
7   Career bureaucrat

The third means for identifying top officials is through the CREON variable Setting (for description see Technical Appendix). This variable concerns whether the action grew out of some meeting between officials of different governments. The following codes would indicate that a top official made the decision:

1   Meeting between heads of state or equivalents
2   Meeting between ministers
3   Meeting between head of state and minister or ambassador
5   Meeting between minister and ambassador

If any of these three configurations occurs in the event, then it is presumed that the decision was clearly that of a top official. If not, then the decision was that of lower officials.

Whether the action was a statement of intent and whether the intent is conditional or unconditional are both indicated by a series of codes in SAS. Conditional intentions are identified by the following codes:

34   Intent: verbal policy–contingent
36   Intent: verbal deed–contingent

Conditional intentions are also indicated by codes of 517 (Threaten) and 610 (Offer) on the CREON Revised WEIS variable (for description see Technical Appendix).

Level 5: Unconditional Statements of Intention by Lower Officials

This point on the scale contains unconditional statements of intention by lower-level officials. Lower-level officials are identified in the same way as in Level 4—that is, by the lack of a clear indication in the data of participation of higher-level officials. Unconditional statements of intention are indicated by two codes in the SAS:

33   Intent: verbal policy–noncontingent
35   Intent: verbal deed–noncontingent

Unconditional intentions are also indicated by the following codes from the CREON Revised WEIS variable:

502 Negative Intention
511 Reject
516 Warn
602 Positive Intention
605 Promise
608 Agree

Level 6: Conditional Statements of Intention by Top Officials

Conditional statements of intention by higher-level officials are identified by a combination of the codes indicating top officials (discussed in Level 4) and the contingent intent codes from SAS and Revised WEIS listed in Level 4.

Level 7: Unconditional Statements of Intention by Top Officials

Unconditional statements of intention by higher-level officials are indicated by the presence of a top official in the decision-making process (as discussed in Level 4) and the noncontingent intent codes from the SAS and Revised WEIS listed in Level 5.

Level 8: Formal International Agreements

The next point on the commitment scale represents pledges made in written international agreements. There were two basic strategies for identifying written international agreements. In the first strategy, if "yes" was coded on the Negotiation/Bargaining Behavior variable (for a description see Technical Appendix), the event was one in which representatives of two or more nations met and substantive discussions occurred. The Revised WEIS scheme was used to supplement this information. The event had to be coded 829 on WEIS, which means "Increase Relationship: Increase economic, military, technical, or cultural exchanges bilaterally; includes the signing of formal agreements involving the transfer of resources." This process eliminates from Level 8 all negotiations that do not come to fruition in some agreement. Finally, there needed to be some way to eliminate from this level those events in which the negotiators were not governmental officials. This was done by including only those cases that were coded 7 or lower on the Setting variable.

The second strategy for identifying written agreements begins with the CREON variable Channel (for description see Technical Appendix), which records the method for announcing the action. Included were events coded 4: "diplomatic communique, text of treaty or other diplomatic document between states or ruling political parties; includes notes and informal letters." From this subset we eliminated events that did not occur in a multilateral context. We did this by excluding those events coded 9 on the Setting variable. However, many events generated from a multilateral meeting could be communicated by diplomatic documents but would not be written agreements. Therefore, events that were not also coded as involving Treaty Behavior (see Technical Appendix) were excluded. Treaty behavior consists of "behavior proposing, discussing, establishing, involving, or altering (including terminating) a contractual relationship between two or more nations in which they are signatories to a written document that (1) does not involve a permanent secretariat or other full-time group to administer the activities of the treaty, and (2) does not involve a one-time loan or other single-exchange economic transaction." Finally, it was necessary to exclude those events that were merely agreements to meet and discuss but did not describe matters of substance. This was done by excluding all events coded 608 on the Revised WEIS scheme. That code is titled Agree and is defined as "accept proposal, agree to meet to negotiate, agree to future action. *Does not include the signing of formal agreements or the transfer of resources*" (C. Hermann et al., 1973: 76; italics added).

Level 9: Reversible Resource Allocations/
No Resource Allocations

This level is defined as reversible resource allocations and other significant nonverbal behaviors that involve no resource allocations. This level on the scale has been operationalized using a number of variables and categories. The primary indicator of this level of commitment was the SAS category "significant deeds." According to the CREON coding scheme, significant deeds are "those deeds that represent a significant budgetary commitment on the part of the acting government, often requiring a special allocation or requiring a relocation of existing budgetary allocations" (C. Hermann et al., 1973: 80).

This level of commitment should also include actions involving military resources, provided that the control of the resources is not transferred to another actor and the resources themselves are not destroyed by use. Such uses of military resources are indicated in a number of ways in the CREON data. First, in SAS there is a category "military nonconflict deeds" defined as "actions involving the use of military resources in nonconflict situations, but for military purposes" (C. Hermann et al., 1973: 80). Second, a variable indicating internal military mobilization, deployment, or alert—named Internal Military Mobilization (see Technical Appendix)—also taps relevant events. Third, three codes on External Use of Military Force (see Technical Appendix) reveal events that should go into this level of the scale:

2   Reinforcement of bases abroad, placement of bases or overseas troops on alert status
3   Actual evacuation or rescue of civilian or nonessential military personnel
4   Show of force in location where actor's forces had not been recently. . . . This category includes war games and military exercises conducted outside actor's country.

Two of the Revised WEIS codes indicate behaviors that belong at this level of commitment. Code 718 (Demonstrate) includes "armed forces mobilization, movement, exercise, display; non-military demonstration sponsored by government" (C. Hermann et al., 1973: 76). Code 723 (Increase Military Capability) includes events that increase military spending, increase troop levels, develop weapons, authorize military action, or call up reserves (C. Hermann et al., 1973: 76).

The last set of events that falls into this level of commitment involves the reciprocal transfer of resources. Because the actor receives something as part of the exchange, we cannot assume that there will be resource constraints in the future. Indeed, the exchange may reduce resource constraints. Thus, we believe that such behaviors are most appropriately treated as equivalent in commitment to other significant deeds that do not entail an increase in resource constraints. Reciprocal transfers of resources are indicated by three categories in the variable Transfer with Foreign Entity:

06   Make sale
07   Purchase
08   Barter
12   Currency—precious metal exchange

Level 10: Partially Reversible Resource Allocations

The tenth level of commitment is represented by those events in which resources are used but the usage is reversible; the resources can either be recovered or recreated at some cost. Such events can occur either by granting partial control over resources to some external entity or by eliminating or reducing some capability. There are two ways to identify such events in the CREON data. The first involves the granting of technical assistance and the use of personnel in another nation. Such actions are clearly reversible because the donor nation maintains ultimate control over these persons. Events of this nature were identified first by Foreign Assistance Behavior (see Technical Appendix) when it was coded 4—actual agreement, announcement, or transfer of foreign assistance (other than loans or credits). This set of events, however, could include many irreversible foreign assistance actions. Technical assistance needs the movement of personnel across national boundaries. This movement was captured by the variable Number of Personnel Moving Temporarily (see Technical Appendix). Any code other than 9 (not applicable) indicated the temporary transfer of personnel across national boundaries. It is possible that a meeting to agree to such a program could meet these two criteria. But such events would more appropriately fall under one of the lower levels of commitment, those that involve statements of intention. Events of this type can be filtered out by using the Setting variable. All actions that occur in a meeting of governmental representatives (coded 1 through 8) are excluded.

The other actions that fall into this level of commitment are those in which the actor reduces his capabilities. In the CREON data, such behaviors primarily concern reductions in military forces. These events are indicated by Adherence to International Agreements (see Technical Appendix), code 7 (limits or destroys part of his country's military capability or armed forces) and by the Revised WEIS scheme, code 826 (Decrease Military Capability: reduce military spending, troop levels, or readiness for military action).

Level 11: Irreversible Resource Allocations

Level 11 actions entail the highest commitment. They use tangible resources in such a way that the resources are destroyed or made irretrievable. One way in which that is done is by sending troops into battle. The SAS allows the identification of such events. On that set of variables, military conflict events are defined as "actions that engage the actor in the use of force in times of actual combat" (C. Hermann et al., 1973: 80). A second method for distinguishing such events is through the following codes of the External Use of Military Force variable:

5   Supply equipment to foreign entity actually engaged in combat
6   Supply military advisers to foreign entity actually engaged in combat
7   Engage in air or sea nonnuclear attacks or bombardments against foreign entity
8   Engage in ground combat and/or nuclear air or sea attacks

A third set of events that involve irreversible resource allocation are found in the Transfer with Foreign Entity variable. The relevant codes are concerned with making grants and loans as well as repaying debts. The particular codes are:

01   Gives grant
03   Makes loan
05   Repays loan
10   Pays reparations
13   Releases detainees/POWs

Computer Program

For the purposes of data analysis in the CREON Project, the commitment scale was generated through a series of data transformations using the SPSS programming package. The statements to produce these transformations are available from the author.

NOTES

1. My thanks to Michael Sullivan for pointing out this ambiguity in an earlier draft of this chapter.

2. This conceptualization of commitment is very similar to the definitions of commitment used by sociologists. Roby (1960: 255) states that "a natural and convenient index of the degree of commitment in a decision is the amount of information it carries about the final response choice." He goes on to say that "it appears to be true, in general, that commitment entails the exchange of potential opportunity for some degree of realized payoff" (1960: 262). Becker (1960) argues that commitment is a central concept for accounting for consistent behavior. "The committed person has acted in such a way as to involve other interests of his, originally extraneous to the action he is engaged in, directly in that action" (1960: 35). He goes on to point out that these "side bets" constrain future activity, and that is the crux of the commitment.

3. If one were not interested in coding discrete actions, one could measure resource allocations using aggregate data and expectations through some content analysis scheme. For a comparable effect, see Martin (1977).

4. For purely operational reasons, in the CREON commitment scale there is no distinction made between conditional and unconditional international agreements.

9

MARGARET G. HERMANN
CHARLES F. HERMANN
GERALD L. HUTCHINS

Affect

I can see, Mr. President, that you also are not without a sense of anxiety for the fate of the world, not without an understanding and correct assessment of the nature of modern warfare and what war entails. What good would a war do you? You threaten us with war. But you well know that the very least you would get in response would be what you had given us; you would suffer the same consequences. And that must be clear to us— people invested with authority, trust and responsibility. We must not succumb to light-headedness and petty passions, regardless of whether elections are forthcoming in one country or another. These are all transitory things, but should war indeed break out, it would not be in our power to contain or stop it, for such is the logic of war. I have taken part in two wars, and I know that war ends only when it has rolled through cities and villages, sowing death and destruction everywhere [Khrushchev, 1973].

The above quotation is from the long and somewhat rambling, pivotal message that Chairman Khrushchev sent to President Kennedy on October 26, 1962 at the height of the Cuban missile crisis. This message has been widely interpreted in the West as having been written personally by Nikita Khrushchev and as having provided a break in the tense confrontation between the United States and the Soviet Union. The message in its entirety offers a variety of insights. As evidenced by this quotation, the author conveys considerable feeling about the issues under consideration. Note his characterization of Kennedy, his statement concerning the misleading nature of transitory events, and his perception of the irreversibility and destruction of war once begun.

The following words and phrases that Khrushchev used—"anxiety," "understanding," "suffer the same consequences," "trust," "sowing death and

AUTHORS' NOTE: We wish to thank William Dixon for his aid with the data analysis for this chapter.

destruction"—express his feelings toward the objects he is discussing. Such terms indicate the affect of the communication—that is, the actor's current sentiments as manifested in his/her behavior toward a recipient or other object. In foreign policy, affect becomes the discernible current feelings of a government toward another government or other external entity. Affect is expressed in all behavior whether it takes the form of words or deeds.

If the reader thinks that foreign policy is the product of careful calculation or emanates from an abstraction identified as the nation, he/she may find it difficult to imagine that the manifestation of emotions or feelings constitutes a very significant property of foreign policy behavior. However, the position taken in this chapter—as indeed throughout this volume—is that foreign policy involves the behavior of individuals and collections of individuals who express affect not only in their personal behavior but also in their public behavior. Such expressions of affect may reflect personal feelings, as those in the message from Khrushchev have generally been assumed to do. Alternatively, the expressed affect may be designed as a calculated effort to convey the current official sentiments of the government and, accordingly, may not reflect accurately the personal feelings of some key individuals within the government. But whether the expressed affect is planned and impersonal or a reflection of individual feelings, it provides clues to the government's present attitude toward another government or actor in the international arena.

Not only does affect provide information about attitudes, it also can give us some indication of a government's intentions toward another government or actor. The feelings expressed suggest the current mood of the government that is acting. The current mood—whether planned or spontaneous—implies the desired or intended outcome. At least, the current mood indicates the direction—whether positive or negative in tone—of the behavior and intensity with which the behavior is being implemented. Because intentions are often obscure, decisions are made based exclusively on an assessment of more discernible and "hard" information, such as capabilities ("They have the military capability to attack; therefore, we must assume they will do so."). Such worst-case analyses can lead to a tragic, self-fulfilling prophecy. Thus, an affect measure that could be shown to be an accurate indicator of a government's current disposition toward another government or international actor could have great significance for analysts and policymakers.

The issue is whether public manifestations of affect are dependable indicators of the feelings and, in turn, the intentions of the actors. What about deception— is deception a problem with public manifestations of affect? It would seem unlikely that the affect expressed in most of a government's behaviors is deceptive. Individuals and governments that are caught being deliberately deceptive pay a price, for example, in international prestige, in increased suspicion from other governments, perhaps even in increased isolation. Moreover, it is difficult to maintain a deceptive expression of affect for long periods. At some point, a government will want to signal to others what it is doing and why—signals that will contradict in affect the deceptive behavior.

It is this contradictory behavior that can provide clues to deception in the manifestation of affect and indicate to the analyst where corrective steps need to be taken. Contradictions can be shown in differences in words and deeds. Thus, the affect expressed in what is being said may not match the affect manifested in what the government is doing. Returning to our Cuban missile crisis example, we note the discrepancy between the reassuring statements given Kennedy by the Soviet ambassador about the lack of emplacement of offensive weapons in Cuba and their actual appearance in Cuba. Discrepancies in the patterning of affect toward another government on an issue across events may also provide clues about deception, particularly if specific events are highly discrepant from a fairly stable pattern. The analyst would want to look more closely at these discrepant events. One other type of contradiction, probably the most prevalent, results from lack of coordination and from disagreements among members of a government. A policymaker may make known his/her own feelings about an activity that are contradictory to the government's official proclamations. An example is the difference in the intensity of affect expressed by Khrushchev in the message cited at the beginning of this chapter and by the Soviet government in a message that came only hours later.

We have suggested here only a few ways of checking for deception. These procedures may in themselves provide interesting data about the current dispositions of governments toward other actors in the international arena. Since we can check for deception, it becomes feasible to assess affect using public expressions of policymakers and governments. Such a measure is important because it will help us learn about governments' intentions. In the rest of this chapter we will develop a measure of affect, first presenting a conceptualization and then an operationalization for this foreign policy output.

CONCEPTUALIZATION OF AFFECT

A discussion of affect is not unique to this chapter. Affect is a common means of referring to emotion for psychologists studying personality (see, Lazarus, 1966; Tomkins, 1962). Affect has also been examined in the international relations literature, particularly with regard to the origins of World War I (for example, Holsti et al., 1968; Zinnes, 1968). Our conceptualization of affect builds on these two types of material.

We define affect as the actor's feelings toward a recipient that are manifested in current behavior. Like the psychologist, we perceive that affect represents a feeling, sentiment, disposition, or emotional state. Affect can be negative or positive in tone. Thus, we can feel happy, satisfied, accepting, joyous, loving—experience positive affect. Or we can feel hostile, angry, frustrated, fearful, suspicious—experience negative affect.

As we have already noted, we are interested in not only the personal feelings of an individual policymaker but also the shared dispositions of a group of policymakers who form a decision-making unit. This usage of affect is similar to that of Holsti et al. (1968) and Zinnes (1968). We believe it is possible to talk about the shared disposition of a set of policymakers who are making the foreign policy decisions for a government. We perceive that policymakers express such shared dispositions all the time. Thus, the affect measure being developed in this chapter is concerned with feelings expressed in the foreign policy behavior of collectivities of individuals as well as the feelings expressed in the foreign policy behavior of individuals.

As we conceptualize affect, it also has several other important characteristics. First, affect has both direction and intensity. We have already said something about direction in noting that there is positive and negative affect. Affect at times can also be neutral—the affect is rather bland with little clues as to emotional content. By intensity of affect we mean the degree of affect that is expressed. How hostile or accepting are the policymakers in what they do or say? Direction and intensity provide us with different ways of looking at affect.

Second, affect is dyadic in nature. For affect to be present there must be an actor who is expressing some feelings and a recipient who is the object of the feelings. The affect is being directed toward someone or something. In the case of foreign policy behavior, affect is usually expressed by one government toward another government or international actor. For example, "the United States government is pleased with the Canadian prime minister's proposed solution to the problem." Someone from the United States government—a spokesman—is indicating positive affect toward the proposal of a policymaker from another government. To be considered affect in the context of this chapter, there must be feelings directed from policymakers in one government toward policymakers or political units in other countries or external organizations. A sentiment is being expressed about or toward something external to the actor's nation.

Third, affect as we define it is relevant only to the immediate action or event. In other words, affect is momentary or transitory, linking an actor's feelings to a recipient at a single point in time. As a result, a government can express negative affect toward an ally and positive affect toward an adversary depending on the circumstances. Affect is situation-specific. We are interested in the policymakers' feelings or dispositions toward another government or international actor at the moment.

Fourth, affect is expressed in both verbal and nonverbal behavior. That is, policymakers indicate their affect both in what they say and what they do. It is probably easier for the reader to see how affect is expressed in what policymakers are saying than in what they are doing. But certain behaviors, such as declarations of war or signing a treaty, suggest accompanying affect. There is probably, however, more inference involved in making affective judgments about a government's deeds if there is no verbal accompaniment to the activity.

As we have conceptualized affect, the reader may see a strong resemblance between it and what is often examined in studies of conflict and cooperation. Although affect can overlap with what we ordinarily consider a conflict behavior (harmful actions or actions with the intent to harm) and cooperative behavior (actions that assist and intend to assist), affect is not identical to these concepts. Cooperative behavior can be accompanied by negative affect ("We are being forced to help you.") and vice versa ("We engaged in the subversive activity for your own good."). However, for affect to be distinguished from cooperation and conflict, deeds must be accompanied by some words. When deeds or physical behaviors occur alone (without any verbal accompaniment), the indicators of affect and cooperation/conflict are the same.

In sum, affect as a foreign policy behavior involves transitory negative and positive emotions regarding another actor in the international arena as shown in the verbal and nonverbal behaviors of policymakers of the acting government. Affect focuses on what the policymakers of a government are feeling toward other governments as reflected in what they are saying and doing at the moment.

MEASURING AFFECT

In moving to measure affect, the characteristics we have been specifying become helpful. We are interested in finding out what policymakers and governments in specific countries are saying about or doing with/to other governments or international actors. More particularly, we want to examine these statements and actions for the feelings they express. And we would like to have such information across a variety of occasions or situations.

One type of data that meets these specifications is event data. Here the researcher has what would appear to be a single activity or statement. Thus, using the event it is possible to focus on a transitory or momentary action. Moreover, events are usually defined to include an acting government (or authoritative representative) and a recipient government or international actor. The recipient can be only one government or international actor, or there can be multiple governments or international actors as recipients.

In ascertaining affect using events, we are interested in noting the types of modifiers that accompany verbal statements and the feeling tone that accompanies deeds (nonverbal actions). Do the modifiers in verbal statements express some sort of feeling or emotion toward the recipient? What is the direction and intensity of this feeling or emotion? For example, consider a statement by Gandhi of India that "we find the behavior of China at our borders reprehensible." Gandhi is expressing negative affect toward China—China's behavior is reprehensible. And the feeling is quite intense. Note the positive affect in a second example: "The United States government is impressed and proud of Israel's accomplishment on this front." Once more the feelings being expressed are fairly intense.

Deeds are considered to have some affective component if they are supportive of the recipient or if they are deliberately nonsupportive of the recipient. Thus, giving aid to another country would involve positive affect, whereas mobilizing troops on the border of another country would indicate negative affect. Particularly with deeds, it may be impossible to ascertain whether or not the action is supportive or nonsupportive. In this case the event would be classified as involving neutral affect. Verbal statements may also involve no expression of affect and, as a result, fall into the neutral category.

The previous two paragraphs suggest that it is possible to develop an affect scale. The scale could run from strong expressions of positive affect to neutral affect to strong expressions of negative affect. Captured in the scale would be both direction and intensity.

There are precedents for developing a scale of affect using event data. We refer to the scales, for example, of Azar (1970), Corson (1969), Moses et al. (1967), Odell (1975), and Richman (1968).

Measuring Affect Using the CREON Data

For purposes of illustration and in a manner similar to treatment of other measures in this book, affect has been operationalized using the CREON event data set. As we noted in Chapter 2, CREON events are defined so that they can include multiple recipients for a behavior. An event has an actor, an action, and one or more recipients (see C. Hermann et al., 1973). Events are considered to have a direct target toward whom the activity is addressed and an indirect object, which is the entity the actor is trying to influence. Often the direct target and indirect object are one and the same countries. But at times they differ. Consider an example: Chou En-Lai, in addressing the Albanian Party Congress, decries U.S. imperialism. The direct target of Chou En-Lai's speech is the Albanian Party Congress; indirect object is the United States.

In coding an event for affect, the event was divided into the pairs of nations (dyads) involved in the event. If the targets and objects differed, there were dyadic events involving the actor and each target, as well as dyadic events involving the actor and the indirect objects. Each dyadic event was scored for affect.

In coding for affect, the coders were asked to judge the emotions and feelings expressed in the statement or deed. Did words in the statement or aspects of the deed suggest the presence of positive or negative affect? If neither positive nor negative affect was present, the event was coded as neutral. Moreover, how strongly was the positive or negative affect expressed? How intense was it? The emphasis for the coders in scoring for affect was "on the feeling or emotion expressed in the action (words or deeds) without any attempt to judge either the actor's sincerity or the affective history between the actor and the target" (C. Hermann et al., 1973: 87). A five-point scale was used in coding for affect. The categories were as follows:

1 = *Strong expression of positive affect:* Use of very favorable modifiers in verbal statements to recipients; deeds are highly supportive of the recipient.

2 = *Mild expression of positive affect:* Verbal statement or deed shows that the actor is positive (friendly, supportive of) toward the recipient, but not strongly so.

3 = *Neutral expression:* Verbal statement or deed indicates nothing about the actor's affect toward the recipient.

4 = *Mild expression of negative affect:* Verbal statement or deed shows disapproval or criticism of recipient, but not strongly so.

5 = *Strong expression of negative affect:* Use of very unfavorable modifiers in verbal statements to recipients; deeds of a violent nature are employed against recipient.

Intercoder reliability for this five-point scale was .80 using the Krippendorff (1971) agreement coefficient.[1] Table 9.1 presents several illustrative dyadic events that were coded at each point on the scale.

One concern in developing a scale like the one just proposed for affect centers on the neutral category. A dyadic event can be coded neutral because there is no affect expressed or because it is hard for the coder to decide whether or not affect was expressed. After all the dyadic events were coded for affect and assigned a score on the affect scale, we made an attempt to separate out these two types of

TABLE 9.1
Illustrative Dyadic Events at Each Point of Affect Scale

Strong Expression of Positive Affect

1. Dyadic event involving France and Czechoslovakia, December 5, 1968: French Defense Minister Messmer in speech to French National Assembly in strong language condems Soviet invasion of Czechoslovakia.

2. Dyadic event involving West Germany and the Netherlands, April 8, 1960: West German Foreign Minister Brentano signs agreement stipulating that West Germany will pay $67,144,000 in claims to citizens of the Netherlands persecuted by Nazis.

Mild Expression of Positive Affect

1. Dyadic event involving United States and India, May 22, 1963: U.S. President Kennedy declares in press conference that U.S. will give further economic assistance to India.

2. Dyadic event involving Norway and Great Britain, February 2, 1965: Norwegian Premier Gerhardsen said while visiting Great Britain that it is in the joint interests of EFTA countries that the British economy and pound should remain strong.

Neutral Affect

1. Dyadic event involving East Germany and Poland, July 21, 1964: East German First Secretary Ulbricht attends meeting in Poland.

2. Dyadic event involving Soviet Union and Rumania, June 21, 1960: Soviet Premier Khrushchev says at Rumanian Party Congress that imperialist wars are inevitable as long as socialism has not triumphed all over the world.

Mild Expression of Negative Affect

1. Dyadic event involving China (PRC) and Yugoslavia, January 20, 1961: China (PRC) officially states that Yugoslavian revisionism is greatest danger to international communist movement.

2. Dyadic event involving Israel and Egypt, May 23, 1967: Israeli Premier Eshkol in speech to Knesset urges major powers to see that Egypt does not restrain Israeli ships from navigating into Gulf of Aqaba.

Strong Expression of Negative Affect

1. Dyadic event involving Soviet Union and United States, June 3, 1960: Soviet Premier Khrushchev at a press conference states that U.S. President Eisenhower is completely lacking in will power and is unfit to be the leader of a great power.

2. Dyadic event involving Guinea and South Africa, April 7, 1960: Guinea with Emergency Conference of all independent African states recommends expulsion of South Africa from Commonwealth.

---

neutral affect. In some of the CREON events governments are merely mentioned as part of an acting government's statement or deed and have little to do with the substance of the event. For example, Cuban Premier Castro charges that the statement by his sister, Cuban exile Juana Castro Ruz, in Mexico was written by the U.S. embassy. Mexico has little to do with the substance of the event—it is merely mentioned; therefore, it is hard to judge the appropriate affect for a Cuba-Mexico dyadic event. Events of this nature, instead of being coded as neutral in affect, were eliminated from the affect scale. International organizations often fell into the mentioned category as they were the setting where the event was occurring. By eliminating these neutral events, we attempted to eliminate recipients who were

TABLE 9.2
Distribution of CREON Events Across Affect Scale
After "Mentioned" Events Deleted

Scale Point	Description	Frequency	Percent
1	Strong Expression of Positive Affect	636	3.4
2	Mild Expression of Positive Effect	6,277	33.2
3	Neutral Affect	7,313	38.6
4	Mild Expression of Negative Affect	4,034	21.3
5	Strong Expression of Negative Affect	675	3.6
	Total	18,935	

more part of the context than of the substance of the event.[2] It was hoped in this way to make the neutral category more reflective of a lack of expressed affect. Table 9.2 shows the distribution of dyadic events across the various scalar points after the "mentioned" dyadic events were deleted. The mean affect score across these CREON dyadic events is 2.88; the standard deviation is .89.

It is possible with the affect scale to separate out intensity and direction. Thus, we can combine scale points 1 and 2 (strong and mild expressions of positive affect) and also 4 and 5 (strong and mild expressions of negative affect) to look at direction. In this way, we would have the following scale: +1 = positive affect, 0 = neutral affect, and −1 = negative affect. To assess intensity of affect, we can combine scale points 1 and 5 (strong expressions of positive and negative affect) as well as 2 and 4 (mild expressions of positive and negative affect) to make the following scale: 0 = neutral affect, 1 = mild affect, 2 = strong affect.

The mean score for direction of affect across the CREON dyadic events is +.12; the standard deviation is .78. The mean score for intensity of affect across the CREON dyadic events is .68; the standard deviation, .60.

In addition to looking at the total distribution of events on the affect scale, we can examine the affective behavior of the nations in the CREON sample. Space does not permit reporting the affect scores for every dyad;[3] therefore, we will look at each nation's affect expression toward various types of recipients. We have divided the recipients into four groups—Western community nations, Brazzaville African and Latin American nations, Afro-Asian nations, and Communist nations—based on the results of Russett's (1967) Q factor analysis of 1963-64 United Nations voting patterns.[4] (The particular nations included in each of these sets of countries are listed in the note to Table 9.3.) Because we are assuming affect will change from situation to situation—that it is transitory—we will also present data for three-year time spans (1960-62, 1963-65, 1966-68) as well as for the entire decade (1959-1968) for which the CREON event data were collected.

Table 9.3 indicates the mean direction of affect for the 38 CREON nations toward these different types of recipients across the decade. The table also indicates the number of events on which the means were based. Several observa-

TABLE 9.3

Mean Direction of Affect Scores for 38 CREON Nations Toward Four Types of Recipients Over Four Time Periods

CREON Nation	Western Community Nations				Brazzaville African and Latin American Nations				Afro-Asian Nations				Communist Nations[a]			
	1959-68	1960-62	1963-65	1966-68	1959-68	1960-62	1963-65	1966-68	1959-68	1960-62	1963-65	1966-68	1959-68	1960-62	1963-65	1966-68
Belgium	+.37 (193)[b]	+.36 (74)	+.30 (43)	+.32 (56)	+.23 (44)	+.18 (22)	+.27 (11)	+.22 (9)	+.55 (22)	+.50 (100)	+1.00 (3)	+.50 (8)	-.11 (36)	-.60 (10)	+.67 (6)	-.12 (16)
Canada	+.32 (293)	+.23 (73)	+.31 (74)	+.34 (135)	+.48 (60)	+.44 (9)	.00 (1)	+.50 (47)	+.17 (64)	+.92 (12)	-.60 (10)	+.15 (41)	-.27 (55)	-.50 (26)	.00 (8)	-.18 (17)
Chile	+.48 (63)	+.52 (27)	+.25 (12)	+.50 (14)	+.53 (91)	+.25 (20)	+.31 (16)	+.70 (53)	+.67 (9)	+1.00 (5)	—[c]	+.33 (3)	-.29 (28)	-.44 (16)	-.14 (7)	-.50 (2)
China (PRC)	-.63 (320)	-.62 (95)	-.65 (139)	-.61 (84)	+.03 (34)	-.10 (10)	+.28 (18)	-.50 (6)	+.01 (189)	-.28 (87)	+.37 (54)	+.07 (27)	-.38 (164)	.00 (49)	-.14 (7)	-.74 (43)
Costa Rica	+.64 (64)	+.33 (12)	+.78 (32)	+.38 (8)	+.61 (33)	+.50 (4)	+.70 (23)	+.20 (5)	+.67 (6)	+1.00 (3)	—[c]	+.33 (3)	-.59 (27)	-.62 (8)	-.79 (14)	-.50 (2)
Cuba	-.42 (217)	-.60 (107)	-.16 (68)	-.43 (23)	.00 (78)	+.16 (56)	+.17 (6)	-.45 (20)	+.61 (23)	+.86 (7)	+1.00 (1)	+.47 (15)	+.31 (139)	+.39 (64)	+.33 (61)	-.27 (11)
Czechoslovakia	+.18 (50)	-.08 (13)	.00 (10)	+.35 (20)	+.06 (17)	+.50 (4)	—[c]	-.60 (5)	+.77 (26)	+1.00 (2)	+.92 (12)	+.70 (10)	+.63 (95)	+1.00 (8)	+.92 (26)	+.67 (30)
East Germany	.00 (30)	+.11 (9)	+.57 (7)	-.36 (14)	-.75 (4)	—[c]	—[c]	-.75 (4)	+.45 (38)	+1.00 (2)	—[c]	+.23 (26)	+1.00 (8)	+.25 (8)	+.88 (25)	+.41 (54)
Egypt	-.10 (210)	-.26 (96)	+.22 (46)	-.23 (56)	-.32 (169)	-.33 (54)	-.14 (36)	-.43 (74)	+.50 (210)	+.31 (85)	+.67 (66)	+.55 (55)	+.25 (35)	+.25 (8)	+.90 (10)	+.67 (15)
France	+.24 (503)	+.48 (177)	+.12 (146)	-.05 (144)	+.30 (114)	+.35 (23)	+.66 (44)	-.10 (42)	+.45 (146)	+.67 (21)	+.60 (35)	+.34 (89)	+.02 (122)	-.11 (37)	-.07 (41)	+.17 (35)
Ghana	-.01 (99)	-.25 (55)	-.10 (20)	+.71 (14)	+.23 (87)	+.04 (57)	+.48 (21)	+.88 (8)	+.58 (67)	+.66 (41)	+.58 (19)	+.14 (7)	+.06 (17)	+.22 (9)	-1.00 (1)	-.07 (41)
Guinea	+.03 (62)	-.17 (30)	+.07 (14)	+.12 (8)	+.22 (59)	+.24 (33)	+.67 (15)	-.67 (9)	+.72 (54)	+.61 (18)	+.87 (15)	+.74 (19)	+.65 (17)	+.80 (10)	-1.00 (1)	-.25 (14)
Iceland	+.40 (70)	+.35 (20)	-.27 (11)	+.43 (21)	+.62 (8)	+.50 (2)	—[c]	+.75 (4)	+.67 (9)	+1.00 (3)	—[d]	+.60 (5)	-.36 (22)	-.62 (8)	-1.00 (1)	.00 (1)
India	+.26 (224)	+.33 (81)	+.28 (74)	+.02 (54)	+.02 (128)	+.10 (69)	-.11 (28)	-.15 (27)	+.41 (73)	+.50 (24)	+.33 (21)	+.38 (26)	+.48 (71)	+.05 (21)	+.71 (28)	+.58 (10)
Israel	+.47 (87)	+.53 (19)	+.36 (25)	+.47 (32)	-.03 (31)	-.14 (22)	-.25 (4)	+1.00 (3)	-.53 (211)	.00 (9)	-.94 (33)	-.47 (165)	-.21 (33)	-.25 (4)	-.30 (10)	-.25 (16)
Italy	+.31 (284)[b]	+.34 (108)	+.27 (41)	+.18 (105)	+.24 (29)	+.57 (7)	.00 (1)	+.27 (11)	+.64 (33)	+.69 (13)	+1.00 (3)	+.53 (15)	+.02 (56)	-.24 (18)	+.46 (13)	+.28 (29)
Ivory Coast	+.11 (146)	+.33 (12)	-.11 (28)	+.67 (6)	+.58 (12)	+.60 (5)	+.43 (23)	+.86 (7)	+.51 (37)	+1.00 (9)	+.35 (20)	+.38 (8)	+.14 (7)	.00 (3)	-1.00 (1)	+.67 (3)
Japan	+.45 (123)	+.45 (38)	+.55 (44)	+.28 (29)	+.41 (22)	+.80 (5)	+.33 (18)	+.27 (15)	+.44 (39)	+.67 (6)	+.71 (7)	+.32 (25)	+.10 (30)	-.40 (10)	+.20 (10)	+.57 (7)
Kenya	+.08 (36)	—[d]	+.04 (28)	+.25 (8)	+.35 (20)	—[d]	-.70 (10)	+.50 (2)	+.70 (37)	—[d]	+1.00 (22)	+.27 (15)	-.25 (4)	—[d]	-.33 (3)	.00 (1)
Lebanon	+.04 (47)	+.05 (19)	-1.00 (1)	-.25 (16)	-.46 (28)	.00 (3)	-.14 (14)	-.54 (13)	+.71 (38)	+.80 (10)	+.69 (16)	+.73 (11)	-.18 (11)	—[c]	-1.00 (2)	.00 (1)
Mexico	+.36 (61)	+.30 (23)	+.42 (12)	+.08 (13)	+.24 (29)	+.57 (7)	—[c]	+.67 (6)	+.46 (24)	+.83 (6)	+.50 (18)	+.22 (9)	-.06 (34)	-.71 (14)	+.46 (13)	-.33 (3)
New Zealand	+.43 (75)	+.52 (23)	+.45 (22)	+.32 (22)	+.58 (12)	+.60 (5)	+.17 (6)	+.60 (5)	+.29 (14)	+1.00 (6)	-1.00 (3)	+.25 (4)	-.27 (11)	-.50 (6)	-.50 (6)	.00 (1)
Norway	+.41 (110)	+.33 (42)	+.25 (28)	+.56 (25)	+.54 (35)	.00 (4)	+.50 (2)	+.60 (5)	+.44 (18)	+1.00 (3)	.00 (5)	+.56 (9)	-.24 (37)	-.23 (13)	.00 (7)	-.58 (12)
Philippines	+.33 (98)	+.22 (27)	+.21 (14)	+.39 (44)	+.23 (13)	+.20 (5)	+.67 (3)	.00 (4)	+.52 (23)	+.75 (4)	+.33 (9)	+.67 (9)	-.36 (14)	-.67 (6)	-1.00 (2)	.00 (3)
Poland	+.17 (81)	+.32 (22)	+.08 (25)	-.05 (22)	-.13 (15)	.00 (2)	+.18 (55)	-.62 (8)	+.50 (24)	+1.00 (3)	+.67 (3)	+.50 (16)	+.62 (90)	+.62 (24)	+.86 (22)	+.40 (35)
Soviet Union	-.31 (744)	-.39 (251)	-.41 (291)	-.21 (163)	-.09 (206)	-.05 (86)	+.18 (55)	-.47 (60)	+.49 (185)	+.25 (56)	+.59 (29)	+.60 (97)	+.49 (201)	+.31 (83)	+.62 (48)	+.55 (60)
Spain	+.17 (69)	+.23 (22)	-.25 (12)	.00 (22)	+.27 (11)	.00 (1)	—[c]	+.25 (8)	+.12 (26)	-.08 (12)	+.60 (5)	+.12 (8)	-.25 (24)	-.83 (6)	-.12 (8)	-.14 (7)
Switzerland	+.12 (40)	+.36 (14)	-.14 (14)	+.17 (12)	+.25 (4)	—[c]	—[c]	+.25 (4)	.00 (2)	+.60 (5)	—[c]	.00 (2)	-1.00 (1)	—[c]	—[c]	.00 (3)
Thailand	+.48 (50)	+.29 (17)	—[c]	+.57 (23)	+.58 (12)	+.50 (4)	+.06 (18)	+.67 (6)	+.69 (16)	+.77 (13)	+.51 (41)	+.30 (27)	-.20 (10)	-.67 (3)	-.67 (3)	.00 (3)
Tunisia	+.20 (112)	+.05 (56)	+.11 (28)	+.62 (13)	+.16 (58)	+.23 (26)	+.04 (52)	+.08 (12)	+.48 (82)	+.83 (6)	+.40 (5)	+.51 (41)	+.18 (11)	+.20 (5)	+.14 (7)	-.20 (15)
Turkey	+.33 (211)	+.44 (34)	+.12 (66)	+.31 (88)	+.21 (86)	+.50 (12)	+.05 (22)	+.41 (17)	+.44 (25)	+1.00 (4)	+.85 (27)	+.50 (10)	-.21 (47)	-.47 (17)	-1.00 (1)	-.20 (15)
Uganda	+.14 (57)	+.20 (10)	+.03 (37)	+.50 (10)	+.03 (29)	-.25 (4)	+.35 (130)	+.33 (3)	+.82 (39)	+.56 (54)	+.44 (59)	+.62 (8)	.00 (6)	+.25 (4)	+.25 (4)	—[c]
United States	+.31 (680)	+.25 (218)	+.22 (203)	+.40 (187)	+.33 (326)	+.18 (99)	+.25 (4)	+.40 (86)	+.31 (229)	+.67 (3)	—[c]	+.03 (98)	-.30 (709)	-.43 (427)	-.24 (173)	+.10 (87)
Uruguay	+.18 (33)	+.11 (9)	-.22 (9)	+.20 (5)	+.39 (18)	+.75 (8)	.00 (5)	+.25 (4)	+.38 (8)	+.83 (6)	—[c]	+.25 (4)	-.45 (22)	-.64 (11)	-.67 (3)	-.50 (2)
Venezuela	+.32 (53)	+.39 (23)	+.11 (9)	.00 (11)	+.55 (71)	-.11 (9)	+.29 (17)	+.74 (54)	+.55 (11)	+.55 (11)	.00 (1)	+.55 (11)	-.60 (39)	-.61 (18)	-.63 (3)	-.79 (14)
West Germany	+.47 (456)	+.58 (151)	+.46 (97)	+.34 (174)	+.47 (47)	+.33 (9)	+.75 (8)	+.67 (21)	+.43 (60)	+.64 (14)	+.14 (22)	+.55 (22)	-.18 (104)	-.61 (28)	+.29 (28)	-.24 (41)
Yugoslavia	+.32 (84)	.00 (26)	+.36 (22)	+.50 (24)	+.17 (30)	+.17 (12)	—[d]	-.50 (8)	+.79 (43)	+.83 (18)	+1.00 (11)	+.55 (11)	+.34 (95)	+.38 (34)	+.53 (17)	+.25 (40)
Zambia	+.11 (35)	—[d]	+.33 (3)	+.09 (32)	+.83 (6)	—[d]	—[d]	+.83 (6)	+.64 (11)	—[d]	+1.00 (2)	+.56 (9)	.00 (3)	—[d]	-1.00 (1)	+.50 (2)

NOTE: The following nations fall into the four clusters of recipients represented in this table. The Western Community nations are: Australia, Austria, Belgium, Canada, China (Taiwan), Denmark, Finland, France, Greece, Iceland, Iran, Ireland, Italy, Japan, Netherlands, New Zealand, Norway, Sweden, Turkey, United Kingdom, United States. The Brazzaville African and Latin American nations are: Argentina, Bolivia, Brazil, Cameroon, Central African Republic, Chad, Chile, Colombia, Congo (Brazzaville), Congo (Leopoldville), Costa Rica, Cyprus, Dahomey, Ecuador, Gabon, Guatemala, Haiti, Israel, Ivory Coast, Jamaica, Liberia, Madagascar, Malaysia, Mexico, Nicaragua, Niger, Pakistan, Panama, Paraguay, Peru, Philippines, Rwanda, Senegal, Sierra Leone, Thailand, Togo, Upper Volta, Uruguay, Venezuela. The Afro-Asian nations are: Afghanistan, Algeria, Burma, Cambodia, Ceylon, Egypt, Ethiopia, Ghana, Guinea, India, Indonesia, Iraq, Mali, Morocco, Nigeria, Somalia, Sudan, Syria, Tanganyika, Tunisia, Uganda, Yugoslavia. The Communist nations are: Albania, Bulgaria, Cuba, Czechoslovakia, Hungary, Mongolia, Poland, Rumania, Soviet Union.

aChina (PRC) is not included in the Communist nations since the PRC was not a member of the United Nations in 1963 and thus was not part of the Russett (1967) factor analysis.
bThe figures in parentheses are the number of events on which the mean scores are based.
cNo mean score is listed because there were no events directed at this type of recipient during this period.
dNo mean score is listed because the country was not independent during this period.

tions can be made about the data in Table 9.3. A comparison of the positive and negative means toward Western Community and Communist nations shows a line-up along alliance lines, particularly for NATO countries. There is a tendency, on the average, for Western nations to direct positive affect toward other Western nations and to direct negative affect toward Communist nations. The reverse is less consistently the case, however. During several of the three-year periods, Czechoslovakia, East Germany, and Poland were positive in affect toward the Western nations. Interestingly, Czechoslovakia is becoming more positive toward the end of the decade, while Poland and East Germany are becoming more negative. The Czechoslovakian change occurs during the short Dubcek liberalization period prior to the Russian invasion. Although the Soviet Union, on the average, shows consistently negative affect toward the United States across the decade, the United States shows a slight change toward positive affect at the end of the decade. We might speculate that this is some evidence of détente or, at least, an attempt at détente on the part of the United States.

There are fewer events directed at Brazzaville African and Latin American nations and at the Afro-Asian nations than at the Western Community and at the Communist nations. Once again, there is a tendency for nations with similar attitudes or voting patterns to be positive to one another. All of the positive affect toward the Afro-Asian nations during this period—when many were becoming independent—may represent some deliberate "wooing" of these countries with hopes of building permanent relationships. Only Israel is pointedly negative toward the Afro-Asian nations.

The most negative affect during the decade toward all the recipients came from China (PRC). For 10 of the 16 time periods (62 percent) across recipients, the mean direction of affect for China was negative. The only positive affect was directed toward Third World nations. This negative affect may indicate the isolationist position of the PRC during this decade.

Egypt's turn toward the East and the Soviet Union (and its disenchantment with the West) is evident in this table. At each time period during the decade Egypt's affect is positive toward the Communist nations, while only during the period 1963-65 was Egypt's affect positive toward the Western Community nations.

India's attempt at neutrality between East and West is suggested by its mean direction of affect during this decade. Its affect on the average is positive during all the time periods toward *both* the Western Community nations and the Communist nations. France shows some evidence of an attempt to play a more neutral role toward the end of the decade. We notice that the mean affect direction score for France is negative in 1966-68 toward the Western Community nations and positive during this same period toward the Communist nations, whereas the opposite had been true up to that point in the decade.

Table 9.4 suggests how intense the positive or negative affect in Table 9.3 was. Table 9.4 presents the mean intensity of affect scores for the 38 CREON nations toward four types of recipients during the 1959-1968 decade. Whereas direction of affect scale scores can vary between -1 and $+1$, intensity of affect scale scores vary between 0 and 2—a 0 indicating neutral affect, a 2 indicating strong affect.

TABLE 9.4

Mean Intensity of Affect Scores for 38 CREON Nations Toward Four Types of Recipients Over Four Time Periods

CREON Nation	Western Community Nations				Brazzaville African and Latin American Nations				Afro-Asian Nations				Communist Nations[a]			
	1959-68	1960-62	1963-65	1966-68	1959-68	1960-62	1963-65	1966-68	1959-68	1960-62	1963-65	1966-68	1959-68	1960-62	1963-65	1966-68
Belgium	.72	.65	.84	.71	.66	.77	.45	.67	.86	1.10	1.00	.62	.81	.90	1.00	.75
Canada	.59	.47	.57	.64	.70	1.00	.00	.66	.62	1.25	1.20	.32	.84	1.00	1.00	.53
Chile	.84	.85	.92	.86	.67	.35	.56	.83	.89	1.20	—[b]	.67	.82	.94	.86	.50
China (PRC)	.85	.88	.81	.88	.74	1.10	.50	.83	.76	.68	.76	.85	.78	.76	.77	.98
Costa Rica	.84	.92	.84	.62	.88	1.00	.83	1.00	1.00	1.33	—[b]	.67	.78	.62	1.00	.50
Cuba	.96	1.06	.76	.87	.67	.64	1.00	.70	.74	1.14	1.00	.53	.57	.61	.49	.82
Czechoslovakia	.74	.85	.20	.95	.88	1.50	.67	.80	.85	1.00	1.00	.70	1.00	.97	1.12	.97
East Germany	.63	.67	.86	.50	.75	—[b]	—[b]	.75	.71	—[b]	.92	.62	.75	1.00	1.08	.52
Egypt	.86	.90	.50	1.05	.78	.81	.83	.72	.67	.47	.80	.80	.74	.50	.90	.80
France	.65	.71	.61	.56	.56	.70	.66	.43	.58	.90	.69	.46	.70	.84	.56	.66
Ghana	.73	.71	.70	.79	.80	.81	.71	1.00	.78	.85	.58	.86	.65	.44	1.00	1.25
Guinea	.87	1.00	.86	.62	.95	.76	1.00	1.67	.78	.61	.87	.89	.71	.90	.00	.00
Iceland	.83	.60	.73	.95	.75	.50	—[b]	1.00	.89	1.33	—[b]	.80	.82	.88	1.00	.78
India	.53	.52	.50	.50	.50	.42	.68	.48	.55	.67	.43	.54	.65	.52	.79	.58
Israel	.67	.84	.76	.47	.71	.77	.25	1.33	.91	1.00	1.18	.86	.85	1.00	.90	.88
Italy	.55	.53	.76	.45	.65	1.00	.00	.55	.91	1.00	1.33	.80	.70	.67	1.00	.69
Ivory Coast	.48	.75	.32	.67	.69	1.00	.52	1.00	.78	1.00	.65	.88	.43	.00	1.00	.67
Japan	.61	.68	.64	.41	.45	.80	—[b]	.33	.51	.83	.71	.40	.57	.80	.40	.57
Kenya	.67	—[c]	.79	.25	.80	—[c]	.78	1.00	.95	—[c]	1.00	.87	.25	—[c]	.33	.00
Lebanon	.87	.74	1.50	.88	1.11	.67	1.20	1.23	.92	1.10	.88	.91	.55	.40	1.00	.33
Mexico	.80	.83	.67	.77	.59	.86	.36	.83	.54	1.00	.50	.33	.64	1.07	.77	.00
New Zealand	.63	.74	.73	.41	1.08	1.60	—[c]	.80	1.07	1.50	1.33	.50	.78	.83	1.00	.75
Norway	.67	.71	.39	.80	.65	1.25	.17	.80	.67	1.33	.40	.67	.64	.85	.86	.67
Philippines	.56	.70	.36	.43	.92	1.40	.50	.75	.74	1.00	.56	.89	.74	.67	1.00	.67
Poland	1.00	.86	1.28	.73	1.07	1.00	1.33	1.12	.88	1.00	.67	.88	.68	.79	1.14	.40
Soviet Union	.84	.85	.81	.84	.56	.50	.40	.78	.70	.75	.69	.68	.68	.54	.90	.63
Spain	.61	.45	.75	.55	.36	.00	—[b]	.38	.58	.83	.60	.25	.67	.83	.88	.43
Switzerland	.42	.36	.43	.50	.25	—[b]	—[b]	.25	.00	—[b]	—[b]	.00	1.20	1.20	—[b]	—[b]
Thailand	.78	1.00	—[b]	.65	.92	1.25	—[b]	.83	.81	.80	—[b]	.90	.60	.67	1.00	.67
Tunisia	.72	.66	.82	.62	.62	.54	.67	.75	.77	.92	.85	.45	.45	.40	.50	.00
Turkey	.61	.79	.77	.35	.74	.75	.81	.59	.76	1.00	.80	.60	.68	.82	.71	.47
Uganda	.67	.70	.70	.50	.76	.75	.77	.67	1.00	1.00	1.04	.88	.33	.25	1.00	.00
United States	.46	.42	.45	.46	.53	.39	.51	.71	.74	.74	.86	.68	.66	.70	.55	.64
Uruguay	.73	.89	.67	.60	.83	1.00	—[b]	.50	.50	.67	1.00	.50	.82	.91	1.00	.50
Venezuela	.87	1.00	.78	.55	1.06	1.44	1.00	1.02	.98	1.00	.00	.67	.95	.94	.67	1.07
West Germany	.66	.69	.88	.50	.74	.67	.65	.86	.84	.93	1.27	.73	.62	.61	.64	.63
Yugoslavia	.74	.65	.82	.71	.67	.50	.75	.88	.73	.83	1.00	.73	.64	.68	.76	.55
Zambia	.83	—[c]	1.00	.81	1.00	—[c]	—[b]	1.00	.73	—[c]	1.00	.67	.67	—[c]	1.00	.50

NOTE: The nations included in each of the four types of recipients are listed in the note to Table 9.3. The number of events used to determine the means in this table are the same as those listed in Table 9.3.

[a]China (PRC) is not included in the Communist nations since the PRC was not a member of the United Nations in 1963 and thus was not a part of Russett's (1967) factor analysis.

[b]No mean score is listed because there were no events directed at this type of recipient during this period.

[c]No mean score is listed because the country was not independent during this period.

Table 9.4 suggests that more intense affect is directed toward a nation's adversaries than toward its allies. For example, the Soviet Union's mean intensity of affect scores are higher for the Western Community nations than for the Communist nations; the opposite is the case for the United States. Other examples are Belgium and Canada, with more intense affect scores toward the Communist nations and less intense scores toward Western Community nations, and Cuba, which shows the reverse pattern.

A count of the mean intensity of affect scores of 1.00 or higher shows more intense affect was expressed during this decade toward Afro-Asian nations and Brazzaville African and Latin American nations than toward Western Community nations and Communist nations. Almost a quarter (24 percent) of the mean intensity of affect scores for the Afro-Asian nations were 1.00 or more; only slightly fewer (22 percent) of the intensity of affect scores for the Brazzaville African and Latin American nations were 1.00 or more. The percentages for the Western Community and Communist nations were 6 percent and 17 percent, respectively.

Five of the nations have no mean intensity of affect score that is 1.00 or higher. In other words, their affect tends more toward neutral than strong. These five countries are France, India, Japan, the Soviet Union, and the United States. With the exception of India, these are among the more industrialized nations in the CREON sample of countries. They are also among the most active of the CREON countries, engaging in more routine, neutral affect actions as well as affect-laden activities. Or perhaps the more routine, neutral affect events of these larger countries are picked up in the press more than are similar events for the smaller, less-developed nations. For the less-developed nations, the event must be somewhat intense in affect before it is reported in the press.

The modal affect scale values for the CREON nations' actions toward these four types of recipients are reported in Table 9.5. In other words, these are the points on the affect scale where the greatest number of events were coded for each CREON country toward each of the four types of recipients. For the most part, the modal scores are 2 (mild expression of positive affect), 3 (neutral affect), and 4 (mild expression of negative affect).

An examination in Table 9.5 of the modal scale values for the Western Community recipients shows that four CREON countries expressed essentially mild negative affect toward these recipients during the 1959-1968 decade. These countries are China (PRC), Cuba, Egypt, and the Soviet Union. Eight countries show mood swings from positive to negative affect (or vice versa) toward the Western Community nations during this decade. Czechoslovakia, Ghana, Guinea, Lebanon, Mexico, Poland, Uganda, and Uruguay fit this pattern. At various points during the decade they are predominantly positive in affect, while at other times they are predominantly negative.

None of the CREON countries was generally negative toward the Brazzaville African and Latin American nations during the decade. Negative affect appears to have been limited to certain time periods. Nine of the CREON nations displayed shifts from positive to negative affect during the decade. These countries are East Germany, Guinea, Israel, Lebanon, Poland, Uruguay, Venezuela, and Yugoslavia. The reader will note some nations in this list which also appear among nations showing shifts in feelings toward the Western Community nations.

TABLE 9.5

Modal Affect Scale Score for 38 CREON Nations Toward Four Types of Recipients Over Four Time Periods

CREON Nation	Western Community Nations				Brazzaville African and Latin American Nations				Afro-Asian Nations				Communist Nations			
	1959-68	1960-62	1963-65	1966-68	1959-68	1960-62	1963-65	1966-68	1959-68	1960-62	1963-65	1966-68	1959-68	1960-62	1963-65	1966-68
Belgium	2 (51%)[b]	2 (49%)	2 (51%)	2 (48%)	3 (46%)	3 (36%)	3 (54%)	3 (56%)	2 (54%)	2 (60%)	2 (100%)	2 (50%)	4 (36%)	4 (60%)	2 (83%)	3 (38%)
Canada	3 (55%)	3 (60%)	3 (47%)	3 (60%)	3 (45%)	1,3 (33%)	3 (100%)	3 (47%)	2 (44%)	2 (58%)	4 (70%)	3 (76%)	4 (49%)	(4 (62%))	2,4 (50%)	3 (47%)
Chile	2 (59%)	2 (63%)	2 (58%)	2 (57%)	2 (58%)	3 (65%)	2,3 (44%)	2,3 (74%)	2 (44%)	2 (80%)	—c	3 (67%)	3 (36%)	3,4 (31%)	3,4 (29%)	3,4 (50%)
China (PRC)	4 (66%)	4 (64%)	4 (69%)	4 (68%)	3 (44%)	3 (30%)	3 (61%)	4 (67%)	2 (32%)	2 (42%)	2 (50%)	2 (44%)	1,2,3 (33%)	1,2,3 (33%)	4 (61%)	3,4 (50%)
Costa Rica	2 (67%)	2 (50%)	2 (81%)	2 (50%)	2 (67%)	2 (75%)	2 (74%)	2 (74%)	2 (74%)	2 (67%)	—c	3 (67%)	4 (63%)	4 (62%)	4 (79%)	3 (36%)
Cuba	4 (41%)	4 (49%)	3 (37%)	4 (56%)	3 (54%)	3 (59%)	4 (100%)	3 (45%)	1,2,3 (33%)	2 (57%)	2 (100%)	2 (70%)	2 (73%)	2 (58%)	2 (85%)	2 (77%)
Czechoslovakia	2 (36%)	3 (46%)	3 (80%)	3 (59%)	3 (35%)	1 (50%)[e]	3 (50%)	3,4 (40%)	2 (48%)	2 (100%)	2 (67%)	2 (42%)	2 (61%)	2 (100%)	2 (68%)	3 (48%)
East Germany	3 (40%)	3 (44%)	2 (71%)	3 (50%)	4 (75%)	—	—c	2 (75%)	2 (69%)	—c	2 (92%)	2 (56%)	3 (36%)	3 (50%)	2 (90%)	2 (73%)
Egypt	4 (32%)	4 (40%)	3 (52%)	4 (43%)	4 (38%)	3 (37%)	3 (39%)	3 (40%)	2 (50%)	2 (58%)	2 (62%)	2 (69%)	3 (36%)	2,3 (30%)	3 (44%)	2,3 (37%)
France	2 (41%)	4 (42%)	3 (43%)	2 (64%)	3 (47%)	2,3 (39%)	2 (66%)	3 (62%)	2 (48%)	2 (71%)	2 (60%)	3 (55%)	3 (55%)	3 (56%)	4 (100%)	5 (50%)
Ghana	3,4 (32%)[d]	4 (37%)	4 (40%)	2 (64%)	2 (38%)	3 (37%)	2 (57%)	2 (75%)	2 (58%)	2 (63%)	2 (58%)	2,3,4 (29%)	2 (59%)	2 (70%)	3 (100%)	4 (56%)
Guinea	2 (37%)	2,4 (36%)	2,4 (36%)	2,3 (38%)	3 (36%)	3 (39%)	2 (60%)	5 (67%)	2 (67%)	2 (61%)	2 (87%)	2 (58%)	4 (59%)	4 (75%)	4 (100%)	2 (58%)
Iceland	2 (53%)	3 (45%)	3 (54%)	3 (50%)	2 (50%)	2,3 (50%)	—c	2 (50%)	2 (67%)	2 (67%)	—c	2,3 (40%)	4 (48%)	4 (50%)	4 (100%)	4 (50%)
India	3 (48%)	3 (50%)	3 (50%)	3 (53%)	3 (39%)	3 (64%)	3 (39%)	3 (57%)	4 (53%)	4 (44%)	4 (70%)	4 (50%)	2 (36%)	2 (56%)	4 (60%)	2 (48%)
Israel	2 (54%)	3 (68%)	2 (52%)	3 (59%)	3 (39%)	3,4 (32%)	3 (75%)	2 (67%)	2 (54%)	2 (62%)	2 (67%)	2 (47%)	2 (36%)	3 (100%)	2,4 (50%)	2 (67%)
Italy	3 (48%)	3 (49%)	2 (49%)	3 (64%)	3 (50%)	1,3 (33%)	3 (100%)	3 (54%)	3 (56%)	2 (100%)	2 (50%)	2,3 (68%)	3 (57%)	2 (60%)	4 (60%)	2 (57%)
Ivory Coast	3 (53%)	2 (42%)	3 (68%)	2 (67%)	2 (57%)	2 (80%)	2,3 (48%)	2 (71%)	2 (60%)	2 (50%)	2 (71%)	2 (40%)	3 (43%)	—d	3 (60%)	3 (100%)
Japan	2 (50%)	2 (53%)	2 (59%)	3 (59%)	3 (59%)	2 (80%)	2 (56%)	3 (73%)	2 (76%)	—d	2 (100%)	2 (40%)	3 (75%)	3 (60%)	3 (67%)	3 (67%)
Kenya	2,3 (36%)	—d	2 (39%)	2 (39%)	2 (50%)	—d	—c	1,3 (50%)	2 (66%)	2 (80%)	2 (69%)	2 (54%)	3 (46%)	—e	4 (100%)	3 (100%)
Lebanon	2 (34%)	3 (42%)	4,5 (50%)	3 (38%)	4 (43%)	2 (71%)	4 (50%)	4 (46%)	2 (66%)	2 (67%)	2 (69%)	3 (78%)	2 (35%)	4 (57%)	2 (62%)	4 (67%)
Mexico	2 (46%)	2 (44%)	2,3 (42%)	2 (59%)	3 (48%)	1 (60%)	—c	2 (50%)	3 (54%)	—c	2,3 (50%)	3 (75%)	2 (46%)	4 (67%)	4 (100%)	2,3 (46%)
New Zealand	2 (51%)	2 (56%)	2 (59%)	2 (68%)	1,2 (33%)	1,2 (33%)	—c	2,3 (40%)	1,3 (29%)	1,2 (50%)	4 (67%)	2,3 (44%)	4 (51%)	4 (54%)	2,4 (33%)	2,3,4 (33%)
Norway	2 (52%)	2 (50%)	3 (61%)	3 (57%)	3 (47%)	2 (40%)	3 (83%)	3 (50%)	2 (44%)	2 (67%)	2,3 (44%)	2 (44%)	4 (50%)	4 (67%)	4 (100%)	3 (60%)
Philippines	3 (47%)	2 (41%)	3 (64%)	4 (36%)	2,3 (31%)	2,3 (31%)	2,3 (50%)	2 (62%)	2 (44%)	2 (50%)	2 (67%)	2 (38%)	2 (57%)	2 (58%)	2 (73%)	2 (57%)
Poland	2 (13%)	2 (50%)	2 (44%)	4 (49%)	4 (40%)	2,4 (50%)	1 (67%)	3 (64%)	2 (42%)	2 (100%)	2 (59%)	2 (52%)	2 (50%)	3 (47%)	2 (48%)	3 (57%)
Soviet Union	4 (42%)	4 (40%)	4 (44%)	3 (46%)	3 (53%)	3 (60%)	3 (64%)	4 (43%)	2 (46%)	2 (43%)	2 (60%)	3 (88%)	4 (46%)	4 (83%)	4 (50%)	3 (57%)
Spain	3 (42%)	3 (59%)	4 (50%)	4 (50%)	3 (73%)	3 (73%)	—c	3 (75%)	2 (50%)	4 (42%)	—c	3 (100%)	4 (80%)	4 (80%)	—c	—c
Switzerland	3 (58%)	3 (64%)	4 (57%)	3 (57%)	3 (75%)	2 (50%)	—c	2 (50%)	3 (100%)	—c	—c	2 (70%)	2,4 (40%)	4 (67%)	—c	—c
Thailand	2 (56%)	2 (53%)	2 (39%)	2 (61%)	2 (50%)	2 (54%)	2 (39%)	2 (50%)	2 (56%)	2 (40%)	—c	3 (56%)	4 (40%)	4 (65%)	4 (50%)	2,3,4 (33%)
Tunisia	2 (38%)	2 (45%)	2 (39%)	2 (62%)	3 (47%)	2 (50%)	2 (35%)	3 (47%)	2 (48%)	2 (62%)	2 (61%)	3 (50%)	4 (45%)	3 (75%)	2 (43%)	3 (100%)
Turkey	2 (43%)	2 (53%)	—c	3 (65%)	2 (40%)	4 (50%)	2 (36%)	3 (67%)	2 (48%)	2 (67%)	2 (60%)	2,3 (38%)	4 (41%)	4 (49%)	2 (60%)	3 (53%)
Uganda	2,3 (37%)	2,3 (40%)	2,3,4 (32%)	2,3 (50%)	3 (34%)	3 (62%)	3 (52%)	2 (48%)	2 (80%)	2 (100%)	2 (89%)	3 (75%)	4 (49%)	—e	3 (49%)	3 (100%)
United States	3 (56%)	3 (60%)	3 (57%)	3 (57%)	2 (50%)	2 (88%)	2,3,4,5 (25%)	3 (75%)	2 (40%)	2 (44%)	2 (52%)	3 (67%)	3,4 (36%)	4 (36%)	4 (67%)	3 (41%)
Uruguay	2 (36%)	2,4 (33%)	4 (44%)	4 (44%)	2 (73%)	2,5 (44%)	2 (40%)	2 (83%)	3 (62%)	2 (67%)	—c	2 (50%)	4 (46%)	4 (61%)	4 (50%)	3,4 (50%)
Venezuela	2 (51%)	2 (56%)	2 (44%)	3 (46%)	3 (40%)	3 (44%)	2 (40%)	2 (48%)	2 (48%)	2 (67%)	3 (100%)	2 (48%)	4 (40%)	4 (61%)	4 (67%)	4 (50%)
West Germany	2 (54%)	2 (62%)	2 (60%)	2 (54%)	2,3 (37%)	3 (40%)	3 (47%)	4 (62%)	2 (48%)	2 (57%)	2 (36%)	2,3 (44%)	2 (48%)	2 (53%)	2 (46%)	4 (44%)
Yugoslavia	2 (49%)	3 (38%)	2 (59%)	2 (38%)	2,3 (37%)	3 (50%)	2 (75%)	2 (75%)	2 (74%)	2 (83%)	2 (100%)	2,3 (44%)	2,3,4 (33%)	2 (53%)	2 (65%)	3 (45%)
Zambia	2 (40%)	—d	2 (67%)	2 (67%)	2 (67%)	—d	—c	2 (67%)	2 (54%)	—d	2 (100%)	2,3,4 (33%)	2 (67%)	—d	4 (100%)	2,3 (50%)

NOTE: The nations included in each of the four types of recipients are listed in the note to Table 9.3. The number of events used to determine the means in this table are the same as those listed in Table 9.3.

a. China (PRC) is not included in the Communist nations since the PRC was not a member of the United Nations in 1963 and thus was not a part of Russett's (1967) factor analysis.

b. The number in parentheses is the percentage of events that had the particular affect score.

c. No modal score is listed because there were no events directed at this type of recipient during this period.

d. This nation has a bimodal distribution during this period. Wherever two scale points are listed, a bimodal distribution was present. If three numbers are listed, the distribution was trimodal.

e. No modal score is listed because the country was not independent during this period.

Israel is the only nation expressing consistently negative affect toward the Afro-Asian nations. These nations, as we have already noted, were the objects of much positive affect from 1959 to 1968 from all of the CREON countries except Israel. Given the presence of many of the Arab nations in this group, the Israeli negative affect is probably understandable. Only four of the CREON countries showed changes from positive to negative affect (or vice versa) toward the Afro-Asian nations during this period. These countries were Canada, Ghana, New Zealand, and Spain.

Turning to the Communist nations as recipients, we note that 14 of the CREON countries exhibited both positive and negative affect toward these nations. Belgium, Canada, Chile, China, Italy, the Ivory Coast, Mexico, New Zealand, Norway, the Philippines, Thailand, Turkey, West Germany, and Zambia show shifts in affect directed at the Communist nations during this decade. Iceland, Israel, and Venezuela show consistently negative modal affect toward the Communist nations from 1959 to 1968. It is interesting that the United States does not fall into this category. Instead, the United States' modal score for the years 1963-68 is 3, or neutral affect. One might wonder if, as we noted earlier, the affect scores are reflecting the signals in U.S. behavior toward détente in the latter part of the decade.

Table 9.6 shows the extreme affect behavior of the CREON nations that was addressed to these four types of recipients. The table reports the direction of the strong expressions of affect when such expressions accounted for more than five percent of a nation's events. An overview of Table 9.6 shows that the extreme expressions of affect toward the Western Community nations tended to be more negative than positive in tone. In general, the countries that exhibited consistently strong expressions of negative affect toward the Western Community nations are not surprises. They were adversaries of the Western Community nations for the most part during this decade—Cuba, Egypt, and the Soviet Union.

The extreme expressions of affect are more positive than negative toward the Brazzaville African and Latin American nations. For some of the CREON countries, however, there was an ambivalence toward these nations not manifested toward the other types of recipients. For 20 of the time periods and for 13 of the CREON nations, both extreme scores accounted for more than five percent of the events. In one period both strong negative *and* positive affect were expressed. This ambivalence is most pronounced for Guinea, which in each time has more than five percent of its events at the extremes on affect toward these particular recipients.

The extreme expressions of affect toward the Afro-Asian nations is the most unbalanced with regard to positive and negative affect. Much more strong positive affect is directed at the Afro-Asian nations than for any of the other types of recipients. Moreover, although there are some indications of ambivalence, they are not as widespread as we found when the Brazzaville African and Latin American countries were recipients. Only five of the CREON nations did *not* have more than five percent of their events in an extreme category across the decade (1959-1968). During this decade a CREON nation was very likely to use a strong expression of positive affect when interacting with an Afro-Asian nation.

The extreme expressions of positive and negative affect toward Communist nations were about evenly divided between the two directions. Moreover, there

TABLE 9.6
Types of Recipients Receiving Most Extreme Affect from 38 CREON Nations Over Four Time Periods
(more than 5% of events in extreme categories)

CREON Nation	Western Community Nations				Brazzaville African and Latin American Nations				Afro-Asian Nations				Communist Nations[a]			
	1959-68	1960-62	1963-65	1966-68	1959-68	1960-62	1963-65	1966-68	1959-68	1960-62	1963-65	1966-68	1959-68	1960-62	1963-65	1966-68
Belgium	—[b]	1 (7%)	—	—	1 (7%)	1 (9%)	—	—	1 (9%)	1,5 (10%)	—	1 (12%)	1 (9%)	5 (10%)	—	1,5 (6%)
Canada	1 (14%)[c]	1 (7%)	—	1 (24%)	1 (15%)	1 (33%)	—	—	1 (12%)	1 (33%)	1,5 (10%)	1 (7%)	—	5 (8%)	—	—
Chile	—	—	—	1 (7%)	1 (12%)d	1,5 (20%)	1 (11%)	1 (33%)	1 (22%)	1 (20%)	—	1 (33%)	5 (18%)	5 (25%)	5 (14%)	—
China (PRC)	—	5 (7%)	—	—	5 (6%)	—	—	—	5 (6%)	5 (9%)	—	—	—	—	—	—
Costa Rica	—	1 (8%)	—	—	1 (15%)d	1 (20%)	—	—	1 (33%)	1 (33%)	—	1 (33%)	—	—	—	—
Cuba	5 (18%)	5 (22%)	5 (13%)	1 (15%)	—	1 (50%)	5 (17%)	—	1 (13%)	1 (29%)	—	1 (7%)	—	—	5 (7%)	5 (18%)
Czechoslovakia	1 (6%)	—	—	—	1,5 (12%)	5 (13%)d,f	—	1,5 (6%)	1 (8%)	—	1 (17%)	—	1 (9%)	1 (15%)	1 (7%)	—
East Germany	—	—	—	5 (14%)	—	1 (9%)	—	—	—	—	—	1,5 (6%)	1 (6%)	—	1 (12%)	—
Egypt	5 (10%)	5 (11%)	—	—	5 (11%)	—	5 (6%)	—	1 (6%)	—	1 (8%)	—	5 (12%)	5 (14%)	1 (20%)	—
France	—	5 (12%)	—	—	—	1 (9%)	—	—	—	—	—	—	—	—	—	—
Ghana	5 (7%)	5 (13%)	—	1 (7%)	1,5 (7%)	1,5 (9%)	—	1 (12%)	1 (6%)	1 (7%)	—	1 (14%)	1 (6%)	1 (10%)	—	5 (50%)
Guinea	5 (9%)	—	5 (27%)	5 (14%)	5 (15%)d	1 (9%)d	1 (13%)d	5 (67%)d,f	1 (6%)	—	—	1 (16%)	—	—	—	—
Iceland	—	—	—	—	1 (12%)	—	—	1 (25%)	1 (22%)	1 (33%)	—	1 (20%)	—	—	—	—
India	—	—	—	—	—	—	5 (7%)	—	1 (8%)	1 (17%)	—	1 (8%)	—	—	—	—
Israel	—	5 (8%)	—	—	5 (6%)	5 (9%)	—	1 (33%)	5 (12%)	1 (11%)	5 (24%)	5 (10%)	1 (9%)	1 (25%)	—	1 (12%)
Italy	—	—	—	—	1 (15%)	1 (33%)	—	1 (9%)	1 (15%)	1 (15%)	1 (33%)	1 (13%)	—	—	—	—
Ivory Coast	—	—	—	—	—	—	—	1 (14%)	—	—	—	1,5 (12%)	—	—	—	—
Japan	—	—	—	—	—	—	—	1 (7%)	1 (8%)	1 (17%)	—	1 (8%)	—	—	—	—
Kenya	5 (17%)c	5 (16%)	5 (50%)	5 (25%)	—	—	—	5 (50%)	5 (6%)	—	—	5 (13%)d	—	—	—	—
Lebanon	1 (8%)	1 (8%)	—	1 (8%)	5 (21%)d	5 (21%)d	5 (30%)	5 (23%)d	1 (8%)	1 (10%)	1 (6%)	1 (18%)	5 (9%)	5 (21%)	—	—
Mexico	—	—	—	—	1 (8%)	—	5 (7%)	1 (17%)	1 (29%)d	1 (17%)	—	1 (11%)	—	—	—	—
New Zealand	—	—	—	—	1 (33%)	1 (60%)	—	1 (20%)	1 (11%)	1 (50%)d	5 (33%)	1 (25%)	—	—	—	—
Norway	—	—	—	—	5 (6%)	5 (25%)	—	1 (20%)	1 (13%)	1 (33%)	—	1 (11%)	—	—	—	—
Philippines	—	—	—	—	1,5 (6%)	1,5 (20%)	—	1 (25%)	1 (17%)	1 (25%)	—	1 (22%)	—	—	—	—
Poland	1 (16%)	—	1 (32%)	—	1 (20%)d	—	1 (67%)	1,5 (12%)	1 (9%)	1 (12%)	—	1 (25%)	1 (8%)	1 (8%)	1 (18%)	—
Soviet Union	5 (10%)	5 (15%)	5 (11%)	—	5 (6%)	5 (6%)	—	5 (12%)	1 (9%)	1 (8%)	—	1 (8%)	1 (6%)	—	1 (19%)	—
Spain	—	—	—	—	1 (9%)	—	—	1 (12%)	—	—	—	1 (12%)	—	—	—	—
Switzerland	—	—	—	—	—	—	—	—	—	—	—	—	5 (20%)	5 (20%)	—	—
Thailand	—	1,5 (6%)	—	—	1 (17%)	1 (25%)	—	1 (17%)	1 (12%)	1 (20%)	—	1 (10%)	—	—	—	—
Tunisia	—	1,5 (6%)	—	—	5 (6%)	—	5 (6%)	1,5 (8%)	1 (10%)	1 (15%)	—	1 (15%)	1 (9%)	1 (20%)	—	—
Turkey	—	1 (6%)	5 (6%)	—	5 (6%)	1 (8%)	5 (10%)	1 (6%)	1 (8%)	1 (17%)	—	1 (10%)	—	—	—	—
Uganda	—	5 (10%)	—	—	5 (7%)	—	5 (9%)	1 (33%)	1 (8%)	—	—	1 (25%)	—	—	—	—
United States	—	—	—	—	—	—	—	—	1 (7%)	1 (13%)	1 (8%)	1 (6%)	—	—	—	—
Uruguay	1 (6%)	1 (11%)	—	—	1,5 (6%)	—	5 (25%)	1 (25%)	1 (12%)	1 (17%)	—	1 (33%)	5 (18%)	5 (27%)	1 (17%)	—
Venezuela	1 (6%)	1 (9%)	5 (6%)	—	5 (10%)	5 (44%)	5 (20%)	—	1 (18%)	1 (14%)	—	1 (9%)	1 (20%)	5 (22%)	—	5 (29%)
West Germany	—	—	5 (6%)	—	1 (15%)	1 (11%)	1 (12%)	1 (19%)	1 (13%)	—	1 (18%)d	1 (18%)	—	—	—	—
Yugoslavia	—	—	—	—	—	—	—	1 (12%)	—	—	—	1 (12%)	—	—	—	—
Zambia	5 (14%)	—	—	5 (16%)	1 (17%)	—	—	1 (17%)	1 (9%)	—	—	1 (11%)	—	—	—	—

NOTE: The nations included in each of the four types of recipients are listed in the note to Table 9.3. The number of events used to determine the figures in this table are the same as those listed in Table 9.3.

[a] China (PRC) is not included in the Communist nations since the PRC was not a member of the United Nations during the 1960s and thus was not a part of Russett's (1967) factor analysis.

[b] Dashes are present in this table when the percent of events in either of the extreme categories is not more than 5%.

[c] The number 1 here means strong expression of positive affect. A 5 would mean strong expression of negative affect. The percentage in parentheses is the percentage of events falling in the extreme category for that type of recipient during that period.

[d] Both extreme categories had more than 5% of the events. The one listed had the larger percentage of events, however.

are few shifts in the direction of these strong expressions of affect across the decade. If a CREON country expresses strong negative affect at one point toward the Communist countries, it is likely to express strong negative affect at another point in time. If the strong affect is positive, it is likely to be strongly positive at another point in time. The shifts in mood that do occur are from three Latin American countries: Cuba, Uruguay, and Venezuela.

Our comments on Tables 9.3 through 9.6 in many ways barely "scratch the surface" of the data. The reader is invited to explore the data for support of his/her hypotheses or hunches. There are certainly many more types of cross-time and cross-national comparisons to be made.

SUMMARY

We have attempted in this chapter to develop a measure of affect that can be assessed from foreign policy behavior. We have defined affect as indicating the feelings of an actor (a policymaker or collectivity of policymakers) toward another government or actor in the international arena at a particular moment. Affect can be positive or negative; it can be mild or strong. Affect is transitory and can change as the situation or recipient changes. Affect is manifested in both verbal statements and physical deeds. Affect is dyadic in nature, in that it involves both an actor and a recipient—the affect is directed toward someone or some entity. We have suggested a way of operationalizing affect and have examined some data using the operationalization with the CREON event data set. The data indicate that, with knowledge about a government's affect toward another government, we can begin to note subtle changes in relationship and signs or signals of desired change. We can begin to learn something about the intent of governments toward other governments.

NOTES

1. We wish to thank Petra and Danny Donofrio and Beverly Gatliff, who coded the CREON events for this variable.

2. In eliminating "mentioned" recipients, we used the Role of Targets and Objects variable described in the Technical Appendix. Before examining any dyadic events for affect, we deleted all events that involved domestic recipients. Because CREON events can have multiple recipients, an event (like the first example in Table 9.1 under strong expression of positive affect) can involve a domestic as well as a foreign recipient. Since, in examining foreign policy behavior, we really are not interested in domestic recipients, such events were deleted in developing the affect measure.

3. The reader will note that reporting the affect data for every dyad among the CREON nations alone would have required a 38 x 38 matrix composed of 703 cells.

4. In classifying the recipients, we were interested in groups of nations with similar orientations toward the foreign policy arena that might have been perceived to be similar by the CREON nations during the decade 1959-1968. The Russett (1967) factor analysis data provided such a classification. Each of the four types of recipients had a different pattern of votes in the United Nations during the 1963-1964 session. The Western Community and the Communist nations offer the most distinctive orientations of the four types of recipients, and probably most nations during this decade perceived this difference. The other two types of recipients include developing and underdeveloped nations that were either more pro-Western (Brazzaville African and Latin American nations) or neutralist (Afro-Asian nations) during this decade.

Specificity

What methods are available to foreign policymakers for bringing about a more desirable future? What elements of one's current action seem particularly important in orchestrating a more favorable environment? This chapter outlines one of many possible responses to these questions by explicating the notion of specificity in foreign policy behavior. The argument is based on the premise that foreign policymaking consists of efforts to shape the future as policymakers conceive of it. Concepts such as choice and decision pervade much thinking about politics, whether one thinks in terms of problems of influence (Lasswell, 1936), conflict over values (Easton, 1965b), goal-oriented behavior (Snyder et al., 1962), action and reaction (McClelland, 1966), or coordination and control (Deutsch, 1963). It is not surprising that academicians and practitioners alike find policymakers' attempts to shape the future among the most fascinating aspects of politics, for the comparison of the present with potential futures supplies an immediate opportunity for getting more or doing better. Thus, policymakers' strategies for shaping the future pose a major research question.

Specificity provides one basis for investigating how decision makers use foreign policy behaviors to shape the future. Specificity is the amount of information in a behavior that a foreign policy actor provides the recipient about the actor's expectations concerning future behaviors. By "expectation" we mean

AUTHOR'S NOTE: I would like to thank my colleagues on the CREON Project, especially Charles Hermann and the editors of this volume, for their assistance and encouragement in this research. Charles Hermann, Chadwick Alger, and Robert Trice guided the dissertation effort of which this chapter is a part. Support for the preparation of this chapter was provided by the National Science Foundation (GS 40536), the Mershon Center at Ohio State, the Centre for Foreign Policy Studies at Dalhousie University, and the Computer Centers at both Ohio State and Dalhousie. This chapter was written before I joined the Department of Commerce; thus, the views expressed are my own and do not reflect those of this or any other government agency.

desired future behaviors defined in terms of the actor's initiatives or those of some external entity. Specificity thus reflects the presentation of the actor's own expectations about future behaviors as a potential influence on the behavior of other actors in the international system. Because we assume that the policy-making process is imbued with purpose(s)—often conflicting—we search for patterns in foreign policy behavior. Because references to future behaviors are often made in current behaviors, it follows that these references, too, may be patterned.

Several concepts related to specificity have been considered by students of foreign policy and international politics. Ambiguity (Schelling, 1960; Wright, 1955), vagueness in signaling (Deutsch, 1963; Iklé, 1964), and specificity all describe the amount of information about future behaviors that is transmitted in foreign policy actions. Degree of uncertainty characterizes the situation confronted by the recipient (McClelland, 1972b; Steinbruner, 1974). Common to all of these concepts is a concern with the amount of information transmitted, whether viewed from the actor's or the recipient's perspective and whether descriptive of the behavior or the situation. Specificity, as defined in this chapter, is measured from the actor's perspective and is descriptive of behavior. That is, specificity defines the degree of precision or vagueness with which the actor signals his expectations rather than the uncertainty in the situation that the recipient confronts.

CONCEPTUALIZATION

Foreign policymakers attempt to influence future states of affairs by providing information about behaviors not yet initiated that may bring those desired future states of affairs closer to realization. Alternative futures are valued differentially according to goals, and certain futures—those more highly valued—are sought by attempting to increase their probabilities. A principal means of influencing the future is to orchestrate the behaviors of relevant actors, including oneself, in a way that will favor those behaviors likely to bring about the preferred future and discourage those behaviors likely to preclude the desired outcome (Schelling, 1960: 37). The orchestration of future behaviors is facilitated by providing information about them. The clarification of the terms of threats and promises, the explication of future behaviors one is attempting to elicit, and the communication of cues reflecting the details about one's own intended actions illustrate attempts to orchestrate future behaviors by controlling the degree of specificity in current behaviors.

Specificity poses the question: "To what extent does the action contain information about what the actor claims he intends to do or desires some external entity to do?" It does not reflect the probability that certain behaviors will actually occur, nor does it reflect the actor's credibility or capabilities. But the recipient must be aware of a foreign policy behavior for specificity to produce any effect on the recipient's behavior. If we think of uncertainty as a situational variable that describes the extent to which the consequences of one's behavior can be confidently predicted (Duncan, 1972), then, from the recipient's perspective, specificity is that part of uncertainty that is manipulable by the initiator of the action. Thus, the actor may manipulate the recipient's uncertainty by increasing or decreasing the level of specificity in his behavior.

It is important to note that specificity does not necessarily describe the actor's genuine expectations and intentions. Nor do we assume that the meaning attached to a signal by recipients is necessarily uniform. The concepts of orchestration and manipulation imply that actors may employ a wide range of strategies, including distortion, deception, controlled release of information, and any other means of making net gains "on the cheap" (Jervis, 1970). Specificity measures the representations made by foreign policy actors. There is no necessary one-to-one correspondence between these representations and "true expectations and intentions." Indeed, perhaps the central paradox of policymaking is that one nearly always regards information received as suspect, while one often hopes that information sent will be regarded as sincere. Both actor and recipient function in this way, and each probably knows that the other does. If this argument is plausible, then we should focus on what policymakers do rather than on what they think. In any case, it is clear that the success of attempts to shape the future is partly dependent on the information concerning expectations that is exchanged by interacting parties. As Singer (1963) has argued, in order to influence a second party whose actions may partly determine some future state of affairs, it helps if the first party conveys a set of expectations about what he intends to do in the future, about what the second party is to do, or both.

Students of foreign policy have long been intrigued with the linkages between the projection of actor expectations and both prior and subsequent situations. Machiavelli (1947) offered Lorenzo Medici much sage advice about decision making under uncertainty created in part by the conflicting expectations projected by the monarchs of fifteenth-century Europe. Nicholson (1939) and other students of diplomacy have offered maxims for negotiators operating under the uncertainty created by their counterparts and have suggested ways of generating uncertainty for one's protagonists when doing so is advantageous.

Uncertainty as a characteristic of the situation has been acknowledged in the international relations literature as both a condition that influences behavior and a condition that behavior can be designed to influence (see Swanson, 1976). The impact of behavior received on his own situation presents a policymaker with a problem of interpretation, whereas the impact of his behavior on the recipient's situation and response presents the policymaker with a problem of strategy. Problems of interpretation are key features in, for example, nuclear deterrence:

> It takes no great perspicacity on the part of the initiator [of a challenge to deterrence] to be aware of the possibility that the defender sometimes engages in calculated ambiguity when signaling a commitment. The more difficult problem the initiator faces is that of accounting for the reasons or strategy behind any particular instance of calculated ambiguity [George and Smoke, 1974: 565].

De Sola Pool (1969: 194) highlights the problem of strategy in the same substantive area by arguing that "a large part of the act of deterrence, as of influence in general, is in the manipulation of certainty rather than the substance of the facts.

Certainty is often much easier to affect than net conclusions." If specificity, a behavioral measure, is an influence on uncertainty, a situational measure, and vice versa, then its significance to students of foreign policy should be considerable.

It follows that the typical degree of specificity in foreign policy behaviors is an intriguing research question. Jervis (1970: 9) has argued that "few actions are unambiguous. They rarely provide anything like proof of how the state plans to act in the future." Moreover, actions seldom indicate how one state's decision makers wish *others* to act in the future. Why should this be the case? A tentative rationale is that specific behaviors entail more risks because they are potentially expensive in terms of professional, organizational, and national interests.

Two lines of argument support the hypothesis that risk considerations make less specific behaviors the rule. First, the maintenance of flexibility is an important consideration in foreign affairs. Flexibility—the capacity to reverse or alter a proposed course of action—is often desirable to preserve as an actor and sometimes desirable to offer to the recipients of one's actions, for example, during a crisis situation. Less specific behavior allows the actor to preserve future options. Therefore, to the extent that actors seek to maintain flexibility, less specific behaviors are the rule. Jervis (1970: 123) also argued: "It is the noise and ambiguity in the signaling system that provide flexibility and protection by reducing the danger to an actor's reputation when he undertakes probes and initiatives." Moreover, because the clear projection of one's expectations renders them susceptible to manipulation by the recipient, keeping them hidden in certain situations may be a desirable strategy (Schelling, 1960).

Maintenance of flexibility has domestic as well as external implications. For example, political regimes may engage in less specific foreign policy actions in an attempt to maintain their domestic positions in the face of political opposition. Situations characterized by high levels of threat should tend to result in less specific actions—that is, actions that preserve future options for both the actor and the recipient. When domestic bureaucracies assume conflicting positions on a policy problem, less specific foreign policy behaviors provide a collective umbrella (Halperin, 1974).

Second, less specific foreign policy behaviors are the rule because policymakers, like everyone else, prefer not to be wrong, particularly when being wrong produces undesirable consequences or reflects poorly on their professional competence. One strategy for avoiding the risks of subsequently being judged wrong is to build ambiguity into one's actions. Later, if needed, "plausible denial" can be used to either shift the blame or reject its appropriateness. In addition, the promotion of one's specialty as an art requiring the good judgment born of experience is aided if the substance of that specialty appears to be complex and full of nuances (O'Leary, 1974: 65-70). If the interpretation of most international relations were starkly obvious, caution induced by uncertainty, for example, would rarely be reflected in foreign policy behaviors. Of course, this is not the case.

The risks of being wrong are also recognized on the organizational level. Thompson (1967: 92) argued that "when cause/effect knowledge is believed incomplete, organizations seek extrinsic measures of fitness for future action," such as professional competence. This is so, he says, because "when outcomes are beyond the organization's control, assessment in terms of outcomes is resisted." That is, where the operating environment is complex and contingencies exist, performance is often measured in terms of the appearance of competence for future action. To initiate a less specific behavior is to preserve flexibility and to reduce the risks of later being blamed for an undesired outcome. If foreign policymaking agencies operate along these lines, then they are likely to exhibit an inclination toward less specific behaviors.

These conceptual and theoretical considerations suggest a general direction for the analysis of specificity in foreign policy behaviors, but the difficult task of operationalization remains. The following sections undertake this task, with the first preparing the way by discussing several measurement issues.

EMPIRICAL BASIS OF SPECIFICITY

Measurement of specificity requires some consideration of the kinds of data appropriate to the task. Specificity refers to the amount of information about the actor's expectations contained in an action. Clearly, the most direct solution would be to gather data in which the actor explicitly states his expectations about his own or another's future behavior. Such statements could be content analyzed to determine how detailed they are (how many bits of information they involve), where greater specificity is equivalent to more detail about the time, conditions for, and nature of the expected behavior. This solution is not adopted here because many foreign behaviors are not explicit statements of expectations about future behaviors even though recipients and observers frequently attempt to infer the actors' expectations. We wish to identify the bases for these inferences.

A second solution adopts an indirect approach to the observation of specificity. Using this solution, we would contend that all behaviors relate to some problem and may concern the use or potential use of resources in dealing with the problem. By resources we mean the human or nonhuman military, financial, technical, diplomatic, or economic capabilities that, at the discretion of policymakers, may be used or whose future use may be discussed in the event. The use of resources may be actual or potential and may have occurred in the past as well as in the present or future. Thus, any statement could conceivably refer to resources and the problem to which those resources were directed. Similarly, physical actions can involve resources.

It is this capacity to refer to problem and resources that provides a common basis for measuring specificity in all events, because events can include a variety of kinds of information concerning resources. Four kinds of information about resources that are central to our later development of this measure are: whose resources are being considered, what kinds of resources are being considered, when the resources will be expended, and what is the problem or issue to be affected by the expenditure of the resources.

In order to link information about resource use to specificity, we need to assume that the more information an actor supplies concerning his expectations about future behavior, the greater the likelihood that reference will be made to the resources used or to be used in the execution of such behavior. If the actor provides much detail about the resources, then, by that fact, he is assumed to have provided information about his expectations concerning future behavior. Thus, the clarity of the actor's expectations projected in current behavior may be indirectly measured through information conveyed about the actual or potential use of resources and the clarity of the demarcation of the problem with which those resources are designed to deal.

The way behavior conveys information concerning resources differs in verbal behavior and in physical actions. Verbal behavior conveys information in a relatively simple fashion—either the information is explicitly stated or it is not. The recipient or analyst need only look to see if the information is present.

Physical actions, such as giving foreign aid or establishing a new embassy, present a more difficult case because they intrinsically use resources. One may observe the information projected by these behaviors about the use of resources: who uses them, the problem or issue to which they are directed, and the kinds and amounts of the resources. Physical actions, however, that are not accompanied by some type of verbal statement can ambiguously reflect future behaviors even though they transmit a great deal of information about resources (see Deutsch, 1963). For example, Allison (1971) shows that several competing inferences might have been drawn from the accidental overflight of the Soviet Union by an American U-2 plane during the Cuban missile crisis. President Kennedy immediately stated that the overflight was accidental. The task of interpreting an actor's expectations on the basis of a physical action requires more inference than is often the case with verbal behavior.

Fortunately, physical actions not only convey bits of information that indicate what the actor is currently doing; they also reveal the level of his concern about the issue. They show that the actor is sufficiently concerned about the issue to expend his own resources in dealing with it. We can argue that this level of concern will generally persist, at least over the short term. Such a belief is supported by the position of those students who argue that future behaviors are a function of current behaviors (Halperin, 1974; Phillips, 1969; and Snyder et al., 1962). Because physical actions reveal concern, recipients of these behaviors and students of foreign policy alike draw inferences about future behavior on the basis of physical actions. That recipients draw information from physical actions is significant; actors are able to modify their physical actions and thus manipulate the information transmitted to recipients, including information about the actor's expectations about future behavior.

An important corollary to this argument is as follows. Most physical actions are known not by direct observation of the deed, but by the actor's announcement of its occurrence. It is relatively easy for the actor to be selective about the information he reveals concerning his actions and thereby to manipulate the information conveyed about his expectations concerning future behavior. Note that this means that physical actions may have very low specificity.

OPERATIONALIZING DEGREE OF SPECIFICITY
USING THE CREON DATA

The first step in operationalizing specificity involved the selection of variables from the CREON data set that reflected information about the problem and the actual or potential use of resources. Variables fitting these criteria were intercorrelated using Yule's Q as a means of weeding out those that did not tap the underlying dimension of specificity.[1] It should be noted that, in the absence of any reasoning to the contrary and for economy of effort, we decided to develop a specificity scale that is unidimensional. If the assumption of unidimensionality is to be valid, items (CREON variables) should correlate both with the scale and, by implication, among themselves. No one item should correlate perfectly with another or else the two are effectively measuring the same thing; on the other hand, items should covary reasonably strongly to the extent that they are partial indicators of a common dimension. The arbitrary criterion imposed in this procedure was that each item correlate at ±.4 or more with all other selected items in order to be included in the scale. The following CREON variables satisfied this requirement:

1. Specificity of problem, issue, or topic (for a description see the Technical Appendix) taps the clarity with which an actor makes known the substantive area currently of concern to him and in which possible change is foreseen as a consequence of his or others' foreign policy behaviors. In effect, it indicates the extent to which an actor defines or "zeros in" on the substantive area that present or future activities may affect.

2. Specificity of kinds of resources (see Technical Appendix) measures the extent to which the actor makes explicit the particular resources he is using or intends to use in the future. This variable refers only to the resources under the control of the actor and not to those of external entities.

3. Specificity as to time or condition for use of resources (see Technical Appendix) also refers exclusively to resources under the control of the actor, but only to those that he indicates may be used in future behaviors. It assesses whether or not the actor describes when he will expend his own resources in future behaviors. Projected actor expectations are more precise if an actor indicates when or under what conditions he will act.

4. Resource use (see Technical Appendix) taps the presence or absence of references to actual or proposed uses of resources controlled by either the actor or other entities. If an actor's projected expectations are relatively clear with respect to behaviors that he desires from others, such clarity is in part reflected in this variable, which requires the actor to describe explicitly the nature of the resources, whatever they may be.

The distributions for these four CREON variables and their intercorrelations are presented in Table 10.1. Collectively, the four selected variables may be used to characterize the amount of information in projected actor expectations. Projected expectations about behaviors that the actor claims he intends to initiate are tapped by the variables reflecting specificity in the problem, kinds of resources, and time or condition for use of resources. Expectations about behaviors

TABLE 10.1
CREON Variables Constituting Specificity Scale

CREON Variable		Value	Absolute Frequency	Absolute Frequency Percentage	Adjusted Frequency Percentage
Specificity of problem, issue, or topic[a]					
yes		1	9886	77.8	77.8
no		2	2824	22.2	22.2
		Total	12710	100.0	100.0
Specificity of kinds of resources					
yes		1	1799	14.2	14.2
no		2	630	5.0	
no (not applicable)		9	10281	80.9	85.9
		Total	12710	100.0	100.0
Specificity of time or condition for use of resources					
yes		1	487	3.8	3.8
no		2	1942	15.3	
no (not applicable)		9	10281	80.9	96.2
		Total	12710	100.0	100.0
Resource use					
yes		1	2780	21.9	21.9
no		2	9930	78.1	78.1
		Total	12710	100.0	100.0

Interitem correlations		Problem	Kinds	Time	Resource Use
(Yule's Q)	Problem	1.00			
	Kinds	.75	1.00		
	Time	.42	.91	1.00	
	Resource Use	.57	.77	.64	1.00

[a]Variables have been dichotomized into yes/no categories for purposes of Guttman scaling (see footnote 3).

that the actor desires from others are tapped by the variables reflecting specificity in the problem and general resource use.

A Guttman scale was developed from the four specificity variables.[2] The variables were ordered in the scale according to the size of the passing set of cases so that "easier" items preceded "more difficult" ones. Events were assigned scores according to the "most difficult" item passed, assuming that all preceding items were passed. Events thus scored displayed perfect response patterns over the items in conformity with the assumption of cumulativeness. Some 11,879 events, or 93.5 percent of the data, had perfect, error-free response patterns (see Table 10.2). That is, a score of X indicates that the event passed *the first* X items. Given a score, one can determine the response pattern, and vice versa. A discussion of the events that did not produce error-free response patterns may be found in Appendix 10.1. Table 10.2 shows the number of events falling at each

TABLE 10.2
Specificity Scale Scores for Error-Free Events and All Scored Events

CREON Variables Used to Generate Scale (in order of Degree of Specificity)		Problem Specified	Resources Specified	Kinds of Resources Specified	Time Specified
Specificity Scale	Least Specific			Moderately Specific	Most Specific
Error-Free Events					
Score	0	1	2	3	4
Frequency	2567	6663	1476	826	347
Percentage	21.61	56.09	12.43	6.95	2.92
		N = 11879			
All Scored Events (see Appendix 10.1)					
Score	0	1	2	3	4
Frequency	2567	6878	2043	855	347
Percentage	20.23	54.20	16.10	6.74	2.73
Cumulative Percentage	20.23	74.43	90.53	97.27	100.0
		N = 12690			

point of the specificity scale for those events with error-free response patterns and for all scaled events. The Coefficient of Reproducibility for the finished scale is .98.

Validity of Specificity Scale

Validation studies of this specificity scale are currently under way, but several perspectives on this question may be offered at this time.[3] First, a return to the issue of whether a focus on information about resources logically guarantees that physical actions are highly specific is clearly germane to the scale's validity. Physical actions—that is, actions entailing more than the spoken or written word —in fact vary considerably with respect to degree of specificity. As a group distributed over the five (increasingly specific) degrees of specificity, the percentage distribution of CREON events involving physical actions is 6.1 at scale point 0, 14.1 at scale point 1, 26.9 at scale point 2, 40.1 at scale point 3, and 12.8 at scale point 4 (N = 1941).

Several other ways of examining the validity of the specificity scale can be offered. Earlier, theoretical arguments were supplied in support of our claim that less rather than more specific behaviors are predominant in foreign policy. This is the case because policymakers act to retain flexibility and to minimize the risk that behaviors may later be viewed as inappropriate. More specific behaviors are relatively expensive in terms of resources as well as the risks to one's reputation for making good on projected expectations. As can be seen in Table 10.2, this expectation is borne out by the specificity scale; there is, indeed, a greater percentage of less specific behaviors than of more specific behaviors. This success-

TABLE 10.3
Illustrative CREON Events for Each Degree of Specificity

Range 0 (least specific)

Ivory Coast President Houphouet-Boigny, at a state dinner attended by the leaders of countries belonging to the Inter-African and Malagasy Organization, discusses a future French Commonwealth with French President De Gaulle. (July 9, 1966)

The United Arab Republic's semiofficial newspaper, *Al Ahram,* in an article for domestic readership, calls the Soviet Union a true friend of the Arabs and praises the People's Republic of China for taking a firm stand in condemning aggression. (June 30, 1967)

Range 1

The Costa Rican delegate to the Law of the Sea Conference attends conference session studying territorial sea limits and fishing limits. (April 26, 1960)

The Belgian foreign minister expresses his country's determination to protect the freedom of West Berliners in a NATO Council final communique. (May 4, 1960)

Range 2 (moderately specific)

United States President Johnson states that the $500 million earmarked for military aid and supporting assistance to South Vietnam and Laos might not be enough and asks for standby authorization from Congress to grant additional sums in these categories if necessary. (January 14, 1965)

Guinea recommends an emergency meeting of the Conference of Independent African States to consider severing diplomatic relations with South Africa. (April 7, 1960)

Range 3

France resumes delivery of arms—helicopters—to Jordan and Saudi Arabia after a nine-year embargo. (March 4, 1965)

Israel enters into an agreement with members of the Inter-American Development Bank and the Pan American Union to accelerate the preparation of rural development projects in Latin America by providing technical assistance personnel for one year. (July 5, 1966)

Range 4 (most specific)

United States Department of State spokesman McCloskey announces that the U.S. is terminating all aid and withdrawing all of its AID officials and their dependents from Yemen. (April 28, 1967)

The German Federal Republic announces grants totaling about $4.6 million to finance residential construction and agricultural development projects in the Ivory Coast, Mali, and Upper Volta, in collaboration with the EEC Development Fund whose total contribution is $581 million. (March 18, 1961)

ful matching of a data distribution with the analyst's understanding of phenomena in the empirical world increases our confidence in the validity of the scale.

Another perspective on validity can be gained by examining the sample events in Table 10.3. Two randomly selected events from the five degrees of the specificity scale are presented in this table. The issue is whether or not the scores of these events intuitively accord with our conceptual definition which is embodied in the question: "How much do we know, based on the event, about the actor's own future behavior or the behavior he desires from others?" Although the reader may draw his/her own conclusions, we believe that these sample events, representing only a few of those examined by the author, intuitively accord with our conceptual definition of degree of specificity. The events also support the contention that our Guttman scale of specificity is valid.

A final and more substantial method for examining the validity of the specificity scale is provided by the results of a study that compared CREON events scaled on specificity with expert judgments of specificity (see Swanson, 1978). Six experts—all specialists in international relations—were recruited for the study.[4] Each expert was asked to sort 50 events which had been assembled by randomly sampling ten events from each range of the specificity scale. The experts were supplied with a set of instructions, highlighted by a discussion of the conceptual definition of degree of specificity, asking that they sort the 50 events into five groups of ten. At no time during the exercise were the experts exposed to the operational procedures used to generate the specificity scale, its component variables, or any discussion of resources or problem areas. Each expert had to develop, independently his own scoring rationale based on the conceptual definition. In essence, then, the study consisted of checking a computer-generated event measure against a set of validity criteria established by expert judgments.

Each expert judgment was compared with its corresponding scale score. Inter-expert agreement was also examined. Pearson product moment correlations were computed between all pairs of experts and between each expert and the computer-generated scale. The comparison of ordinal distributions using an interval level statistic constitutes a very stringent test, but it is appropriate to impose stringent demands on tests of validity. The results of the test are presented in the intercorrelation matrix in Table 10.4.

As the first row of Table 10.4 indicates, the judgments of every expert correlate with the computer-generated scale scores at .60 or higher. Interexpert correlations range from a low of .53 to a high of .70. With only two exceptions, all of the intercorrelations lie within the range of .59 to .74, revealing a considerable degree of clustering. The table suggests not only that the instructions were sufficient to produce reasonably high agreement between judgments and computer scores, but that experts were able to internalize the connotations of the concept and to apply them in a fairly consistent manner.[5] The results from these various ways of exploring the validity of the specificity scale are encouraging.

Variations in Degree of Specificity for CREON Nations

Are there any differences between countries in terms of the specificity of their actions in a given period of time? Table 10.5 provides a basis for answering this question by presenting specificity profiles of CREON actor countries for the entire time span of the data—1959-1968. With a possible range of zero to four, Table 10.5 shows that the actor with the least specific mean score was Yugoslavia with .91 and the actor with the most specific mean score was Zambia with 1.513. There are differences between countries on the measure averaged over the decade, but these differences are modest.

An examination of the percentages in Table 10.5 at the various scale points along the specificity scale, however, reveals some interesting differences. Al-

TABLE 10.4
Intercorrelations of Computer Scores and Expert Judgments[a]

	Computer	Judge A	Judge B	Judge C	Judge D	Judge E
Computer	—	.74	.72	.67	.66	.60
Judge A		—	.61	.70	.66	.64
Judge B			—	.65	.63	.53
Judge C				—	.56	.60
Judge D					—	.59
Judge E						—

[a] First-order Pearson product moment coefficients are given; N = 50, all standard deviations are equal. The reader may note that attrition claimed one expert.

though for most of the CREON countries a scale score of one predominates, the percentage of events having this score ranges from 44.9 percent to 65.3 percent. In other words, roughly one-half to two-thirds of the countries' events have a scale score of one. Those countries that have more than 60 percent of their events at scale point one appear generally to be the developing countries in the CREON sample—for example, Ivory Coast, Kenya, Mexico, Uganda, and Uruguay. On the other hand, among the countries with about 50 percent of their events at scale point one are the more industrialized societies, such as France, Japan, the Soviet Union, and the United States. A closer look at the other 50 percent of the events of these more modernized nations reveals different emphases. For France and the Soviet Union, for instance, more of these events fall at the least specific end of the specificity scale, whereas for Japan and the United States more of these events fall at the more specific end of the specificity scale. France and the Soviet Union during this decade were less likely than Japan and the United States to telegraph their expectations concerning future behavior.[6] Combining the percentages of events at scale scores three and four for the countries, we find the following six nations have the largest percentage of events at the more specific end of the scale: Israel, Japan, Lebanon, the United States, West Germany, and Zambia. Three out of every 25 of the events of these nations were highly specific during the decade 1959-1968.

There is another way of analyzing variations in the degree of specificity in CREON nations' foreign policy behavior. This procedure involves tracking specificity profiles through time. Although the CREON data are not well suited to this task because of their noncontiguous time slices, an illustration of this kind of analysis is possible using an episode whose duration and principal actors are matters of general agreement and which is included in the data set. The episode is the Cuban missile crisis, which occurred in October 1962.

Figure 10.1 presents the profiles of the average daily specificity scores for the Soviet Union and the United States during the last three months of 1962.[7] The "thirteen days" of the missile crisis (Kennedy, 1968) spanned October 16 through 28 and are marked in the figure. Note that a value on the ordinate axis (specificity) has been allocated to days on which there were "no events" in order

TABLE 10.5
Specificity Profiles of CREON Actor Countries

CREON Nation	Mean Score	Least Specific 0	1	Moderately Specific 2	3	Most Specific 4
Belgium	1.220	66[a]	223	50	26	16
		17.3	58.5	13.1	6.8	4.2
Canada	1.101	96	202	50	35	5
		24.7	52.1	12.9	9.0	1.3
Chile	1.182	39	105	55	8	2
		18.7	50.2	26.3	3.8	1.0
China (PRC)	1.071	128	274	55	35	13
		25.3	54.3	10.9	6.9	2.6
Costa Rica	1.256	25	88	40	6	5
		15.2	53.7	24.4	3.7	3.0
Cuba	1.304	49	170	71	31	5
		15.0	52.1	21.8	9.5	1.5
Czechoslovakia	1.083	45	120	22	17	2
		21.8	58.3	10.7	8.3	1.0
East Germany	1.262	39	102	37	17	7
		19.3	50.5	18.3	8.4	3.5
Egypt	1.286	82	234	89	24	25
		18.1	51.5	19.6	5.3	5.5
France	1.045	229	456	92	53	23
		26.8	53.5	10.8	6.2	2.7
Ghana	1.150	43	164	55	4	7
		15.8	60.1	20.1	1.5	2.6
Guinea	1.153	41	116	35	13	4
		19.6	55.5	16.7	6.2	1.9
Iceland	1.176	28	88	34	5	4
		17.6	55.3	21.4	3.1	2.5
India	1.152	95	267	100	26	6
		19.2	54.0	20.2	5.3	1.2
Italy	1.195	73	253	56	29	14
		17.2	59.5	13.2	6.8	3.3
Ivory Coast	1.054	27	94	20	3	3
		18.4	63.9	13.6	2.0	2.0
Japan	1.351	40	141	57	21	12
		14.8	52.0	21.0	7.7	4.4
Kenya	1.253	7	62	22	3	1
		7.4	65.3	23.2	3.2	1.1
Lebanon	1.409	19	78	33	10	9
		12.8	52.3	22.1	6.7	6.0
Mexico	1.168	24	121	37	8	1
		12.6	63.4	19.4	4.2	0.05
New Zealand	1.050	45	112	35	7	2
		22.4	55.7	17.4	3.5	1.0
Norway	1.133	42	135	33	6	9
		18.7	60.0	14.7	2.7	4.0

(Continued)

TABLE 10.5   Continued

CREON Nation	Mean Score	Least Specific 0	1	Moderately Specific 2	3	Most Specific 4
Philippines	1.226	35 17.6	108 54.3	38 19.1	12 6.0	6 3.0
Poland	1.060	57 24.5	130 55.8	24 10.3	19 8.2	3 1.3
Soviet Union	1.047	274 27.3	517 51.5	135 13.4	48 4.8	30 3.0
Spain	1.201	29 17.2	90 53.3	40 23.7	7 4.1	3 1.8
Switzerland	1.230	11 14.9	46 62.2	10 13.5	3 4.1	4 5.4
Thailand	1.142	36 22.2	78 48.1	38 23.5	9 5.6	1 0.6
Tunisia	1.109	52 19.0	163 59.5	43 15.7	9 3.3	7 2.6
Turkey	1.224	58 18.3	165 52.1	66 20.8	21 6.6	7 2.2
Uganda	1.145	20 13.8	92 63.4	28 19.3	2 1.4	3 2.1
United States	1.261	380 19.9	988 51.6	277 14.5	205 10.7	64 3.3
Uruguay	1.196	16 11.6	87 63.0	29 21.0	4 2.9	2 1.4
Venezuela	1.226	30 14.4	118 56.7	45 21.6	13 6.3	2 1.0
West Germany	1.197	142 22.0	347 53.9	70 10.9	56 8.7	29 4.5
Yugoslavia	.910	88 34.4	120 46.9	35 13.7	9 3.5	4 1.6
Zambia	1.513	9 11.5	35 44.9	23 29.5	7 9.0	4 5.1
Totals	1.186	2567 20.2	6878 54.2	2043 16.1	855 6.7	347 2.7

[a]For each CREON country and degree of specificity, the top figure is a raw frequency and the bottom figure is the percentage which the frequency is of that country's total number of events.

to distinguish these cases from days on which mean specificity was zero. The proper interpretation for these cases is that they yielded no recorded events and are therefore undefined in terms of specificity.

Several points can be made about this illustration. In general, the oscillations of the two profiles during the 13 days of the crisis and immediately thereafter appear to be different from those in the rest of the period. For 17 of the 23 days (from October 16 to November 7) the United States was more specific than

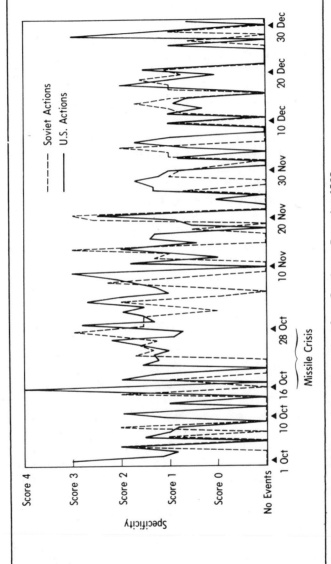

Figure 10.1 Specificity profiles of Soviet and American actions from October to December 1962.

the Soviet Union on an average daily basis. Although their "vocabulary" was the same, the two actors seem to have been making different uses of it. In Robert Kennedy's (1968: 126) words, "President Kennedy dedicated himself to making it clear to Khrushchev by word and deed—for both are important—that the U.S. had limited objectives and that we had no interest in accomplishing those objectives by adversely affecting the national security of the Soviet Union or by humiliating her." Moreover, during the 13 days and for a while after, both countries tended to avoid inactivity. During the crisis, the Soviet Union was inactive on five days, all in the first half of the crisis. The United States was inactive on two days, again in the first half of the crisis. Furthermore, there seems to be a difference in the relationship between the two countries' fluctuations during the crisis and at other times. Whereas before October 21 and after November 10 there is no consistent relationship between specificity averages, there are two patterns within this time span. From October 21 to November 2, one country's peak tends to correspond to the other's valley. The profiles are out of synchronization, and, although it is open to interpretation, this patterning may reflect one mode of crisis resolution through alternating increases in the clarity of the antagonists' projected expectations. The period November 3-10 contains a reversal of this pattern and shows a marked consistency in the relationship between oscillations.

This illustration raises as many questions as it answers, but it serves to demonstrate that, even though foreign policymakers may seem to exercise similar degrees of specificity in their behavior across a span of time, particular circumstances give rise to actions that may vary widely in specificity. Empirically uncovering the sources of this variation is a future task.

SUMMARY AND CONCLUSIONS

This chapter has defined, discussed, operationalized, and examined the validity of degree of specificity as one of many possible measures of foreign policy behavior. The interest that is grounded in the notion of specificity arises from a concern over increasing our understanding of international influence, especially the efforts of policymakers to shape the future, as they conceive it, through foreign policy actions. It would be difficult to identify evidence of the earliest concern in this area. In contrast, the systematic empirical investigation of projected actor expectations is quite recent. It is no surprise, therefore, that both prospects and problems attend the opportunities for future research.

Perhaps the most outstanding need is to design a strategy for gathering data that more directly assess actor expectations than the data used here. It bears repeating that, although degree of specificity is designed around the notion of projected actor expectations, neither CREON nor any other data set of which the author is aware provides direct measurement of this type of data. In our judgment, this paucity should not be allowed to preclude analysis. On the other hand, one should use indirect indicators—such as those used here to operationalize specificity—with caution.

Not only would a reduction in the level of inference required be desirable in and of itself, but three additional reasons may be offered which underscore this need. First, it is well known that the validity of a given measure is increased if similar results are obtained by means of an independent measure of the same phenomena (Campbell and Fiske, 1959). An alternative measure would thus supply another fix on the validity of the existing measure. Second, the experience and results of constructing a parallel measure would not only broaden the data base for research on projected actor expectations, but would possibly supply operational improvements for the measure as it exists in the CREON data. Finally, some of the more intriguing prospects for future research share the need for the capability of tracking a country's specificity through time. The CREON data set with its sampled time slices is ill-suited for this research, and the notion of an event as a discrete behavior may also be somewhat confining to the notion of specificity. Continuous data are required for such avenues of future research.

Degree of specificity is a very simple measure, simpler than the concept it is designed to measure. We hope that more elaborate and more robust measures may be employed which use degree of specificity as a starting point. The task of investigating the efforts of policymakers to shape the future through foreign policy behaviors has only begun. Much work remains to be done. With this crude beginning, however, perhaps systematic empirical study can accompany measurement improvement, and both can stimulate conceptual development.

APPENDIX 10.1
Disposition of Scale Errors

Some 811 events, or 6.5 percent of the data, did not have error-free response patterns. The perennial question for the scale builder is whether to drop these events from the analysis or, if not, how to score them with respect to the scale. Two widely used procedures for dealing with response errors exist—the Goodenough (1944) and Guttman (1944) techniques. The Goodenough (1944) technique is simply to assign scores to cases based on the number of items passed regardless of which items are passed. Proponents of this technique argue that if the assumptions of unidimensionality and cumulativeness are satisfied sufficiently for purposes of the particular analysis, then ease of use and acceptable levels of distortion recommend this technique. An alternative was suggested by Guttman(1944) and consists of correcting the minimum number of errors required to produce an error-free response pattern for each case.

The identification and disposition of scale errors are dependent on the selected scoring technique. For example, if the response pattern over a four-item scale is yes/no/no/yes, the Goodenough technique would identify two errors (responses 2 and 4) in order to assign a score of 2. The Guttman technique would identify one error (response 4) and assign a score of 1. The selection of a scoring technique has implications both for the identification of errors and for the scoring of cases. Because of these implications, the nature of the data and what they are measuring should be considered in making the selection. In the case just discussed, for example, is the error(s) produced by the fourth response more likely to be a result of random error in the original data used to measure the underlying dimension or inapplicability of the Guttman scaling assumptions? Because each item is only a partial indicator of the underlying concept, all items together are unlikely to measure it with no error. Moreover, when an overwhelming percentage of cases scale without producing errors, those that do not are more likely to be the result of random errors than systematic ones. Hence, for the degree of specificity scale developed in this chapter, events that did not

TABLE A10.1
Specificity Scale Scores for Events with One Scaling Error

Items Used to Generate Scale	Problem Specified	Resources Specified	Kinds of Resources Specified	Time Specified
Specificity Scale	Least Specific	Moderately Specific		Most Specific
Score	0	1	2	3	4
Frequency	0	215	566	30	0
Percentage	0.0	26.51	69.79	3.70	0.0

N = 811

produce perfect response patterns were scored using the Guttman technique where error-free patterns could be acheived with the correction of a single error. It may be noted that the Guttman scoring technique sometimes identifies errors in response patterns that yield nonunique scale scores. In such cases, the OSIRIS program assigns the median score. These events, along with all others that could be scored with the correction of a single error, are distributed along the specificity scale in Table A10.1. When they are added to the error-free events, 12,690 events, or 99.8 percent of the data, may be arrayed on the scale (see Table 10.2). The Coefficient of Reproducibility (CR) for this final scale is .98 [where CR = 1 − (number of errors/number of items times number of cases)]. Twenty CREON events had more than one error in their response patterns and have been dropped from the scale.

NOTES

1. Over 20 items were initially selected as candidates for the specificity scale, all providing information in one way or another concerning an actor's behavior. Many were dropped because they failed to reflect the actor's representations about the future. That is, they measured the amount of information in behavior in an indiscriminate manner. Thus, as the concept of specificity developed, the initial candidate items were constantly reconsidered, and some were judged to have lost their relevance for the concept. Others were dropped because of weak intercorrelations with selected items or negligible independent contributions to the specificity scale. Yule's Q was used here because it has been called the "dimensioning coefficient" since it can achieve maximum value in either of two ways: (1) the relation is linear (all cases pass on both or neither of the variables) or (2) the relation is curvilinear (all cases pass both variables, neither variable, or pass only the less restrictive variable). These results are available from the author on request and are not presented here.

2. The items were scaled with the aid of the Guttman Scaling Program in OSIRIS III, Release 2. In brief, the Guttman (scalogram) model assumes that items or raw variables can be identified that measure in different ways or to different degrees a single, underlying dimension. This is the assumption of unidimensionality. The second assumption requires that the items be ordered on the scale in terms of restrictiveness or difficulty. That is, a case that "passes" or satisfies the criteria of a given item must have passed all preceding items on the scale. This is the assumption of cumulativeness. Thus, if cases are scored according to the number of items passed on a four-item scale, a case with a score of 2 means that it passed the first two items but not the last two, a case with a score of 3 means that it passed the first three items but not the last, and so forth. Together, these assumptions allow one to say that a case with a score of 3 has more of the property that defines the entire scale than does a case with a score of 2. A scalogram facilitates measurement along an underlying dimension; the individual items can measure it only partially and inadequately because they measure *portions* of the dimension.

3. A more complete consideration of the validity of the specificity scale may be found in Swanson (1976, 1978).

4. The author is grateful to the following colleagues at Dalhousie University for their participation: Professors Roger Dial, Michael McGwire, Don Munton, Timothy Shaw, Denis Stairs, and Gilbert Winham.

5. A second round of event sorting and comparison was carried out following a group discussion of events that had elicited discrepant judgments in the first round. With the exception of the loss of one expert to attrition, the difference in results between the two rounds was negligible. On balance, the second round of sorting revealed little change in the experts' scoring rationales, or, at least, those changes that did occur tended to cancel each other out.

6. The reader may have noted a marked similarity between the discussion here of specificity and that for commitment in Chapter 8. Both are concerned with the problem of expectations and rely heavily in their conceptual development on the impact of physical deeds and resource allocations. Despite these similarities, there are two primary characteristics that distinguish the two measures. First, commitment relates to the expectations of recipients and of other observers resulting from the foreign policy behavior; specificity relates to the actor's expectations. Second, the commitment scale makes an analytical distinction between symbolic and significant deeds; specificity does not. The former will be very low on the commitment scale but may be quite high on the degree of specificity scale, depending on the extent to which the actor reveals his expectations. The conceptual differences between the two are reinforced by the empirical distinction; the correlation (Gamma) between the two is only .47.

7. Each country's actions in Figure 10.1 are undifferentiated by target. Thus, the profiles represent all Soviet and all U.S. actions during the period, including those not targeted to each other.

11
MARGARET G. HERMANN

Independence/Interdependence of Action

A basic tenet of most governments is maintenance of control over their nation's destiny. The goal is to sustain the nation as a separate or autonomous entity. Governments, however, are more or less successful at maintaining their autonomy, particularly in the international arena. Independence/interdependence of action focuses on the amount of autonomy a government tries to maintain in its foreign policy actions.

An examination of nations' foreign policy behavior indicates that governments do differ in the degree of autonomy they are able to sustain in their foreign policy activities. This difference is most evident when we compare a dependent nation with a neutral or unaligned nation. Governments in dependencies have little control over their foreign policy. Policy is determined by the dominant power. When dependent nations attempt to go off on their own, the consequences can be quite severe. Witness the experiences of Czechoslovakia in 1968 and Cuba in the early 1960s. They have very little autonomy in the foreign policy arena. At the other extreme is the neutral or unaligned nation that supposedly acts in all foreign policy matters as a free agent. Such a nation maintains a high degree of autonomy in its foreign policy activity.

Focusing on dependent nations and unaligned nations, however, suggests that autonomy is continuously maintained at a certain level, which is probably not the case. It seems more likely that certain kinds of behaviors allow a government to act autonomously in dealing with foreign policy problems while other behaviors limit such autonomy. What is the nature of activities where autonomy is maintained? Two conditions appear critical to acting autonomously or on one's own. The first concerns acting alone or unilaterally. Autonomy is maintained if the government makes and implements a foreign policy decision itself without involving other governments or foreign policy actors. The government assumes sole responsibility for the behavior. The second condition involves taking the initiative. The government does not wait for other governments to set the stage but acts. In effect, it generates stimuli for other governments to respond to. Once again, the government takes sole responsibility for the action. If a government both takes the initiative and acts alone, it is displaying the most autonomous kind of behavior. With a unilateral initiative, a government is "calling the shots." It is directing the activity. The government is acting independently.

Governments also engage in foreign policy actions that limit or forfeit some of their autonomy with regard to policy. Multilateral actions—actions taken with other nations—are of this nature. The action is no longer the sole responsibility of one nation. The governments of the other nations that are involved can, and probably do, influence the choice of activity. The governments share in the responsibility for the action. Governments also forfeit some of their autonomy when they respond to direct demands or requests of other governments or international actors. In effect, the governments react to the desires of others rather than their own desires. Moreover, demands and requests reduce policy options, eliminating some alternatives. A government that acts with others or collectively and in response to others' agendas forfeits the most autonomy in the foreign policy arena. It is no longer directing the action. Coordination and consultation become important. What the government may have desired is likely to be modified to arrive at a reaction approved by all and appropriate to the situation. Responsibility is shared. Governments acting in this manner become highly interdependent.

An analogy to a driver and passenger in a car may help the reader understand how we are using autonomy here. The driver of a car is in charge of making the car run. He/she steers the car as well as stops and starts it. The driver can make the car go when he/she wishes it to go (providing, of course, he/she has the keys and the car has fuel and will run). A passenger, however, is not in charge of steering the car or of stopping and starting it. The passenger can request changes in direction and express a desire for a stop but cannot be assured that his/her wish will prevail. When the government of a nation takes an independent action, it is like the driver of the car. The government is in charge of what happens— good or bad—to the nation in foreign policy. When the government of a nation acts interdependently, it is like the passenger of the car, able to propose, suggest, attempt to persuade, and cajole the driver about what should be done but not able to take charge of the action.

By examining the percentage of a government's behaviors that are independent and interdependent over a length of time, we learn which governments are likely to trigger incidents in international affairs and which nations are likely to play a more passive or supportive role in the international arena. Governments engaging in a large number of independent behaviors probably act as instigators of activity or as active third parties in international affairs. Governments engaging in a large number of interdependent behaviors are more involved in an interactive mode of behavior, consulting on and coordinating activity. By enabling a government to remain autonomous in its foreign policy, the independent action indicates a certain assertiveness on the part of the actor. Moreover, the independent action suggests a certain risk orientation toward policymaking because the source of the action is unmistakable. The interdependent behavior, on the other hand, is less risky for the individual government but may indicate a greater sensitivity to the international environment and what other nations have to offer. Governments may be prepared to forfeit some autonomy in foreign policy if, in turn, they can gain resources they lack, credibility or legitimacy they lack, or political support they need.

By assessing the amount of independence or interdependence in a government's behavior, we can also begin to investigate the charges of some historians and political scientists that certain nations respond to but do not initiate foreign policy activity while others generally initiate what is going on in the international system. Soviet-American interactions during the Cold War have often been discussed in this way (see O. Holsti, 1974). Some (for example, Strausz-Hupe et al., 1959) feel the Soviets initiated most Cold War situations while the Americans only responded; others (see Kolko, 1969; Kolko and Kolko, 1972) suggest just the reverse. Moreover, with a measure of independence/interdependence of action we can check the match between government leaders' statements about their nation's foreign policy roles (for example, K. Holsti, 1970) and their actual foreign policy behavior. For example, do governments that conceive of themselves as bloc leaders or neutrals engage in a large amount of independent activity? Furthermore, information on independence/interdependence of action allows us to study those issues on which governments are willing to forfeit some autonomy and those on which they maintain their autonomy. If independence/ interdependence of action is issue-specific, are there underlying reasons which explain the relationships? For instance, is lack of resources an important factor in determining when a government acts interdependently?

CONCEPTUALIZATION

As our discussion suggests, independence/interdependence of action is conceptualized as the degree of autonomy a government tries to maintain in its foreign policy actions. We propose two dimensions to independence/interdependence of action. The first dimension focuses on the location of the stimulus for the action. Is the stimulus for the action internal to the acting government, or was the stimulus directed at the acting government by another government? In other words, has the acting government set its own priorities regarding problems to be addressed, or are the priorities being set by other actors' demands or requests? The acting government forfeits some autonomy when its actions are based on other governments' goals and problems. We will call this dimension the "initiative-reactive" dimension. The initiative-reactive dimension is intended to tap the extent to which the content of a government's present behavior is structured for it by entities outside its control. Examples of initiative behavior are third party interventions, proposals, warnings, and threats; examples of reactive behavior are agreements, denials, grants resulting from loan or aid requests, and negotiations.

The second dimension concerns the number of actors involved in the action. Does the government act on its own, or does it collaborate with other governments in the action? In collaborating with other governments, the acting government forfeits some autonomy. Although the acting government has input into any decision that is made, so do the collaborators. The acting government's impact on the final decision will depend on such factors as status among the collaborating nations, the resources of the collaborating nations, the nature of

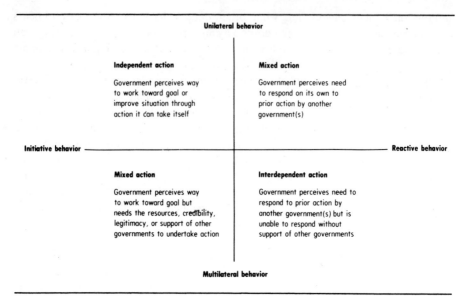

Figure 11.1   The components of independence/interdependence of action.

any treaties or alliances among the collaborators, and past behavior among the group of collaborating nations. By acting alone a government maintains its autonomy. The government decides what to do and acts on the decision. We shall call this dimension the "unilateral-multilateral" dimension. Unilateral refers to acting alone, multilateral to acting in a collaborative way with other governments.

Figure 11.1 presents the four types of actions that result from combining these two dimensions. Some characteristics defining the activity in each quadrant are also found in Figure 11.1. The most independent action is a unilateral, initiative behavior. Here a government perceives a way to work toward a goal by doing something on its own. The government is working on its own problems by itself. In effect, the government is setting its own foreign policy agenda and pursuing that agenda. As a consequence, the government maintains autonomy in its foreign policy activity.

The least autonomous action—the interdependent action—occurs when a government feels the need to respond to a prior action directed toward it or problem posed to it by another actor but is unable to act without the collaboration of others. This action involves multilateral, reactive behavior. The foreign policy agenda is set for the government by other actors in the international system. Further limiting the government's maneuverability is the fact that in order to act it must work with other governments or international actors. If it acts, and there is external pressure to act, the government forfeits considerable autonomy over the action. Control over the decision is shared, responsibility is shared, and any benefits are shared. Thus, we refer to this type of behavior as "interdependent."

The other two types of behavior in Figure 11.1—the unilateral, reactive behavior and the multilateral, initiative behavior—we call "mixed actions." In each type of behavior the government both forfeits some autonomy and maintains some autonomy over the action. In the unilateral, reactive behavior, the government perceives a need to respond to a prior action or problem posed to it by another government or international actor. The issue is not necessarily among the government's priorities, but there is external pressure to act on it. Although the government has had little influence over selection of the problem at hand, the decision makers do perceive a means of dealing with it on their own. By acting on their own they maintain some autonomy in their behavior. The situation may be externally imposed on them, but they are able to deal with it on their own. Similarly, in a multilateral, initiative behavior, decision makers maintain some autonomy over their behavior. Policymakers in the government perceive a way to work toward a goal of their nation but lack the resources, credibility, legitimacy, or political support needed to take any action without the help of other governments. The idea is theirs, but execution is dependent on the collaboration of others.

As the discussion suggests, the four types of behavior in Figure 11.1 appear to form a scale. Thus:

unilateral initiative	=	independence of action
unilateral reaction or multilateral initiative	=	some independence/interdependence of action
multilateral reaction	=	interdependence of action

In the unilateral initiative, governmental decision makers maintain their autonomy in their foreign policy behavior. In unilateral reactions and multilateral initiatives, governmental decision makers retain some autonomy over their own foreign policy behavior but also forfeit some autonomy. In multilateral reactions, governmental decision makers forfeit autonomy over their own foreign policy behavior. Instead, problem definition, decision making, responsibility for the action, and any benefits are shared with others.

OPERATIONALIZATION

Because independence/interdependence of action consists conceptually of two dimensions, operationalizing the concept requires us to find information on these two dimensions: (1) unilateral versus multilateral behavior and (2) initiative versus reactive behavior. To determine whether a foreign policy action is unilateral or multilateral, one can ascertain the number of governments participating in an action. Did the acting government act alone, or did it collaborate or act jointly with other governments? If the government acted alone, the action is considered unilateral. If, however, the government collaborated or acted jointly with another government or governments, the action is considered multilateral.

Several steps are necessary to determine whether an action is an initiative or a reaction. To simplify the task, we will focus on delimiting what a reaction is. All other actions will be considered initiatives. In general, a reaction is an explicitly elicited behavior—an action that appears to be a response to a prior behavior directed at the government by another government or external entity, or an action that is characterized as part or the result of a set of interchanges between governments. The following questions seem appropriate in ascertaining what a reaction is:

(1) Was the action elicited—that is, is the action a response to the behavior of another government or external entity which explicitly requested a response from the actor?
(2) Is the action a public vote by a government representative in an international organization?
(3) Does the action involve an actual agreement to, announcement of, or transfer of a loan, credit, or other foreign assistance?
(4) Does the action involve an actual agreement to, announcement of, or execution of an economic transaction?
(5) Is the action a denial, a rejection of or agreement to a prior proposal, or a protest of a prior activity directed at the acting government by another government or external entity?
(6) Does the action involve negotiation, consultation, or a response dictated by a treaty?

If any of these six questions can be answered yes, the behavior or action in question is considered reactive. If any action does not fit into any of these six categories, it is considered an initiative.

Combining these two dimensions, one can construct a scale for independence/ interdependence of action. Actions that are unilateral initiatives and indicate independence are scored 1. Actions that are either unilateral reactions or multilateral initiatives—indicative of mixed actions—are scored 2. Actions that are multilateral reactions and indicate interdependence of action are scored 3. In addition to examining mean behavior using this three-point scale, one could study each dimension separately. What percentage of the behaviors or actions are initiatives (or reactions); what percentage of the behaviors are unilateral (or multilateral)? And the researcher could look at each of the four categories of actions that result from combining the dimensions; for example, the percentage of unilateral initiatives, the percentage of multilateral initiatives, the percentage of unilateral reactions, or the percentage of multilateral reactions.

OPERATIONALIZATION USING CREON EVENT DATA

As with other behavior measures in this book, in order to examine independence/interdependence of action in more detail we have operationalized this variable using the CREON data set. The following CREON variables were used to operationalize the two dimensions of independence/interdependence of action. To assess whether an event was unilateral or multilateral, the CREON variable indicating the Number of Nations Participating in the Action was used (for a description of this variable, see the Technical Appendix at the end of the book). This variable was dichotomized to denote when a government acted alone and when it acted jointly with governments of other nations.

To assess when an event was a reaction as opposed to an initiative, the following CREON variables were used. These variables were selected because they appeared to exhaust the ways in the CREON data set of answering the questions raised earlier that delimit a reaction. An event was considered a reaction (1) when coded elicited on the Sequential Action Scheme; (2) when coded public vote on the Channel variable; (3) when coded actual agreement to, announcement of, or transfer of loan, credit, or other foreign assistance in the Foreign Assistance Behavior variable; (4) when coded actual agreement to, announcement of, or execution of economic transaction on the Economic Transaction Behavior variable; (5) when coded other than not applicable on the Transfers with Foreign Entity variable; (6) when coded denial, consult, negotiate, reject, or agree on the revised WEIS (World Event/Interaction Survey) coding scheme; or (7) when coded present on the Response variable *and* coded as either protest or carry out agreement on the revised WEIS scheme or as treaty behavior present on the Treaty Behavior variable. If an event satisfied any of these conditions, it was counted as a reaction. All other events were considered initiatives. The variables used to define a reaction are described in detail in the Technical Appendix. Reliabilities for these variables are presented in the Technical Appendix.

Each of the events in the CREON data set was coded as either unilateral or multilateral and as either an initiative or a reaction. Events were then sorted into four categories: unilateral initiatives, multilateral initiatives, unilateral reactions, and multilateral reactions. An independence/interdependence of action scale was developed by giving all unilateral initiatives a score of 1, all multilateral initiatives *and* unilateral reactions a score of 2, and all multilateral reactions a score of 3. Sample events falling into each of the four types of behavior will help illustrate the nature of the independence/interdependence of action variable.

Unilateral Initiatives (Independent Actions):

(1) East German First Secretary Ulbricht proposes a nonaggression treaty between NATO and Warsaw Pact countries. (September 1, 1964)
(2) People's Republic of China official newspaper, *The People's Daily,* congratulates Indonesia on its decision to withdraw from the United Nations. (January 6, 1965)

Unilateral Reactions (Mixed Actions):

(1) The United States government agrees to give India the $43.7 million grant it requested for the expansion of Indian elementary education. (January 21, 1965)
(2) French President De Gaulle tells the United States ambassador that France responds negatively at this time to the U. S. request for its support in pressing for a solution to the German problem. (April 19, 1960)

Multilateral Initiatives (Mixed Actions):

(1) The Swiss representative in a communique with the Group of Ten and IMF endorses West Germany's decision to maintain the parity of the deutsche mark. (November 22, 1968)

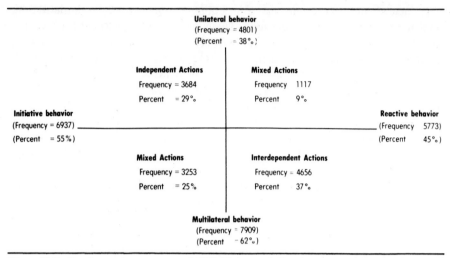

Figure 11.2 Number and percentage of CREON events falling into each of the independence/ interdependence of action categories.

(2) Belgium and a majority of NATO nations request the U.S. to increase its monetary support of NATO. (May 19, 1960)

Multilateral Reactions (Interdependent Actions):

(1) Mexico votes no with a majority of the other nations in the UN General Assembly on the Soviet Union's proposal to remove Taiwan from the UN and replace it with the People's Republic of China. (October 30, 1962)

(2) Switzerland's representative, with other representatives of Western European countries at an official meeting of bankers and economists, issues a communique suggesting several remedies to quell the speculation in three West European currencies that is particularly evident in Switzerland. (November 22, 1968)

Figure 11.2 displays the number and percent of events that were found in the CREON data set in each of the four categories of behavior involved in the independence/interdependence of action variable. Roughly one-third of the events are independent actions, one-third are interdependent actions, and one-third are mixed actions. There are more initiatives than reactions, although each accounts for almost half the events. Multilateral behavior occurs more often than unilateral behavior; in a little over three-fifths of the events governments acted jointly, while in about two-fifths of the events governments acted alone. An examination of the individual cells in Figure 11.2 shows the following rank order based on number of events from least to most events: (1) unilateral reactions, (2) multilateral initiatives, (3) unilateral initiatives, and (4) multilateral reactions. As this rank ordering suggests, there is some relationship between the two dimensions. The correlation, .35 (phi coefficient), however, is not high enough to indicate no difference between the two dimensions. Combining the two dimensions to form a three-point independence/interdependence of action scale, we find a mean score

of 2.08 across the 12,710 events in the CREON data set. (Remember that independent actions are scored 1, mixed actions 2, and independent actions 3.) The
standard deviation for the scale is .81.

Table 11.1 presents the mean scores and standard deviations on the independ-
ence/interdependence of action scale for the 38 nations in the CREON sample.
These data are averages for events across a ten-year period, 1959-1968. Although
the nations are listed in alphabetical order in Table 11.1, ranks for each nation
are given in column 3 of the table.

According to Table 11.1, during the decade 1959-1968 among the 38 CREON
nations, the People's Republic of China displayed the most independent behavior,
while the Ivory Coast displayed the most interdependent behavior with Uruguay
a close second. Among the six CREON nations displaying the most independent
behavior we find the two superpowers (the Soviet Union and the United States),
more countries with closed as opposed to open political systems (the People's
Republic of China, Cuba, East Germany, the Soviet Union) and nations that
appear to have been fairly isolated during this period (the People's Republic of
China, Cuba, Israel.) Among the six CREON nations that acted the most interdependently during this decade, we find developing countries (Costa Rica,
Guinea, Ivory Coast, and Uruguay). Iceland and Norway probably appear so
highly interdependent because of the large amount of their behavior that occurs
in a NATO context. The finding that nations like the People's Republic of China,
Cuba, and Israel exhibit some of the highest levels of independence suggests a
degree of face validity for the measure, since these nations had few friends with
whom to collaborate during this decade. Moreover, they tend to launch out at
others rather than to respond to others' demands.

The standard deviations in Table 11.1 suggest that we might learn even more
by separating out events that are independent, mixed, and interdependent. Table
11.2 provides us with this breakdown of the actions of the 38 CREON nations
during the 1959-1968 decade. The percentage as well as the frequency of a
nation's events that were independent, mixed, and interdependent are listed.
About one-half of the events of the six nations displaying the most independent
actions according to Table 11.1 (China, Cuba, East Germany, Israel, the Soviet
Union, the United States) were independent. For another six nations—Egypt,
France, India, Poland, West Germany, Zambia—roughly one-fourth to one-third
of their events were independent. All other CREON countries (26 nations) acted
independently less than 20 percent of the time. More of the actions of these
nations were interdependent (some two- to three-fifths of them). To maintain
some autonomy in their nation's foreign policy behavior, however, we note that
governments of the more interdependent countries also have 30 percent to 40
percent of their events as mixed. They are unable to maintain the complete
autonomy denoted by an independent action but manage about one-third of the
time to have *some* control over what they do.

The behavior of two of the nations in Table 11.2 is distinctly different from
that of the other countries. France and India, instead of emphasizing one type of
behavior, used all three types of behaviors, acting about one-third of the time
interdependently, independently, and mixed. Since the governments of these
nations at this time were striving to be neutral in their foreign policies, one wonders

TABLE 11.1
Mean Scores on Independence/Interdependence of Action Scale
for 38 CREON Nations, 1959-1968

CREON Nation	Mean Scale Score	Standard Deviation	Rank
Belgium	2.44	.63	31
Canada	2.27	.76	15
Chile	2.45	.59	32
China (PRC)	1.41	.66	1
Costa Rica	2.46	.61	33
Cuba	1.72	.87	3
Czechoslovakia	2.41	.72	27
East Germany	1.80	.79	6
Egypt	1.89	.75	7
France	2.07	.81	9
Ghana	2.28	.76	16
Guinea	2.48	.68	35
Iceland	2.48	.59	35
India	2.04	.82	8
Israel	1.74	.82	4.5
Italy	2.43	.61	29.5
Ivory Coast	2.62	.50	38
Japan	2.34	.71	24
Kenya	2.25	.70	12.5
Lebanon	2.35	.72	25
Mexico	2.42	.68	28
New Zealand	2.43	.63	29.5
Norway	2.48	.62	35
Philippines	2.32	.68	20
Poland	2.25	.80	12.5
Soviet Union	1.74	.82	4.5
Spain	2.32	.72	20
Switzerland	2.26	.60	14
Thailand	2.33	.66	22.5
Tunisia	2.33	.72	22.5
Turkey	2.30	.67	17.5
Uganda	2.39	.68	26
United States	1.70	.79	2
Uruguay	2.60	.52	37
Venezuela	2.32	.75	20
West Germany	2.09	.77	10.5
Yugoslavia	2.30	.75	17.5
Zambia	2.09	.80	10.5

NOTE: A score of 1 on the independence/interdependence of action scale indicates independence; a score of 3, interdependence.

TABLE 11.2
Percentage of Independent, Mixed, and Interdependent
Events for 38 CREON Nations, 1959-1968

CREON Nation	Percent Independent	Percent Mixed	Percent Interdependent
Belgium	8 (29)[a]	40 (154)	52 (198)
Canada	19 (75)	35 (135)	46 (178)
Chile	5 (10)	45 (95)	50 (104)
China (PRC)	68 (346)	22 (109)	10 (50)
Costa Rica	6 (10)	42 (68)	52 (86)
Cuba	56 (181)	17 (56)	27 (89)
Czechoslovakia	14 (28)	31 (65)	55 (113)
East Germany	43 (87)	34 (69)	23 (46)
Egypt	34 (156)	42 (191)	24 (107)
France	29 (251)	34 (290)	37 (314)
Ghana	19 (51)	34 (94)	47 (128)
Guinea	11 (22)	30 (64)	59 (123)
Iceland	5 (8)	42 (67)	53 (84)
India	32 (157)	32 (162)	36 (177)
Israel	49 (172)	27 (94)	24 (82)
Italy	6 (26)	45 (190)	49 (209)
Ivory Coast	1 (1)	36 (54)	63 (93)
Japan	14 (38)	38 (103)	48 (130)
Kenya	15 (14)	45 (44)	40 (38)
Lebanon	15 (22)	35 (53)	50 (75)
Mexico	10 (20)	37 (70)	53 (101)
New Zealand	7 (15)	42 (84)	51 (102)
Norway	7 (15)	38 (86)	55 (124)
Philippines	12 (24)	44 (88)	44 (87)
Poland	22 (52)	30 (70)	48 (111)
Soviet Union	50 (499)	26 (265)	24 (242)
Spain	15 (25)	39 (67)	46 (79)
Switzerland	8 (6)	58 (43)	34 (25)
Thailand	10 (17)	47 (76)	43 (70)
Tunisia	15 (40)	37 (103)	48 (133)
Turkey	12 (37)	46 (147)	42 (133)
Uganda	11 (16)	39 (57)	50 (73)
United States	50 (966)	29 (560)	21 (390)
Uruguay	1 (2)	36 (50)	62 (86)
Venezuela	17 (35)	35 (72)	48 (101)
West Germany	25 (164)	40 (259)	35 (223)
Yugoslavia	18 (45)	34 (89)	48 (123)
Zambia	28 (22)	35 (27)	37 (29)

[a]The numbers in parentheses indicate the number of a nation's events falling into that category.

if equal division among these three types of behaviors is indicative of a neutral posture.

For most of the nations (29, or 76 percent), the percentage of events falling into these three categories is scalar. In other words, the percentage of events that is mixed falls between the percentage of events that is independent and the percentage of events that is interdependent. However, six of the nations—Egypt, Kenya, Switzerland, Thailand, Turkey, West Germany—had a greater percentage of their actions mixed than either independent or interdependent. To the extent that they could, decision makers in these nations tried to maintain a degree of autonomy over their governments' behavior. Some degree of control of their destiny appears important to these governments. On the other hand, they may recognize the importance of not appearing too different or "off on their own." Thus, they lean more often toward the choice of a mixed behavior.

In addition to looking at the independence/interdependence of action scale and the percentage of activity at each point on the scale, we can separate the two dimensions of independence/interdependence of action and examine the CREON nations' behavior on each dimension. Table 11.3 displays the percentages and frequencies of the CREON nations' events that were reactions as opposed to initiatives and unilateral as opposed to multilateral. In Table 11.3 we note that for 23 of the 38 nations (61 percent) in the CREON sample the percentage of events that were initiatives and the percentage of events that were reactions approximates 50 percent. Behaviors were about equally split between these two types of activity. Initiatives were taken about as often as the nations responded to others' demands and requests. For the other 15 nations the behavior was split two-thirds initiatives to one-third reactions or vice versa. Eight of the nations—the People's Republic of China, Cuba, East Germany, Egypt, Israel, the Soviet Union, Switzerland, and the United States—usually engaged in initiative behavior during this decade, while seven of the nations—Chile, Costa Rica, Guinea, the Ivory Coast, Mexico, Norway, and Uruguay—generally reacted during this same period.

The differences between unilateral and multilateral behavior are more dramatic than those for initiative versus reactive behavior. Some 30 of the 38 nations (79 percent) in the CREON sample engaged at least two-thirds of the time in multilateral behavior. Only five of the nations—the People's Republic of China, Cuba, Israel, the Soviet Union, and the United States—generally acted on their own. Three of the countries perceived some choice between acting unilaterally and multilaterally. East Germany, Egypt, and India engaged about 50 percent of the time in unilateral behavior and 50 percent in multilateral behavior.

SUMMARY

Independence/interdependence of action has been conceptualized as the amount of autonomy a government tries to maintain in its foreign policy actions. We have proposed that there are two dimensions to independence/interdependence of action—an initiative versus reactive dimension and a unilateral versus multilateral dimension. The initiative versus reactive dimension focuses on the location of the occasion for a decision. The unilateral versus multilateral dimension refers to the number of actors involved in the action. These two dimensions combine to form a three-point scale. The behavior that most maintains a government's autonomy is the

TABLE 11.3
Percentage of Events that were Initiatives vs. Reactions and Unilateral vs. Multilateral for 38 CREON Nations, 1959-1968[a]

CREON Nation	Percent Initiatives	Percent Reactions	Percent Unilateral	Percent Multilateral
Belgium	45 (171)[a]	55 (210)	11 (41)[b]	89 (340)
Canada	44 (172)	56 (216)	29 (113)	71 (275)
Chile	40 (84)	60 (125)	15 (31)	85 (178)
China (PRC)	77 (387)	23 (118)	82 (414)	18 (91)
Costa Rica	39 (64)	61 (100)	15 (24)	85 (140)
Cuba	63 (205)	37 (121)	65 (213)	35 (113)
Czechoslovakia	42 (86)	58 (120)	17 (35)	83 (171)
East Germany	71 (143)	29 (59)	50 (100)	50 (102)
Egypt	67 (306)	33 (148)	43 (197)	57 (257)
France	57 (485)	43 (370)	36 (307)	64 (548)
Ghana	50 (136)	50 (137)	22 (60)	78 (213)
Guinea	37 (77)	63 (132)	15 (31)	85 (178)
Iceland	42 (66)	58 (93)	11 (17)	89 (142)
India	53 (261)	47 (235)	43 (215)	57 (281)
Israel	62 (216)	38 (132)	64 (222)	36 (126)
Italy	47 (199)	53 (226)	10 (43)	90 (382)
Ivory Coast	35 (52)	65 (96)	3 (4)	97 (144)
Japan	44 (119)	56 (152)	22 (60)	78 (211)
Kenya	53 (51)	47 (45)	22 (21)	78 (75)
Lebanon	47 (70)	53 (80)	18 (27)	82 (123)
Mexico	40 (77)	60 (114)	17 (33)	83 (158)
New Zealand	47 (94)	53 (107)	10 (20)	90 (181)
Norway	40 (90)	60 (135)	12 (26)	88 (199)
Philippines	52 (104)	48 (95)	16 (32)	84 (167)
Poland	49 (113)	51 (120)	26 (61)	74 (172)
Soviet Union	63 (634)	37 (372)	63 (629)	37 (377)
Spain	48 (82)	52 (89)	21 (35)	79 (136)
Switzerland	62 (46)	38 (28)	12 (9)	88 (65)
Thailand	53 (87)	47 (76)	14 (23)	86 (140)
Tunisia	48 (132)	52 (144)	19 (51)	81 (225)
Turkey	44 (141)	56 (176)	25 (80)	75 (237)
Uganda	46 (67)	54 (79)	15 (22)	85 (124)
United States	66 (1275)	34 (641)	63 (1217)	37 (699)
Uruguay	32 (44)	68 (94)	7 (10)	93 (128)
Venezuela	47 (97)	53 (111)	22 (45)	78 (163)
West Germany	54 (349)	46 (297)	37 (238)	63 (408)
Yugoslavia	43 (110)	57 (147)	27 (69)	73 (188)
Zambia	58 (45)	42 (33)	33 (26)	67 (52)

[a] The numbers in parentheses indicate the number of a nation's events falling in that category.

unilateral initiative. The government acts by itself on its own agenda. This behavior we have called an independent action. The behavior that forfeits autonomy most completely is the multilateral reaction. Here the government responds to another actor's agenda with the help of other actors. This behavior indicates interdependent behavior. The unilateral reaction and the multilateral initiative both maintain some autonomy and forfeit some autonomy. These we have called mixed actions. Using the CREON event data set to operationalize independence/interdependence of action, we found some face validity for the variable and learned which governments among the 38 nations represented in this data set tended to be the instigators of activity in the international system during the 1960s and which governments tended to play a more supportive or interactive role in this decade.

PART V

Outcome Properties of Foreign
Policy Behavior

Editors' Introduction

Whereas the previous section dealt with the class of measures most commonly developed and used in foreign policy research (output properties), this section concerns the measures developed and used least frequently. By and large, students of comparative foreign policy do not attend to the consequences or effects of behavior. This hiatus is partly explained by the difficulty of assessing the effect of a policy. However, an entire academic field has grown around the problem of developing methods for assessing policy impact, so assessment studies can be done. That they are not done more frequently in foreign policy research is probably attributable to the genesis of foreign policy analysis out of decision-making studies. Traditionally, foreign policy analysis has focused on explaining the reasons why a decision is made, rather than on understanding what its consequences are. Explaining decisions requires an exploration of the psychological milieu of decision makers; explaining consequences requires examining the operational milieu of the nation. The former was the realm of foreign policy analysis; the latter, of international politics.

The members of the CREON Project, along with others, believe the boundary between the subfields is arbitrary and, if made impermeable, impedes the search for understanding. The impacts of behavior have to be drawn into foreign policy research. This needs to be done, first, because of the normative/evaluative function of research; it would be desirable to be able to assess performance and prescribe policy changes. Moreover, even at the explanatory level, the outcomes of behavior must be considered. Foreign policy is a dynamic process. The inputs to decision making at one time are partly determined by the feedback from or the outcomes of prior actions.

During the CREON measurement efforts, serious consideration was given to three potential outcome property measures. As Callahan pointed out in Chapter 2, two of the concepts considered candidates for operationalization were situation generation and external consequentiality. Situation generation refers to the nature of the situation posed for the target by the actor's activity. It is closely related to output properties, in that the quality of output affects the nature of the resulting situation; but it is conceptually different, in that situation generation concerns the effects of behavior. To illustrate, specificity is an output property which shapes the clarity or ambiguity of the situation. Also, affect is an output property that feeds into the threatening or nonthreatening nature of the situation. The distinction between output properties and situation generation is not merely one of perspective. Situation generation would rest on a multidimensional taxonomy, whereas output properties are intentionally unidimensional. As part of the collective effort, work on situation generation never went past the idea stage. Conceptual and operational problems seemed overwhelming, so it lost its priority position. Based on the CREON conversations, however, C. Hermann and Mason (1980) have followed up with some initial research on the kinds of behaviors that tend to produce crisis situations for others.

External consequentiality, unlike situation generation, moved well into the operational stage before it was abandoned. It concerned the likelihood that an action would stimulate decision-making activity in a wide range of other entities in the system. External consequentiality would thus serve as a measure of impact or expected impact. After considerable labor, the measure was stillborn. Anticipating the impact of an action requires a solid body of grounded theory on the effects of actions. Such theory is currently lacking, as was indicated before. As a result, the measure that was developed was of dubious validity at best. Moreover, the measure that was produced was dependent on the capabilities of the actor in its operationalization. Since national actor capabilities was one of the theoretical perspectives members of the CREON Project hoped to use to explain foreign policy behavior, this dependence was seen as a fatal flaw.

Therefore, the only outcome property that was finally developed by the CREON Project involved the acceptance and rejection measures that M. Hermann presents in the next chapter. Initially intended to be an indicator of goal achievement, the measure has been changed, because of currently insurmountable operational problems, to a monitoring of the positive feedback (acceptance) and negative feedback (rejection) a nation receives from the environment, as reflected in its own and others' behavior. Although acceptability of policy is something other than success, we believe that it clearly is an interesting and important quality of the outcomes of policy.

Feedback

Acceptance and Rejection

What happens after a nation acts in the international arena? A government makes and implements a series of foreign policy decisions. What are the consequences of this foreign policy activity? As these questions suggest, in the present chapter we are changing our focus. Whereas previous chapters have sought to characterize or describe governmental foreign policy actions, in this chapter we are interested in the outcomes of foreign policy behavior. We will suggest a way of examining the effects of governmental actions on the international arena,

In research on foreign policy behavior we are concerned not only with what governments do but with what differences their actions make. We want to know about the results of the actions—the impacts, if any, of the actions on other national and international actors. As Rosenau (1968: 320-321) has noted:

> a concern for foreign policy cannot be sustained without the question of its effectiveness and consequences arising. Some conception of the receptivity of the international system to the behavior of the national actor being examined is necessary. . . . Not only do the responses that unfold in the environment provide a means of assessing the effectiveness of foreign policy undertakings, but they also lead the analyst to treat the foreign policy process as dynamic rather than static.

There are at least three different ways of approaching the study of foreign policy outcomes. One can (1) focus on the *potential* consequences of an action, (2) investigate the *intended* consequences of an action, or (3) study the *actual* consequences of an action. In examining the potential consequences of an action, the idea is to ascertain what can or probably will happen as the result of a certain activity. Policy planning staffs continuously pose this question as they discuss the possible outcomes of the actions they consider and propose. "If our nation does X, how likely is it that certain other nations will respond with Y?" Simulation studies such as those by Brody (1963) on the spread of nuclear weapons and Forrester (1971) on world dynamics provide information on the potential consequences of specific actions.

The second approach considers what policymakers intended in taking the action. What is the expected impact of the behavior on other nations? Research on intended effects often focuses on the goals of policymakers or the ends toward which policymakers are directing their actions. Policymakers in nation X are doing Y with the hope of achieving Z. Literature on national interest is relevant here, as are case studies on what C. Hermann (1971a) calls "strategic or grand designs" for example, containment, disengagement, detente, wars of liberation. The Brady chapter on goals in this volume (Chapter 6) examines the intended consequences of a foreign policy action.

The third approach to studying outcomes focuses on the actual consequences of a foreign policy action. The researcher asks what *did* happen. When the policymakers in a nation acted, what *were* the responses of other governments? What kind of feedback did the policymakers of the acting government receive? Of interest here is what the impact of the behavior actually was on the target government and third parties. Studies in international politics that use interaction analysis (for example, McClelland, 1972; Pruitt, 1969) illustrate how one might examine actual outcomes.

The present chapter follows the third approach. It focuses on the actual consequences of a government's foreign policy behavior. Specifically, we will examine the type of feedback a government receives on its behavior. One way for a government to learn about the effects of its foreign policy actions is by the feedback that comes from other governments. Through feedback, policymakers learn how their actions are being interpreted by others. Moreover, policymakers learn which other governments are paying attention to them and on whom they are having an impact. In effect, feedback provides policymakers with some clues concerning their government's foreign policy performance—some hints about what is succeeding and what is failing.

The relevance of feedback for foreign policy is most easily perceived in international negotiations or crises where each party eagerly awaits and responds to the other's moves. Each party judges the appropriateness of its behavior based on the feedback it receives on prior moves. Although feedback may not be as evident or eagerly sought in day-to-day foreign policymaking, governments still assess their next moves by the effects previous moves have had.

Feedback is usually of two kinds—positive and negative. It is favorable and accepting ("we back you in your proposal to extend the territorial limits to 200 miles") or it is unfavorable and rejecting ("one more military move and we will be forced to mobilize against you"). When feedback is positive or favorable, policymakers are likely to assume some measure of success. If the policymakers are pursuing a goal of long-term policy, they are likely to proceed to next steps. In any case, under similar circumstances policymakers will probably use the behavior which produced positive feedback again. When feedback is negative or unfavorable, policymakers are likely to perceive some sense of failure (unless, of course, the objective of the behavior was to get such negative reinforcement).[1] They are less likely to try that behavior again under similar circumstances. Moreover, policymakers may be forced to rethink next steps in working toward their goals or policies in light of the rejection. If a behavior receives no feedback, policymakers may be forced to consider more drastic action or, at least, to try repeating the behavior in hopes of guaranteeing feedback.

By learning about the nature of the feedback a government receives from other governments, we can begin to assess its foreign policy performance. We know which other governments and international actors are giving feedback. We can ascertain whether what the government is doing is generally acceptable to other governments or whether it is behaving in such a way as to arouse the general indignation of other governments. Perhaps neither of these extremes characterizes reactions to the government's behavior—in effect, feedback is mixed, some positive, some negative, depending on the target. In a sense, we can begin to say something about a government's success rate—namely, whether it is experiencing a high rate of acceptances per rejection. Feedback provides us with information about the "vibrations" from other actors that policymakers are receiving.

We make no pretense at being the first to propose feedback as a relevant dimension in examining the policy process. Some of the more persuasive "paradigms" in political science—for example, Easton's (1965a, 1965b) systems model, Almond and Powell's (1966) structural-functional model, and Deutsch's (1963) cybernetics model—include feedback processes. In writings on foreign policy and international relations, the Holsti et al. (1968) "mediated S and R" model and McClelland's (1966) systems model both incorporate feedback loops. In all these proposals there is a presumption that we should explore the impacts of behavior and that one of the relevant indicators of such impacts is feedback. Unfortunately, although it is perceived as important to an examination of the policy process, there have been few attempts to study feedback systematically, particularly that feedback which a government receives from other actors in the international system. The measure we are proposing in the present chapter may help us begin to fill this gap.

CONCEPTUALIZATION

We are using feedback to refer to the responses of other governments and international actors to an acting government's foreign policy behavior. In particular, we are interested in whether the feedback is positive or negative in tone. Do other governments and international actors react favorably or unfavorably to the acting government's foreign policy behavior? Do they accept or reject the acting government's behavior? We have developed acceptance and rejection ratios to provide information on the nature of a government's feedback.

The acceptance ratio is conceived as an indicator of the degree of favorable reaction a government's foreign policy behavior receives from other governments and from international actors. How well are the policymakers of a nation doing in having their foreign policies accepted by other actors in the international arena? The emphasis here is on positive feedback from the external environment. Acceptance occurs when the policymakers of a nation direct some activity toward other national or international actors and these actors react favorably to it. The rejection ratio, on the other hand, indicates the degree of negative reaction a government's foreign policy behavior receives from other actors in the international environment. The emphasis is on negative feedback. Rejection occurs when the policymakers of a nation direct activity toward other national and international actors and these actors react negatively or unfavorably to it.

How is acceptance signaled in the foreign policy arena? That is, what kinds of behaviors constitute positive feedback from national and international actors? The *Random House Dictionary of the English Language* indicates the following meanings for acceptance: "The act of taking or receiving something offered, granting a favorable reception or giving approval, assenting to a proposal." The definition suggests several types of behavior that probably denote acceptance: (1) responding positively to specific requests (for example, for loans, grants, or trade), (2) expressing pleasure with a prior interaction even though no specific request for a response was made (for instance, a target government indicates pleasure with an acting government's change of policy toward them), (3) reaching an agreement, (4) voting for a nation's proposal in an international organization, and (5) as a third party for another government's position. In each instance the behavior of the initiating government is attended to by another government or international actor and acted on positively. The policymakers in the acting nation are rewarded for their efforts.

Are there conditions or circumstances which make an accepting response (positive feedback) more likely? Several conditions come to mind. One condition which heightens the chances of acceptance occurs when a government directs its behavior toward other national or international actors who have been generally supportive of such behavior in the past. For instance, the nations are allies or co-signers of a previous agreement on the issue under consideration. A nation's allies will usually be supportive of its behavior unless the behavior clearly contradicts their goals or interests. As a second condition, consider the nation that has skills and resources needed by other nations. The nation receiving positive feedback has raw materials and/or technical expertise which the accepting nations need for production or industrialization. A third reason for acceptance might be the attempt to create good will between the two interacting nations. For example, they are about to begin long-term negotiations. Or, perhaps, further interaction is possible only after some initial positive feedback. By being accepting the nation indicates its willingness to have further interaction. It is conceivable, as a fourth condition, that the behavior of the acting nation helps the accepting nation to move toward its own goals or objectives. The acting nation "plays into the hands" of the accepting nation whose policymakers are quite willing to react favorably. A final condition occurs when one nation threatens another nation. With the expectation of harm if it is not accepting, the target nation may have no alternative but to provide the positive feedback which is requested. Because of differentials in size, military capability, or natural resources, the threatening nation has the power to coerce the target nation into acceptance. Knowledge about the conditions that facilitate positive feedback (or acceptance) helps us to explain why certain governments have higher acceptance ratios than others.

Rejection is signaled to actors in the foreign policy arena in the same way that acceptance is, but the feedback is negative rather than positive in tone. The following behaviors suggest rejection: (1) responding negatively to specific requests such as those for trade and aid, (2) indicating displeasure with a prior interaction even though there was no specific request for a response, (3) terminating an agreement, (4) voting against a nation's proposal in an international organization, and (5) as a third party expressing opposition to an actor's position. In each case, the behavior of the acting government is attended to by another government or international actor and acted on unfavorably. The policymakers in the acting nation are *not* rewarded for their efforts.

Four conditions seem likely to promote one nation's rejection of another nation's (or international actor's) behavior. First, foreign policy behavior is more likely to be rejected by traditional enemies or nations in opposing alliances. Negative feedback is almost a requisite of being an opponent. Second, when nations are competing for scarce resources, they are more likely to reject another's attempts at cooperation—particularly if one is receiving less of the commodity at present. A third condition centers on propaganda. A nation may show disapproval or displeasure with the behavior of a second nation in order to gain favor with a third nation or with its own countrymen. Finally, the nations may be following a "tit for tat" strategy—"You reward me and I will reward you; you reject me and I will reject you."

In the previous discussion we have relied on input variables (for example, the nature of the situation, the nature of the relationship between the government and its targets) to explain why the outcome is acceptance or rejection. Acceptance and rejection may also be the result of certain types of outputs. In other words, some of the behavior measures that are covered in this book may be more likely to trigger acceptance than rejection. One proposition that comes immediately to mind concerns behaviors that are positive in affect. Such behaviors will probably lead to more positive feedback than behaviors that are negative in affect. Other propositions are possible, linking feedback to goals, specificity, and independence/interdependence of action. The more articulated the goals of a particular set of actions or the more specific the behaviors, the more likely acceptance is as opposed to rejection. Policymakers usually are not willing to risk articulating goals or using specific behaviors unless they are fairly sure such actions will receive approval in the international environment. With articulated goals and specific behaviors, there is no way out for the policymakers if such actions are rejected. Interdependent actions would also seem more likely to lead to acceptance than rejection. Other national and international actors will consider carefully before they reject an action that has been endorsed by more than one government. In a sense, there is safety in numbers. These propositions are suggestive of the linkages that can be made between the output (behavior) measures described in other chapters in this book and the outcome measure being developed in this chapter.

OPERATIONALIZATION

In order to operationalize acceptance and rejection, we need to learn when governments respond to other governments' actions. For some behaviors—such as when a nation receives a loan or grant or makes a sale—we know there has been a response. But in most cases, we learn nothing about the environmental response to the acting government's behavior by focusing on that government's actions. It is the behavior of the recipients of an action and third parties that we must examine for acceptance or rejection.

To assess acceptance and rejection, a government's behavior is scanned for its responses to other national and international actors. The following question is asked: Is the behavior a response to another government's request or action? If the behavior is a response, does it indicate acceptance or rejection of that other government's request or action? Acceptance is characterized by such actions as responding affirmatively to requests or proposals, promising help and support, yielding to demands, signing and carrying out agreements, and expressing pleasure with a prior behavior. Rejection occurs when governments terminate agreements, oppose proposals, turn down or ignore requests, express displeasure with prior behaviors, or launch a military attack. If any of these behaviors are found, the target of the response is credited with having received some feedback—either acceptance or rejection.

Acceptance ratios and rejection ratios can be calculated from the acceptance and rejection scores. The acceptance and rejection ratios are determined by ascertaining the percentage of a nation's foreign policy actions that are accepted or rejected by other nations. Using a ratio helps to control for differences in overall activity among nations. The acceptance and rejection ratios represent an aggregation of events for a nation across a certain period (for example, a month, a year, or a decade).

With information on acceptance and rejection we have the possibility of using several indices in addition to the acceptance and rejection ratios. For example, we can examine the rate of acceptance per rejection. Is the government receiving more acceptance of its foreign policy behavior than rejection, or vice versa? We can also analyze the amount of acceptance (or rejection) to total feedback. What percentage of a government's total feedback is accepting (or rejecting) in nature? Moreover, we can study the rate of feedback relative to activity. What percentage of the time does the nation receive feedback on its behavior?

Operationalization Using CREON Event Data

As with other foreign policy behavior measures in this book, we have operationalized the acceptance and rejection ratios using the CREON event data set. In determining the presence of acceptance, the following sequence of questions was asked of each event in the CREON data set. (The CREON variables mentioned in these questions are described in more detail in the Technical Appendix at the end of this book; reliabilities for the variables also appear in the Technical Appendix.)

(1) Does the event indicate receipt of foreign assistance on the Foreign Assistance Behavior variable, receipt of an economic transaction on the Economic Transaction Behavior variable, or receipt of materials, services, or currency on the Transfers with Foreign Entity variable? If the answer is yes, the nation on the receiving end of the grant, trade, or transfer is credited with one feedback event indicating acceptance. If the answer is no, question 2 is asked.

(2) Are any of the recipients of the event actually participants in the event with the acting government? (See the Role of Targets and Objects variable in the Technical Appendix.) In other words, have governments of other nations cooperated with the acting government in carrying out the foreign policy behavior? We make the assumption here that, by participating with the government of another nation, each cooperating government is giving positive feedback to that government. The government that is the focus of the event receives credit for one positive feedback event for each of the recipients participating with it in the activity. If

there are no other participants in the event beside the acting government, question 3 is asked. Question 3 is also asked for each recipient of the event that *is not* participating with the acting government in the event.

(3) Is the event coded as present on the Response variable? In other words, was the action in the event triggered or stimulated by previous actions of other external actors? If this question can be answered yes, the event is a response. Is it a response to a request? If the event is a response and it is coded as a response to a request that either partially fulfills or fulfills the request, the nation toward whom the response is directed is credited with one feedback event indicating acceptance. Or, if the event is a response but is not a request and yet is scored as indicating the actor's pleasure with a recipient's prior behavior, the nation toward whom the response is directed receives credit for one feedback event denoting acceptance. If the event is not a response, question 4 is asked. If the event is a response but neither of the two conditions mentioned above is present, the event is considered no further in scoring for acceptance.

(4) Is the event coded in one of the following eight Revised WEIS (World Event/Interaction Survey) categories—approve, promise, agree, yield, carry out agreement, reward, increase relationship? If any of the eight categories are coded, the nation that is the recipient of the behavior in the event is given credit for one feedback event showing acceptance. If none of the categories is coded, question 5 is asked.

(5) Is the event coded for any of the categories on the Adherence to International Agreement variable? The Adherence to International Agreement variable is coded if a government enters into agreements that restrict its sovereignty—for example, permits use of territory for military bases or signs an agreement creating privileges for others with regard to economic transfers. If any of the categories of the Adherence to International Agreement variable are coded, the nation co-signing the agreement is credited with one feedback event involving acceptance. If none of the categories is coded, the event is considered no further in scoring acceptance.

The scoring sequence for acceptance is summarized in Figure 12.1. Since a CREON event can have multiple recipients, questions 2 through 5 of the scoring sequence are repeated for each recipient. It may help the reader to understand this scoring sequence by going through several examples. How would we code an event which states that the Canadian government endorses the position of the United States in the Cuban missile crisis? Using the coding scheme for acceptance outlined in Figure 12.1, we note first that Canada is not receiving a grant or trade or making a sale. Moreover, there are no other participants in the event with Canada, so we ask whether the event involves a response. The answer is yes. The response, however, is not to a request but is a statement indicating pleasure with a prior behavior. The actor is pleased with the position (prior behavior) that another government (the U.S. government) took with regard to the Cuban missile crisis. In this case Canada is giving the United States positive feedback, and the United States is credited with one acceptance.

In another example, suppose the event we are examining is a joint communique from Premier Gerhardsen of Norway and Premier Khrushchev of the Soviet Union expressing support for expanded Norwegian-Soviet trade. Consider that the Norwegian government is the actor on which we are focusing in this event. Going through the sequence in Figure 12.1, we observe that Norway is not receiving a

Does event involve:

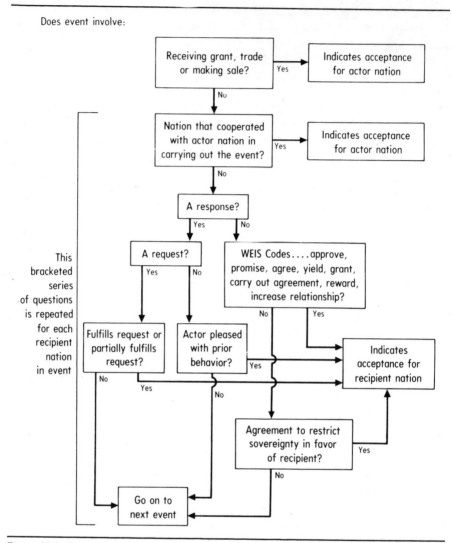

Figure 12.1 Summary of scoring sequence for acceptance using the CREON event data set.

grant or trade or making a sale. There is, however, another government participating with Norway in this event—the Soviet Union. Given our assumption that participation with the government of another nation in an event constitutes giving positive feedback to that government, Norway receives credit for one acceptance. Here, unlike the previous example, the acting government—not the recipient government—is having its behavior accepted.

The number of events indicating acceptance were summed for each of the 38 CREON nations over a period of one year. The acceptance ratio was calculated for these periods by dividing the acceptance score for a government for a year by the number of foreign policy actions the government engaged in during that year.

In coding for rejection we followed a set of coding steps similar to the set used in coding for acceptance. The following sequence of questions was asked of each event in the CREON data set in coding for rejection. (The CREON variables mentioned in these questions are described in more detail in the Technical Appendix; reliabilities for the variables also appear in the Technical Appendix.)

(1) Does the event indicate the termination of an economic transaction on the Economic Transaction Behavior variable, or does it involve reported opposition by entities outside the nation on the Opponents of Action variable? If the answer is yes, the nation whose economic transaction is terminated or whose behavior is receiving external opposition is credited with one feedback event involving disapproval or rejection. If the answer is no, question 2 is asked.

(2) Are any of the recipients in the event participants with the acting government in the foreign policy activity? If the answer is yes, these recipients are no longer considered in coding for rejection. If the answer is no, question 3 is asked. Question 3 is asked for each recipient nation that did not participate with the acting government in the event.

(3) Is the event coded present on the Response variable? In other words, is the event a response to previous actions of other national or international actors? If the event is a response, is it a response to a request? If the answer again is yes and the request is ignored or rejected, the nation whose response is ignored or rejected is credited with one feedback event indicating rejection. If the event is a response but not to a request, we are interested in whether it denotes displeasure on the part of the nation making the response with the prior action of another nation. If the response does indicate displeasure, the nation that is the target of the displeasure is credited with a feedback event involving rejection. If the event is not a response, question 4 is asked. If the event is a response but does not fit either the request or displeasure conditions just described, it is considered no further in coding for rejection.

(4) Is the event classified in any of the following five Revised WEIS categories: deny, warn, reject, reduce relationship, or expel? If the event is coded in any of these WEIS categories, the recipient of the action is credited with one feedback event indicating rejection. If the event is not coded in any of these categories, question 5 is asked.

(5) Is the event coded as an attack on the External Use of Military Force variable? (Attack means air or sea bombardment or ground combat against a foreign entity.) If the answer is yes, the target of the attack is credited with one feedback event involving rejection. If the answer is no, the event is considered no further in coding for rejection.

The scoring sequence for rejection is summarized in Figure 12.2. As with acceptance, questions 2 through 5 are repeated for each recipient listed for an event. Let us go through the rejection scoring sequence with an example. Suppose the French UN ambassador votes against Resolution 395, which is sponsored by the Soviet Union. Turning to the questions in Figure 12.2, we observe that France is not having a grant, trade, or sale terminated, nor is there any external opposition to its behavior. The Soviet Union is not operating with the French ambassador in carrying out the event. This event, however, does involve a request—a request that is rejected. The call for a vote in the UN finds France voting against the Soviet Union's proposal. The Soviet Union receives one rejection.

Does event involve:

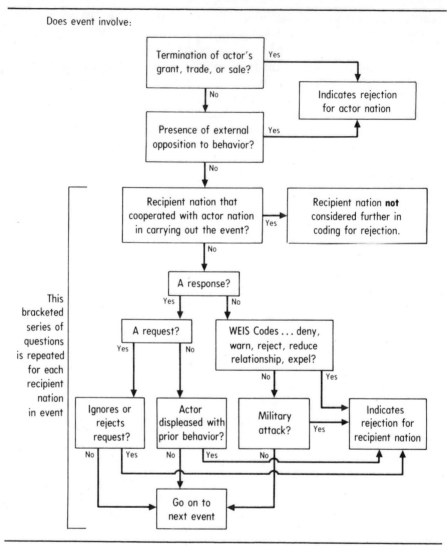

Figure 12.2 Summary of scoring sequence for rejection using the CREON event data set.

The number of events involving rejection were summed for each of the 38 nations across one year. The rejection ratio was calculated for these periods by dividing the rejection scores for a government for a year by the number of foreign policy actions the government engaged in during that year.

Variations in Feedback for CREON Nations

Table 12.1 presents the acceptance and rejection ratios as well as three other indices that we have developed from the acceptance and rejection scores for the 38 nations in the CREON project. The data were collected for the decade 1959-1968. The means in Table 12.1 are averages across the ten years. As we have already noted, the acceptance and rejection ratios indicate the relative amount of acceptance or rejection a nation receives per action. The other indices show the amount of acceptance a government receives relative to rejection (acceptance relative to rejection), the relative feedback a government receives given its activity in the international system (feedback relative to activity), and the percentage of a government's feedback that involves acceptance (percentage of feedback indicating acceptance). Feedback here refers to the sum of the acceptance and rejection scores for a government for a year. The way these three indices were calculated is explained in the note to Table 12.1.

What do we learn from Table 12.1 about the behavior of the governments of the CREON nations during the decade 1959-1968 when we examine the feedback they received from other CREON nations? Focusing first on the acceptance ratio, we note that the Soviet Union has the highest acceptance ratio. The Soviet government received positive feedback for approximately one out of every two events. Three other Communist nations also had some of the highest acceptance ratios during this period—East Germany, Cuba, and China (PRC). When we add Israel to this set of nations with the highest acceptance ratios, we have a list of the predominant crisis areas of the 1960s: the continuing Berlin confrontations; the Cuban missile crisis and Cuban revolutionary activity in Latin America; Israel's persistent attempts to maintain its autonomy and territory; Soviet interventions in Eastern Europe, the Middle East, and the Third World; and the Sino-Soviet rift. These nations may receive high rates of positive feedback because their behavior is threatening. Acceptance behavior may be seen as placating or diverting the potentially damaging activity. Or, perhaps, the positive feedback is from allies and friends, supporting what they are doing and urging them on.[2]

Interestingly, these same nations also have among the highest rejection ratios. These nations received mixed signals from other nations. They were successful in some interactions and unsuccessful in others. They were getting "good news and bad news" from the international environment.

For most of the nations in the CREON sample, the acceptance ratios are higher than the rejection ratios. The governments received a higher rate of positive feedback on their foreign policy behavior. For seven of the nations, however, this was not the case. Belgium, China (PRC), Cuba, Egypt, Israel, Lebanon, and the United States have higher rejection ratios. China's ratios are the most discrepant.

The figures for acceptance relative to rejection compare the amount of acceptance to rejection more directly. What this figure indicates is the amount of positive feedback a government is receiving per negative feedback. The data for this index lend support to the observation that the CREON nations generally received more acceptance than rejection of their foreign policy activity from 1959 to 1968. For only five of the nations was the acceptance relative to rejection index less than one. These five nations are China (PRC), Cuba, Egypt, Switzerland, and Uruguay. Four other nations—Iceland, Lebanon, the Soviet Union, and Venezuela—received about as much negative as positive feedback. Their ratios of acceptance to rejection are about 1.00. The other 29 nations received more positive than negative feedback— many almost two acceptances for every rejection. Canada, Italy, and Turkey received over four acceptances for every rejection. Most of the CREON nations experienced positive reinforcement from their environment.

TABLE 12.1

Means (Mn) and Ranks of 38 CREON Nations for Acceptance and Rejection Ratios, Acceptance Relative to Rejection, Feedback Relative to Activity, and Percentage of Feedback Indicating Acceptance

CREON Nation	Acceptance Ratio[a]		Rejection Ratio[b]		Acceptance Relative to Rejection[c]		Feedback Relative to Activity[d]		Percentage of Feedback Indicating Acceptance[e]	
	Mn	Rank[f]	Mn	Rank	Mn	Rank	Mn	Rank	Mn	Rank
Belgium	.35	7	.47	4	3.65	4	.82	5	.60	24.5
Canada	.21	18	.12	17	4.08	3	.33	18	.75	8.5
Chile	.24	17	.06	24.5	2.75	9	.30	20	.84	4
China (PRC)	.43	3	.65	1	.57	38	1.08	1	.34	38
Costa Rica	.45	2	.33	9	2.30	14.5	.78	6	.76	6.5
Cuba	.41	5	.53	2	.84	36	.94	3	.42	36
Czechoslovakia	.10	33	.03	33.5	1.12	29	.13	34.5	.78	5
East Germany	.40	6	.37	6.5	2.54	11	.77	7	.54	26.5
Egypt	.29	13.5	.37	6.5	.98	34	.66	9	.45	33
France	.30	12	.25	10	2.32	13	.55	10.5	.60	24.5
Ghana	.16	22.5	.05	27.5	2.55	10	.32	24.5	.67	19
Guinea	.10	33	.06	24.5	1.82	21	.16	30.5	.70	17
Iceland	.09	35	.04	30	1.05	31	.13	34.5	.53	28
India	.25	16	.20	13	2.27	17	.45	13.5	.61	23
Israel	.42	4	.45	5	2.29	16	.87	4	.54	26.5
Italy	.28	15	.11	19	5.97	1	.39	15	.71	15.5
Ivory Coast	.08	36.5	.06	24.5	1.42	25	.14	32	.42	36
Japan	.33	10	.17	14	3.60	5	.50	12	.74	11
Kenya	.15	25.5	.03	33.5	2.80	8	.18	29	.87	2
Lebanon	.15	25.5	.22	11	1.03	32	.37	16	.46	32
Mexico	.16	22.5	.09	20	1.89	20	.25	22.5	.68	18
New Zealand	.15	25.5	.04	30	1.22	27	.19	27	.74	11
Norway	.11	30	.05	27.5	1.57	24	.16	30.5	.76	6.5
Philippines	.11	30	.02	36.5	2.30	14.5	.13	34.5	.73	13.5
Poland	.08	36.5	.03	33.5	1.16	28	.11	37	.73	13.5
Soviet Union	.52	1	.52	3	1.01	33	1.04	2	.43	34
Spain	.19	20	.06	24.5	2.05	19	.25	22.5	.62	21.5
Switzerland	.15	25.5	.04	30	.83	37	.19	27	.48	31
Thailand	.10	33	.03	33.5	1.60	23	.13	34.5	.75	8.5
Tunisia	.11	30	.08	21	2.18	18	.19	27	.71	15.5
Turkey	.33	10	.12	17	5.44	2	.45	13.5	.74	11
Uganda	.29	13.5	.07	22	3.33	6	.36	17	.86	3
Uruguay	.33	10	.34	8	1.27	26	.67	8	.50	30
Uruguay	.07	38	.02	36.5	.87	35	.09	38	.42	36
Venezuela	.14	28	.12	17	1.09	30	.26	21	.51	29
West Germany	.34	8	.21	12	2.48	12	.55	10.5	.62	21.5
Yugoslavia	.17	21	.15	15	1.65	22	.32	19	.66	20
Zambia	.20	19	.01	38	3.00	7	.21	24.5	.96	1
Overall Average	.24		.18		2.18		.42		.63	

[a] Acceptance ratio is number of acceptance events for a government during a year divided by total number of events for that government during the year.

[b] Rejection ratio is number of rejection events for a government during a year divided by the total number of events for that government during the year.

[c] Acceptance relative to rejection is number of acceptance events for a government in a year divided by the number of rejection events for that same government and year.

[d] Feedback relative to activity is acceptance events plus rejection events during a year for a government divided by that government's total number of events during the year.

[e] Percentage of feedback indicating acceptance is number of acceptance events in a year for a government divided by the sum of the acceptance and rejection events for that government during a year.

[f] Ranks are assigned so that 1 accompanies the highest score and 38 the lowest score.

Examining in Table 12.1 the percentage of the CREON nations' foreign policy behavior that received any feedback (feedback relative to activity), we note some governments' behavior generated much more attention than others. For thirteen of the nations, less than one out of every five of their events received any feedback. On the other hand, for nine of the nations at least two out of every three events received some feedback. Four of the nine nations with high feedback rates are Communist nations—China (PRC), Cuba, East Germany, and the Soviet Union. Both superpowers—the Soviet Union and the United States—appear among these nine nations, as do Egypt and Israel. The behavior of certain nations appears to have more impact on the international system. Or perhaps these nations act in a way that ensures feedback—their behaviors may be more dramatic. Moreover, since the nations with the most feedback were also those nations involved in the disputes during this decade that could have precipitated nuclear war, their behaviors were probably closely monitored by others.

When we examine those nations with a high percentage of their feedback involving acceptance, we find among the top-ranked nations three African countries that achieved independence during this decade—Kenya, Uganda, and Zambia. The positive feedback in this instance may reflect other nations' attempts to influence the direction of the foreign policy behavior of these three nations. Feedback was being used in this case as the psychologist uses it to train a rat to run a maze or a pigeon to select its food. Those giving the feedback were employing it as a tool of statecraft, hoping to gain the favor of the new governments.

Besides looking at all the CREON nations, we can compare individual nations. A comparison of the feedback indices of the two superpowers during this decade, the United States and the Soviet Union, proves interesting. Both nations received about as much negative as positive feedback. However, on the average, the United States received less total feedback than the Soviet Union. Whereas one-third of the U.S. events were either accepted or rejected, one-half of the Soviet events were either accepted or rejected. Overall, two-thirds of the U.S. events received some type of feedback, while all of the Soviet events received some type of feedback. Soviet foreign policy behavior appears to have generated more response from the other CREON countries during this decade than U.S. foreign policy behavior. But both nations' behavior was not unequivocally condoned or repudiated during this period.

Relationships Among Feedback Indices

Table 12.2 shows the intercorrelations (Pearson product moment correlations) among the five feedback indices. The correlations indicate that nations with high acceptance ratios also have high rejection ratios. Acceptance during the decade under study went hand in hand with rejection for the CREON nations. Moreover, CREON countries receiving a lot of feedback from the international arena were getting both negative and positive feedback. The correlations in Table 12.2 suggest that rejection may be more important to study than acceptance given the stronger correlations of rejection with feedback relative to activity and with percentage of feedback indicating acceptance. None of the correlations in Table 12.2 is large enough to indicate an overlap in the variables.

TABLE 12.2

Intercorrelations Among Types of Feedback Indices

	1	*2*	*3*	*4*	*5*
(1) Acceptance Ratio	—				
(2) Rejection Ratio	.60	—			
(3) Acceptance Relative to Rejection	.29	−.22	—		
(4) Feedback Relative to Activity	.66	.76	−.13	—	
(5) Percentage of Feedback Indicating Acceptance	.12	−.34	.51	−.27	—

Relationships with Other Behavior Measures

As we noted in discussing the conceptualization of the feedback measure, feedback is probably partly determined by what a nation has done—by its output—as well as by who the nation is. Let us explore how two of the behavior measures discussed in previous chapters—commitment and independence/interdependence of action—influence feedback.

It is possible to argue that the more willing a nation is to commit itself in foreign policy, the more positive the feedback it will receive. Nations are interested in being able to count on one another. When the government of a nation makes a commitment, it is suggesting what its future behavior will be. Such behavior will be reinforced by governments of other nations, particularly those desiring the commitment. The correlation (Pearson product moment) between commitment and the acceptance ratio is .30, while between commitment and the rejection ratio it is .18.

We hypothesized earlier in this chapter that interdependent actions would be more likely to lead to acceptance than to rejection. The reasoning was that other national and international actors would carefully consider rejecting an action that was endorsed by more than one government. There would be safety in numbers. Recall from Chapter 11 that interdependent actions are activities with other nations and in response to an external stimulus, while independent actions are taken on one's own and at one's own initiative. The independence/interdependence of action scale (score of 1 indicates independence; score of 3, interdependence) correlates −.14 with the acceptance ratio and −.40 with the rejection ratio. Although the relationship between independence/interdependence of action and the acceptance ratio is minimal, it does appear easier to reject independent behavior than interdependent behavior. There would seem to be safety in numbers. At least the CREON nations were less likely to risk rejection the more interdependent their behavior.

We have focused here on only two of the output measures in this book. But these two variables suggest that output and outcome are related.

SUMMARY

In this chapter we have examined the outcomes of foreign policy behavior, studying what happens when a government acts in the international arena. Instead of describing foreign policy behavior as we have in previous chapters, we have asked what the impact of the behavior is. We have proposed a way to assess such impacts by analyzing the feedback a government receives on its actions. In particular, is the feedback positive or negative—does it represent acceptance or rejection of the acting government's foreign policy behavior? We have developed five indices of acceptance and rejection: (1) the amount of acceptance relative to activity, (2) the amount of rejection relative to activity, (3) the amount of acceptance relative to rejection, (4) the relative prevalence of feedback based on activity in the international system, and (5) the percentage of feedback that involves acceptance.

NOTES

1. There may be times when a government's goal is to elicit a rejecting response from another government—for example, an adversary. Thus, a rejection is positive feedback. Similarly, there may be times when receiving acceptance is actually negative feedback. It is much more difficult to ascertain events of this nature; therefore, the conceptualization in this chapter focuses on acceptance and rejection when such were sought.

2. *The reader should keep in mind during this discussion* of the data in Table 12.1 that the feedback measures presented here represent the feedback *CREON nations* gave one another. In other words, the feedback is not from all other nations in the international system but only from the other CREON countries. Because of the way the CREON data were collected, it was possible to get only the responses that sampled nations gave one another. Feedback may therefore be underestimated for some of the countries whose more salient dyadic partners are *not* included in the *CREON* sample of nations—for example, for India since Pakistan is excluded, for Turkey since Greece is excluded.

PART VI

Future Directions:
Additional Uses for Behavior Measures

Editors' Introduction

The chapters up to this point have focused on trying to fulfill the task set out in Chapter 1: to conceptualize and to operationalize diverse properties of foreign policy behavior in such a way that comparisons can be made across nations or across time along theoretically interesting or policy-relevant dimensions. The measures that have been described (or the improved ones that are sure to replace them in the future) enable researchers to make comparisons beyond those which were previously possible, simply because there are now a larger number of concepts developed to the operational stage. Most of the comparisons discussed in this volume involve calculating for nations either average scores on a measure or the proportion of behavior falling into the various categories of the measure. Although these ways of using the behavior measures are important, they do not cover the full range of possible uses.

Some additional ways of working with the data were addressed in earlier chapters. C. Hermann and Coate in Chapter 4, for example, discuss a "range of concern" indicator representing the proportion of international problems that a nation addresses. East and M. Hermann propose a similar "scope of action" measure in Chapter 5, using the dispersion of attention across targets as the core of the measure. C. Hermann in Chapter 7 proposes measuring the diversity of instrumentalities a nation uses to indicate the degree of its reliance on one or a few tools of statecraft. These ideas begin to suggest the potential range of ways of working with the behavior measures.

In the two chapters in this section, Callahan undertakes a more systematic consideration of the potential uses of the behavior measures. Chapter 13 deals with higher-order measures which concern properties of a pattern of events, rather than single events, and which represent concepts that transcend events. Three statistical procedures that may be used to generate higher-order measures are reviewed and assessed: measures of dispersion/concentration, inductive clustering, and a priori clustering.

In Chapter 14, Callahan probes the question of whether event data can be used to develop measures of policy. In so doing, he reassesses one of the basic assumptions of the CREON measurement effort (summarized in Chapter 2)—namely, that the phenomenon to be explained is behavior rather than policy. While acknowledging the difficulties inherent in the idea of policy, Callahan argues that event data can be brought to bear on the study of policy. In making this argument, he reviews sundry definitions of policy and derives the definition that policy is a standard used in the making of decisions. The policy may have varying degrees of vagueness or concreteness, generality or particularity. No matter what, its effect is probabilistic. From this conceptualization flows the position that the study of policy should not be a debate over the existence or the lack of a policy, but over the strength of the policy in determining decisions. The potential role of event data in such an inquiry is considered, as well as checks against error in ascribing an effect to a policy.

13

PATRICK CALLAHAN

Measurement Strategies for Higher-Order Behavior Properties

Although the simple aggregated statistics calculated and presented in the main substantive chapters of the book provide valuable tools for comparing the foreign policy behavior of nations, they realize only part of the potential usefulness of event data. Simple aggregation produces measures whose interpretation is made in terms of the concept measured at the event level. For example, "average commitment level" creates no new concept for analyzing foreign policy behavior; its values are understood in terms of the original concept. In addition, as we move toward using measures of foreign policy behavior to construct measures of foreign policy, we must be sensitive to a possible need to portray a more complex pattern of activity than simple aggregation can provide.

This chapter surveys some additional ways of using the behavior measures to create comparative indicators of foreign policy behavior. To be specific, it considers the problem of characterizing behavior in ways that are not tied conceptually to the event. These behavioral properties which transcend the event are here called *higher-order* concepts. They build on first-order measures, which characterize properties of discrete events (such as commitment, affect, goals), but the resulting measures tap qualities of patterns of events rather than qualities of the events themselves. There are two defining criteria for higher-order measures. First, they must establish values for sets of events rather than for single events. Second, they must represent concepts that transcend events; that is, higher-order measurement must be more than simple aggregation of data across a number of events along a dimension that characterizes the discrete event. Measures of central tendency in a nation's behavior, such as mean level of commitment or mean level of independence of action therefore are not higher-order measures.

As an illustration of the distinction between first- and second-order measures, consider the differences between two measures of the information content of foreign policy behavior: Swanson's measure of specificity (Chapter 10) and the uncertainty measure (H-rel) developed and used by McClelland and others (McClelland, 1968, 1972b; Phillips and Crain, 1974). Specificity concerns the amount of information provided by the actor about his expectations; H-rel concerns the variety of events making up the foreign policy behavior of a nation for some time period. Specificity is a measure of the information communicated by an event. It measures a quality of an event and is a first-order measure of behavior. H-rel, on the other hand, is a measure of the information communicated by a series of events. It taps a quality of a pattern of events and is considered a higher-order measure.

A thorough treatment of the topic of higher-order measures of foreign policy would require a full volume in itself. This chapter, therefore, adopts a more modest goal: to identify some of the statistical techniques that may be used to measure higher-order behavior concepts. For each method, we will discuss some salient features of the statistic as it relates to creating higher-order measures. We will try to highlight the potential for applying these statistics to create additional measures of foreign policy. It should be kept in mind, however, that the creation of a valid measure of any complex phenomenon is never simple. Therefore, this chapter will also consider some of the problems that might be confronted in creating higher-order measures of policy using these statistics.

Unlike the previous chapters, this chapter focuses on techniques rather than on concepts. Concepts are employed to illustrate the use of the methods, but we are not focusing on the development of any concepts. The justification for this concentration on method is that each method may be employed to develop measures of more than one higher-order behavior concept. Nevertheless, we want to emphasize that these methods should be used only when they illuminate important concepts or allow research on important problems. The methods may be used to spin off countless "measures," but before that is done, the researcher should ask: "What is the significance of the concept represented by this measure?" If no persuasive answer can be given to this question, then the measure should be ignored in the research process.

In this chapter we will examine three classes of methods for measuring higher-order behavior properties: measures of dispersion and concentration, inductive clustering, and a priori clustering.

DISPERSION AND CONCENTRATION

Dispersion and concentration are complementary qualities of the distribution of an actor's output along some first-order property of foreign policy behavior. Level of dispersion is the degree of scatter in the distribution; that is, how evenly distributed the data are into the categories that comprise the behavior property. Concentration taps the opposite characteristic—the extent to which the data cluster into a few categories.

Measures of dispersion and concentration may reveal important tendencies in an actor's foreign policy behavior. High dispersion and low concentration indicate tendencies to choose widely across the repertoire of possible behavior options; low dispersion and high concentration suggest constraints that narrow the perceived range of viable options available to the actor. In Chapter 7, for example, C.

Hermann argues that a measure of concentration of instrumentalities could indicate dependence on one or a few means for creating and executing policy. Similarly, the measure of dispersion in the discussion of the substantive problem area scheme (Chapter 4) indicates the degree to which actors were motivated to concern themselves with many or a few issues in the international system.

As East and M. Hermann have noted in Chapter 5, one of the areas in which concentration measures might prove most useful is the study of targeting behavior—that is, the pattern of recipient selection in a nation's foreign policy behavior. That a nation chooses to direct a foreign policy action at another entity indicates some degree of interest in and attention to that recipient. Thus, measures of concentration of event recipients reveal important information about how the nation attends to its environment. A low level of concentration reveals wide-ranging interest and perhaps a cosmopolitan view of the nation's role in the global system. A high level of concentration indicates preoccupation with a few relationships, which implies that external forces or internal resource limitations constrain the range of a nation's foreign relations. A measure of recipient concentration could provide empirical evidence of the validity of the Deutsch and Singer (1964: 396) argument on stability in the international system. They assume that "any nation's total attention—that is, its information-processing and resource-allocating capabilities—will be distributed among all others in the international system according to a normal distribution." Armed with a measure of recipient concentration, we could determine the accuracy of this assumption, especially for those nations with the greatest capability to disturb the system.

Measures of dispersion—the range, mean deviation, standard deviation, and coefficient of variability—indicate the degree of scatter in a distribution. The range is the least informative of the three, revealing only the difference between the extreme low and high values in the distribution. The mean deviation and the standard deviation more fully describe the entire set of cases because both are based on the difference between each case and the mean of the set. Of the two, the standard deviation, which is also more commonly used, is more sensitive to the values of cases that vary greatly from the group norm. The coefficient of variability adjusts the standard deviation by dividing it by the mean, thereby taking into account the differences in standard deviations necessitated by the measurement of different variables using different metrics.

Measures of concentration examine a distribution of data from the opposite perspective. Rather than describing the degree of scatter in the distribution, they describe the extent to which the data fall into one or a few categories on a nominal or ordinal scale. Table 13.1 illustrates the logic of concentration measures. Actor A shows the least concentration of behavior; its events are evenly distributed across the four categories of the first-order behavior measure. Actor C, in turn, shows the most concentration of behavior.

A number of statistics measure concentration. The measurement of concentration across categories of a behavior variable is essentially equivalent to the measurement of inequality (concentration of wealth) in a society. A helpful review of measures of inequality is provided by Alker and Russett (1965). The simplest statistic would be the proportion of cases falling into the modal category. Referring back to Table 13.1, the concentration scores for the three actors are .25, .40, and

TABLE 13.1

Illustration of Concentration Using Hypothetical Data on
Independence/Interdependence of Action for Three Actors

	Actors		
Independence/Interdependence of Action	*A*	*B*	*C*
Initiative, unilateral	25%	20%	0%
Initiative, multilateral	25	40	60
Reactive, unilateral	25	20	40
Reactive, multilateral	25	20	0
Total	100	100	100

.60 for A, B, and C, respectively. The difficulty with this statistic is illustrated by these two displays:

D	E
0	10
0	10
60	20
40	60

Although D and E have the same proportions in their modal category, most observers would say that nation D has a higher level of concentration than E. Therefore, a more frequently used statistic is the Gini index, which incorporates all the information about the distribution. In highly simplified terms, the Gini index is based on the difference between the actual distribution of data and a postulated equal distribution. Equality is assumed to be a condition in which group shares of a value are proportional to group size. If groups are equally large, they should have equal shares. In an application to event data, the assumption is that each category in the classification scheme should have equal numbers of events. The Gini index is computed by cumulating across groups the differences between the supposed equal distribution and the actual distribution, then dividing that absolute measure of inequality by the maximum possible inequality. This procedure yields a statistic with values ranging from zero (perfect equality, minimal concentration) to one (complete concentration).

One research problem that may arise is whether to choose a measure of dispersion or a measure of concentration. Sometimes there may be conceptual reasons to guide the choice; the theoretical logic may lead to framing the hypothesis in terms of dispersion or concentration. Complementing this aspect of the problem is a methodological consideration. The common measures of dispersion assume that the variable is measured on an interval scale. Some variables meet that criterion—for example, the CREON feedback measure (Chapter 12), the cooperation-conflict scale developed by Azar (Azar et al., 1972a), and measures derived from factor analysis. If the variable is measured on an ordinal or nominal scale, then either of two options may be adopted. The researcher may aggregate the data by time as an intermediate step in the research design, which transforms the nominal or ordinal scale into an interval scale, or he/she may use measures of concentration, which are compatible with nominal or ordinal data.

Measures of dispersion and concentration are quite simple statistics which, in many instances, will provide reasonably valid measures of a concept. In other instances, however, their simplicity may lead to their being relied on when more sophisticated measurement and research strategies are called for. One example of this is the recent work that has been done on continuity.

Continuity

Questions of change or lack of change such as those involved in determining continuity have long been central concerns of foreign policy analysts. Rosenau (1976) has argued that instances of change should be a primary target of research; Rosen (1974) has examined the extent to which policy output changes when the political leadership changes. Examining the lack of change or stability in policy, Phillips and Crain (1974) and Tanter (1972) have described how well a state's behavior at one time predicts its behavior in a subsequent time period (see also Kegley and Wittkopf, 1979 and Phillips, 1978).

As a concept, continuity entered the foreign policy literature in the form of a question: Are certain forms of government better or less well equipped to persevere in a course of action to achieve a goal? De Tocqueville analyzed constraints between democracies and monarchies; more recently, scholars have been concerned with the differences between authoritarian and nonauthoritarian systems (Brzezinski and Huntington, 1964) and between presidential and parliamentary systems (Waltz, 1967). If it is true that continuity varies systematically with the structure of the government, this fact would have profound implications for our understanding of how foreign policy is made, the relative importance of internal and external forces, and the viability of nations in an increasingly interdependent world. Thus, research on continuity is a matter of some importance.

Unfortunately, the concept presents serious operational problems. As the concept has been used in theoretical discussions, it usually refers to steadiness in the application of means to the achievement of goals. In this case, change is compatible with continuity, provided that the fulfillment of goals triggers the change in behavior. This perspective on change is reinforced by Deutsch's (1963) discussion of self-steering mechanisms that respond to negative feedback. A nation may approach its goal and modify its behavior in order to avoid overshooting its goal. Or, if the system overshoots its goal, alterations in means would be mandated to approach the goal. Change in foreign policy behavior may also be compatible with continuity in policy if a change in the external environment of the nation alters the challenges and opportunities it faces. Then, a steady pursuit of a goal should require a change in behavior. Otherwise, it might be more appropriate to consider the nation's behavior as rigid rather than as continuous.

These problems suggest that continuity might be examined best through a series of case studies that consider the goal, the means being employed, and any changes in the environment or in the degree of goal fulfillment. If two simplifying assumptions are made, however, a less burdensome research design might be employed. The assumptions are that the environment is basically stable and that

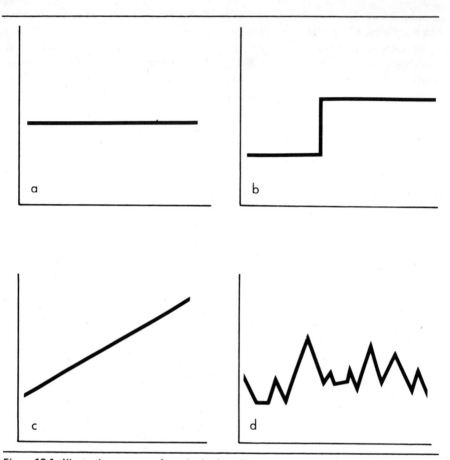

Figure 13.1   Illustrative patterns of continuity in policy.

nations rarely fulfill or overshoot their foreign policy goals. With this assumption, changes in behavior must be related to changes in goals or to changes in the means used to pursue goals. Thus, with an acceptable level of imprecision, one may examine continuity by studying patterns of behavioral output without explicitly controlling for national goals, levels of goal fulfillment, or characteristics of the situation.

If one chooses to study continuity through patterns of behavioral output, then continuity refers to the extent to which an actor's behavior at one time is similar to its behavior in the preceding and following time periods. An illustration is provided in Figure 13.1. The horizontal axis in each frame represents time and the vertical axis is some measure of policy. Figure 13.1a represents a maximum in continuity; the "line of policy" is stable through time. Figures 13.1b and 13.1c show lower levels of continuity. Figure 13.1b displays a pattern of high continuity interrupted by a major change, which, in turn, gives rise to another period of high continuity. Figure 13.1c represents a pattern in which behavior is constantly changing, but in a consistent direction and at a consistent rate. Figure 13.1d shows a very low level of continuity, as indicated by the marked and erratic fluctuations from one time to another.

Empirical research has followed two tracks in measuring continuity. In one, correlational methods have been used. A nation's behavior, along a variety of dimensions, is correlated with its behavior during the following period. A high correlation coefficient indicates high continuity. This approach has been used by Phillips and Crain (1974) and by Tanter (1972). Butler and Taylor (1975: 6-7) criticize this method, saying:

> What is important in that approach is the prediction of variation over time. The more predictable the change, the more consistent the actor is said to be. The problem with this approach is that vast changes in behavior over time can be equated with consistency as long as those changes can be predicted.

In Figure 13.1, the patterns displayed in 13.1a and 13.1c would be considered to have equal levels of continuity, because in each the value of the line at one time can be predicted with knowledge of the slope of the line and the value of the preceding time.

The second approach to measuring continuity employs a measure of dispersion. In a paper using CREON data, Butler and Taylor (1975) argued that continuity should be examined in terms of absolute variability or dispersion. The higher the variability in behavior across time, the lower the continuity. They aggregated the CREON nations' behavior along 32 dimensions for two-year periods. Because the CREON data covered a ten-year period, there were five data points for each nation for each dimension. For each nation, the standard deviation of the data points on each dimension was calculated and produced a measure of foreign policy continuity on that dimension.[1] The lower the standard deviation, the higher the continuity was considered to be.

To what extent is it valid to measure continuity as the dispersion in a nation's foreign policy output across time? It may be argued, first, that any discussion of continuity presumes the prior development of a general theory of change, which identifies a threshold in change below which policy is said to be the same and above which it is said to be different. This problem is analogous to the one facing students of the international system who attempt to demarcate the beginnings and ends of different international systems.[2] This argument is appropriate, however, only if the researcher is interested in demarcating identifiable periods of policy separated by meaningful discontinuities. (The problems in attempting to do this are discussed in the next chapter.) Both the correlational and dispersion approaches to measuring continuity assume, however, that continuity is a variable quality that is always present to some degree in the foreign policy of all nations. Given such an understanding of the meaning of continuity, it is more appropriate to search for statistical procedures that can summarize the degree of *relevant* fluctuation in foreign policy behavior. Returning to the assumptions we made earlier—the environment has remained stable and there has been no change in the degree to which goals have been fulfilled—measures of dispersion, such as the standard deviation, should provide reasonably valid measures of continuity, because a low degree of continuity should be associated with dispersion around the norm of a nation's behavior.

Although measures of dispersion *in principle* may be used to create a valid measure of continuity, in actual application a number of statistical problems may arise to frustrate such use. For many data sets, there may be too few data points to yield statistically meaningful results. To have a large enough number of data points, a lengthy time series of data is necessary. To illustrate the problem, Butler and Taylor were producing measures based on five data points for each nation. A measure of dispersion using such a small number of data points may be unstable.

The apparent solution to the problem is to reduce the time frame for aggregation, so that each data point represents a smaller segment of time while the time series yields more data points. For example, Butler and Taylor could have aggregated across one-year rather than two-year segments, giving them ten rather than five data points. However, for many data sets—especially event data sets—such an alternative is likely to produce even more serious problems. Many nations act infrequently. To aggregate data by smaller time periods risks having data points representing few events. Perhaps more significantly, reducing the time frame for aggregation amplifies the instability in the data, for the shorter the period considered, the greater the effect of forces idiosyncratic to that period. That is why more sophisticated time-series analysis expands the aggregation period through such devices as moving averages.[3]

A second problem in the measurement of continuity is the choice of behavior dimensions along which preliminary data aggregation is to take place. Some dimensions are relatively insensitive to changes in policy and are therefore less revealing in a study of continuity. As an illustration, Butler and Taylor examined continuity along 32 dimensions, such as total number of events, number of conflict acts, number of actions in a world organization, and number of acts directed at Communist nations. Although in most cases there will be no serious problems using such dimensions, problems can arise. For example, suppose a nation undergoes a major shift in alignment, so that at one time it is actively hostile to the United States and in the next period it is actively friendly to it. We would expect a high volume of behavior directed at the United States before and after the shift, the result being the appearance of a high degree of continuity in behavior—or, at least, the operationalization would overestimate the degree of continuity. C. Hermann (1978: 43-44) has made a recent proposal that would alleviate this problem:

> One might define foreign policy continuity as a government's attention through time to the same problems with the same or equivalent strategies or means. To specify this concept in terms of the behavior properties discussed above, we might look at the extent to which, in a given *substantive problem area,* the same *goals* were enumerated with reference to the same entities *(entity identification)* using approximately the same mix of *instrumentalities.*

There is evidence to suggest that such a strategy would work. Kegley and Wittkopf (1979) and Blechman and Kaplan (1978) have been able to examine continuity and change in U.S. foreign policy by examining one aspect at a time in isolation from others. However, for studies using event data, following this suggestion may exacerbate the first problem (too few cases) because each data point would represent a subset of each nation's events rather than all of its events for that period.

Thus, there seems to be a serious dilemma in empirical research on continuity. In order to minimize statistically induced instability in the continuity measure, one must aggregate the data; but aggregation risks obscuring important evidence of actual policy discontinuity. The steps that can be taken to reveal more actual policy discontinuity increase the chances of measuring a lower level of continuity than is substantively warranted.

Two possible ways out of the dilemma can be suggested. First, research can be limited to those nations that are relatively frequent actors. Although such a procedure excludes from the analysis most small states, we can begin to learn something about continuity by bounding the analysis in this way. Second, the analysis could focus on the set of issues to which each nation paid most attention. Thus, the dependent variable would be continuity of policy on a specific issue where the issue could be different for each nation. Those nations that are frequent actors could have more than one issue checked for continuity. This suggestion means, however, that one would be unable to make statements about the degree of continuity in a nation's foreign policy in general.

In conclusion, the discussion has identified some major dangers in using a measure of dispersion to operationalize the degree of continuity in a nation's foreign policy. Perhaps the most serious problem involves the powerful assumptions one must make: that nations rarely approach fulfillment of their foreign policy goals and that they confront an environment presenting a rather consistent set of challenges and opportunities over time. In the ideal situation, one would want to exert some control over these two factors in order to distinguish between spurious and real discontinuity in policy. In addition, for most event-based measures of foreign policy behavior, one must aggregate the data prior to calculation of the measure of dispersion. Unfortunately, there will usually be such a small number of data points that the resulting statistic may be highly unstable. It seems clear, then, that research on continuity in foreign policy must employ multiple, alternative research designs. Within that context, calculations of dispersion or concentration may serve to complement the other types of research. They are, however, unlikely to serve well standing alone.

INDUCTIVE CLUSTERING

Higher-order measures build on the first-order measures of events. In the case of measures of dispersion and concentration, each higher-order property is based on a single first-order property. Thus, each of the first-order behavior dimensions is treated as an isolated phenomenon. To a certain extent that is appropriate. In each of the preceding chapters the author has pointed out why the behavior being developed warrants research—why it is important to understand, for example, specificity on its own merits. Nevertheless, we need to keep in mind that behavior which is specific or nonspecific also has other characteristics that can be related in important and complex ways to specificity. At some point, it would seem desirable to be able to treat the first-order behavior properties as a set rather than as isolated phenomena. Clustering mechanisms draw on the multidimensional nature of behavior to develop integrated characterizations of an actor's foreign policy behavior.

In a clustering procedure each case (actor) is first described by a multidimensional profile of behavior. For example, a particular nation may employ a very high level of commitment, moderately negative affect, high independence of action, low specificity, and infrequent articulation of goals. This profile can be compared to the profile for other nations. Similarity in profiles would indicate that the nations tend to have similar patterns in their relations with the larger system. If a number of nations share a similar pattern, then we could argue that the pattern constitutes a syndrome of behavior, some sort of logical stance toward the outside world. If a number of such commonly occurring stances could be found, we would have generated a new nominal variable along which nations could be compared.

Of course, merely discovering groups of nations that share a common profile of behavior falls short of creating a useful new variable for further analysis. The clusters must first be interpreted to determine the common thread that holds them together. Interpretations will often be quite difficult, because interesting clusters, those that are not self-evident, may have some puzzling members. However, cracking the puzzles posed by the clusters should stimulate theoretical development. And if the clusters can be interpreted, they make an easily manageable dependent variable amenable to intensive case analysis and focused comparison (see George and Smoke, 1974).

Implicit in the previous discussion was the suggestion that clusters be found by "eyeballing" the nation's profiles. Such a procedure has two drawbacks: (1) it is extremely tedious to examine in detail the profiles for each of a large number of actors; and (2) such a method is liable to produce errors through human failings, partly because people tend to see order even when it does not exist, and partly because they tend to see those things that conform to their expectations, even when the basis for those expectations is false. Therefore, most clustering analyses use some form of computerized data reduction technique. The underlying logic of such procedures can be stated briefly. The behavior dimensions that constitute the profile define a multidimensional space within which each actor can be located. In Figure 13.2 five actors have been located in a space defined by two dimensions (X, Y). The dissimilarity in their profiles can be represented by the distance between the actors—the more dissimilar the profiles, the greater the distance. The distances serve to define the clusters. Thus, Actors A and B as well as Actors C and D constitute two tight clusters because of the short distances between the members. If the requirements for a cluster are loosened somewhat, then Actor E would enter the cluster with Actors C and D. If the bounds of the cluster are made very loose, then all five actors would fit into the same cluster. Indeed, one class of algorithms for clustering—hierarchical decomposition and taxonomy creation systems—will automatically partition the sample in such a way that each case is a member of a small, tight-knit cluster, with the tight-knit clusters combined into ever more inclusive, looser clusters until the whole set is combined into one universal cluster.

Despite their convenience and power, such computerized clustering techniques have some limitations. First, the programs force the discovery of clusters. The researcher must still make the independent decision whether the clusters make any sense; this may require an examination of the raw data. Second, the programs define all clusters on the basis of the same dimensions. Such uniformity is unnecessary to produce meaningful clusters. If we were to discover a cluster of nations sharing the same behavior patterns on specificity, commitment, and instrumentalities, but not on affect and independence of action, we could still treat the nations as a cluster sharing a syndrome of behavior. Other clusters could reasonably be defined in terms of other syndromes of behavior. Such flexibility in the definition of clusters would be inhibited by the use of computer routines for clustering. It

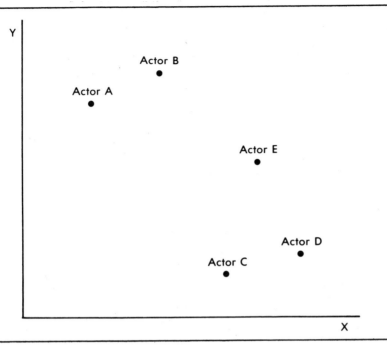

Figure 13.2 Hypothetical clustering space.

should be noted, however, that the creation of clusters based on subsets of behavior dimensions creates the additional requirement that the researcher explain why those behavior dimensions constitute a syndrome.

One particularly attractive feature of clustering analysis needs to be highlighted: It can be used to approximate the reconstruction of policy if the dimensions used to define the nation profiles are appropriately chosen. It would seem that one of two classes of variables is required: substantive problem area or the target of the behavior. Substantive problem area provides a surrogate for national goals, so that the clusters identify nations that process the same or similar issues using behavior that is similar on a number of dimensions. For example, one might find a cluster of nations sharing a tendency to address security issues in a highly interdependent fashion, using highly specific behavior. Such a cluster might indicate a policy of multilateral deterrence to preserve the status quo. Inclusion of the target in the clustering allows one to generate clusters based on policy toward certain kinds of actors. For example, a cluster might share a high level of attention to the Western community combined with moderate affect, low commitment behaviors, and high independence of action. Such a cluster would probably define active neutrals attempting to serve as buffers in the Cold War.

A PRIORI CLUSTERING

The capacity of inductive clustering to advance the qualtitative measurement of policy is enhanced by the methods previously discussed in this chapter, which have let the measure fall out of the data with a minimum of guidance from the researcher. A priori clustering provides close conceptual guidance to methods. In a prior clustering, the researcher provides a conceptual description of a pattern of behavior that should exist given a strategy or general foreign policy that a nation is assumed to have. For example, the foreign policy of a satellite nation may be expected to show these characteristics: low independence of action, moderately high commitment (to cement ties between the satellite and the dominant state), generally positive affect (to appease the dominant state), preponderant attention paid to the dominant state, and a high concentration in the mix of instrumentalities. Armed with this expected profile, the researcher consults the data to determine if the pattern actually holds up. If so, the procedure has defined a cluster of nations.

Clearly, the end products of a priori and inductive clustering are the same—groups of nations sharing certain behavioral tendencies. The advantage of a prior clustering is that theoretical considerations lead the analyst to concentrate on certain actors and specific variables. Such a focus greatly simplifies the search for meaningful clusters of actors. Moreover, the theoretical insights help clarify the meaning of the clusters. After arriving at the clusters of actors via an inductive clustering analysis, the analyst must engage in post hoc explanation of why the nations cluster as they do. Finally, because a priori clustering proceeds from theory, it approximates the testing of hypotheses. Arrayed against these advantages are two disadvantages to this approach. Because it is less likely than inductive clustering to reveal unexpected combinations of actors and variables, it is less likely to produce the serendipitous results that are so beneficial in advancing research. A priori clustering also is not widely applicable in a field lacking adequate theory to explain foreign policy. The analyst must develop theory prior to addressing the data. Inductive clustering is less impeded by a paucity of theory.

Within the CREON Project, one extended effort at a priori clustering has been attempted by Hagan (1977). The remainder of this section closely follows his discussion of the research. He began by defining two strategies for developing states: a strategy of development and a strategy of independence. The foreign policy of development is characterized by the desire to mobilize external resources for internal development. The foreign policy of independence, on the other hand, concentrates on the problem of maintaining autonomy and inner control when the society suffers external penetration and vulnerability to international markets. From those working hypotheses, Hagan proceeded to infer the patterns of behavior that should flow from each orientation.

1. *Affect-direction.* The independence orientation should be associated with more frequent negative behaviors, because hostility toward the external world is a major component of this orientation. Development-oriented states, on the other hand, will be required to engage in extensive cooperative actions in order to execute a shift in resources.

2. *Affect-intensity.* The themes of national independence and external hostility should induce states with the independence orientation to behave with very intense levels of affect. "In contrast, the development orientation necessitates moderate and restrained behavior in order to project the image of stability so attractive to Western governments and private enterprise" (Hagan, 1977: 4).

3. *Goals.* States with a development orientation will tend to profess short-term goals, because of their immediate purpose of extracting resources from the environ-

ment. States with an independent orientation are likely to phrase their goals in long-range, perhaps millennial, language.

4. *Independence of action.* Clearly, nations that pursue a policy of independence should be expected to show high independence of action, especially through the assertion of national will by the initiation of interaction. Conversely, the foreign policy of development should require that a nation act collaboratively and thus with more interdependence of action.

5. *Commitment.* The development orientation requires the investment of material and political resources in order to cement relations and ensure the continued flow of resources from the environment. The independence orientation, on the other hand, suggests a marshaling and conserving of resources in order to avoid being constrained. Thus, the development orientation implies much higher levels of commitment.

6. *Basic value-issue area.* The development orientation should imply a greater degree of attention to economic issues than to other issues, whereas the independence orientation should involve somewhat greater emphasis on security and status issues, because these issues assert the nation's independence and importance in the international system.

7. *Instrumentalities.* Because states with a development orientation seek to extract economic resources from the environment, such states should employ economic skills and resources more frequently than will states having an independence orientation.

Hagan generated data on each of these dimensions to determine whether nations' profiles fit the pattern he expected. He performed the analysis comparing four regimes: the Nkrumah regime of Ghana and the Sekou Toure regime of Guinea, both having the independence orientation; the Houphouet-Boigny regime of the Ivory Coast and the Ankrah regime of Ghana, both having the development orientation. The results are presented in Table 13.2. For five variables—affect intensity, commitment, proportion of economic issues, proportion of security issues, and proportion of economic instrumentalities—the pattern is as expected, with both of the regimes having a development orientation either higher or lower on the variable than either regime having an independence orientation. For the other variables the pattern fails to hold, although only in the case of affect direction does there appear to be no relationship between the orientation and the behavior.

Hagan's analysis demonstrates the methodology for creating higher-order measures using a priori clustering. It is by no means a complete analysis. Additional actors and additional variables need to be considered before the final product is reached. Nevertheless, these results provide strong hope that this approach will prove fruitful.

SUMMARY

This chapter has examined approaches for developing higher-order measures— that is, measures of qualities of patterns of events that represent concepts which transcend events. Higher-order measures produce values that can be neither attached to single events nor interpreted in terms of variables that constitute measures of events. Four approaches were considered. Measures of concentration or

TABLE 13.2
Behavior Profiles for Four African Regimes

Behavior Measure	Independence Orientation		Development Orientation	
	Toure (N=203)	Nkrumah (N=229)	Ankrah (N=42)	Houphouet-Boigny (N=144)
Mean affect intensity[1]	1.63	1.55	1.30	1.36
Rank among CREON nations	4	10	36	31
Mean affect direction[2]	.97	.73	.74	.94
Rank among CREON nations	27	14	15	23
Proportion second-order goals	.34	.33	.46	.31
Rank among CREON nations	15	14	35	12
Mean independence of action	3.33	3.01	3.26	3.58
Rank among CREON Nations	30	14	27	37
Mean commitment	2.83	2.63	3.79	3.09
Rank among CREON Nations	36	37	8	28
Proportion economic issues	.24	.21	.47	.37
Rank among CREON nations	28	33	6	16
Proportion security issues	.26	.33	.07	.22
Rank among CREON nations	19	12	36	24
Proportion status issues	.41	.35	.36	.38
Rank among CREON nations	2	17	15	10
Proportion economic instrumentalities[3]	.25	.19	.38	.33
Rank among CREON nations	25	30	7	10

[1] Higher number indicates more extreme expressions of affect.
[2] Higher number indicates a greater proportion of cooperative action.
[3] Implementation stage only.

dispersion tap the propensity of an actor to select widely or narrowly from a range of possible options. Attention is a commonly used concept based on concentration or dispersion. Various statistical techniques were summarized in a nontechnical fashion. Continuity was evaluated as a concept appropriately treated as a problem of dispersion of behavior over time.

The other two techniques considered were variants of clustering analysis. In inductive clustering, the data are dissected to determine whether a group of nations behave similarly on a set of behavior properties. If so, they constitute a cluster. The dissection may be by computer routine or by hand and eye. The latter is more flexible and allows greater theoretical guidance but is infinitely more laborious. In either case, once the cluster is identified, the researcher must ascertain the concept that defines it and makes it theoretically interesting. When that is done, membership in a cluster may be treated as a nominal level behavior measure amenable to explanation.

A priori clustering uses theoretical concepts to structure the search for clusters. That is, a theory or model is used to identify the nations that should be members of a cluster and the variables that should define the cluster. The data are then examined to determine whether the expected pattern occurs. The advantages of a priori clustering are that theoretical concepts (1) simplify the search for clusters and (2) clarify their interpretation. Disadvantages are (1) a priori clustering impedes discovery of unexpected relationships and (2) it cannot proceed without adequate theory. A priori clustering is illustrated by an example of research on the foreign policy strategies of four African regimes.

A recurring theme in the chapter is the use of measures of foreign policy behavior to yield measures of foreign policy. The consideration of policy measures takes us far afield from the initial assumptions of the CREON project into a problem requiring extensive analysis on its own. The next chapter undertakes that task.

NOTES

1. Butler and Taylor normalized the data for each of the dimensions before calculating the standard deviation in order to reduce the internation differences in the absolute frequency of action. They refer to the standard deviation as a measure of continuity. The use of the coefficient of variability would have had the same effect as the normalization of the data.

2. I would like to thank Charles Kegley for pointing out this argument to me.

3. That the CREON data are events from sampled quarters rather than a continuous time series further impedes the sort of crosstime analysis that the study of continuity requires.

14   PATRICK CALLAHAN

Event Data and the Study of Policy

One of the most remarkably useful inventions in the history of man is the Boy Scout pocketknife. The basis of its usefulness is its multipurpose nature. Including such implements as spoon, can opener, screwdriver, and scissors, as well as large and small knife blades, it is a tool sufficient for almost any task. No wonder Scouts can "Be Prepared." As a general rule, the value of an implement increases with the number of its uses.

This rule applies to data as well as to physical tools. The value of event data varies with the range of intellectual tasks to which such data can be put.[1] This volume has examined a number of ways to use event data to study foreign policy activity. Tapping multiple properties of behavior with multiple classification schemes expands the set of concepts falling within the range of our studies. Simple aggregations of behavior allow us to apply the concepts we use to think about national decisions to compare the output of national governments. Creation of higher-order measures allows us to create and measure concepts that apply to patterns of foreign policy activity.

The previous chapter raised the possibility that the behavior measures could be used to develop representations of policy. That was a significant shift from the previous assumption of a fundamental distinction between foreign policy *behavior* and foreign *policy*. Foreign policy behavior refers to the observable acts of individuals serving in an official governmental capacity. Policy, on the other hand, is usually understood to include both behavior and the underlying purposes and strategies that are presumed to give some coherence to behavior. Attempts to describe foreign policy, therefore, usually describe the goals and intentions that underlie behavior, whereas one can readily describe foreign policy behavior without any reference to such psychological constructs.

Because of the dichotomy between policy and behavior, analysts must choose whether to begin research by attempting a description of foreign policy or by describing patterns of behavior. The authors of this book have chosen the latter approach for a number of reasons. In the first place, the description of foreign policy behavior is more readily operationalized than is the description of foreign policy, because policy description relies so heavily on goals, purposes, intentions, and other psychological phenomena that cannot be easily observed.

But, beyond this practical consideration, sound conceptual grounds justify the study of behavior. Very often, theories concern the nature of a nation's behavior rather than the nature of its policy. To choose an unoriginal example, students of conflict and peace are intensely interested in which nations are likely to instigate conflicts in the world. If we knew what kinds of nations have that tendency and we could forecast whether they were likely to increase or decrease in number, we would be in a better position to anticipate increases or decreases in global political and military stability. A measure of affect and a measure of initiative/reactive tendencies in behavior give us some leverage on this problem.

Furthermore, an examination of patterns of behavior provides a holistic picture of a nation's foreign relations that is difficult to obtain by describing policy. A nation's policy toward one nation may not be closely related to its policy toward another nation. Perhaps more important, the positions nations take on issues can be unrelated, as has been demonstrated repeatedly in the factor analyses of roll call data (for example, Alker, 1969; Russett, 1967). Thus, describing policy toward one target, or on one issue, may reveal very little about the totality of a nation's foreign relations. Yet the totality must be grasped somehow if one is to raise a variety of crucial questions, such as the following: What priorities does a nation place on its relationships with other nations? Which nations occupy the bulk of an actor's attention? To what issues does the actor pay most attention? To what extent does the nation have a singleminded concentration on one issue; to what extent does it participate broadly in world political life? The study of foreign policy behavior helps us to examine these questions. The description of policy may not.

Despite the distinction between behavior and policy, it may be useful to look at behavior and policy as ultimately complementary foci of examination. More specifically, progress in our capacity to measure behavior may improve our capacity to study policy. There are strong reasons to hope that will be the case. Many important theoretical problems concern policy. After all, the field of foreign policy analysis developed out of a desire to understand, to predict, and ultimately to improve foreign policy. Thus, to abandon permanently an interest in analyzing foreign policy would be to abandon some fundamental intellectual and moral concerns. In addition, scholars with a commitment to traditional research methods surely will continue to examine foreign policy. If the quantitatively oriented scholars abandon the study of foreign policy entirely, the nascent fissure of the discipline into mutually exclusive schools will be complete. Valuable communication and reality-testing between the two research traditions will be prevented. This chapter will attempt an initial consideration of some of the problems involved in using event data in an attempt to describe foreign policy and, where possible, will pose some solutions.

AMBIGUITIES IN THE CONCEPT OF POLICY

One of the major impediments to describing foreign policy is the extraordinary range of meanings of the term. The distinction between foreign and domestic policy also poses conceptual problems, but these are relatively small compared with the problems involved in the concept of policy. In this section, I will attempt to point out some of the ambiguities and clarify matters where possible.

The first source of ambiguity arises in the purpose of the definitions of foreign policy. Many are intended to mark out the boundaries of the field, to identify the legitimate subject matter of inquiry. A particularly clear example of a field-demarcating definition is provided in a dictionary of political science terms (Joynt, 1964: 189). There foreign policy is defined as

> courses of action in pursuit of national objectives beyond the limits of the jurisdiction of the state. It includes objectives in the sense of specific goals, principles or guides to action and conduct, commitments or specific undertakings, and the strategy and tactics suitable to the attainment of the ends sought.

Such definitions are of limited analytic value. They distinguish the set of phenomena related to foreign policy from the rest of the universe of social phenomena. But they provide no means for making distinctions among things falling into the realm of foreign policy. Indeed, they would seem to obliterate changes in foreign policy except when those changes coincide with the temporal boundaries of a particular study (French foreign policy under DeGaulle versus French foreign policy under the Fourth Republic, for example). They also distract attention from possible interesting differences in policies toward different targets or on different issues. By labeling all things as policy, they obscure the possibility that some aspects of foreign activity may not constitute a policy.

Other definitions seek not to define the field of foreign policy, but to provide some criteria specifying the components of a policy. These definitions may be classified into four groups. Definitions in the first group equate policy with official aspirations. For example, Zadrozny (1959: 126) defines foreign policy as "the principles and aims of a government in dealing with the governments of other nations." According to Allison and Halperin (1972: 46), policy is "authoritative aspirations, internal to a government, about outcomes" where outcomes refer to conditions in the environment, not to the actions of the government. Relevant terms include "goals," "objectives," "values," "preferences," "intentions." These terms concern purposes. They are the information needed to identify the reasons for state action. As important as goals are for some analysis tasks, definitions that equate policy with aspirations are not completely helpful. All aspirations are treated equally, whether or not there is any connection with action. A pious hope has the same claim to being a policy as does a principle that directly guides all behavior. This distinction would seem worth mentioning, however, as a way of weeding out vacuous, hypocritical, or deceitful assertions of governmental or national purposes because they do not define a nation's foreign policy (although, perhaps, they constitute an element in foreign policy behavior).

If action must be considered in a definition of policy, then why not define policy as action? Plano and Riggs (1973: 76) claim, for example, that "foreign policy consists of governmental actions with respect to foreign governments and their nationals and international agencies." Thus, a nation's policy is what it does. By choosing to ignore purposes, this definition has operational value, but some serious costs. Policy becomes conceptualized in terms of the behavior measures that are used to characterize action. A nation's policy, perhaps controlling for target or issue, is some aggregate characteristic of its behavior along dimensions of affect, commitment, independence/interdependence, and so on. One gains operationalizability at the cost of conceptual richness. And the definition allows no ground for criticism or evaluation, because there are no purposes against which one might assess the quality of action. For these reasons, a total concentration on action is likely to deepen the split between quantitative and nonquantitative scholars.

The third and fourth groups of definitions attempt to bring together both aspirations and actions, ends and means. The third group defines policy as a course of action. Harrison (1964: 509) defines policy as "a course of action or intended course of action conceived as deliberately adopted, after a review of possible alternatives, and pursued, or intended to be pursued." Wilkinson (1969: 18) uses quite similar language: Policy is "a specific, deliberate course of action for achieving some objective." Others relate policy to the existence of a plan of action. "Policy is a projected program of goal values and practices" (Lasswell and Kaplan, 1950: 71), "Policy is an explicit set of preferences and plans drawn up in order to make the outcomes of a series of future decisions more nearly predictable and consistent" (Deutsch, 1978: 88).

Defining policy as a course of action in pursuit of some end has persuasive qualities. By distinguishing among ends, one may be able to make distinctions among policies. Thus, the field is opened to rich conceptualization and description. Second, by taking conscious note of action, the definitions allow the researcher to assess whether a supposed policy has any actual significance for behavior. On the other hand, the definitions seem to require a great deal of consistency in behavior. Action that is not directed toward achieving a particular goal or that contradicts previous behavior calls into question the existence of the policy. Recent theorizing on decision-making processes calls into question any assumption that behavior is likely to be consistent. Individual decision making is characterized by constrained search for alternatives (Braybrooke and Lindblom, 1963: Simon, 1957) and constrained information-processing capabilities (Steinbruner, 1974). Organizational decision making consists of interaction among bureaucratic units, each having a parochial bias on the ends to be pursued in a situation. Others, especially those with extensive participation in government, contend that there is very little planning or other programmatic activity in foreign affairs (see Kissinger, 1977). Behavior, rather, tends to be ad hoc responses to immediate problems. The ultimate consequence of all this is that a definition of foreign policy that equates policy with a fairly consistent pattern of behavior in pursuit of some end will prove to be sterile because such a large proportion of behavior is left outside the purview of research.

The fourth class of definitions considers policy as a standard for behavior, a criterion for choice. Thus, Snyder et al. (1962: 84-85) define policy as follows:

> We suggest that for the purposes of the analytic scheme being outlined here, policy be considered to have two components. . . . One component is action as defined. . . . The other component is rules, that is, guides to action. Rules have a threefold aspect: (1) the substance of a response to some future situation . . . (2) the occasion for a response or the conditions under which a particular response will be made . . . (3) the interpretation of future events and circumstances. . . . Thus policy embraces action and rules of action, reaction or interpretation. Accordingly, policy can be anticipatory, cumulative, specific, and general. "To have a policy" means action and/or rules with respect to a problem, contingency or event which has occurred, is occurring, or is expected to occur.

Standard operating procedures are an extreme example of what the definition refers to. This also is the sense of Meehan's (1971) extensive discussion of the concept. He sees the problem of foreign policy as a matter of choice from among alternative courses of action in a situation. Each alternative generates an outcome that may be characterized by its anticipated values on a set of normative variables. Policy, then, is "the instrument needed to make a reasoned choice in a specified situation" (1971: 279). More specifically, policy identifies the relevant normative variables and stipulates which configuration of projected values and, thus, which option is to be selected. "Policies must take the form 'In situation S, prefer X to Y' where S is defined in terms of normative variables and X and Y are specific values for those variables" (1971: 279).

Besides the differences in explicit definitions of the concept of foreign policy, there are three additional disagreements in the way the concept is treated which give rise to ambiguity. The first concerns whether policy is authoritatively stated or not. Some of the definitions cited above (for example, Allison and Halperin, Deutsch, Lasswell and Kaplan) require that some person in authority enunciate the policy, however policy is defined. Other definitions (Wilkinson's or Plano and Riggs's), although allowing behavior to follow some conscious plan, do not require that the decision makers state the nature of the policy. The distinction has research consequences. If the policy must be formally stated, either publicly or privately, by officials, then the conceptualization of policy is in the hands of governmental officials. On the other hand, if policy need not be explicitly stated, then policy is an analytic construct to be fashioned by the researcher. The researcher may adopt official proclamations of policy if that serves to advance inquiry, but he/she need not be so limited.

The second disagreement concerns whether the effect of policy on behavior is deterministic or probabilistic. One of Kurt Vonnegut's characters in the novel, *Player Piano*, says: "If policy is iron-clad, why not let a machine make the decisions? Policy isn't thinkin, it's a reflex." The idea that policy determines behavior also arises in the foreign policy literature, although in a less colorful formulation. Meehan (1971: 274), for example, asserts:

> The set of standards used to produce a choice in a situation must be sufficiently comprehensive to *force* a choice—a result that is *compatible*

with a policy is not enough. Policies must provide calculated solutions to particular choice problems.

Definitions that equate policy with plans, programs, or rules make a similar assumption; once the policy is in place, the policy-related action of the government follows logically.

Others avoid making strong demands on policy. Treating policy as deterministic, or nearly so, tends to make it a sterile concept. For a policy to operate deterministically, policymakers must anticipate a set of occasions for decision that are sufficiently alike in terms of important properties that the same alternative course of action will consistently have the same desired effect. But it is rare that occasions for decision arise having enough similarities to allow the uniform application of policy to determine action. In addition, the values underlying a nation's relations often conflict in particular instances. In such situations, disagreements arise among lower-level officials attempting to formulate a response to the problem. The disagreements frequently are sent up to higher levels in the bureaucracy for an ad hoc decision by an official who can determine the priorities in the particular case. In sum, there is likely to be little that can be called policy if it must operate deterministically.

Hence, other researchers discuss the term in ways that allow action that is inconsistent with policy. Deutsch (1978) offers an extended discussion of how policy affects behavior probabilistically. When a decision is being made, the actors involved in making the decision attend to a variety of pieces of information, but their attention is not equally distributed across all pieces of information. Some characteristics of the context for decision emerge as more important —that is, they are given greater weight. Elements of the "memory" of the decision-making unit determine the weight assigned to particular pieces of information. Policies—as well as goals, purposes, and values—are parts of the memory. Thus, if a policy exists, it will amplify the importance of some pieces of information, making a particular kind of behavior more probable. This view is similar to Snyder et al.'s notion of policy as involving rules of interpretation. The more important the policy, the greater is the weight given by policymakers to information, and the greater the effect on the probability of the kind of subsequent behavior. Thus, other things being equal, the strength of a policy will be revealed by the distribution of behavior over some period of time.

The third source of ambiguity in the term foreign policy centers on the problem of the level of generality. Wilkinson (1969: 18) draws the useful distinction between policy, defined above, and the "general line of policy," which is "the unifying and overriding strategic imperative that connects area policies (for example, Far Eastern, European) and functional policies (for example, military, economic), and subordinates them to objectives of higher and lower priority, of shorter and longer run." Policies may be nested, so that a general policy may contain within it (imply) a number of more particular policies. For example, at a general level, a nation may have a status quo policy under which is subsumed a policy toward a particular issue—for instance, opposition to nuclear proliferation —which may include an even more particularistic policy, such as opposition to the spread of technology used to reprocess nuclear waste into plutonium. Different students of foreign policy conceive of policy as more or less general. Policy as a program of action is quite particularistic. Policy is least general in Meehan's treatment of the concept. By tying policy to a particular configuration of values in normative variables, he makes it quite improbable that a policy would ever apply to more than one situation. Other definitions are more general.

To summarize the discussion, the ambiguity in the concept of policy can be traced to a number of sources. Definitions serve different purposes: to enunciate the boundaries of a field of study or to state the elements that constitute a policy. Within the class of definitions having the latter purpose, four approaches to defining policy can be distinguished: (1) policy as aspirations, (2) policy as action, (3) policy as a course of action in pursuit of certain ends, and (4) policy as a standard for decision making. Cutting across these classes of definitions are three additional differences in use of the term which add to its ambiguity: (1) some definitions require that policy be explicitly stated by officials, others do not; (2) some definitions require policy to have a deterministic effect on action, others allow the effect to be probabilistic; and (3) definitions vary in the level of general applicability of policy to decision situations.

A CONCEPTION OF FOREIGN POLICY

For the remainder of this chapter, policy will have the following meaning: Policy is a standard used in the making of decisions. Logically, it exists prior to the decision being made, although one policy can lead a decision maker to adopt another policy to be used in making later decisions. For example, at various times during the Vietnam war, presidents of the United States made decisions about the way air power would be used. Those decisions established standards by which field commanders could decide on targets to be bombed. The presidents made policy in one sense. But the policy decisions also reflected other standards (policies). Johnson chose not to hit Hanoi because such bombing was deemed detrimental to other aspects of U.S. foreign relations. Those other aspects of U.S. foreign relations provided standards for Johnson's decision making and thus would here be construed as policy.

Policy operates probabilistically. The existence of a policy makes some kinds of behavior more likely and other kinds of behavior less likely. Rarely does policy completely prohibit a particular class of action or dictate another kind of action. Thus, for the analyst, the study of policy poses two research problems. Does the actor in question have a discernible policy? If so, how strong is the effect of the policy on behavior? This distinction might have the beneficial consequence of deflecting a number of sterile debates over whether a nation has a particular policy into the much more researchable and less polemical question of how significant a particular policy is in determining the nature of the nation's foreign policy activity. Of course, in some cases, analysts will still confront the knotty problem of whether a nation actually has a specific policy. Policy has to have some effect on behavior. Otherwise it makes no sense to speak of policy as a standard for decision. The question, then, is this: What is the lowest boundary in the strength of the effect of policy on behavior below which it makes no sense to speak of a policy as existing? This is an important issue that cannot be given a definitive answer in the confines of this chapter.

Finally, as a standard for making decisions, policy may range from the most general formulation to the most particular rules for decision. Thus, it makes sense to speak of a very broad human value, such as economic equality for individuals, as a policy for a nation if it provides a standard by which that nation makes foreign policy decisions. Similarly, a rule as specific as refusal to negotiate with international terrorists can also be a policy if it leads the nation to refuse negotiations when presented with such a demand.

Before turning to the question of how this conception of foreign policy might be given empirical application, let us consider one implication of accepting such a conception of foreign policy. This definition makes little distinction between domestic and foreign policy. A policy is a foreign policy if it serves as a standard for determining activity toward entities outside the borders of the nation-state. A standard such as reduction of domestic unemployment is a foreign policy if it leads the actor to choose particular options in its trade negotiations, for example. Conversely, what would seem to be a foreign consideration—such as maintaining good relations with another nation—may become a domestic policy if it is used as a standard in making decisions about the treatment of ethnic nationals of the other nation. The distinction between domestic and foreign policy becomes totally arbitrary, serving only to provide a convenient division of labor among students of governmental activity.

USING EVENT DATA TO STUDY FOREIGN POLICY

Whether this conceptualization of foreign policy has any value depends on its a priori persuasiveness and on whether it permits sound empirical research on foreign policy to be carried out. Therefore, this section of the chapter will examine whether policy as conceived here can actually be studied using event data measured by the classification schemes presented in this book.

According to the definition of policy, one must examine patterns of activity to get a real measure of the strength of a policy. A single act may announce a policy, or it may be seen in retrospect to exemplify a policy. But one can study policy only by examining patterns of behavior. The question, then, is whether one can use the pattern of aggregated output along some behavior property as a measure of a nation's policy. For example, can one calculate for each nation the mean affect level of its behavior and use that statistic as the measure of its policy on positive and negative affect? Unfortunately, no. As illustrated in Figure 14.1, policy has a causal effect on the kinds of decisions a state makes, but it is not the only causal force. The foreign policy literature suffers an embarrassment of riches in terms of the number and variety of causal forces that have been identified. Those causal forces have a dual effect on behavior—direct as well as indirect—through their impact on policies which, in turn, have an impact on behavior. Thus, the affect output of a government reflects the hostility of the world around it, as well as its own desires for friendly or hostile relations.[2]

The problem is that policy is an unmeasured construct. As an unmeasured construct, it cannot be used directly in empirical research. The first task for the researcher is to give policy some independent meaning. There are two ways to go about this. The researcher may draw on different evidence to indicate that the

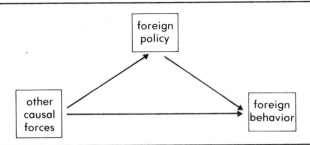

Figure 14.1 Schematic representation of the relationships among foreign policy, foreign policy behavior, and other causal forces

government does indeed have a particular policy and to show roughly how strong that policy is. Possibilities might be to take the policymakers' word at face value *at this first stage of research* or to draw on the accounts of journalists or other observers. Or the researcher may stipulate the working assumption that a nation has a particular policy. It is best, but not necessary, that there be good reasons for such a stipulation.

Once a policy is stipulated, the researcher spells out the behavioral implications of that policy and then uses the data to see if the implications are valid. For example, the change in U.S. presidents from Ford to Carter is generally supposed to have brought with it a change in U.S. foreign policy, from traditional, Great Power balancing to a "world order" policy. If this intended change in policy had any effect on decision making within the U.S. government, it should be reflected in some simple aggregated statistics for U.S. behavior. A world order policy suggests that greater significance is attached to relationships with nations other than the Great Powers. Hence, more behavior should be directed toward other actors and less attention should be paid to the Soviet Union. Likewise, under a world order policy rather than under a traiditional Great Power balancing policy, basic values such as economic wealth, well-being/welfare, and enlightenment should be rated above military/security and respect/status values, and one should see a higher percent of behavior addressing these areas. If these predictions are incorrect, then one might question whether the supposed change in policy did occur. (A more extensive example of the kind of analysis being proposed here was presented in Chapter 13 under the heading "A Priori Clustering." The reader may want to look at that discussion again, not only to see a careful elaboration of the steps involved in carrying out such research, but also to see evidence that such research can produce results with prima facie plausibility.)

Of course, such a simple research design cannot produce conclusive evidence, given the problems discussed above. We will return soon to this point to offer some ideas on how to alleviate the problems. But first let us ask whether the behavior measures proposed in this volume show any possibility of being linked theoretically to conceptions of policy. If so, their theoretical utility, one of our criteria for a good classification scheme, is enhanced. In general, the answer is affirmative. The following are examples of linkages between conceptions of policy and the behavior measures described earlier. One would expect that a policy of autarchy, isolationism, or neoisolationism would be associated with a standard of rejecting requests for high-level commitment acts which would be granted under other policies. Conversely, an attempt to assert leadership will require that the nation undertake more high-level commitment actions. Independence/interdependence of action is probably affected by policies of coalition formation (increase independence by decreasing collective activity), isolationism (increase independence by decreasing collective activity), containment (increase reactive behavior), or a "forward strategy" (increase initiative behavior). Affect may be influenced by either a policy to "get tough" with another entity or a policy of "responsiveness" (see Pruitt, 1964). One of the things we might expect from an authoritative policymaker is the establishment of broad guidelines to identify those problems in the external environment which should be given priority. The flurry of bureaucratic activity stirred up by Kissinger's National Security Council apparatus during the first months of the Nixon administration provides an apt illustration. It is also obvious that policy may be used to determine the mix of a nation's instrumentalities. A war policy compared to a policy of peace provides only the most extreme example of the way in which different instrumentalities may be needed.

On the other hand, a measure of policy success such as the ratio of positive to negative feedback is an implausible candidate for a measure of policy. Although one can imagine a nation's leadership consciously striving to increase positive feedback, devising strategies to further that end, and communicating its strategy via orders to the government, the feedback received from the environment is too dependent on forces beyond the control of the leadership for the values on this measure to be very sensitive to policy choices.

It is also doubtful that policy measures can be built on specificity. The mind does not quickly recall cases in which policymakers sought to increase or to decrease specificity of behavior as a matter of general policy. Indeed, Swanson's arguments suggest that the incentives are slanted toward unspecific behavior for all decision makers. If behavior is to be specific, situational variables rather than policy guidelines probably are the determining consideration.

Conceptually, then, the behavior measures described in this book do increase our ability to develop empirical tests of the proposition that a nation has a certain policy and to estimate the strength of that policy. But before we claim to have made a breakthrough, the operational problems raised earlier must be considered. Unfortunately, no single, definitive solution is possible. Ultimately, the examination of policy must be based on inconclusive evidence. Fortunately, there are ways to shorten the length of any inferential leaps.

First, the behavioral implications of the supposed policy can be more fully articulated. To do this we could specify distinctive patterns of expected behavior built on more than one behavior measure. Returning to an earlier example, a shift to world order policies from traditional power-balancing policies should entail changes in behavior besides a shift in the targets and issues commanding the attention of U.S. policymakers. World order policies should require a decrease in the use of military resources in the implementation phase of action and, possibly, an increased use of economic resources. Further, given the belief that the new world order requires a sharing of responsibility for global decision making, the shift from power balancing to world order policies should involve an increased use of multilateral decision-making processes and an increased relative frequency of reactive over initiatory actions. Thus, the independence/interdependence of action dimension of behavior should throw some light on the question of whether and to what extent the United States reoriented its foreign policy with the advent of the Carter administration.

Along the same lines, we could also attempt to determine which behavior properties should *not* be strongly related to a policy. World order policies, for example, should not radically change the average levels of commitment aggregated across all behavior. If the level of commitment in U.S. behavior was stable from the Ford to the Carter administrations, that would strengthen the assumption that the other changes in behavior were due to the postulated change in policy. The underlying assumption of this argument is that, as more dimensions of behavior are theoretically related and empirically demonstrated to vary with a supposed policy, the less likely it is that any single dimension's relationship is an artifact of chance and the more persuasive is the explanation of the relationship as a consequence of the different behavioral demands of different policies.

A second way to increase confidence in any apparent relationship between policy and behavior is to conduct the analysis controlling for substantive problem area or target. Most discussions of foreign policy employ substantive or geographic classifications as ways of dividing the foreign policy universe. Similarly, foreign ministries are organized on both geographic and functional bases. This suggests that policies are often differentiated along such lines, especially the more narrowly applicable policies. If we can argue that the policy actually applies only to a limited set of targets in the international environment or to a limited set of problems, then we can rerun the analysis for two subsets of data: one consisting only of those events falling into the relevant target or problem set, the other, all remaining events. If the predicted pattern of behavior occurs for the first subset of events but does not occur for the second, then the researcher would be on solid ground in concluding that the actor had a policy that was affecting its behavior. On the other hand, if the analysis showed the predicted pattern of behavior for both subsets, then the researcher would conclude that something other than policy was producing the observed pattern of behavior. Of ocurse, a possible alternative interpretation that might deserve further investigation in at least some cases would be that the policy should be reconceptualized by the researcher to give it broader application because the original conceptualization may be more narrowly conceived than that guiding the decision makers. If policy is reconceptualized to become more general, however, the researcher must devise additional tests. Otherwise, the study of policy loses falsifiability and ceases to be a scientific enterprise.

The third way that we can increase our confidence in interpreting patterns of behavior as reflecting policy is to make comparisons across time. Thus, we look for moments when policy is believed to have changed and compare the patterns of behavior before and after the supposed change. In essence, we execute an interrupted time-series form of quasi-experimental design. The advantage of the approach is that one is holding constant the effects of variables that do not experience a change simultaneously with the supposed change in policy. Thus, for example, a change in U.S. foreign activity following a change in presidential administrations cannot be attributed to a change in such variables as national attributes or the basic structure of the government. The danger with this type of analysis is the too-facile assumption that the supposed change in policy produced the change in behavior patterns. Other variables may also change at the same time as the supposed change in policy. It may be that the change in these other variables, rather than the change in policy, produces the change in behavior. In our example, the change in presidential administrations brought not only a supposed change in policy, but also a change in the personalities of the top governmental leadership—at least in the executive branch—and a change in the procedures used in making decisions. Changes in behavior may be the result of these or other unmentioned variables rather than a change in policy.

One other question deserves consideration in this context. Does marked, discontinuous change in a behavior pattern follow a change in policy, or can the behavior pattern change be more gradual, extending over a period of time? If one assumes that policy has a deterministic effect on behavior, then one should look for sudden changes in behavior following a change in policy. On the alternative assumption, however, that policy has only a probabilistic effect on behavior and that the degree of this effect reflects the strength of the policy, it makes sense to expect the change in the pattern of behavior to be more gradual. Not only must those who change the policy announce the change to the bureaucracy; they must also persuade the members of the organization to incorporate the new policy into their calculations. Presumably, this could be a lengthy process. The following propositions can be made about this process. The more frequently the new policy is reiterated, the more it is given emphasis in official pronouncements, and the more often it is used as the basis for decision, the more thoroughly socialized members of the decision-making apparatus will be to the new policy and the more the policy will affect the nature of the decisions that are made. To be more specific, what is predicted here is a kind of S-curve in the pattern of change in behavior. Shortly after the policy is changed, behavior will begin to change, but at a relatively slow pace. Then there will be a period of quickened change until some upper boundary is reached, after which the rate of change will slow and eventually stop.

The previous three suggestions have assumed that the researcher is studying patterns in the aggregated behavior of an actor along a series of separate but related properties of behavior. The final idea proposed here requires the disaggregation of the data to the event level. With this final suggestion the theory about the behavioral consequences of a particular policy is used to identify a set of configurations of behavior characteristics that an event should satisfy to qualify as an instance of the application of a policy and a set of configurations that would qualify as evidence of the failure of the policy to have an effect on behavior. To illustrate with an example somewhat beyond the temporal boundaries of most existing event data sets, the policy of isolationism followed by the United States during the first dozen decades of its own life involved a variety of criteria for proper behavior by the nation. The United States was to avoid entangling itself with European nations in ways that were likely to draw it into Europe's wars. The United States was supposed to pay a great deal of attention to affairs in the western hemisphere, with no particular limitations on the kinds of interactions that could be undertaken. And the United States was supposed to avoid conflicts with European nations and seek friendly relations with all. From these standards, certain kinds of behavior can be identified that either exemplify the policy or contradict it. Any behavior toward another nation in the Americas would be acceptable. Actions showing positive, neutral, or weak negative affect toward European targets would be consistent with isolationism, but actions showing strong negative affect toward a European nation would be a deviation from the policy. One could engage in a variety of high-commitment behaviors with European nations as long as the substantive problems were of an economic nature, but high commitment behaviors with European nations on political or military issues would mark a significant departure from isolationism. The test of the operation of a policy, then, would be to array the data to see the relative frequency of policy-consistent and policy-contradictory actions in terms of these event-level policy indicators. A preponderance of policy-consistent actions would be evidence of the decision-making significance of the policy, whereas a preponderance of policy-contradictory behaviors would indicate that the policy was moribund.

The preceding discussion has presented four different data analysis strategies for making stronger inferences about the relationships between hypothesized policy and observed patterns of behavior. At the danger of belaboring the obvious, we should note that these strategies are not mutually exclusive. Indeed, it is to be hoped that the researcher will make creative use of a number of these strategies as well as others that may be devised. However, even extensive use of a variety of analysis techniques will not eliminate the inferential nature of the task of using data to study policy. Caution must always be exercised.

SUMMARY

Foreign policy is a seminal concern of those involved in foreign policy analysis. But a variety of conceptual and empirical problems have deterred systematic, quantitative research on policy. Conceptually, policy is riddled with ambiguities. A review of the literature reveals four different classes of definitions of policy as well as disagreements over the requirements for asserting that a policy exists. Empirically, policy often is interpreted to require a specification of the actor's goals. As Brady pointed out in Chapter 6, this is generally an impossible mission. Consequently, research has tended to emphasize behavior rather than policy, or, to use a distinction introduced in Chapter 1, style rather than substance.

In this chapter, the argument was made that policy can be a researchable topic if policy is conceived as a standard used in the making of decisions, which, rather than determining the decision, operates probabilistically to make certain kinds of actions more or less likely. The research problem becomes assessing the strength of the effect of some presumed policy rather than determining whether a particular policy has been adopted. With this approach, event data sets, incorporating many of the variables presented in this volume, can be most helpful. The more behavior properties are presumed to be affected by a policy, the more varied the possible tests of the effects of that policy. Also, measures of substantive problem area and of the targets of action allow one to check whether the presumed effects of policy appear in behavior directed toward appropriate problems or targets and only in such behavior. Having data across time enables the use of interrupted time series quasi-experiments. And, finally, policy indicators can be created to reveal the occurrence of actions that are either consistent or inconsistent with a policy. The balance of consistent and inconsistent behaviors reveals the strength of the policy.

NOTES

1. This eagerness to exploit as fully as possible the usefulness of event data must be tempered, however, by an awareness of the danger of fulfilling the "law of the instrument"—that is, using the data because they are convenient even though they may not be appropriate for the task at hand.

2. The relationships among behavior, policy, and other causal factors are further complicated if one takes into consideration the feedback effects behavior can have on policy and on the other causal factors. Whether one chooses to analyze those feedback effects or to ignore them, it remains true that one cannot equate the stream of foreign policy behavior with policy. My thanks to Charles Kegley for pointing this out.

PATRICK CALLAHAN

Epilogue

It has now been more than a decade since foreign policy researchers began to use event data in their studies. In that time, we have learned a great deal about the kinds of bias present in various event data sources and the dimensional bases of event data sets using the most common coding schemes. Scholars have developed and tested various conflict and cooperation scales. And we have inherited a number of event data sets held in data libraries. In sum, we have progressed far in the development of event data as a tool of foreign policy research.

Despite the forward movement on many fronts, the conceptualization *and* measurement of the properties of foreign policy activity, other than affect, have been relatively stagnant. That is the problem to which this book has been addressed. Following the early and repeated calls of Charles Hermann for sustained thinking about the nature of foreign policy, we have set out to develop measures that meet four criteria: they must be based on rigorous, a priori conceptualization; they must be theoretically significant or policy relevant; they must facilitate comparison; and collectively they must represent the diversity of foreign policy activities and the rich body of concepts used in traditional, nonquantitative scholarship. To represent the predecisional context of behavior, we have offered measures of the substantive problem areas of action and of the scope of a nation's actions— the distribution of its attention across external entities. To represent the decision-making process, we have developed classification schemes for nonsubstantive properties of goals and for the instruments used in generating action. To portray the nature of foreign policy outputs, we have created scales of commitment, affect, specificity, and independence/interdependence of action. To monitor feedback, we devised the acceptance/rejection ratios. For each measure, we have made a determined effort to design and use an a priori conceptualization of the measure prior to indicator construction and to identify its theoretical or policy import. And we have produced for each measure tables showing cross-national comparisons. In addition, the last two chapters suggested strategies for using the behavior measures to develop ways of assessing "higher-order" properties and of studying foreign policy, thereby amplifying the value of the measures as tools of comparison.

Thus, on the criteria that we advanced, this volume has tried to move toward the closing of one gap in the measurement of foreign policy activity. Nevertheless, considerable work remains before we can be completely satisfied with the quality of the event-based measurement of foreign policy described in this volume. What follows is a cursory discussion of some of the kinds of follow-up work that need to be pursued. The tasks can be grouped into three areas: (1) establishing the validity of the individual event measures reported in this book, (2) improving the quality of the cross-national comparative indicators produced from the measures, and (3) testing the quality of the set or repertoire of measures now available to the analyst.

ESTABLISHING THE VALIDITY OF THE MEASURES

The prerequisite for a successful measurement effort is that the measures must tap the concepts they are supposed to tap. Thus, we return to the issue of validity discussed at some length in Chapter 2. At present, assessment of the validity of the individual measures rests largely on impressions of the plausibility of the reasoning behind the measure and the intuitive appeal of the data that result. Judgments of validity should rest on stronger, more systematically generated evidence. Thus, more extensive validity testing is required.

Devising appropriate validity tests requires considerable creativity, however, and, as was shown in Chapter 2, the results of such tests are often full of ambiguities. The use of event data further complicates the problem because a measure can become invalid at either of two levels: at the event level—that is, in the assignment of a score on the measure to the individual event—and at the aggregate level, in the generation of scores on the measure for nations or other units of analysis. A measure may be valid in the scores that it assigns to individual events but invalid when aggregated to higher levels of analysis because of flaws in the data set or in the aggregation technique.

Usually, a measure that is invalid at the event level will not generate valid indicators at a higher level of analysis, but exceptions are possible. If the errors at the event level are randomly distributed and if the aggregation is based on a fairly large number of events, the errors should cancel out. Even if the errors are not randomly distributed but, rather, reflect some degree of bias, aggregation may still yield useful comparative indicators. The crucial assumption that must be made here is that the degree of bias is not differential; that is, it is not greater or lesser for different cases at the higher unit of analysis. If this assumption is correct, then the scores generated by aggregation will all be inaccurate in terms of revealing the "true" level of the variable but will be accurate in revealing the relative position of the cases. To illustrate, suppose the specificity scale tends to overstate the degree of specificity in the foreign policy behavior of all events. As a result, the calculation of a specificity score for a nation will overstate the specificity in its activities. The relative position of each nation, however, may be quite accurate, so that analyses designed to test the sources of cross-national variation in specificity would be appropriate.

Keeping these provisos in mind, we can suggest some alternative routes to validity testing. For at least two of the measures, affect and scope of action, comparable indicators in other data sets exist to allow concurrent validity testing. Many event data sets have measures of either affect or cooperation and conflict. If the CREON affect variable measures affect, there should be positive correlations between affect scores generated by the CREON data and scores generated by the other data. The strengths of the correlations should vary with the degree to which the other data sets define their measures as measures of affect or measures of cooperation and conflict. Correlations should be stronger with other measures of affect. In addition, the multiplicity of affect and cooperation/conflict measures removes one source of ambiguity in validity testing. If the CREON measure were poorly correlated with *only one* of the other indicators, we would have strong grounds for concluding that it was the other measure that was inadequate; whereas if the CREON affect measure were poorly correlated with them all, then one would feel more confident that the CREON measure was flawed.

Similar tests should be possible for the scope of action measures. If, as East and M. Hermann imply, scope of action measures reveal the importance or salience of external entities to an actor, then one might expect to find such measures highly correlated with the pattern of diplomatic exchange between pairs of nations (as found in Alger and Brams, 1967). In addition, scope of action might be correlated with the measures of the diplomatic importance of states developed by the Correlates of War Project (Singer and Small, 1968; Small and Singer, 1973). We would not expect such correlations to be perfect, however, because the patterns of diplomatic exchange reflect many influences other than the importance of the receiving state to the sending state. Bitter enemies, for example, are quite important to each other but may not have diplomatic relations simply as a reflection of their mutual hatred. Or a state may use its diplomatic presence in another nation to monitor developments in a third nation bordering the receiving state. The U.S. diplomatic presence in Iran and Turkey during the 1950s and 1960s is an excellent example of this phenomenon. The correlations may also be less than perfect because events and diplomatic exchanges indicate different kinds of attention. The staff of large embassies and consulates is responsible for managing many of the transactions carried on between two nations. Most of those transactions make up the normal flow of relations between nations and are less likely than other levels of relations to provoke the kinds of decision-making activities by political authorities that are recorded as events. In other words, a large diplomatic staff may indicate more directly the level of economic salience of one nation to another, whereas a heavy event flow from one nation to the other may indicate more directly the level of political salience.

Other evidence about validity may be gained by examining the correlations among the behavior measures themselves. For example, we might look to see if certain classes of basic values are associated with certain classes of instruments. If these two measures validly tap what they are purported to tap, we would expect to find events concerned with security values more likely to be carried out with military instruments than are events involving the other basic values. We would similarly expect that events in the wealth basic value area would be more likely than other events to involve the use of economic instruments, that events in the enlightenment problem area would be associated with the use of science and technology instruments, and that events in the respect/status basic value area would be associated with promotive instruments. In addition to checking for positive associations, one could also check to see if associations that should not occur do not, in fact, occur. For example, we would not expect to see military instruments being used in events in either the enlightenment or well-being basic value problem areas. Moreover, we would expect that events involving respect/status basic values would be associated with the use of military instruments, but to a lesser extent than promotive instruments and to a lesser extent than the use of military instruments in events dealing with security values.

In addition to checking the patterns of association between categories of nominal-level measures, we should also be able to develop validity tests based on the correlations between entire measures. For example, one might expect that affect will be poorly correlated with commitment and specificity and that commitment and specificity will be inversely correlated with the time frame for realization of goals.

A third approach to validity testing might involve checking one or a few categories of a variable against some external criterion. For example, level 8 of the commitment scale purports to capture the making of formal, binding agreements. We could see if the relative frequency of such actions by a nation as recorded in the CREON data corresponds to the relative frequency of formal agreements that some nation reports to the United Nations as part of the UN treaty series.

A final approach to the validity testing of these measures might involve plotting various patterns in a variable across time. For example, if the feedback measure accurately measures the degree to which a nation experiences positive or negative feedback, and if it is the case that the world has been less positive toward the United States since the early 1960s, then the measure should show declining scores for the United States during the decade for which CREON has data. Perhaps one might also see an increase in the positive feedback received by China as a result of the breakdown of its isolation from the world.

Shifts in the relative frequency of attention to various issues could also shed light on the validity of the substantive problem area variable. One would expect to see, during the decade 1959-1968, a decrease (or, at least, not an increase) in the number of events concerned with the problems of colonialism, as well as complete and general disarmament, but an increase (or, at least, not a decrease) in the frequency of events concerned with the problems of nuclear proliferation and drug traffic and abuse.

Other cross-time tests of validity could be fashioned for the behavior measures. All such tests, however, are susceptible to certain problems that need to be considered. One problem is that such tests involve a comparison of patterns in the data with some intuitively or impressionistically derived belief about trends and changes in the "real world." Such beliefs may, in fact, be false. Therefore, such trend analysis should be limited to those instances in which one feels confident about the truth of the beliefs, either because the evidence for the belief, although assessed impressionistically, is so overwhelming as to preclude other interpretations, or because there is virtual consensus among experts.

A second problem with such cross-time validation tests, at least for the CREON data, stems from the fact that the CREON Project gathered its event data from sampled quarters of different years rather than as a continuous time series. As a result, the data for different years represent different months of the year. Assuming that there is some cyclical fluctuation in foreign policy behavior throughout the year caused by such things as the meetings of the UN General Assembly during the autumn, the central tendencies in the data for any one year represent both long-term trends and quarter-specific fluctuations. By grouping years together, the analyst might be able to cancel out those cyclical fluctuations.

To summarize the argument in this section, validity testing of the measures presented in this volume is a priority research task. It is not a task, however, for which there are solutions that are both satisfying and uncomplicated. Nevertheless, four approaches that might prove useful for some of the measures involve correlating the measures with some external indicator of the same or similar concepts, examining patterns of correspondence between individual measures, comparing the correlations between categories of variables with external criteria, and examining cross-time trends in the data for correspondence with trends known through other means.

IMPROVING THE QUALITY OF CROSS-NATIONAL INDICATORS

In their study of success and failure in the United States' use of force to supplement its diplomacy, Blechman and Kaplan (1979: 203) discovered, among other things:

> Political uses of the armed forces were often associated with favorable outcomes when U.S. objectives were at least loosely consistent with prior U.S. policies. The purpose of discreet political uses of force must fit within a fundamental framework of expectations held by decision makers both in this country and abroad if the military activity is to be associated with a favorable outcome. . . . Similarly, the aggregate analyses suggest that prior U.S. military engagement in conflicts in a region was often associated with favorable outcomes when subsequent demonstrative uses of military force took place.

These findings have startling implications for any planned use of, for example, the CREON commitment scale for the creation of cross-national indicators of commitment, since they suggest that the expectations created by an action depend not only on the qualities of the action but also on the historical context of the action—that is, how it relates to events undertaken at the same time as well as to events that came before it. As a further illustration with reference to commitment, it would be implausible to assume that the reiteration of a pledge for the thousandth time is just as constraining as the reaffirmation of a pledge for the second time.

Similar difficulties probably arise in the attempt to measure specificity and affect as qualities of a nation's foreign policy behavior. The specificity scale provides a means to grasp the amount of information (about the actor's expectations of others) communicated by an event. But when we attempt to measure differences in nations' propensities to reveal or hide their expectations, we may need to take into account the likelihood that different events reveal different, though complementary, information about expectations. With affect, how we interpret the disposition of the actor toward the target should probably depend on the configuration of events undertaken at the time. It is reasonable to presume, for instance, that an expression of mildly positive affect by itself has different implications from a similar expression accompanying an event of strongly negative affect.

The argument, in other words, is that the movement from measures appropriate for characterizing the qualities of an event to measures appropriate for characterizing the foreign policy behavior of a nation is in no way a simple, straightforward process. The movement from one level to the other may be especially complicated for concepts—such as commitment, specificity, and affect—whose values depend heavily on the behavioral context of the event.

By and large, in this book we have aggregated event data to yield indicators for nations by simple statistics such as means and proportions. Because such aggregations of the data can be executed relatively easily, there is a general tendency to use them to produce indicators of cross-national differences in foreign policy behavior without devoting careful attention to what such indicators represent. Generating statistics such as the "proportion of events concerned with security/military values" in no way guarantees that the indicator is related closely to any theoretically or practically important concept. Of course, the use of such simple statistics does not preclude the development of useful measures. The point is that some thought should be devoted to moving the measurement effort from the event level to the nation level.

Measures of social phenomena usually incorporate two kinds of variation: that which is relevent to the concept being measured and that which is irrelevant. Improving measurement involves discovering the first kind while reducing the influence of the second. One approach to excluding irrelevant variation is what is called "indexing" by Webb and his colleagues (1966). An example of indexing is the seasonal adjustment of economic statistics.

Most indexing done in measuring foreign policy activities of nations is intended to exclude from the measures the effects of size or capability differences among nations. Thus, defense effort is usually measured by dividing defense expenditures by GNP. Most measures created from event data use a proportion, percentage, or mean, all of which remove from the statistical results the effects of different levels of activity among nations. Another type of measurement that uses the indexing approach is the calculation of residuals during a regression analysis. The residuals represent the value of a case on the dependent variable once the variation attributable to the independent variable has been removed.

Despite these fairly common ways of normalizing data to remove irrelevant variation, the creation of index measures remains a largely unexplored frontier in the measurement of foreign policy. Perhaps it will prove, as some frontiers have proven, to be barren. Nevertheless, the possibilities are enticing. For instance, if one conceives of foreign policy behavior as representing the decisions of an actor in a context, then it would be immensely helpful if we could remove from our measures of foreign policy output the effects of variation due to differences in the contexts within which different nations must act. Perhaps one could adjust an indicator of affect for differences in the level of hostility or amicability concurrent in the environment. Similarly, one might be able to adjust a measure of independence/ interdependence of action to take into account the differing extents to which nations are members of international organizations and thus have thrust upon them the opportunity (or necessity) to act interdependently. The most utopian vision for the use of index numbers would involve being able to remove source bias from event data through some kind of indexing adjustment.

The type of measurement program proposed here in many cases may be impossible given our current state of knowledge of foreign policy. Such a program would require, first, that we have a measure which validly captures the relevent variation in the property to be assessed before we can justify much effort in seeking to rid the measure of irrelevant variation. Once this requirement is met, we need a valid way of measuring the irrelevant variation before we can take it out of the measure. For many, if not most, properties of foreign policy behavior, these requirements are not met well at this juncture in the comparative study of foreign policy.

TESTING THE QUALITY OF
THE SET OF MEASURES

The preceding two areas of unfinished work dealt with how well one can measure some aspect of foreign policy behavior, either at the event level or at the national actor level. Here we return to one of the criteria that was first raised in Chapter One: The successful measurement of foreign policy will require the creation of a diverse set of measures. Although the set of variables presented in this book does indeed represent a diverse set of foreign policy properties, it is reasonable to assume that the repertoire of measures can be further expanded and improved.

In thinking about expanding the set of foreign policy activities that are conceptualized and measured, we agreed that one area of high priority would seem to be the creation of additional concepts and measures of the outcomes or impacts of foreign policy behavior. Whereas we were able to assess several types of foreign policy behavior involved in the predecisional context, decision-making process, and as outputs, we were able to operationalize successfully only one measure of outcomes of foreign policy behavior.

The other important kind of work that is needed to improve the quality of the set of measures presented here is rigorous testing of hypotheses to see whether the measures can be systematically related to other foreign policy phenomena. If the measures cannot be related to other things, we would be tempted to question their theoretical importance and to deemphasize them.

Several cautions are in order, however, before any of the measures are pruned from the set because they have failed to bear theoretical fruit. First, there may be a fundamental difference between measures as to the levels of analysis at which they reveal variation. Most of the measures produce considerable variation at both the event and nation levels of analysis. Some, however, such as commitment and specificity, produce negligible variation when aggregated to the nation level. This is probably the case because characteristics of the context of action, which fluctuate at a fairly rapid pace, have an effect on these behaviors. Second, as Callahan and

Swanson argue in their chapters on commitment and specificity, respectively, there are important reasons for believing that nations may experience similar constraints about commitment and specificity which tend to produce cross-national homogeneity rather than diversity. If these arguments are correct, it would be inappropriate to use a cross-national study of measures, such as those for commitment and specificity, as a basis for drawing conclusions about their theoretical import and about their value as members of the set of foreign policy characteristics to be examined.

CONCLUSION

As we reach the end of this volume, we find ourselves not fully capable of judging the contribution that it has made to the measurement of foreign policy. Tough tests of validity remain to be conducted. Actual use of the measures in research is an agenda item for the future. The intense scrutiny of our disciplinary colleagues has scarcely begun. Certainly, we would be surprised, and perhaps disappointed, to find other scholars using these measures without modifications. For some variables, the operationalization, especially, is too closely tied to and constrained by the nature of the CREON data. Adaptation for other data sets should occur. But even when our operationalizations prove wanting, we hope and believe that the conceptualizations and the attempts at operationalization should persuade other scholars to begin thinking about these properties of foreign policy. We hope our efforts will provide guidance for their work.

Although the focus of this volume has been on the development of behavior measures through the use of event data, this concentration does not mean that progress toward a rigorous, data-based study of foreign policy or foreign policy behavior can emerge solely from the analysis of event data. Event data are useful for the things they highlight, such as political-level decisions of sufficient significance that they become public; for the operational convenience of providing an opportune, bounded unit of observation; and for their frequency of occurrence, which allows extensive statistical manipulation in the analysis stage. But event data also have weaknesses as descriptive devices. They represent the episodic rather than the persistent aspects of international politics. They better reflect decisions to begin or to cease some activity, or to increase or decrease the level of activity, than they reflect continuation of that activity. This is especially noticeable when looking at such concepts as commitment or independence/interdependence of action, where the lack of a decision to alter the level of resource expenditures or the lack of a decision to join or leave an alliance may be of equal importance to the making of such a decision.

Event data are also inherently incapable of yielding a rich representation of the substance of a foreign policy decision, in the sense of the semantic meaning of a communication. The coding schemes used to develop event data must be phrased at a fairly general level to be applicable to all instances of foreign policy action. They cannot incorporate the specific description unique to a particular, narrowly defined issue. For instance, we can note that an action is the making of a demand; we can note with varying degrees of generality the problem about which the demand is being made; and we can note whether the demand reflects friendly or hostile feelings toward the target of the demand. However, we cannot note what was demanded. Such a description of the substance of behavior, one would expect, would be a powerful kind of data for testing notions about what policy is and how strongly it affects behavior, but it cannot be derived from event data. (For an elaboration of this argument, see Callahan and Succari, 1978.)

This, however, is not to deny the potential value of foreign policy research using event data. Some years ago, two eminent social scientists (Campbell and Fiske, 1959) warned their colleagues against the fallacy of trying to devise the single, best, error-free measure of any phenomenon. One could equally well set out to tilt with windmills. Instead, they urged that research should employ multiple, differing measures having compensating biases and should compare the results that emerge with the hope that the empirical findings would converge. We therefore believe that the use of event data scored to represent multiple characteristics of behavior (as we have done in this book) and used in conjunction with other kinds of data, such as UN roll calls and budget allocations, should prove of great value in the description and analysis of foreign activity and foreign policy.

Technical Appendix

CREON Variables Used to Create the Behavior Measures

INTRODUCTION

The purpose of this appendix is to present in more detail the specific variables from the CREON event data set that were used in developing the foreign policy behavior measures described in this book. We will present a brief description of the variable and its coded categories, the number of events that fall into each category of the variable, and the reliability for the variable.

If the reader seeks more in-depth explication of the variables or the means by which they were coded, he/she should consult the appropriate coding manual. Two manuals were used in identifying events: "Procedures for the Identification of Foreign Policy Events: A Manual" (CREON Publication 1A) and "Procedures for Coding Military Conflict Events: Revision of a Manual" (CREON Publication 18B). Information on the coding of numeric variables is found in "Code Manual for Analytic Deck of Comparative Foreign Policy Events: Revised" (CREON Publication 8B). All requests for such manuals should be sent to: CREON Project, Mershon Center, Ohio State University, 199 West 10th Avenue, Columbus, Ohio 43201.

The format of this appendix is as follows. A reference number for each variable appears first, followed by the name of the variable. To the right of the formal name and in parentheses is the key word for the variable. Next to the key word is the variable number. (Any communication with the authors concerning a variable should use the formal name and variable number, not the reference number in the left margin.) Where applicable, the reliability coefficient for the variable is supplied next to the variable number. On the next line following this identification information begins a description of the variable. This description may be one line or quite extensive. Code numbers (the identification number of each category within a variable) and definitions of the categories used in coding for the variable appear below the variable description. To the left of each coding category are listed the raw frequency and percentage of events which were coded in that category.

Before presenting the variables several general comments are warranted about the CREON event data set. The data set contains two types of variables, numeric and alphabetic. The numeric variables have set values into which events are distributed. Numeric values are assigned to each of the coding categories for these variables. The alphabetic variables provide a verbal description of one particular aspect of an event. There are no code values for these variables. They are accessed through the use of key words. In order to provide some information on the alphabetic variables, they have been converted to numeric variables by ascertaining whether each variable is present (coded "one") or absent (coded "zero") in any given event. Some variables have both numeric and alphabetic forms.

At the end of the coding categories for many of the variables listed here are two codes which require further explanation: "not applicable" and "insufficient information." "Not applicable" is assigned when a particular event is a member of a class of events which cannot have the property indicated by the coding rules. "Insufficient information" occurs when the particular event must logically have the property identified by the variable, but there is not enough information to choose an appropriate category. Referring to the example in Figure A.1, one can see the difference between these two codes. In order for an event to be "not applicable," one must answer the first question "no"—that is, the event does not involve a meeting. If answered "no," the event is logically excluded from consideration on this variable. If the answer is "yes" (the event is a meeting), then the variable is coded into one of the substantive categories (1-8). If the answer is "yes" but there is insufficient information to place the event in an appropriate substantive category, then the variable is left blank. In general, "not applicable" is coded 9,99 or 999 depending on the column width of the item. "Insufficient information" is left blank or coded zero.

The method used in determining reliabilities for the variables in the CREON data set is described in Chapter 2. One reason noted there for using the Krippendorff (1971) coefficient of agreement is that the CREON data set contains some variables that involve decision trees or multilevel coding rules. Figure A.1 presents an example of a variable which forms a decision tree. In this illustration, the decision tree has two contingent decisions: did a meeting take place, and, if so, what type of meeting was it? The Krippendorff coefficient of agreement allows us to determine a single reliability for the decision tree as a whole, taking into account agreement at each decision point. It is this single agreement coefficient which is reported for variables involving decision trees.

Because the CREON Project team has been engaged in cleaning and updating the data set for a period of time, we have assigned version numbers to each new update. By referring to the version number, the reader of a particular paper using the CREON data set knows whether that form of the data set is comparable to the one used in any other CREON publication. This appendix is based on version 6.01 of the data set. The digit "six" indicates that this data set represents the sixth major expansion of the total number of events. The two digits following the decimal point refer to the number of relatively minor updates performed since the large number of new events were added. This particular version of the data set contains 12,710 events for 38 countries (see Chapter 2 for a list of the countries).

LIST OF APPENDIX CONTENTS

(Variables appear in this appendix in the order in which they are listed below and can be found by use of the reference number in the left margin.)

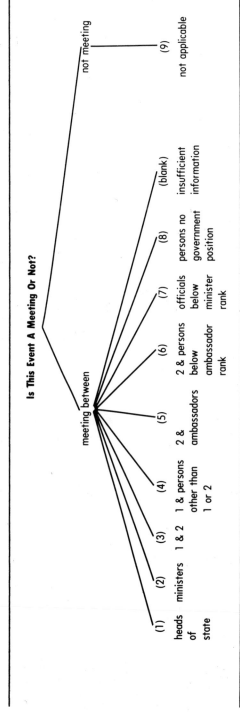

Is This Event A Meeting Or Not?

meeting between / not meeting

| (1) heads of state | (2) ministers | (3) 1 & 2 | (4) 1 & persons other than 1 or 2 | (5) 2 & ambassadors | (6) 2 & persons below ambassador rank | (7) officials below minister rank | (8) persons no government position | (blank) insufficient information | (9) not applicable |

Figure A.1 Example of a decision tree using variable, "Setting for Multinational Collaboration."

15. External Use of Military Force
16. Nature of Recipients
17. Role of Recipients
18. Sequential Action Scheme
19. Military Behavior
20. Negotiation/Bargaining Behavior
21. Treaty Behavior

22. Foreign Assistance Behavior
23. Economic Transaction Behavior
24. Head of State Involved
25. Resources Used
26. Goals
27. Response

1. Revised WEIS (WEIS REV) Var. = 6, Rel. = .84

Description: These categories constitute a revised version of the World Event/Interaction Survey (WEIS) developed by Charles McClelland and his associates (see Fitzsimmons et al., 1969) to classify the foreign actions of nations. Actions are divided first into verbal actions (words) and nonverbal actions (deeds). The verbal category is further separated into three subdivisions assumed to represent an increasing commitment toward physical action (that is, deeds). The least degree of commitment is present in those categories labeled as the actor's evaluation, or perception, of past or current international action. A higher degree of commitment is present in the categories dealing with the actor's desire for future action by self or other. Finally, the verbal categories labeled as intent include the actor's statements that he will undertake foreign action himself in the future. Intent statements contain the highest commitment possible in any verbal action. Both verbal and nonverbal actions are divided into conflictual and cooperative actions with respect to the actor's orientation toward the first foreign direct target. If no direct target is a foreign entity, then the cooperation or conflict is coded with respect to the first foreign indirect object. If the action is neutral, it is classified with the cooperative actions. These distinctions (three types of verbal behavior versus nonverbal behavior plus conflictual behavior versus cooperative/neutral behavior) locate each action in one of the eight major cells shown in Table A.1. Coders then select the most appropriate specific type of action noted in each major subdivision of Table A.1. Brief descriptions of each type of action are presented below under the eight basic divisions.

I. Evaluative Categories (perceptions of past or current action by self or target)

Raw Freq.	*%*	*1. Conflict*
936	7.4	102 = Negative Comment: Comment on situation, explain policy undesired by actor or target
666	5.2	112 = Accuse: Charge, criticize, blame, disapprove, denounce, denigrate
90	0.7	114 = Deny: Deny accusation, attributed action, or policy
		2. Cooperation
2295	18.1	202 = Positive Comment: Comment on situation, explain policy desired by actor or target, abstain on vote
531	4.2	203 = Consult: Make or receive official visit; participate in meeting involving foreign travel for at least one participant—protocol, non-substantive meetings only

TABLE A.1

Revised WEIS Categories Organized into Eight Basic Divisions

	Verbal (Words) (increasing commitment to deeds)			Nonverbal (Deeds)
	Actor's Evaluation, Perception of Past or Current Action	Actor's Desire for Future Action by Self or Target	Actor's Intent Regarding Own Possible Future Action	
Conflict	1. 102 Negative Comment 112 Accure 114 Deny	3. 309 Negative Request 310 Negative Propose 313 Protest 315 Demand	5. 502 Negative Intention 511 Reject 516 Warn 517 Threaten	7. 718 Demonstrate 719 Reduce Relationship 720 Expel 721 Seize 722 Force 723 Increase Military Capability 724 Aid Opponent 728 Subvert
Cooperation	2. 202 Positive Comment 203 Consult 204 Approve	4. 409 Positive Request 410 Positive Propose 425 Negotiate	6. 602 Positive Intention 605 Promise 608 Agree 610 Offer	8. 801 Yield 806 Grant 807 Reward 826 Decrease Military Capability 827 Carry Out Agreement 829 Increase Relationship

NOTE: The eightfold division for organizing these WEIS categories was devised by Corson (1970). At a meeting in New Brunswick, New Jersey in the spring of 1970 attended by Walter Corson, Patrick McGowan, Maurice East, Stephen Salmore, and Charles Hermann, the Corson organizing scheme was adopted for those event data projects represented that planned to use WEIS. Additional categories not included in the original 22 WEIS categories were proposed. Those additional categories appear underscored in this table. These added categories included three types of action (comment, request, and propose) that appeared in the original WEIS classification, but were not differentiated between conflictual and cooperative actions.

| 1518 | 11.9 | 204 = Approve: Praise, hail, applaud, endorse, support |

II. Desire Categories (desire for future action by self or target)

Raw Freq.	%	3. Conflict
12	0.1	309 = Negative Request: Ask for information undesired by target
271	2.1	310 = Negative Propose: Offer proposal, suggest, urge action or policy undesired by target
116	0.9	313 = Protest: Make formal or informal complaint
68	0.5	315 = Demand: Order, command, insist, demand compliance

Raw Freq.	%	4. Cooperation
39	0.3	409 = Positive Request: Ask for information desired by target
1205	9.5	410 = Positive Propose: Offer proposal, suggest, urge action or policy desired by target
642	5.1	425 = Negotiate: Participate in substantive talks, negotiations on a specific issue or interest area

III. Intent Categories (regarding actor's possible future action vis-à-vis target)

Raw Freq.	%	5. Conflict
159	1.3	502 = Negative Intention: Explain future policy undesired by target
394	3.1	511 = Reject: Turn down proposal, vote against, protest, demand, threaten; refuse, oppose, harden position
175	1.4	516 = Warn: Warn of future situation or action undesired by target; warn against action by target undesired by actor; a less specific, non-contingent category than threaten
114	0.9	517 = Threaten: Threaten to take future action against the target with or without sanction

Raw Freq.	%	6. Cooperation
476	3.7	602 = Positive Intention: Explain future action desired by target
151	1.2	605 = Promise: Assure of future action desired by target; ensures a definite commitment which is not contingent

| 790 | 6.2 | 608 = Agree: Accept proposal, agree to meet or negotiate, agree to future action; does not include the signing of formal agreements or the transfer of resources |

| 104 | 0.8 | 610 = Offer: Offer an explicit proposal for future action desired by target (of a contingent if-then nature) |

IV. Nonverbal Categories (deeds)

Raw Freq.	%	7. Conflict
48	0.4	718 = Demonstrate: Armed forces mobilization, movement, exercise, display; non-military demonstration sponsored by government
112	0.9	719 = Reduce Relationship: Cancel or postpone proposed event, meeting, boycott or walkout, reduce routine international activity, recall officials, halt negotiations, break diplomatic relations
40	0.3	720 = Expel: Expel organization, group, or personnel
49	0.4	721 = Seize: Seize position or possessions, detain or arrest personnel
96	0.8	722 = Force: Forceful or violent use of military resources, equipment to achieve objectives; military engagement, nonmilitary destruction, non-injury destruction
32	0.3	723 = Increase Military Capability: Increase military spending, troop levels; develop weapons; authorize action, reserve callups
9	0.1	724 = Aid Opponent: Give aid to opponents of target outside the borders of the target, such as granting asylum to opponents of target
9	0.1	728 = Subvert: Aid to insurgents in their own country; nonverbal attempts to influence internal politics of the target

		8. Cooperation
12	0.1	801 = Yield: Surrender, submit, retreat, evacuate
66	0.5	806 = Grant: End negative sanctions, conflict action, threat of conflict action; express regret, apologize, release or return prisoners or property

243	1.9	807 = Reward: Give or receive economic, technical, or military aid unilaterally
30	0.2	826 = Decrease Military Capability: Reduce military spending, troop levels; reduce readiness for military action
87	0.7	827 = Carry Out Agreement: Implement a previous agreement
1125	8.9	829 = Increase relationship: Increase economic, military, technical, or cultural exchanges bilaterally; includes the signing of formal agreements involving the transfer of resources

2. Number of Nations Participating in Action (ACTORNUM)
Var. = 17, Rel. = .88

Description: Although, by definition, every event has only one actor, we recognize that nations often act jointly—in conferences, alliances, and the like. If the action was taken by the actor alone, this item was coded 001; if the actor collaborated with other nations, then the total number of participants was recorded. If the action was a joint communique between two nations, it was coded as 2 participants (that is, 002). In international organizations or alliances if a divided vote occurred, then only the number of nations that voted with the actor, not the total membership, was recorded.

Raw Freq.	%	
4778	37.6	1 = Actor acts alone
2023	15.9	2 = Two nations act jointly
153	1.2	3 = Three nations act jointly
71	0.6	4 = Four nations act jointly
126	1.0	5 = Five nations act jointly
536	4.2	6 = Six nations act jointly
296	2.3	7 = Seven nations act jointly
213	1.7	8 = Eight nations act jointly
57	0.4	9 = Nine nations act jointly
166	1.3	10 = Ten nations act jointly
2327	18.3	11-79 = Eleven thru seventy-nine nations act jointly
1964	15.5	80+ = Eighty or more nations act jointly

3. Setting for Multinational Collaboration (SETTING)
Var. = 21, Rel. = .76

Description: If the action occurred in the presence of representatives from one or more other actors, then the most applicable description of the setting was coded.

Raw Freq.	%	
1326	10.4	1 = Meeting Between Heads of State or Equivalents: The delegation of each participating nation

is led by a head of state. In nations ruled by a committee recognized by the international diplomatic community as officially equal in status, any member is considered a head of state. In nations where the government is controlled by a single party, the head of the party may be regarded as equivalent in rank to the head of state. This item also includes meetings which involve the delegated representative of a head of state.

1268	10.0	2 = Meeting Between Ministers: Each country's delegation is headed by one or more ministers of a major department of the government. An official of this rank is usually identified by his title as Minister or Secretary of some named bureaucratic organization.
602	4.7	3 = Meeting Between Head of State and Minister or Ambassador: To be classified as an ambassador, the individual in question must have specific title of Ambassador.
176	1.4	4 = Meeting Between Head of State and Individuals other than Heads of State, Ministers, or Ambassadors: If one delegation is led by a head of state, and the others do not fall into categories 1,2, or 3, then this code is used.
88	0.7	5 = Meeting Between Minister and Ambassador: One delegation must involve individual of ministerial rank and others must be headed by men of ambassadorial rank.
191	1.5	6 = Meeting Between Minister and Individuals Below Ambassador Rank: This category includes meetings between a minister and any individuals without diplomatic status as well as those with a rank below ambassador.
3263	25.7	7 = Meeting Between Governmental Officials Below Ministerial Rank: All delegations led by government people but below rank of minister (could include meeting of ambassadors).
13	0.1	8 = Meeting Between Individuals with No Permanent Governmental Position: Includes contacts between private citizens and between private individuals appointed by the government to represent the country in a short-term conference or meeting.
5389	42.4	9 = Not applicable
394	3.1	Blank = Insufficient information

4. Channel Through which Action Is Announced (CHANNEL)
Var. = 23, Rel. = .76

Description: This item refers to the communication channel (as opposed to the individual) used to announce the action. This variable also appears in alphabetic format under the key word CHANNEL.

Raw Freq.	%	
1572	12.4	1 = Address or speech (even if presented to a closed group)
577	4.5	2 = Press conference or interview with an identified official
550	4.3	3 = Written message or statement, not delivered in person, to sources within the society (e.g., message to Congress); press release
2064	16.2	4 = Diplomatic communique, text of treaty or other diplomatic document between states or ruling political parties; includes notes and informal letters
360	2.8	5 = Official newspaper—that is, one controlled by rulers
50	0.4	6 = News story attributed to a government official (official need not be referred to by name, but there must be a specific reference to an official)
119	0.9	7 = News story attributed to another news source (e.g., *The New York Times* reported ...”).
149	1.2	8 = Other—identified source explicitly stated in the data source
1962	15.4	9 = Public vote
5307	41.8	Blank = Insufficient information

5. Official Position of Announcer of Action (ANNOUNCR)
Var. = 24, Rel. = .64

Description: This item identifies the individual who reports that the action has been taken. The list of categories is ordered: that is, the coder began with the first category and used it if the announcer fit the description. If not, the coder proceeded to the second category, etc.

Raw Freq.	%	
242	1.9	1 = Source outside the acting nation (including foreign journalist). IF NOT 1, THEN 2.
3784	29.8	2 = Political executive (head of government or of ruling political party or minister within acting state). IF NOT 2, THEN 3.
65	0.5	3 = Nonexecutive government official (member of legislature, judge, municipal or regional leader, etc.). IF NOT 3, THEN 4.
29	0.2	4 = Communications personnel (press secretaries, public relations officials). IF NOT 4, THEN 5.

81	0.6	5 = Military personnel. IF NOT 5, THEN 6.
8	0.1	6 = Political party official (must not have any governmental post of significance). IF NOT 6, THEN 7.
2578	20.3	7 = Career bureaucrat, including a ministerial or departmental spokesman (must not be a significant military or party official). IF NOT 7, THEN 8.
42	0.3	8 = Journalist, press or other nongovernmental source such as lobbyist (must have no known governmental, political party, or military position).
5881	46.3	Blank = Insufficient information

6. Specificity of Problem, Issue, or Topic (SPECPROB)
Var. = 26, Rel. = .74

Description: The coder is asked to answer the following questions: What problem, issue, or topic is the action intended to affect? More exactly, does the party to whom the action is addressed know what is expected of him?

Raw Freq.	%	
9886	77.8	1 = Yes
2824	22.2	2 = No

7. Specificity of Kinds of Resources (KINDRES)
Var. = 28, Rel. = .94

Description: Does the action involve more than assurance to do "something" or "talk with someone" about the issue? That is, are specific kinds of people or resources (e.g., currency) mentioned? The action need *not* be a physical deed to be coded specific. A conditional statement (threat) or any other statement of intent (offer) may be specific in terms of the kinds of resources that will be expended. Evaluative statements or other verbal statements (desire for action on the part of another nation) not involving the possibility of future resource exchange are coded not applicable.

Raw Freq.	%	
1799	14.2	1 = Yes
630	5.0	2 = No
10281	80.9	9 = Not applicable

8. Specificity as to Time or Conditions for Use of Resources (CONDITAL)
Var. = 30, Rel. = .81

Description: If the action involves the use or transfer of resources that does not occur simultaneously with the announcement of the action, does the actor specify either the time when the resources will be committed or the necessary condition for their use? If there was no transfer of resources involved, then not applicable was coded. This variable also appears in alphabetic form under the key word CONDITAL.

Raw Freq.	%	
487	3.8	1 = Yes
1942	15.3	2 = No
10281	80.9	9 = Not applicable

9. Adherence to International Agreement (AGREEMENT)
Var. = 31, Rel. = .62

Description: This item concerns those actions of states in which they enter into an agreement that in some way regulates or restricts their behavior and/or that of their citizens—in other words, agreements that restrict their sovereignty. Obviously, many international agreements do not fall into this category. Excluded are all agreements that require no real change in the behavior of the actor. Also excluded are all "simple," one-time transfers (trades, assistance loans, grants, etc.) and agreements devoid of any long-term obligation.

Raw Freq.	*%*	
34	0.3	1 = Grants access to actor's territory and the population within it for limited purposes under control of actor's government (e.g., commercial air rights)
6	0.0	2 = Permits use of territory for military noncombat purposes (e.g., leasing territory for military bases)
226	1.8	3 = Enters agreement creating privileges to others concerning transfers (e.g., tariff reductions)
32	0.3	4 = Forms alliance or "peacekeeping" arrangement which commits actor's military forces to defense of another country or government and/or allows other country to place its forces on his soil when actor's nation is threatened (e.g., Sweden enters agreement with UN to provide peacekeeping troops in Middle East)
91	0.7	5 = Agrees to regulations governing his country's use of international territories, rights of his nationals in other countries, and/or his government's participation in international organizations (e.g., sign treaty on use of outer space)
4	0.0	6 = Submits a dispute to which the actor's country is a party to binding arbitration (e.g., submits case to International Court of Justice and agrees to abide by court's decision)
12	0.1	7 = Limits or destroys part of his country's military capability or armed forces (e.g., Nuclear Non-Proliferation Treaty); if both this category and 5 are applicable, this category is given priority
10	0.1	8 = Yields partial or complete control of the right to govern a population (excluding foreign nationals) and property currently under one's jurisdiction (e.g., grant independence to colony)
12290	96.7	9 = Not applicable
5	0.0	Blank = Insufficient information

10. Transfers with Foreign Entity (TRANSFER)
Var. = 32, Rel. = .79

Description: Does the action involve the transfer of materials, services of personnel or currency to or from some foreign entity either as a grant, trade, or loan? If yes, one of the categories below indicates the nature of the transfer from the perspective of the actor. If several kinds of transfers are involved in the same transaction, the category that accounts for the largest share of the total value of the transaction is coded.

Raw Freq.	*%*		
209	1.6	01 =	Gives Grant: Actor gives materials, currency, or service of personnel to foreign entity without expectation of any payment in return; grants do not include nonreciprocal payments for war costs or other penalties paid by the actor
80	0.6	02 =	Receives Grant: Same as 01, except the actor receives something from another entity for which he is not expected to pay
143	1.1	03 =	Makes Loan: Actor lends currency or credits (an account against which goods and services can be charged) for which full immediate payment is not required, but which must be paid, usually with interest, at some future point
148	1.2	04 =	Receives Loan: Same as 03, except actor receives currency or credits from another entity for which repayment is deferred
6	0.0	05 =	Repays Loan: Actor pays for all or part of the currency or credits he obtained from another actor at some point in the past
42	0.3	06 =	Makes Sale: Actor sells materials or services of personnel for which payment in currency or precious metal is required; includes sales of goods and services for which payment is deferred (those "bought on time") or for which payment is in installments
60	0.5	07 =	Purchase: Actor buys materials or services of personnel from another entity and agrees to pay for them (at time of purchase, in installments, or with deferred payments) with currency or precious metal
164	1.3	08 =	Barter: Actor exchanges with a foreign entity one kind of commodity or service for others; in other words, the transaction occurs without currency or precious metal. If one of the parties to the transaction provides barter for part of the cost and currency for the other, code under whichever category covers the largest share of the cost
5	0.0	10 =	Pays Reparations: Actor pays foreign entity for damages the latter incurred as a result of behavior of actor, such as settlement of war damages or the like

1	0.0	11 = Receives Reparations: Same as 10, except actor receives reparations
2	0.0	12 = Currency/Precious Metal Exchange: Actor exchanges with a foreign entity one currency for another, or exchanges precious metal (gold bullion) for currency and vice versa
8	0.1	13 = Releases Detainees/POWs: Actor releases prisoners of war or other foreign individuals (e.g., persons accused of spying) without receiving any payment or individuals in return
6	0.0	14 = Exchanges Detainees/POWs: Actor exchanges with foreign entity POWs or other individuals held in the country for release of individuals held in foreign entity or for some form of payment or vice versa
11831	93.1	99 = Not applicable
5	0.0	Blank = Insufficient information

11. Opponents of Action (OPPONENT)
Var. = 33, Rel. = .72

Description: Is the action known to be opposed by a group within the nation or by external entities? The opposition must be explicitly mentioned by the actor or the data source. This variable is also available in alphabetic form under the key word OPPONENT.

Raw Freq.	%	
7	0.1	1 = Reported opposition within the society, but no external opposition is mentioned
130	1.0	2 = Reported opposition includes generally friendly or allied states, but no opposition within actor's country is mentioned
37	0.3	3 = Reported opposition by other external entities but not by generally friendly or allied governments
0	0.0	4 = Reported opposition both within actor's country and external to it, including governments friendly or allied with actor
1	0.0	5 = Reported opposition both within actor's country and external to it, but not including generally friendly or allied governments
835	6.6	6 = Relationship between actor and opponent not known; coded also in the event of a divided vote in the context of an international organization
11700	92.1	Blank = Opponent unidentified or nonexistent

12. Acting Agency Has Needed Authority (OKNEEDED)
Var. = 34, Rel. = .66

Description: Assuming that some operational bureau or department (e.g., foreign ministry) was given responsibility for the present action, was the cost or the gravity of the situation such that approval from the highest authorities of government was required? More specifically, the coder was asked the following questions: (a) Does the action appear to have far-reaching consequences for the future of the present government or its basic policies? (b) Does the action involve real financial expenditures considerably in excess of what it would cost to send a two- or three-man delegation to a meeting anywhere in the world? (c) Is the action one that neither occurs regularly for this country nor one that the government likely anticipated months in advance? If the answer to all three questions was yes, then category 1 was coded. If question (a) was answered yes, but either (b) or (c) was answered no, then category 2 was coded. If question (a) was answered no, but both (b) and (c) were answered yes, then category 3 was coded. If all three questions were answered no, then category 4 was coded. If the head of state was specifically mentioned as involved in the decision, then category 5 was coded.

Raw Freq.	%	
667	5.2	1 = Approval of higher authority probably necessary on both substance of action and financial expenditures
3480	27.4	2 = Approval of higher authority probably necessary on substance of action
249	2.0	3 = Approval of higher authority probably necessary for financial expenditures
4631	36.4	4 = No approval of higher authority probable
3236	25.5	5 = Head of state or highest authority participated directly in the decision or the execution of the action; hence, no appeal to higher internal authority possible
447	3.5	Blank = Insufficient information

13. Number of Personnel Moving Temporarily (TEMPMOVE)
Var. = 36, Rel. = .82

Description: Does the action involve temporary assignment across national boundaries of governmental representatives? (Excluded are military personnel with the exception of high-level military decision makers and military personnel assigned to diplomatic duty.) If no, then the item is not applicable. If yes, that category is chosen which best indicates the approximate number of policymaking individuals.

Raw Freq.	%	
3497	27.5	1 = 1 to 2 individuals
177	1.4	2 = 3 to 5 individuals
60	0.5	3 = 6 to 10 individuals
131	1.0	4 = 11 to 15 individuals
11	0.1	5 = 16 to 20 individuals
1	0.0	6 = 21 to 30 individuals
0	0.0	7 = 31 to 50 individuals
7	0.1	8 = More than 50 individuals
8821	69.4	9 = Not applicable
5	0.0	Blank = Insufficient information

14. Internal Military Mobilization (INTMOBIL)
Var. = 38, Rel. = 1.00

Description: Does the behavior involve preparation for military action within the actor's own country, such as increasing the number of men in the armed forces, relocating nonessential civilians, deploying military forces to borders or staging points, or putting forces on "alert" status? Notice that such internal behavior can take place even if the action also involves other activity outside the boundaries of the acting nation.

Raw Freq.	*%*	
34	0.3	1 = Yes
12676	99.7	9 = Not applicable (no mobilization)

15. External Use of Military Force (EXTFORCE)
Var. = 39, Rel. = 1.00

Description: Does the action directly involve any use of military force outside the actor's nation? If no, then the item is not applicable. If yes, the most appropriate category is chosen. This variable is also available in alphabetic form under the key word EXTFORCE.

Raw Freq.	*%*	
1	0.0	1 = Use of military equipment or personnel for nonmilitary purposes, such as search for crash victims
17	0.1	2 = Reinforcement of bases abroad, placement of bases or overseas troops on alert status
9	0.1	3 = Actual evacuation or rescue of civilians or nonessential military personnel
34	0.3	4 = Show of force in location where actor's forces had not been recently. Shows of force that do not violate other nation's sovereignty by staying in international territory or by having permission from host government should be included. This category includes war games and military exercises conducted outside actor's country.
32	0.3	5 = Supply equipment to foreign entity actually engaged in combat
17	0.1	6 = Supply military advisers to foreign entity actually engaged in combat. (This category is used if equipment is being supplied in addition to advisers.)
57	0.4	7 = Engage in air or sea nonnuclear attacks or bombardments against foreign entity
45	0.4	8 = Engage in ground combat and/or nuclear air or sea attacks
12498	98.3	9 = Not applicable
0	0.0	Blank = Insufficient information

16. Nature of Recipients (Targets and Objects) NATTARG 1-9) (NATOBJ 1-9) Var. = 59-77, Rel. for Targets = .64, Rel. for Objects = .80

Description: This set of categories indicates the nature of the recipients of the action—that is, a description of the targets and objects toward which the activity is directed by the actor. Data were recorded for up to nine targets and nine objects. The frequencies and percentages reported here represent a summation across targets and objects. Given the possibility of multiple targets and objects for an event, the total number of recipients (30,209) exceeds the total number of events (12,710).

Raw Freq.	%	
247	0.8	1 = Domestic readership of official newspapers
439	1.5	2 = Domestic political meeting, conference, rally, etc.
430	1.4	3 = Other domestic audience
12596	41.7	4 = External governmental participants in conference or other setting with the actor
974	3.2	5 = External governmental officials *not* in same setting with actor (must be mentioned by name, position, or as "the government of nation X")
942	3.1	6 = External populations, publics, or colonies— this category should be for mass publics not differentiated into organized groups (for those, see Category 8)
264	0.9	7 = External officials of international or regional organizations (must be mentioned by name or position)
1636	5.4	8 = External nongovernmental (i.e., nonruling) individuals, groups, or organizations
12681	42.0	9 = Undifferentiated target

17. Role of Recipients (Targets and Objects) (ROLETARG 1-9) (ROLEOBJ 1-9) Var. = 96-113, Rel. = .83

Description: This variable classifies recipients (targets and objects) of an action according to the logic or rule which makes them a part of the event. What is the nature of the role the recipient is playing in the event? Data were recorded for up to nine targets and nine objects. The frequencies and percentages reported here represent a summation across targets and objects. Given the possibility of multiple targets and objects for an event, the total number of recipients (30,209) exceeds the total number of events (12,710).

Raw Freq.	%	
2248	7.4	1 = Special Rules: recipients not explicitly referenced by the actor's behavior nor found in the event's context are coded here if they fit under special rules regarding crises, ongoing conflicts, and the Berlin situation
725	2.4	2 = Mentioned: recipients explicitly referenced by actor's behavior but unrelated to substance of event

237	0.7	3 = Facilitator: recipient whose sole purpose in event is to make the action of the event easier or more convenient
1062	3.5	4 = Recipient's Policy Subject: target or object which one of the recipients of the present event is trying to influence through its past, present, or future behavior
1995	6.6	5 = Indirect Addressee: recipient that the actor refers to in an event without mentioning specific policies or behaviors of said recipient and without establishing direct contact or communication with them in the event
7679	25.4	6 = Indirect Policy: recipient whose policies or behavior the actor mentions in the event without establishing direct contact or communication with them in the event
2483	8.2	7 = Direct Addressee: recipient the actor is clearly trying to influence by its behavior
4459	14.8	8 = Direct Policy: recipient whose policies or behavior actor is explicitly trying to influence in the event
9321	30.9	9 = Participants: foreign entities that are acting jointly with the actor in the event

18. Sequential Action Scheme

The Sequential Action Scheme (SAS) provides information on a series of properties of the action, target(s), and object(s) in every event. An overview of the scheme is presented as a flow diagram in Figure A.2. One of the distinctive features of the SAS appears in Figure A.2: a large number of nominal categories have been organized into clusters that are coded in a chain or sequence. Many of the decisions in subsequent sections of the scheme are partly determined by the coder's previous choices. The entire set of properties in the scheme is represented by a six-column field with the first four columns characterizing the action and a two-column code summarizing each direct target and indirect object in the event.

The individual categories with their frequencies and percentages are presented by column and section following the organization shown in Figure A.2. Each column of the SAS is treated as a variable with its own range of values and its own identifying information for the variable numbers. Reliabilities for the scheme pose a special problem and are reported after all the categories in the scheme have been presented.

Word/Deed—Column 1 (WORDEED) Var. = 114

Description: Column 1 of the SAS is subdivided into three sections. Section 1 concerns whether an event is a word or a deed, Section 2 deals with what kind of word it is, and Section 3 deals with what kind of deed it is. Word is defined as behavior which does not involve the actual commitment of resources. Deeds always involve the use of actual resources, or regulations governing the use of the society's resources. Because the word/deed distinction is revealed in the difference between Sections 2 and 3, no frequencies or percentages are displayed for Section 1.

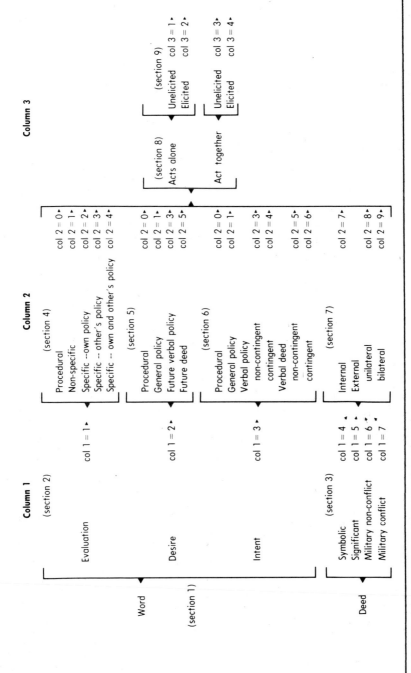

Figure A.2 A flow diagram of the sequential action scheme.

(Continued)

Column 4
(section 10)

Verbal act — col 4 = 0

(section 11)
- Resource use completed with announcement
  - Increase or initiate — col 4 = 1
  - Same — col 4 = 2
  - Decrease — col 4 = 3

(section 12)
- Resource use continues to definite date
  - Increase or initiate — col 4 = 4
  - Same — col 4 = 5
  - Decrease — col 4 = 6

(section 13)
- Resource use continues to indefinite date
  - Increase or initiate — col 4 = 7
  - Same — col 4 = 8
  - Decrease — col 4 = 9

Column 5
(section 14)

(for each target and object)
- Domestic target or object — col 5 = 0
- Actor sees action as desired by external entity — col 5 = 1
- Action neutral — col 5 = 2
- Actor sees action as undesired by external entity — col 5 = 3

Column 6
(section 15)

(for each target and object)
- National entity (in general) or authoritative actor — col 6 = 1
- National entity -- non-authoritative, supportive — col 6 = 3
- National entity -- non-authoritative, non-supportive, internal — col 6 = 4
- National entity -- non-authoritative, non-supportive, external — col 6 = 5
- International organization — col 6 = 6
- Domestic audience -- governmental or political — col 6 = 7
- Domestic audience -- other — col 6 = 8
- Colony — col 6 = 9

Figure A.2 (Continued)

Section 2: Verbal Behavior

Raw Freq.	%	
5349	42.1	1 = Statements of Evaluation (Word): Evaluative statements are those that imply no action on the part of the actor; nor do they express any action desired by the actor of an external entity
3759	29.6	2 = Statements of Desire (Word): Those statements that express the actor's wishes as to what they would like (want, desire) an external entity to do in the future
1654	13.0	3 = Statements of Intent (Word): Statements that mention possible future action by the actor

Section 3: Nonverbal Behavior

865	6.8	4 = Symbolic Deeds: Those deeds involving only minor resource commitment which would be regarded as "insignificant" given the total income of the actor government; in other words, the necessary resources can be readily absorbed by the actor within its existing budget and without special allocation
707	5.6	5 = Significant Deeds: Those deeds that represent a significant budgetary commitment on the part of the acting government, often requiring a special allocation or requiring a relocation of existing budgetary allocations
212	1.7	6 = Military Nonconflict Deeds: Actions involving the use of military resources in nonconflict situations, but for military purposes
164	1.3	7 = Military Conflict Deeds: Actions that engage the actor in the use of force in times of actual combat

Word/Deed Properties—Column 2 (PROPERTIES) Var. = 116

Description: Column 2 is strictly dependent on the first column of the scheme and is broken down into four sections (4 through 7) according to the type of word or deed specified in Column 1.

Section 4: Extension of Evaluative Category

Raw Freq.	%	
395	3.1	0 = Procedural: Events having to do with the physical formalities and arrangements by which some activity is to be carried out, even when the activity itself is substantive

| 1164 | 9.2 | 1 = Nonspecific: Evaluative comments that refer to a past or present behavior, situation, or policy in abstract or general terms and contain no mention of any identifiable event or series of events and no allusions to specific known occurrences |

| 519 | 4.1 | 2 = Specific—Own Policy: The actor comments on a specific past or present behavior, situation, or policy that involves decision making by the actor's government |

| 1334 | 10.5 | 3 = Specific—Other's Policy: The actor comments on a specific past or present behavior, situation, or policy involving decision making by an external entity |

| 1937 | 15.2 | 4 = Specific—Own and Others: The actor comments on a specific past or present behavior, situation, or policy that involves decision making by the actor and one or more external entities; both the actor and an external entity having decision-making authority or responsibility, have taken action in the situation being discussed in the event, and the substance of the event includes comment on both entities' roles |

Section 5: Extension of Desire Category

Raw Freq.	*%*	
33	0.3	0 = Procedural: Events having to do with the physical formalities and arrangements by which some activity is to be carried out, even when the activity itself is substantive
512	4.0	1 = General Policy: Statements that express a future policy hoped for or expected of an external entity, but expressed in vague or general terms so that the external entity cannot tell what is expected of it
1523	12.0	3 = Future Verbal Policy: A specific verbal activity that the actor hopes or expects of an external entity
1691	13.3	5 = Future Deed: A specific deed (i.e., a resource use) that the actor hopes or expects an external entity to undertake

Section 6: Extension of Intent Category

Raw Freq.	*%*	
48	0.4	0 = Procedural: Events having to do with the physical formalities and arrangements by which some activity is to be carried out, even when the activity itself is substantive

287	2.3	1 = General Policy: A statement in which the actor describes its own future policy in vague or general terms so that it is not clear what specific activities the actor intends to undertake
447	3.5	3 = Verbal Policy Noncontingent: A specific verbal activity the actor states it will do without implying any conditions or contingency
86	0.7	4 = Verbal Policy Contingent: A specific verbal activity the actor explicitly states will happen only if there is a specific future action or nonaction on the part of an external entity or entities
521	4.1	5 = Verbal Deed Noncontingent: A future deed by the actor without any conditions involved
265	2.1	6 = Verbal Deed Contingent: A specific future action by the actor contingent on some explicit action or nonaction on the part of an external entity or entities

Section 7: Extension of Deeds Category

Raw Freq.	%	
222	1.7	7 = Internal: Deeds whose aspects for the actor take place wholly within the borders of the actor even though the effects of the action will be on an external entity
397	3.1	8 = External Unilateral: Actions that involve the actor's resources actually crossing its borders, and that the actor can complete alone without any concomitant act on the part of a target or object
1329	10.5	9 = External Bilateral: Actions that involve the actor's resources actually crossing its borders, and require simultaneous behavior by both the actor and either target or object in order to be completed or executed

Collaborative and Elicited Actions—Column 3 (ELICIT) Var. = 117

Description: Column 3 of the SAS concerns whether the actor's nation acts alone or with some other entity (Section 8), and whether the action was elicited from some other entity or was unelicited (Section 9). Elicited actions are the actor's responses to the behavior of another authoritative actor who explicitly requested some response from the present actor. Unelicited actions are all others. Unlike the previous column, this one is not contingent on previous coding decisions. Although coders first make decisions about collaboration and then about whether the behavior was elicited, the two sections are combined to create a single set of categories.

Sections 8-9: Collaborative and Elicited Actions

Raw Freq.	%	
4638	36.5	1 = Acts alone unelicited

483	3.8	2 = Acts alone elicited
6801	53.5	3 = Act together unelicited
788	6.2	4 = Act together elicited

Resource Commitment—Column 4 (COMITRES) Var. = 118

Description: Column 4 concerns the commitment of resources and their level. Distinctions are made among (a) verbal actions involving no resources (Section 10), (b) deeds consuming resources only simultaneously with the announcement of the deed (Section 11), (c) deeds committing resources for a specific length of time (Section 12), and (d) deeds committing resources for an indefinite period (Section 13). Because verbal acts are defined as not involving resources, these behaviors are identified in order to eliminate them from further differentiation in Column 4. Sections 11-13 distinguish among three levels of resource commitment in relation to past efforts.

Section 10: Eliminating Verbal Acts

| *Raw Freq.* | % | |
| 10755 | 84.6 | 0 = Verbal act |

Section 11: Resource Use Completed with Announcement or Within One Year

Raw Freq.	%	
599	4.7	1 = Increase or initiate new level of commitment
18	0.1	2 = Same—maintain past level of commitment
130	1.0	3 = Decrease past level of commitment

Section 12: Resource Use Continues to Definite Date of More Than One Year

Raw Freq.	%	
135	1.1	4 = Increase or initiate new level of commitment
28	0.2	5 = Same—maintain past level of commitment
13	0.1	6 = Decrease past level of commitment

Section 13: Resource Use Continues Indefinitely

Raw Freq.	%	
952	7.5	7 = Increase or initiate new level of commitment
24	0.2	8 = Same—maintain past level of commitment
56	0.4	9 = Decrease past level of commitment

Anticipated Desirability to Recipient—Column 5 (DESIRE) Var. = 119-136

Description: Column 5 (Section 14) asks the question: "Does the actor believe that the foreign target or object will view this action as desirable, undesirable, or neutral?" This question, which is recording information on hostility and friendliness and therefore is related to the Affect variable, is answered with respect to each separate direct target and indirect object in the event. The coding of anticipated desirability constitutes a separate variable for each object and target in the event with a maximum of nine targets and nine objects. Because events can have multiple targets and objects, the total number of recipients exceeds the total number of events.

Section 14: Anticipated Desirability

Raw Freq.	%	
1122	3.7	0 = Domestic Target or Object: Actions directed toward groups within actor's nation, but which have effects on foreign entities
17233	57.0	1 = Desired Actions: Those actions which the actor believes the target will view as desirable
5319	17.6	2 = Neutral Actions: Those actions which the actor believes the target will view as neutral
6535	21.6	3 = Undesired Actions: Those actions which the actor believes the target will view as undesirable

Recipient Differentiation—Column 6 (RECEIVER) Var. = 137-154

Description: Column 6 (Section 15) consists of a series of categories for grouping different kinds of targets and objects. As such, it is related to the Nature of Recipient variable. In every event each target up to a maximum of nine and each object up to a maximum of nine are separately coded into one of the eight recipient differentiation categories. Because events can have multiple targets and objects, the number of recipients exceeds the number of events.

Section 15: Recipient Differentiation

Raw Freq.	%	
16587	54.9	1 = National Entity (in General) or Authoritative Actor: Includes names of entire nations or government officials; i.e., an individual who speaks on behalf of the government
291	1.0	3 = National Entity—Nonauthoritative, Supportive Actor: Includes anyone who is not an official spokesman for the government
1225	4.1	4 = National Entity—Nonauthoritative, Nonsupportive Actor, Internal: Includes internal opponents of the regime (e.g., Vietcong, East Pakistani rebels)
121	0.4	5 = National Entity—Nonauthoritative, Nonsupportive Actor, External: Includes external opponents of the government (e.g., Cuban rebels in Florida, black Rhodesian exile groups in Zambia)
10047	33.3	6 = International Organizations: Any international grouping; includes both organizations and alliances
442	1.5	7 = Domestic Audience—Governmental or Political: Any group of government officials, elected officeholders, political party members (whether or not the party is in power)

| 674 | 2.2 | 8 = Domestic Audience—Other: Any domestic audience other than governmental or political |
| 822 | 2.7 | 9 = Colony: Any governmental entity whose foreign policy is legally under the control of another entity and is not recognized as an independent nation |

Reliabilities for the Sequential Action Scheme: Because of the large number of possible, theoretically interesting combinations that can be derived from groupings of various columns of the action scheme, no single reliability score exists for each column. Rather, various cuts from the action scheme have been devised to meet the needs of the principal investigators' theoretical interests, and reliabilities have been computed for these cuts. At present, nine separate reliabilities exist, but it is important to note that any number of reliabilities is possible depending on which segments of the action scheme one might be interested in analyzing. For simplicity, the reliabilities computed to date are listed 1 through 9. The segments used are listed below. Referring back to the decision tree idea developed earlier, the first column or word listed represents the first coder decision and the following column (or bracketed words) indicates the contingent coding decision. In reading through these, the reader should refer to the discussion of the action scheme.

(1) Column 1, word [evaluative (1), desire (2), intent (3)] versus deed [symbolic (4), significant (5), military (6 and 7)]. Reliability = .84.
(2) Column 1, word [evaluative (1), desire (2), intent (3)] and column 2 [all items that follow from column 1 (word)]. Reliability = .64.
(3) Column 1, deed [symbolic (4), significant (5), military nonconflict (6), military conflict (7)] and column 2 [all items that follow from column 1 (deed)]. Reliability = .76.
(4) Column 1 [word (1, 2, 3) and deed (4, 5, 6, 7)] and column 4 [0 if word, 1-9 if deed]. Reliability = .73.
(5) Column 5, domestic (0) versus external [desired (1), neutral (2), undesired (3)]. Reliability = .90.
(6) Column 3, acts alone [unelicited (1), elicited (2)] versus act together [unelicited (3), elicited (4)]. Reliability = .83.
(7) Column 1 [word (1, 2, 3) and deed (4, 5, 6, 7)] and column 6 [internal target (7, 8, 9) and external target (1, 3, 4, 5, 6)]. Reliability = .91.
(8) Column 6 [all targets uncombined, noncontingent on any other column]. Reliability = .96.
(9) Column 1 [word (1, 2, 3) and deed (4, 5, 6, 7)] and column 5 [desired (1), neutral (2), undesired (3)]. Reliability = .78.

19. Military Behavior (MILITARY) Var. = 159, Rel. = .73

Description: Military Behavior is any past, present, proposed, or planned behavior involving the use of military resources or military personnel. This pertains to actor, target, or object.

Raw Freq.	%	
1461	11.5	1 = Propose or request military behavior
932	7.3	2 = Actual agreement for or execution of military behavior
10317	81.2	5 = Military behavior not present

20. Negotiation/Bargaining Behavior (BARGAIN) Var. = 161, Rel. = .81

Description: Negotiation/Bargaining Behavior is defined as behavior in which representatives of the actor's country meet representatives of other entities and substantive issues or problems are discussed (that is, the interaction is not described in strictly social or protocol terms). This excludes signing of treaties.

Raw Freq.	%	
7347	57.8	1 = Negotiation behavior present
5363	42.2	5 = Negotiation behavior not present

21. Treaty Behavior (TREATY) Var. = 164, Rel. = .82

Description: Treaty Behavior is behavior proposing, discussing, establishing, involving, or altering (including terminating) a contractual relationship between two or more nations in which they are signatories to a written document that (1) does not include a permanent secretariat or other full-time group to administer the activities of the treaty, and (2) does not involve a one-time loan or other single exchange economic transaction.

Raw Freq.	%	
916	7.2	1 = Treaty behavior present
11794	92.8	5 = Treaty behavior not present

22. Foreign Assistance Behavior (ASSIST) Var. = 167, Rel. = .82

Description: Foreign Assistance Behavior is behavior that involves currency or resources furnished by one country or group of countries to one or more other countries for which either *no* payment in currency or resources is required or payment is deferred; that is, it involves establishing a loan or the granting of credits.

Raw Freq.	%	
96	0.8	1 = Propose or request loan or credit
324	2.5	2 = Actual agreement, announcement, or transfer of loan or credit
173	1.4	3 = Propose or request other foreign assistance
253	2.0	4 = Actual agreement, announcement, or transfer of other foreign assistance
11864	93.3	5 = No foreign assistance behavior present

23. Economic Transaction Behavior (ECONTRAN) Var. = 169, Rel. = .77

Description: Economic Transaction Behavior is behavior involving an announcement, actual execution of activity, or consideration of rules governing activity dealing with the exchange of currency or resources between nations or groups of nations. In contrast to foreign assistance, economic transactions must be reciprocal; that is, all parties to the transactions are recipients as well as suppliers.

Raw Freq.	%	
229	1.8	1 = Propose or request economic transaction
351	2.8	2 = Actual agreement, announcement, or execution of economic transaction
24	0.2	3 = Propose termination of economic transaction
10	0.1	4 = Actual termination of economic transaction
12096	95.2	5 = No economic transaction behavior present

24. Head of State Involved (HEAD) Var. = 175, Rel. = .91

Description: This variable indicates whether presidents, prime ministers, premiers, vice presidents, their press secretaries, or ruling party secretaries of one-party systems were involved in making a particular decision.

Raw Freq.	%	
9366	73.7	0 = Head of state absent
3344	26.3	1 = Head of state present

25. Resources Used (RESOURCES) Var. = 187, Rel. = .64

Description: This variable records in specific amounts all proposed and actual uses of resources. Resources expended by the actor, targets, or objects are coded. The nation expending the resources and the nature of the resources are explicitly described. If no resources are utilized in the event, then the item is left blank. There are two locations in the data set for the listing of the resource variable. The presence or absence of the variable is reported in numeric form as indicated in the frequency distributions below. The other listing is in alphabetic form and can be accessed by using the key word RESOURCE. It includes the country expending the resources and the exact quantity of resources reported by the data source.

Raw Freq.	%	
9930	78.1	0 = Resources absent
2780	21.9	1 = Resources present

26. Goals (GOALS) Var. = 202, Rel. = .63

Description: A goal is a statement of a future condition of domestic or international affairs desired by the acting nation. The future condition may require a change in the present state of affairs or may involve the maintenance of the present state. Two types of goals have been distinguished. First-order goals deal with the immediate purposes of the action. Second-order goals concern broader, long-term purposes which the action is designed to serve. In order to indicate the frequency with which first- and second-order goals appear in the alphabetic data, we have accessed the subkey words FIRST and SECOND and reported the frequencies and percentages found for each directly below the present-absent distributions. The presence or absence of goals for a particular event is in numeric form and the frequency distribution appears below. The substance of the goals is in alphabetic form using the key word GOALS to access the data. The alphabetic data include, in the following order: (a) whether the goal was first order (FIRST) or second order (SECOND); (b) what the goal was; and (c) the rule used by the coder to justify the inclusion of the goal. A goal may indicate negative as well as positive desires.

Raw Freq.	%	
5142	40.5	0 = Goal absent (present/absent variable)
7568	59.5	1 = At least one goal present (present/absent variable)
4840	64.0	1 = First-order goals (type of goal variable)
2727	36.0	2 = Second-order goals (type of goal variable)

27. Response (RESPONSE) Var. = 227 & 228, Rel. = .75

Description: Response concerns the linkage between the present event and some prior activity. In response, the previous occurrence must involve an entity other than the government which initiates the present event. In brief, response asks: Is the present event triggered or stimulated by the previous actions of external actors or the prior internal activity of some entity other than the governmental actor identified in the present event? The presence or absence of response appears in numeric form in the frequency distribution below. The substance of the response is in alphabetic form which can be accessed through the use of the key word RESPONSE. The alphabetic data include, in the following order: (a) whether a response was inferred by the coder (CODER INFERS) or related explicitly by the source (SOURCE RELATES) or the actor (ACTOR RELATES); (b) whether the source of the prior behavior was inside the nation (INTERNAL) or outside (EXTERNAL); (c) whether the prior action was a request (REQUEST) or not (NO REQUEST); (d) the affect (PLEASED, DIS-PLEASED, or INDIFFERENT) of the prior behavior from the present actor's perspective; and (e) if a request was made, how the present action answers the request (IGNORES REQUEST, PARTIALLY FULFILLS REQUEST, FULFILLS REQUEST, REJECTS REQUEST). Since the affect of the prior behavior from the actor's perspective and whether or not the present actor answered a request were used in generating the acceptance and rejection measures, the frequency distributions for these variables are also listed below.

Raw Freq.	%	
8502	66.9	0 = Response absent
4208	33.1	1 = Response present
2289	54.4	1 = No request
308	7.3	2 = Rejects request
94	2.2	3 = Ignores request
228	5.4	4 = Partially fulfills request
1289	30.6	5 = Fulfills request
1908	45.3	1 = Actor pleased
207	4.9	2 = Actor indifferent
2093	49.7	3 = Actor displeased

References

Agnew, A. C., & Kegley, C. W., Jr. *Reciprocity and symmetry in interstate interactions: An attribute foreign policy behavior in dyadic relationship?* Unpublished manuscript, Department of Government and International Studies, University of South Carolina, 1977.

Alexandroff, A., Rosecrance, R., & Stein, A. History, quantitative analysis, and the balance of power. *Journal of Conflict Resolution,* 1977, *21,* 35-56.

Alger, C. F., & Brams, S. Patterns of representation in national capitals and intergovernmental organizations. *World Politics,* 1967, *19*(4), 646-663.

Alker, H. R. Supranationalism in the United Nations. In J. N. Rosenau (Ed.), *International politics and foreign policy* (2nd ed.). New York: Free Press, 1969. Pp. 697-710.

Alker, H. R., & Russett, B. M. *World politics in the general assembly.* New Haven: Yale University Press, 1965.

Allison, G. T. *The essence of decision: Explaining the Cuban missile crisis.* Boston: Little, Brown, 1971.

Allison, G. T., & Halperin, M. H. Bureaucratic politics: A paradigm and some policy implications. In R. Tanter & R. H. Ullman (Eds.), *Theory and policy in international relations.* Princeton: Princeton University Press, 1972. Pp. 40-79.

Almond, G. A., & Powell G. Bingham, Jr. *Comparative politics: A Developmental approach.* Boston: Little, Brown, 1966.

Aron, R. *Peace and war.* New York: Praeger, 1966.

Azar, E. E. Analysis of international events. *Peace Research Review,* 1970, *4* (1).

Azar, E. E. *Conflict and peace data bank: A codebook.* Chapel Hill: Studies of Conflict and Peace, University of North Carolina, 1971.

Azar, E. E. *Probe for peace: Small state hostilities.* Minneapolis: Burgess Publishing, 1973.

Azar, E. E., Cohen, S. H., Jukam, T. O., & McCormick, J. M. Making and measuring the international event as a unit of analysis. In E. E. Azar, R. A. Brody, & C. A. McClelland (Eds.), *International events interaction analysis.* Beverly Hills, CA: Sage, 1972. Pp. 59-77. (a)

Azar, E. E., Cohen, S. H., Jukam, T. O., & McCormick, J. M. Problems of source coverage in the uses of international events data. *International Studies Quarterly,* 1972, *16,* 273-88. (b)

Babbie, E. R. *The practice of social research.* Belmont, CA: Wadsworth, 1975.

Bailey, T. A. *The art of diplomacy: The American experience.* New York: Appleton-Century-Crofts, 1968.

Barghoorn, F. C. *Soviet foreign propaganda.* Princeton: Princeton University Press, 1964.

Becker, H. S. Notes on the concept of commitment. *American Journal of Sociology,* 1960, *66,* 32-40.

Bemis, S. F. *A diplomatic history of the United States* (5th ed.). New York: Holt, Rinehart & Winston, 1965.

Blau, P. M. Interaction: Social exchange. In D. L. Sells (Ed.), *International encyclopedia of the social sciences* (vol. 7). New York: Free Press, 1968. Pp. 452-57.

Blechman, B. M., & Kaplan, S. S. *Force without war: U.S. armed forces as a political instrument.* Washington, DC: Brookings Institution, 1978.

Blechman, B. M., & Kaplan, S. S. U.S. military forces as a political instrument. *Political Science Quarterly*, 1979, *95* (2), 193-209.

Bloomfield, L. P. *The foreign policy process: Making theory relevant.* Beverly Hills, CA: Sage, 1974.

Brady, L. P. *Threat, decision time and awareness: The impact of situational variables on foreign policy behavior.* Unpublished doctoral dissertation, Ohio State University, 1974.

Brady, L. P. Explaining foreign policy using transitory qualities of situations. Paper presented at the American Political Science Association meeting, Los Angeles, California, September 2-5, 1975.

Brady, L. P. The situation in foreign policy. In M. A. East, S. A. Salmore, & C. F. Hermann (Eds.), *Why nations act: Theoretical perspectives for comparative foreign policy studies.* Beverly Hills, CA: Sage, 1978. Pp. 173-190.

Braybrooke, D., & Lindblom, C. E. *A strategy of decision.* New York: Free Press, 1963.

Brecher, M. *The foreign policy system of Israel: Setting, images, process.* New Haven: Yale University Press, 1972.

Brecher, M. Toward a theory of international crisis behavior: A preliminary report. *International Studies Quarterly*, 1977, *21*, 39-74.

Brewer, T. L. *Foreign policy situations: American elite responses to variations in threat, time, and surprise.* Beverly Hills, CA: Sage, 1972.

Brody, R. A. Some systemic effects of the spread of nuclear weapons technology. *Journal of Conflict Resolution*, 1963, *7*, 663-753.

Brunner, R. D., & Brewer, G. D. *Organized complexity: Empirical theories of political development.* New York: Free Press, 1971.

Brzezinski, Z., & Huntington, S. P. *Political power: USA/USSR.* New York: Viking Press, 1964.

Burgess, P., & Lawton, R. W. *Indicators of international behavior: An assessment of events data research.* Beverly Hills, CA: Sage, 1972.

Burrowes, R. Mirror, mirror on the wall . . . A comparison of sources of external event data. In J. N. Rosenau (Ed.), *Comparing foreign policy: Theories, findings, and methods.* New York: Halsted Press, 1974.

Butler, F. F., & Taylor, S. Toward an explanation of consistency and adaptability in foreign policy behavior: The role of political accountability. Paper presented at the Midwest Political Science Association meeting, Chicago, Illinois, May 1-3, 1975.

Callahan, P. *Third party response behavior in foreign policy.* Unpublished doctoral dissertation, Ohio State University, 1975.

Callahan, P. Value deprivation, value indulgence, and foreign policy: An initial analysis. Paper presented at the International Studies Association meeting, St. Louis, March 16-20, 1977.

Callahan, P., & Succari, E. Foreign policy positions in UN conferences: Measurement and interpretation. Paper presented at the Midwest Political Science Association meeting, February 22-25, 1978.

Campbell, D. T., & Fiske, D. W. Convergent and discriminant validation by the multitrait—multimethod matrix. *Psychological Bulletin*, 1959, *56*, 81-105.

Campbell, J. F. *The foreign affairs fudge factory.* New York: Basic Books, 1971.

Cimbala, S. J. Foreign policy as an issue-area: A roll call analysis. *American Political Science Review*, 1969, *63*, 148-56.

Clausen, A. R. *How congressmen decide: A policy focus.* New York: St. Martin's Press, 1973.

Coate, R. *Logical interdependencies in the CREON data set.* Mimeographed. Columbus: Mershon Center, Ohio State University, 1974.

Cobb, R. W., & Elder, C. *International community: A regional and global study.* New York: Holt, Rinehart & Winston, 1970.

Coombs, P. H. *The fourth dimension of foreign policy: Educational and cultural affairs.* New York: Harper & Row, 1964.

Coplin, W. D., Mills, S. L., & O'Leary, M. K. The PRINCE concepts and the study of foreign policy. In P. J. McGowan (Ed.), *Sage international yearbook of foreign policy studies* (vol. 1) Beverly Hills, CA: Sage, 1973. Pp. 73-106.

Corson, W. H. Measuring conflict and cooperation intensity in international relations. Paper presented at the First Events Data Conference, Michigan State University, February-March, 1969.

Corson, W. H. Conflict and cooperation in East-West crises: Measurement and explanation. Paper presented at the American Political Science Association meeting, Los Angeles, California, September, 1970.

Crabb, C. V., Jr. *Policy-makers and critics: Conflicting theories of American foreign policy.* New York: Praeger, 1976.

Cyert, R. M., & March, J. G. *A behavioral theory of the firm.* Englewood Cliffs, NJ: Prentice-Hall, 1963.

Dahl, R. *Who governs? Democracy and power in an American city.* New Haven: Yale University Press, 1963.

Dean, M. A., Dean, P. D. O'Leary, M. K., and Shapiro, H. B. *Instructions for abstracting and coding issue position statements.* Syracuse: International Relations Program, Syracuse University, September 1972.

DeRivera, J. H. *The psychological dimension of foreign policy.* Columbus, OH: Merrill, 1968.

de Sola Pool, I. Deterrence as an influence process. In D. G. Pruitt & R. C. Snyder (Eds.), *Theory and research on the causes of war.* Englewood Cliffs, NJ: Prentice-Hall, 1969. Pp. 189-96.

Deutsch, K. W. *The nerves of government.* New York: Free Press, 1963.

Deutsch, K. W. *The analysis of international relations.* Englewood Cliffs, NJ: Prentice-Hall, 1968.

Deutsch, K. W. *The analysis of international relations* (2nd ed.). Englewood Cliffs, NJ: Prentice-Hall, 1978.

Deutsch, K. W., & Singer, J. D. Multipolar power systems and international stability. *World Politics,* 1964, *16,* 390-406.

Doran, C. F., Pendley, R. E., & Antunes, G. F. A test of cross-national event reliability: Global versus regional sources. *International Studies Quarterly,* 1973, *17,* 175-203.

Duncan, R. B. Characteristics of organizational environments and perceived environmental uncertainty. *Administrative Science Quarterly,* 1972, *17,* 313-27.

East, M. A. Size and foreign policy behavior: A test of two models. *World Politics,* 1973, *25,* 556-76.

East, M. A. Explaining foreign policy behavior using national attributes. Paper presented at the American Political Science Association meeting, Los Angeles, California, September 2-5, 1975.

East, M. A., & Winters, B. K. National attributes and scope of action measures: A study of the targets of foreign policy behavior. Paper presented at the International Studies Association meeting, Washington, D.C., February 19-22, 1975.

East, M. A., & Winters, B. K. Targeting behavior: A new direction. In J. N. Rosenau (Ed.), *In search of global patterns.* New York: Free Press, 1976. Pp. 361-69.

East, M. A., Salmore, S. A. & Hermann, C. F. (Eds.). *Why nations act: Theoretical perspectives for comparative foreign policy studies.* Beverly Hills, CA: Sage, 1978.

Easton, D. *A framework for political analysis.* Englewood Cliffs, NJ: Prentice-Hall, 1965. (a)

Easton, D. *A systems analysis of political life.* New York: John Wiley, 1965. (b)

Fitzsimmons, B., Hoggard, G., McClelland, C., Martin, W., & Young, R. *World event-interaction survey handbook and codebook.* World Event-Interaction Survey Technical Report 1, University of Southern California, January 1969.

Forrester, G. W. *World dynamics.* New York: Wright Allen, 1971.

Froman, L. A., Jr. The categorization of policy contents. In A. Ranney (ed.), *Political science and public policy.* Chicago: Markham, 1968.

Galtung, J., & Ruge, M. H. The structure of foreign news. *Journal of Peace Research,* 1965, *1,* 64-91.

Gamson, W. A., & Modigliani, A. *Untangling the cold war.* Boston: Little, Brown, 1971.

Gatliff, B. *The use of deadline data sources.* Unpublished manuscript, Mershon Center, Ohio State University, 1974.

George, A. L., & Smoke, R. *Deterrence in American foreign policy.* New York: Columbia University Press, 1974.

George, A. L., Hall, D. K., & Simons, W. E. *The limits of coercive diplomacy: Laos, Cuba, Vietnam.* Boston: Little, Brown, 1971.

Goodenough, W. H. A technique for scale analysis. *Educational and Psychological Measurement,* 1944, *4,* 179-90.

Guttman, L. A basis for scaling qualitative data. *American Sociological Review,* 1944, *9,* 139-50.

Hagan, J. *Can CREON foreign policy behavior measures describe the foreign policy strategies of three African countries?* Unpublished manuscript, CREON Project, University of Kentucky, July 14, 1977.

Halperin, M. H. *Bureaucratic politics and foreign policy.* Washington, DC: Brookings Institution, 1974.

Hanreider, W. F. Compatibility and consensus: A proposal for the conceptual linkage of external and internal dimensions of foreign policy. *American Political Science Review,* 1967, *61* (December), 971-82.

Harf, J. E. Inter-nation conflict resolution and national attributes. In J. N. Rosenau (Ed.), *Comparing foreign policies: Theories, findings, and methods.* New York: Halsted, 1974.

Harrison, W. Policy. In J. Gould & W. L. Kolb (Eds.), *A dictionary of the social sciences.* New York: Free Press, 1964.

Hazelwood, L. A. and West, G. T. Bivariate associations, factor scores, and substantive impact: The source coverage problem revisited. *International Studies Quarterly,* 1974, *18* (September), 317-38.

Hermann, C. F. International crisis as a situational variable. In J. N. Rosenau (Ed.), *International politics and foreign policy* (rev. ed.). New York: Free Press, 1969. Pp. 409-421.

Hermann, C. F. Policy classification: A key to the comparative study of foreign policy. In J. N. Rosenau, V. Davis, & M. A. East (Eds.), *The analysis of international politics* New York: Free Press, 1971. Pp. 58-79. (a)

Hermann, C. F. What is a foreign policy event? In W. Hanrieder (Ed.), *Comparative foreign policy.* New York: David McKay, 1971. Pp. 295-321. (b)

Hermann, C. F. *International crises: Insights from behavioral research.* New York: Free Press, 1972.

Hermann, C. F. *Substantive problem area coding manual.* Unpublished manuscript, Mershon Center, Ohio State University, 1974.

Hermann, C. F. Foreign policy behavior: that which is to be explained. In M. A. East, S. A. Salmore, & C. F. Hermann (Eds.), *Why nations act: Theoretical perspectives for comparative foreign policy studies.* Beverly Hills, CA: Sage, 1978. Pp. 25-47.

Hermann, C. F., & Mason, R. E. Identifying behavioral attributes of events that trigger international crises. In O. R. Holsti, R. Siverson, & A. L. George (Eds.), *Change in the international system.* Boulder, CO: Westview Press, 1980.

Hermann, C. F., & Salmore, S. A. The recipients of foreign policy events. Paper presented at the Peace Research Society meeting, Ann Arbor, Michigan, November 15-16, 1971.

Hermann, C. F., & Swanson, D. E. *Procedures for coding military conflict events.* Unpublished manuscript, Mershon Center, Ohio State University, 1972.

Hermann, C. F., East, M. A., Hermann, M. G., Salmore, B. G., & Salmore, S. A. *CREON: A foreign events data set.* Beverly Hills, CA: Sage, 1973.

Hermann, M. G. Explaining foreign policy behavior using personal characteristics of political leaders. *International Studies Quarterly,* 1980, *24,* 7-46.

Hilsman, R. *To move a nation.* New York: Dell, 1967.

Hilsman, R. *The politics of policy making in defense and foreign affairs.* New York: Harper & Row, 1971.

Hilton, G. *A review of the dimensionality of nations project.* Beverly Hills, CA: Sage, 1973.

Hirschman, A. O. *National power and the structure of foreign trade.* Los Angeles: University of California Press, 1945.

Hoggard, G. D. *Comparison of reporting for New York Times Index, Asian Recorder, and Deadline Data–Chinese interactions January through October, 1962.* Unpublished manuscript, University of Southern California, 1967.

Hoggard, G. D. An analysis of the 'real' data: Reflections on the uses and validity of international interaction data. In E. E. Azar & J. D. Ben-Dak (Eds.), *Theory and practice of events research: Studies in inter-nation actions and interactions.* New York: Gordon and Breach, 1975.

Holsti, K. J. National role conceptions in the study of foreign policy. *International Studies Quarterly,* 1970, *14* (September), 233-309.

Holsti, K. J. *International politics: A framework for analysis* (3rd ed.). Englewood Cliffs, NJ: Prentice-Hall, 1977.

Holsti, O. R. *Crisis, escalation, war.* Montreal: McGill-Queen's University Press, 1972.

Holsti, O. R. The study of international politics makes strange bedfellows: Theories of the radical right and the radical left. *American Political Science Review,* 1974, *68,* 217-42.

Holsti, O. R., & North, R. C. Perceptions of hostility and economic variables. In R. Merritt & S. Rokkan (Eds.), *Comparing nations.* New Haven: Yale University Press, 1966. Pp. 169-190.

Holsti, O. R., North, R. C., & Brody, R. A. Perception and action in the 1914 crisis. In J. D. Singer (Ed.), *Quantitative international politics: Insights and evidence.* New York: Free Press, 1968. Pp. 123-158.

Hoole, F. W., & Zinnes, D. A. (Eds.). *Quantitative international politics: An appraisal.* New York: Praeger, 1976.

Hopkins, R. F., & Mansbach, R. W. *Structure and process in international politics.* New York: Harper & Row, 1973.

Huntington, S. P. *The common defense.* New York: Columbia University Press, 1961.

Hutchins, G. L. *The public foreign policy behavior of heads of government: The character of leader behavior and its effect on the behavior of other decision-makers.* Unpublished doctoral dissertation, Ohio State University, 1977.

Iklé, F. C. *How nations negotiate.* New York: Harper & Row, 1964.

Jacob, P. E., & Toscano, J. V. (Eds.). *The integration of political communities.* Philadelphia: J. B. Lippincott, 1964.

Janowitz, M. *The professional soldier: A social and political portrait.* New York: Free Press, 1960.

Jervis, R. *The logic of images in international relations.* Princeton: Princeton University Press, 1970.

Joynt, C. B. Foreign policy. In J. Dunner (Ed.), *Dictionary of political science.* New York: Philosophical Library, 1964.

Kahn, H. *On escalation: Metaphors and scenarios.* New York: Praeger, 1965.

Kaplan, A. *The conduct of inquiry.* San Francisco: Chandler, 1964.

Kegley, C. W., Jr. *A general empirical typology of foreign policy behavior.* Beverly Hills, CA: Sage, 1973.

Kegley, C. W., Jr. Selective attention: A general characteristic of the interactive behavior of nations. Paper presented at the Southern Political Science Association meeting, New Orleans, Louisiana, November 8-10, 1974.

Kegley, C. W., Jr., & Wittkopf, E. R. *American foreign policy: Pattern and process.* New York: St. Martin's Press, 1979.

Kegley, C. W., Jr., Salmore, S. A., & Rosen, D. Convergences in the analysis of the structure of interstate behavior. In P. J. McGowan (Ed.), *Sage yearbook of foreign policy studies* (vol. 2). Beverly Hills, CA: Sage, 1974. Pp. 309-39.

Kennedy, R. F. *Thirteen days.* New York: New American Library, 1968.

Keohane, R., & Nye, J. S. *Power and interdependence: World politics in transition.* Boston: Little, Brown, 1977.

Khrushchev, N. Letter to John F. Kennedy during the Cuban missile crisis, October 26, 1962. *Department of State Bulletin,* (November 19), 1973, 643-45.

Kissinger, H. A. *American foreign policy: Three essays.* New York: W. W. Norton, 1969.

Kissinger, H. A. Domestic structure and foreign policy. In *American foreign policy* (expanded ed.). New York: W. W. Norton, 1974.

Kissinger, H. A. Secretary Kissinger discusses Egypt-Israel agreement. *Department of State Bulletin* (October 27), 1975, 609-13.

Kissinger, H. A. *American foreign policy* (3rd ed.). New York: W. W. Norton, 1977.

Kolko, G. *The roots of American foreign policy: An analysis of power and purpose.* Boston: Beacon, 1969.

Kolko, J., and Kolko, G. *The limits of power: The world and United States foreign policy 1945-1954.* New York: Harper & Row, 1972.

Krippendorff, F. K. Reliability of recording instructions: Multivariate agreement for nominal data. *Behavioral Science,* 1971, *16,* 228-35.

Lasswell, H. D. *Politics: Who gets what, when, how.* New York: Whittlesey House, 1936.

Lasswell, H. D. *A pre-view of policy sciences.* New York: Elsevier, 1971.

Lasswell, H. D. Research in policy analysis: The intelligence and appraisal functions. In F. I. Greenstein & N. W. Polsby (Eds.), *Policies and policy making* (vol. 6), *Handbook of Political Science.* Reading, MA: Addison-Wesley, 1975. Pp. 1-22.

Lasswell, H. D., & Kaplan, A. *Power and society.* New Haven: Yale University Press, 1950.

Lazarus, R. S. *Psychological stress and the coping process.* New York: McGraw-Hill, 1966.

Leng, R. J. *Coder's manual for identifying and describing international actions* (5th ed.). Middlebury, VT: Middlebury College, 1975.

Leonhard, W. The domestic politics of the new Soviet foreign policy. *Foreign Affairs,* 1973, *52* (October), 59-75.

Lerche, C. O., Jr. *Foreign policy of the American people* (2nd ed.). Englewood Cliffs, NJ: Prentice-Hall, 1961.

Lowenthal, A. F., & Baldwin, H. W. *A new treaty for Panama?* Washington, DC: American Enterprise Institute Defense Review, 1977.

Lowi, T. Making democracy safe for the world: National politics and foreign policy. In J. N. Rosenau (Ed.), *Domestic politics and foreign policy.* New York: Free Press, 1967. Pp. 295-331.

Machiavelli, N. *The prince* (G. R. Bergin, trans. and ed.). New York: Appleton-Century-Crofts, 1947.

McClelland, C. A. *Theory and the international system.* New York: Macmillan, 1966.

McClelland, C. A. Access to Berlin: The quantity and variety of events. In J. D. Singer (Ed.), *Quantitative international politics.* New York: Free Press, 1968. Pp. 159-86.

McClelland, C. A. Some effects on theory from the international event analyses movement. In E. E. Azar, R. A. Brody, & C. A. McClelland (Eds.), *International events interaction analysis.* Beverly Hills, CA: Sage, 1972. Pp. 15-44. (a)

McClelland, C. A. The beginning, duration, and abatement of international crises. In C. F. Hermann (Ed.), *International crises: Insights from the behavioral sciences* New York: Free Press, 1972. Pp. 83-108. (b)

McClelland, C. A., & Hoggard, G. Conflict patterns in the interactions among nations. In J. N. Rosenau (Ed.), *International politics and foreign policy* (2nd ed.). New York: Free Press, 1969. Pp. 711-24.

McGowan, P. J., & Shapiro, H. B. *The comparative study of foreign policy: A survey of scientific findings.* Beverly Hills, CA: Sage, 1973.

Martin, W. R. The measurement of international military commitments for crisis early warning. *International Studies Quarterly,* 1977, *21* (March), 151-80.

Meehan, E. J. The concept "foreign policy." In W. F. Hanrieder (Ed.), *Comparative foreign policy: Theoretical essays* New York: David McKay, 1971. Pp. 265-94.

Michaely, M. *Concentration in international trade.* Amsterdam: North-Holland, 1962.

Montgomery, J. N. *Foreign aid in international politics.* Englewood Cliffs, NJ: Prentice-Hall, 1967.

Moore, D. W. Repredicting voting patterns in the General Assembly: A methodological note. *International Studies Quarterly,* 1975, *19* (June), 199-211.

Morgenthau, H. J. *In defense of the national interest.* New York: Macmillan, 1951.

Morgenthau, H. J. *Politics among nations.* New York: Alfred A. Knopf, 1973.

Moses, L. E., Brody, R. A., Holsti, O. R., Kadane, J. B. & Milstein, J. S. Scaling data on inter-nation action. *Science,* 1967, *156* (May 26), 1054-59.

Mosteller, F. Errors: Nonsampling errors. In *International encyclopedia of the social sciences* (vol. 5) (2nd ed.). New York: Macmillan, 1968.

Munton, D. *Measuring international behavior: Public sources, events, and validity.* Halifax, Canada: Centre for Foreign Policy Studies, Dalhousie University, 1978.

Nelson, J. M. *Aid, influence, and foreign policy.* New York: Macmillan, 1968.

Neustadt, R. *Alliance politics.* New York: Columbia University Press, 1970.

Nicholson, H. *Diplomacy.* London: Oxford University Press, 1939.

North, R. C. *The foreign relations of China* (2nd ed.). Encino, CA: Dickenson, 1974.

North, R. C., Brody, R., & Holsti, O. R. Measuring affect and action in international reaction models: Empirical materials from the 1962 Cuban case. In J. N. Rosenau (Ed.), *International politics and foreign policy* (2nd ed.). New York: Free Press, 1969. Pp. 679-96.

Odell, J. S. The hostility of U.S. external behavior: An exploration. In P. J. McGowan (Ed.), *Sage international yearbook of foreign policy studies.* (vol. 3). Beverly Hills, CA: Sage, 1975.

O'Leary, M. K. Foreign policy and bureaucratic adaptation. In J. N. Rosenau (Ed.), *Comparing foreign policies: Theories, findings, and methods.* New York: Halsted, 1974. Pp. 55-70.

O'Leary, M. K. The role of issues. In J. N. Rosenau (Ed.), *In search of global patterns.* New York: Free Press, 1976. Pp. 318-25.

O'Leary, M. K., & Shapiro, H. B. *Instructions for coding foreign policy acts.* Unpublished manuscript, International Relations Program, Syracuse University, 1972. (a)

O'Leary, M. K., & Shapiro, H. B. A codebook of international transactions, issue-specific interactions and power. *PRINCE Research Studies,* No. 10, Syracuse University, December 1972. (b)

Organski, A.F.K. *World politics.* New York: Alfred A. Knopf, 1968.

Ostgaard, E. Factors influencing the flow of the news. *Journal of Peace Research,* 1965, *1,* 39-63.

Phillips, W. R. *Dynamic patterns of international conflict.* Unpublished doctoral dissertation, University of Hawaii, 1969.

Phillips, W. R. Prior behavior as an explanation of foreign policy. In M. A. East, S. A. Salmore, & C. F. Hermann (Eds.), *Why nations act: Theoretical perspectives for comparative foreign policy studies.* Beverly Hills, CA: Sage, 1978. Pp. 161-72.

Phillips, W. R., & Callahan, P. Dynamic foreign policy interactions: implications for a non-dyadic world. Paper presented at the Midwest Political Science Association Meeting, Chicago, Illinois, May 3-5, 1973.

Phillips, W. R., & Crain, R. C. Dynamic foreign policy interactions: Reciprocity and uncertainty in foreign policy. In P. J. McGowan (Ed.), *Sage international yearbook of foreign policy studies* (vol. 2). Beverly Hills, CA: Sage, 1974. Pp. 227-66.

Pipes, R. Détente: Moscow's view. In R. Pipes (Ed.), *Soviet strategy in Europe.* New York: Crane, Russak, 1976.

Plano, J. C., & Riggs, R. E. *Dictionary of political analysis.* Hinsdale, IL: Dryden Press, 1973.

Poteat, G. H. The intelligence gap: Hypotheses on the process of surprise. *International Studies Notes,* 1976, *3* (3), 14-18.

Pruitt, D. G. National power and international responsiveness. *Background,* 1964, *7,* 165-78.

Pruitt, D. G. Stability and sudden change in interpersonal and international affairs. In J. N. Rosenau (Ed.), *International politics and foreign policy* (rev. ed.). New York: Free Press, 1969. Pp. 392-408.

Przeworski, A., & Teune, H. *The logic of comparative social inquiry.* New York: Wiley-Interscience, 1970.

Richman, A. *A scale of events along the conflict-cooperation continuum.* Research Monograph Series No. 10. Philadelphia: Foreign Policy Research Institute, University of Pennsylvania, 1968.

Roby, T. B. Commitment. *Behavioral Science,* 1960, *53,* 253-64.

Rosen, D. J. Leadership change and foreign policy. Paper presented at the American Political Science Association meeting, Chicago, Illinois, August 29-September 2, 1974.

Rosenau, J. N. Pre-theories and theories of foreign policy. In R. B. Farrell (Ed.), *Approaches to comparative and international politics.* Evanston, IL: Northwestern University Press, 1966. Pp. 27-92.

Rosenau, J. N. (Ed.). *Domestic sources of foreign policy.* New York: Free Press, 1967. (a)

Rosenau, J. N. Foreign policy as an issue-area. In J. N. Rosenau (Ed.), *Domestic sources of foreign policy.* New York: Free Press, 1967. (b)

Rosenau, J. N. Comparative foreign policy: Fad, fantasy, or field? *International Studies Quarterly,* 1968, *12,* 296-329. (a)

Rosenau, J. N. Moral fervor, systematic analysis, and scientific consciousness in foreign policy research. In A. Ranney (Ed.), *Political science and public policy.* Chicago: Markham, 1968. Pp. 197-236. (b)

Rosenau, J. N. *The adaptation of national societies: A theory of political system behavior and transformation.* New York: McCaleb-Seiler, 1970.

Rosenau, J. N. Restlessness, change, and foreign policy analysis. In J. N. Rosenau (Ed.), *In search of global patterns.* New York: Free Press, 1976. Pp. 369-376.

Rosenau, J. N., & Hoggard, G. D. Foreign policy behavior in dyadic relationships. In J. N. Rosenau (Ed.), *Comparing foreign policies: Theories, findings, and methods.* New York: Halsted, 1974.

Rosenau, J. N., Burgess, P. M., & Hermann, C. F. The adaptation of foreign policy research. *International Studies Quarterly,* 1973, *17,* 119-144.

Rummel, R. J. A social field theory of foreign conflict behavior. *Papers of the Peace Research Society (International),* 1966, *4,* 131-50. (a)

Rummel, R. J. Some dimensions in the foreign behavior of nations. *Journal of Peace Research,* 1966, *3,* 201-224. (b)

Rummel, R. J. The relationship between national attributes and foreign conflict behavior. In J. D. Singer (Ed.), *Quantitative international politics.* New York: Free Press, 1967. Pp. 187-214.

Rummel, R. J. Indicators of cross-national and international patterns. *American Political Science Review,* 1969, *63* (March), 127-47.

Rummel, R. J. *The dimensions of nations.* Beverly Hills, CA: Sage, 1972.

Russett, B. M. Cause, surprise and no escape. *Journal of Politics,* 1962, *3* (February), 3-22.

Russett, B. M. The calculus of deterrence. *Journal of Conflict Resolution,* 1963, *7,* 97-109.

Russett, B. M. *International regions and the international system: A study in political ecology.* Chicago: Rand-McNally, 1967.

Salmore, B., & Brady, L. P. *CREON supplemental and descriptive coding manual.* Unpublished manuscript, Mershon Center, Ohio State University, 1972.

Salmore, B. G., & Salmore, S. A. Regime constraints and foreign policy behavior. Paper presented at the American Political Science Association meeting, Los Angeles, California, September 2-5, 1975.

Salmore, S. A., & Munton, D. Classifying foreign policy behaviors: An empirically based typology. In J. N. Rosenau (Ed.), *Comparing foreign policies:Theories, findings, and methods.* New York: Halsted, 1974. Pp. 329-52.

Schelling, T. C. *The strategy of conflict.* New York: Oxford University Press, 1960.

Schelling, T. C. *Arms and influence.* New Haven: Yale University Press, 1966.

Schroeder, P. W. Quantitative studies in the balance of power: An historian's reaction. *Journal of Conflict Resolution,* 1977, *21* (March), 3-22.

Sherwin, R. G. *WEIS project final report.* Los Angeles: School of International Relations, University of Southern California, 1973.

Shively, W. P. *The craft of political research: A primer.* Englewood Cliffs, NJ: Prentice-Hall, 1974.

Simon, H. A. *Models of man.* New York: John Wiley, 1957.

Simon, H. A. *The science of the artificial.* Cambridge: MIT Press, 1969.

Simon, H. A. *Administrative behavior* (3rd ed.). New York: Free Press, 1976.

Singer, J. D. Inter-nation influence: A formal model. *American Political Science Review,* 1963, *57,* 420-30.

Singer, J. D. War and other problems in the global system. *International Organizations,* 1977, *31* (Summer), 565-78.

Singer, J. D., & Small, M. The composition and status ordering of the international system, 1815-1940. *World Politics,* 1968, *18,* 236-82.

Singer, J. D., & Small, M. National alliance commitments and war involvement, 1815-1945. In J. N. Rosenau (Ed.), *International politics and foreign policy* (rev. ed.). New York: Free Press, 1969. Pp. 513-42.

Singer, J. D., & Small, M. *The wages of war, 1816-1965.* New York: John Wiley, 1972.

Small, M. Doing diplomatic history by the numbers: A rejoinder. *Journal of Conflict Resolution, 1977, 21* (March), 23-34.

Small, M., & Singer, J. D. The diplomatic importance of states, 1816-1970: An extension and refinement of the indicator. *World Politics, 1973, 25,* 577-99.

Small, M. & Singer, J. D. Conflict in the international system, 1816-1977: Historical trends and policy futures. In C. W. Kegley, Jr., & P. J. McGowan (Eds.), *Challenges to America: United States foreign policy in the 1980s.* Beverly Hills, CA: Sage, 1979. Pp. 89-115.

Smith, R. F. On the structure of the foreign news: A comparison of the New York *Times* and the Indian White Papers. *Journal of Peace Research, 1969, 1,* 23-36.

Snyder, R. C., Bruck, H., & Sapin, B. *Foreign policy decision making: An approach to the study of international politics.* New York: Free Press, 1962.

Spiro, H. J. Foreign policy and political style. *The Annals of the American Academy of Political and Social Science, 1966, 266,* 139-48.

Sprout, H., & Sprout, M. *Toward a politics of the planet Earth.* New York: Van Nostrand Reinhold, 1971.

Steinbruner, J. D. *The cybernetic theory of decision.* Princeton: Princeton University Press, 1974.

Stoessinger, J. G. *Why nations go to war.* New York: St. Martin's Press, 1974.

Strausz-Hupé, R., Kintner, W.R ., Dougherty, J. E., & Cottrell, A. J. *Protracted conflict.* New York: Harper & Row, 1959.

Sullivan, M. P. Commitment and the escalation of conflicts. *Western Political Quarterly, 1972, 25* (1), 28-38.

Swanson, D. *Degree of specificity: Actor expectations in foreign policy behaviors.* Unpublished doctoral dissertation, Ohio State University, 1976.

Swanson, D. Analyzing foreign policy goals: The need for a policy relevant approach. Paper presented at the International Studies Association meeting, St. Louis, Missouri, March 16-20, 1977.

Swanson, D. Measurement validity through expert judgment: A method and a preliminary application. In D. J. Munton (Ed.), *Measuring international behavior: Public sources, events, and validity.* Halifax, Nova Scotia: Dalhousie University Centre for Foreign Policy Studies, 1978.

Szyliowicz, J. S., & O'Neill, B. E. (Eds.). *The energy crisis and U.S. foreign policy.* New York: Praeger, 1975.

Tanter, R. International system and foreign policy approaches: Implications for conflict modelling and management. In R. Tanter & R. H. Ullman (Eds.), *Theory and policy in international relations.* Princeton: Princeton University Press, 1972. Pp. 7-39.

Tanter, R., & Ullman, R. H. (Eds.). *Theory and policy in international relations.* Princeton: Princeton University Press, 1972.

Teune, H., & Synnestvedt, S. Measuring international alignment. *Orbis, 1965, 9* (Spring), 171-89.

Thompson, J. D. *Organizations in action.* New York: McGraw-Hill, 1967.

Tomkins, S. S. *Affect, imagery, and consciousness.* New York: Springer, 1962.

Vincent, J. Predicting voting patterns in the general assembly. *American Political Science Review, 1971, 65* (June), 471-98.

Waltz, K. N. *Foreign policy and democratic politics: The British and American experience.* Boston: Little, Brown, 1967.

Webb, E. J., Campbell, D. T., Schwartz, R. D., & Sechrest, L. *Unobtrusive measures: Nonreactive research in the social sciences.* Chicago: Rand McNally, 1966.

Weinstein, F. B. The concept of a commitment in international relations. *Journal of Conflict Resolution, 1969, 13* (1), 39-56.

Wilkenfeld, J. Some further findings regarding the domestic and foreign conflict behavior of nations. *Journal of Peace Research, 1969, 2,* 147-56.

Wilkenfeld, J. A time-series perspective on conflict behavior in the Middle East. In P. J. McGowan (Ed.), *Sage international yearbook of foreign policy studies* (vol. 3). Beverly Hills, CA: Sage, 1975.

Wilkenfeld, J., Lassier, V. L. & Tahtinen, D. Conflict interactions in the Middle East, 1949-67. *Journal of Conflict Resolution,* 1972, *16* (June), 135-54.

Wilkinson, D. O. *Comparative foreign relations: Framework and methods.* Belmont, CA: Dickenson, 1969.

Winters, B. K. Monitoring activity in the international system. Paper presented at the Southern Section Meeting of the Peace Science Society, Raleigh, North Carolina, 1975.

Wittkopf, E. R. *Western bilateral aid allocations: A comparative study of recipient state attributes and aid received.* Beverly Hills, CA: Sage, 1972.

Wittkopf, E. R., & Ferris, E. Dyadic analysis of issues and issue-areas in Latin American foreign policy. Paper presented at the Southern Political Science Association meeting, New Orleans, Louisiana, November 7-9, 1974.

Wolfers, A. *Discord and collaboration.* Baltimore, MD: Johns Hopkins University Press, 1962.

Wright, Q. *The study of international relations.* New York: Appleton-Century-Crofts, 1955.

Yarmolinsky, A. Bureaucratic structures and political outcomes. *Journal of International Affairs,* 1969, *23,* 225-35.

Zadrozny, J. T. *Dictionary of social science.* Washington, DC: Public Affairs Press, 1959.

Zimmerman, W. Issue area and foreign-policy process: A research note in search of a general theory. *American Political Science Review,* 1973, *67* (December), 1204-12.

Zinnes, D. A. The expression and perception of hostility in prewar crisis: 1914. In J. D. Singer (Ed.), *Quantitative international politics.* New York: Free Press, 1968. Pp. 85-119.

Index

About the Authors and Editors

LINDA P. BRADY is a defense analyst in the Europe Division of Regional Programs, Office of the U. S. Assistant Secretary of Defense, Program Analysis and Evaluation. Formerly Special Assistant for MBFR Policy in the Office of the Deputy Undersecretary of Defense (Policy Planning), she has twice been a member of the U. S. delegation to the MBFR talks in Vienna, Austria. Before joining the Department of Defense, Brady taught at Goucher College and Vanderbilt University. In addition to papers on MBFR and theater nuclear force issues, Brady has written extensively in the comparative foreign policy area.

PATRICK CALLAHAN is Associate Professor of Political Science at DePaul University. He has also been a visiting faculty member at Northwestern University. Callahan's research focuses on foreign policy issues, particularly the impact of values on nations' foreign policy behavior. He served three years as editor of *Comparative Foreign Policy Notes* and currently serves as education editor of the Comparative Foreign Policy Section of the International Studies Association. Recently Callahan compiled a bibliography of comparative foreign policy studies, which was published in *The Political Economy of Foreign Policy*.

ROGER A. COATE is Assistant Professor of International Organization and Ocean Space in the Department of Government and International Studies at the University of South Carolina. He is author of the book, *Global Issue Regimes* (Praeger, forthcoming). Coate's main research interests are global political economy, international organization, and development policy.

MAURICE A. EAST is Professor of Political Science at the University of Kentucky. He has been associated with the CREON Project since its inception and is the senior author-editor of another CREON Project book, *Why Nations Act: Theoretical Perspectives for Comparative Foreign Policy Studies* (Sage, 1978). East is interested in examining the foreign policy behavior of small states and is currently working on a study of foreign policymaking in the Nordic countries.

CHARLES F. HERMANN is Director of the Mershon Center for Research and Education in National Security and the Policy Sciences at The Ohio State University. He began the CREON Project a decade ago with the twin objectives of developing a variety of measures of foreign policy behavior and of constructing multivariate explanations of such foreign policy behavior. Hermann has published widely in the areas of the comparative study of foreign policy and foreign policy crises. Among his current research projects is the development and testing of several models of foreign policy behavior that link nations' external relations with domestic political and economic variables.

MARGARET G. HERMANN is Senior Research Associate at the Mershon Center for Research and Education in National Security and the Policy Sciences at The Ohio State University. A psychologist, Hermann has just completed a term as editor of *Political Psychology*. She has written extensively on political leadership and political personality, including *A Psychological Examination of Political Leaders*, (Free Press, 1977). Hermann's research focuses on how political leaders' personalities affect what they do politically and, in particular, how their personalities influence their nations' foreign policy behavior.

GERALD L. HUTCHINS is a senior urban studies analyst and Coordinator of Computer Services at the Urban Studies Center of the University of Louisville. Affiliated with the CREON Project as a graduate student, Hutchins was responsible for much of the initial analysis of the event data set and for the initial attempts at combining variables to make indicators of foreign policy behavior.

BARBARA G. SALMORE is Professor of Political Science at Drew University. Recently President of the Northeastern Political Science Association, her previous work in the area of foreign policy includes articles in *Why Nations Act, Events Data and Foreign Policy*, the *Policy Studies Journal*, and *Society*. Among Salmore's research interests is a concern with how the nature of the political regime influences nations' foreign policy behavior.

STEPHEN A. SALMORE is Professor and Chair of the Political Science Department at Rutgers University. He was a coeditor and contributer to *Why Nations Act* and has written other articles on comparative foreign policy and events data. He was Director of the Eagleton Poll from 1971 to 1979 and is currently working in the areas of campaigns and elections and New Jersey politics.

DEAN SWANSON is Conservation Program Manager, Office of Marine Mammals and Endangered Species, National Marine Fisheries Service, National Oceanic and Atmospheric Administration, U. S. Department of Commerce. Prior to joining the Department of Commerce, he was a research fellow at the Centre for Foreign Policy Studies, Dalhousie University, Halifax, Canada. Swanson has written articles in *World Politics, Measuring International Behaviour,* and *Canada's Foreign Policy*. His principal research interest is in international marine environmental policies.